VISUAL QUICKSTART GUIDE

3DS MAX 6

FOR WINDOWS

Michele Matossian

 PEACHPIT PRESS

Visual QuickStart Guide
3ds max 6 for Windows
Michele Matossian

Peachpit Press
1249 Eighth Street
Berkeley, CA 94710
510/524-2178
800/283-9444
510/524-2221 (fax)

Find us on the World Wide Web at http://www.peachpit.com
To report errors, please send a note to errata@peachpit.com

Peachpit is a division of Pearson Education.

Copyright © 2004 by Michele Matossian

Acquisitions Editor: Elise Walter
Senior Project Editor: Sarah Kearns
Technical Editor: Jon McFarland
Compositor: Gloria Schurick
Indexer: Lisa Stumpf
Cover Design: Aren Howell

ISBN: 0-7357-1391-X

9 8 7 6 5 4 3 2

Printed and bound in the United States of America

Dedication

To my cats,

Metta and McCoy,

whose antics and affection

bring me such joy!

Acknowledgments

Thanks to my dear friends and family for all
their support in completing this project:
Dr. Garo S. Matossian, Dr. Mary K. Matossian,
Chris Thralls, Jude Levinson, Marc Libarle,
Donna Thomson, and Suzanne Grahn.

A special thanks goes to Jude Levinson for
guiding me through the quirks of Quark and
for invaluable lessons on the layout of books.

May all beings be peaceful, happy, and free
of suffering.

Michele Irene Matossian
January 15, 2004

CONTENTS AT A GLANCE

TABLE OF CONTENTS

TABLE OF CONTENTS

INTRODUCTION

Figure i.1 The cadaceus is an ancient symbol of power and healing. 3ds max 6 gives you all the tools you need to quickly make images such as this.

3ds max is one of the most powerful and popular desktop 3D graphics programs available today. It is used for a wide variety of commercial and artistic applications, including architecture, computer games, film production, web design, forensics, medical visualization, scientific visualization, virtual reality, and fine art.

This book was written for artists, designers, students, teachers, working professionals, and anyone who wants to build their dreams. At the beginning of each chapter, the introduction gives you a sense of the possibilities. The section headings present the theory you need just in time to do the step-by-step tasks that follow. Tips and tables give you important clues about pitfalls, shortcuts, and advanced techniques. By studying both the theory and the mechanics, you will be equipped not only to push the right buttons, but also to create art, solve problems, and invent solutions.

Like other Visual QuickStart Guides, this book is designed to be as clear as possible and presumes no prior experience on the part of the reader. To assist your learning, over 1400 figures show you what to do and how to do it. By the end of this book, you will have learned how to create, model, map, animate, and render objects in 3ds max 6.

To get the most out of this book, you should be familiar with the Windows environment and have access to an installation of 3ds max 6. You should also have a good understanding of 2D graphics programs, such as Adobe Photoshop and Fractal Design Painter.

There are as many ways to work in 3ds max as there are artists who use the program. Throughout this book, I have tried to select the most effective way to get things done, while showing you the larger design of how the program works. By breaking down complex ideas into plain English and carefully organizing the information, I have tried to present the material in such a way that you can quickly find what you need and apply it.

I present this book with particular pride because it is the first edition that I revised in layout. Working in layout allowed me to tailor each page to better communicate the content, both verbally and visually. Along the way, I designed many new figures and expanded the text to present new ideas and make it all look nice. I hope you enjoy this book as much as I enjoyed creating it for you.

The chapters of the book are meant to be followed in order, but each one is designed to be able to stand alone. If you are new to 3ds max, the best thing to do is start at the beginning and work your way through the topics in order. More advanced students may want to skip to areas of particular interest. To use this book as a "how to" reference, look up your task in the table of contents or look up topics in the index. Extensive tables of commands may be found in the chapters as well as in the appendices.

Chapter 1 gets you up and running, from installing the program to navigating the interface and learning essential file commands.

Chapters 2–4 teach you how to create and select objects, control the display, render images, and navigate 3D scenes. Since the last edition of this book, new objects, group commands, and sidebars have been added.

Chapters 5–7 show you how to manipulate and animate objects using transforms, modifiers, and animation controllers. The sequence of topics has been significantly revised, in accordance with changes to the user interface as well as for clarity.

Chapters 8–10 explain more advanced modeling techniques, including sub-object editing and compound objects. New to this edition are sections on polymesh editing in Chapter 8 and AEC Objects in Chapter 10.

Chapters 11 and 12 describe the use of lights and cameras for illuminating and composing views of your scenes. The section on animating cameras in Chapter 12 has been expanded to include more on walk-through, flythrough, and flyby animations.

Chapters 13 and 14 cover materials and mapping, so that you can make your scenes realistic as well as beautiful. Special care went into these chapters to make the figures larger and more beautiful.

Chapter 15 rounds out the book with rendering and shows you how to add effects to produce high-quality pictures and movies. Many new figures have been added here for clarity, beauty, and visual interest.

Note: In this edition, I enlarged the inline graphics of the buttons from' one line high to two lines high. I did this in order to provide stronger visual cues of what to look for, and what to do. Let me know if you find this helpful. I always enjoy hearing from readers, and welcome your suggestions.

Best of luck,
Michele Matossian
3dsmax@lightweaver.com

1

GETTING STARTED

Figure 1.1 By combining 3D objects with 2D bitmaps, you can build your own paradise using 3ds max 6.

Welcome to the world of 3ds max, where you can create alien planets, towering ruins, heroes, and villains, or build your own paradise (**Figure 1.1**). By harnessing your imagination to 3D animation, you can make animals prowl and mountains tumble, as people run through quivering jungles. You are not bound by the rules of this sphere: pigs can fly, and fleas rumble.

Before you start creating chaos and conquest, you need to learn some basic skills. This chapter starts at the very beginning: how to install and configure the program; how to manage files; and how to get around the user interface. Once you have mastered these skills, you will learn to create, navigate, and animate scenes. Toward the end of the book, you will find out how to change the entire look of a scene by setting up lights and cameras, applying maps and materials, and by adding special effects.

As with other Visual QuickStart books, procedures are short and to the point; each step is designed to get you from point A to point B by the shortest possible route. Tips provide information on keyboard shortcuts, common pitfalls, advanced practices, and related tools. By paying close attention to these, you will soon be able to create your dreams.

Installing 3ds max 6

3ds max 6 is designed to run on the Windows XP or Windows 2000 platform using an AMD or Intel-compatible processor. It may also run on older Windows operating systems, but it is not supported on these platforms. See the "System Requirements" sidebar on the next page for details.

The following steps guide you in setting up a typical installation of 3ds max 6.

To install 3ds max:

1. Close any open programs, including anti-virus programs, and make sure sufficient disk space is available on the hard drive.

2. Place the 3ds max 6 CD-ROM in the CD-ROM drive and double-click on the CD-ROM drive letter.

3. In the Welcome to 3ds max 6 screen, choose 3ds max 6 install.

4. Select the components that you wish to install. Then click Install (**Figure 1.2**).

5. Following the steps in the 3ds max 6 installation wizard, accept the license agreement and click Next.

6. Enter your personal information and your 3ds max 6 serial number, which is found on the product packaging (**Figure 1.3**). Click Browse if you want to install the program to a different folder or location. Leave the license type set to Stand Alone. Then click Next.

7. After the program finishes installing, click Finish to exit the installation wizard. Then click additional installs.

8. Install each program that you do not already have installed (**Figure 1.4**).

9. Click Exit. To start the program, double-click the 3ds max 6 icon on your desktop.

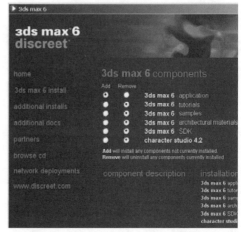

Figure 1.2 Choose the components you wish to install.

Figure 1.3 Enter your personal information and the serial number from the product packaging.

Figure 1.4 Install additional programs and documents that you need to run 3ds max 6.

System Requirements

Operating Systems and Software

◆ Windows XP Professional (SP1), Windows 2000 (SP4), or XP Home (SP1).

◆ Internet Explorer 6

◆ DirectX 9 recommended (minimum requirement is DirectX 8.1), Open GL.

Hardware

◆ AMD or Intel PIII processor running at a minimum speed of 300 MHz (a Dual Intel Xeon or dual AMD Athlon system is recommended).

◆ 512 MB RAM and 500 MB swap disk space (1 GB RAM and 2 GB swap disk space recommended).

◆ 664 MB hard drive space (to install all 3ds max 6 components).

◆ A graphics card that supports 1024 × 768 pixels per inch at 16-bit color with 64 MB RAM (OpenGL and Direct3D hardware acceleration supported; 3D graphics accelerator that supports 1280 × 1024 ppi, 24-bit color and 256 MB RAM preferred).

◆ A mouse or other pointing device (optimally a Microsoft Intellimouse). A Wacom Intuos or other pressure-sensitive tablet is recommended for using the vertex paint feature.

◆ A CD-ROM drive.

◆ Optional: sound card and speakers, cabling for a TCP/IP-compliant network, 3D graphics hardware acceleration, video input and output devices, joystick, MIDI instruments, three-button mouse.

✔ Tips

■ The DirectX 9.0 installs a program that tests, diagnoses, and configures DirectX components and drivers. If you don't have any of this type of hardware, DirectX can improve the performance of your system by emulating hardware services with software drivers.

INSTALLING 3DS MAX 6

Setting Up 3ds max 6

When you first start up 3ds max, you will be prompted to choose a display driver and authorize the program with a code that you obtain from Autodesk. If you do not authorize the program, it will run for only 14 days.

To configure the display driver:

1. Open 3ds max 6 by double-clicking the icon it installed on your desktop. You can also choose Start > Programs > discreet > 3dsmax6 > 3dsmax6.

2. In the 3ds max Graphics Driver Setup dialog box, choose a display driver appropriate to your hardware setup (**Figure 1.5**).

   Unless you have OpenGL, Direct3D, or another hardware accelerator card, choose "Software" to install the Heidi software driver. If you have Direct 3D, click Advanced Direct3D to set up your driver, or accept the defaults (**Figure 1.6**).

3. Click OK.

✔ Tips

- If you subsequently install a new hardware accelerator card, you can install a new driver by choosing Customize > Preferences > Viewports.

- Additional graphics driver configuration settings can be accessed by choosing Customize > Preferences > Viewports > Configure Driver.

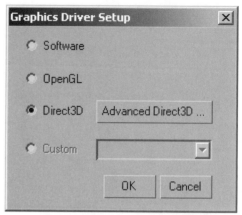

Figure 1.5 Choose a display driver to match your graphics hardware set up.

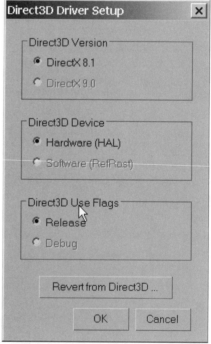

Figure 1.6 Access these Direct3D driver settings by clicking the Advanced Direct3D button.

Authorizing 3ds max from North America

Web: https://register.autodesk.com

Email: authcodes@autodesk.com

Phone: (800) 551-1490 or (415) 507-4690

Fax: (800) 225-6490

Mail: Product Registrations
       Autodesk Inc.
       111 McInnis Parkway
       San Rafael, CA 94903

Authorizing 3ds max from Europe

Web: https://register.autodesk.com

Email: authcodes@eur.autodesk.com

Phone: +41-32-723-9100

Fax: +41-32-723-9399

Mail: Autodesk Development BV
       Rue de Puits-Godets 6
       Case Postale 35
       Neuchatel CH-2005
       Switzerland

To authorize the program:

1. Start up 3ds max 6.

2. In the Product Authorization dialog box, choose Authorize the product.

3. Register the program by filling in all the required fields in the Register Today routine.

   When you have filled out all the information, you will be asked how you want to contact Autodesk. If you have an online connection, choose Connect directly via the Web. You will then be prompted to connect. The registration program uploads the information you entered, plus the CD Key and serial number of the program. It then downloads your authorization code and enters it automatically.

4. If you choose one of the other options, you will be given directions and contact information for submitting your registration and obtaining your authorization code. For your convenience, the contact information for North America and Europe is provided here.

5. Click Finish. The program starts.

SETTING UP 3DS MAX 6

Accessing Tech Support

If you have any problems with your 3ds max installation or use, the following resources are available to help you:

◆ The Installation Notes in the Readme file located in the 3ds max 6 main directory.

◆ The Authorized Reseller who sold you the product. To obtain the number of an Authorized Reseller, call (800) 879-4233 or go to www.discreet.com/support.

◆ The 3ds max User Reference files, located in the Help menu (**Figure 1.7**).

◆ The Discreet Support Pages on the Web at www.discreet.com/support.

◆ The Product Support HelpFile in the 3ds max Help menu under Additional Help.

◆ Product Support. From the United States and Canada: 1-800-225-6531 or 1-425-489-7519, Monday through Friday, 6 AM–5 PM PST.

◆ From Europe, the Middle East, or Africa, 00.800.3472.7338 or +44.207.851.8090 Monday to Friday, 8 AM – 6 PM GMT. The 800 number is toll-free within UK, France, Germany, Italy, and Spain.

◆ Have your product serial number ready when you call. Installation and configuration support is available for free for 30 consecutive business days after your first call. After 30 days, telephone support costs $65 per incident.

◆ Autodesk 24-hour FAX Support Information System at 1-514-954-7254.

◆ Discreet Presales at 1-800-869-3504.

For display problems, make sure that you have the latest display driver and video card BIOS installed by checking the technical support pages of your video card manufacturer's Web site. If problems persist, contact the manufacturer directly.

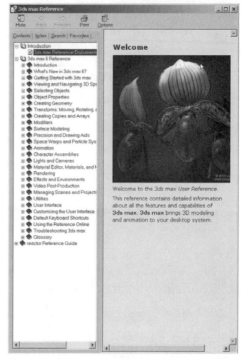

Figure 1.7 The User Reference describes the features of the program.

Touring the Interface

3ds max 6 is a very powerful program that includes tens of thousands of commands. To save desktop real estate, many commands are initially hidden from view. Consequently, learning their location can take a while. This section takes you on a tour of what you typically see as you work with the program.

The 3ds max interface is visually organized by function. Commands are layered in menus, toolbars, tab panels, modules, and dialog boxes to maximize screen real estate without compromising workspace. Icons and right-click menus supply handy shortcuts to the most commonly used commands.

The main user interface is organized into five main regions, as shown in **Figure 1.8**.

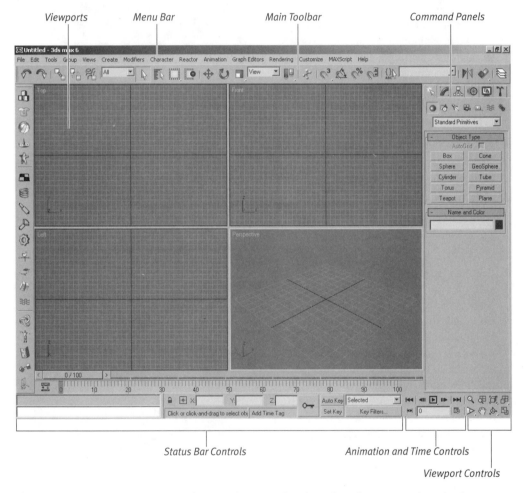

Viewports   Menu Bar   Main Toolbar   Command Panels

Status Bar Controls   Animation and Time Controls

Viewport Controls

Figure 1.8 The default 3ds max user interface contains a menu bar, the Main toolbar, command panels, viewports, status bar controls, animation and time controls, viewport controls, and an assortment of other features.

Special Controls

A few special controls of the user interface make the program easier to use:

◆ **Tooltips (Figure 1.9)** are pop-up labels that appear when you rest your cursor over a button without clicking it.

◆ **Drop-down menus (Figure 1.10)** are indicated by an inverted black triangle just to the right of the current menu item.

◆ **Context-sensitive menus (Figure 1.11)** are extensive hidden menus that exist throughout 3ds max 6. You access these menus by right-clicking, by holding down the Ctrl key and right-clicking, or by holding down the Alt key and right-clicking.

◆ **Floaters (Figure 1.12)** are modeless dialog boxes that stay on top of the interface until you close them.

◆ **Cursors (Figure 1.13)** in 3ds max change to indicate the selected action. They usually match the icon of the selected tool.

◆ **Rollouts (Figure 1.14)** contain additional commands. The title bar of a rollout displays a plus sign (+) when the rollout is closed; clicking the title bar opens the rollout and changes the plus sign to a minus sign (-). To scroll a long rollout so that you can see all the commands, place the cursor over an empty area so that it changes to a panning hand. Then drag up or down. As an alternative, you can drag the thin gray scrollbar that appears to the right of the rollout.

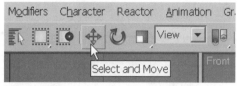

Figure 1.9 If you rest the cursor over a button, tooltips appear to tell you what the button represents.

Figure 1.10 Downward-pointing triangles indicate the presence of a drop-down menu.

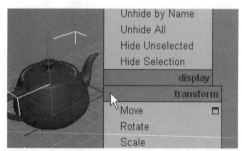

Figure 1.11 Context-sensitive menus appear throughout the 3ds max program interface.

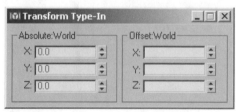

Figure 1.12 Floaters are dialog boxes that stay on top of the interface. Many are found in the Tools menu.

Figure 1.13 The cursor changes shape to indicate which tool is active.

SPECIAL CONTROLS

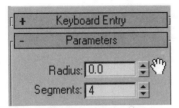

Figure 1.14 Scrolling a Parameters rollout by dragging a panning hand. The Keyboard Entry rollout is closed.

Figure 1.15 Numeric input fields set the dimensions of a box.

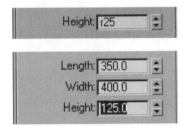

Figure 1.16 Incrementing the height parameter by a relative amount (top) and the result (bottom).

Figure 1.17 Dragging a spinner.

Figure 1.18 You can find flyouts on the Main toolbar, the status bar, and in the Material Editor.

- ◆ **Numeric input fields (Figure 1.15)** allow you to enter parameter values from the keyboard. To increment a parameter value by a certain amount, enter the letter "r" and the amount you want to add into the field. Then press the Enter key (**Figure 1.16**). To decrement a value, enter "r-" instead of "r," and the amount you want to subtract. Then press Enter.

- ◆ **Spinners (Figure 1.17)** are a pair of small up- and down-facing triangular arrows to the right of an input field that give you a quick way to change parameter values. Click or drag the up arrow to increase a parameter. Click or drag the down arrow to decrease a parameter. Holding down the Ctrl key speeds the rate of change. Holding down the Alt key slows the rate of change. Right-clicking a spinner resets it.

- ◆ **Flyouts (Figure 1.18)** are sets of related tool icons that appear when you click and hold any button that displays a small black triangle in its lower-right corner. You pick a tool from the flyout by rolling the cursor over its icon and then releasing the mouse button.

- ◆ **Toolbars (Figure 1.19)** are groups of commands that float in the foreground. Drag a toolbar to detach it, move it, or dock it at the edge of the display.

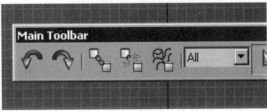

Figure 1.19 You can drag toolbars around the interface or attach them alongside the viewports.

The menu bar

Fifteen drop-down menus are available from the menu bar (**Figures 1.20** and **1.21**). Commands that cannot be used with the current selection are grayed out.

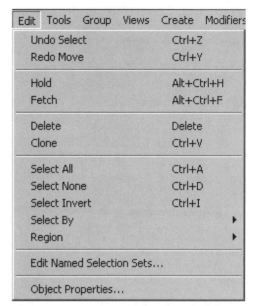

Figure 1.21 Menus contain commands, keyboard shortcuts, and arrows that lead to submenus.

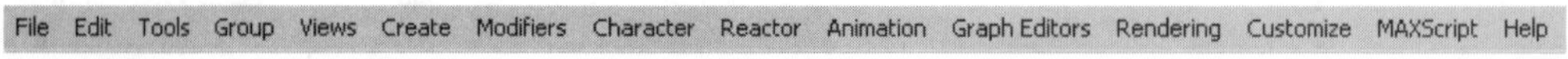

- The **File menu** contains commands for managing files and viewing file information.

- The **Edit menu** includes commands for selecting and editing objects. It also contains the Undo, Redo, Hold, and Fetch commands.

- The **Tools menu** accesses tools and tool modules. Many of these tools (but not all) are also found in the toolbar.

- The **Group menu** contains commands for grouping and ungrouping objects.

- The **Views menu** contains commands that control viewport display.

- The **Create menu** contains shortcuts to the Create panel rollouts for creating most of the objects in 3ds max.

- The **Modifiers menu** has commands for modifying and editing objects.

- The **Character menu** contains commands for managing character assemblies and bones.

- The **Reactor menu** contains commands for dynamically simulating complex physical reactions.

- The **Animation menu** includes advanced commands for character animation.

Figure 1.20 The 3ds max menu bar contains 13 menus that work just like other Windows menus.

SPECIAL CONTROLS

◆ The **Graph Editors menu** commands access modules that manage hierarchies and animations.

◆ The **Rendering menu** commands access modules that control the rendered appearance of objects and backgrounds.

◆ The **Customize menu** contains commands that allow you to customize the user interface and set program preferences.

◆ The **MAXScript menu** contains commands for working with MAXScript, the program's built-in scripting language.

◆ The **Help menu** provides access to the 3ds max 6 help system.

The Main toolbar

The Main toolbar contains buttons and drop-down menus that access the most important tools (**Figure 1.22**). To see all of the buttons at once, your display must be set to a minimum resolution of 1280 × 1024. If the resolution is set lower, some of the buttons will disappear off to one side or the other. To view the hidden buttons, place the cursor in an empty area of the Main toolbar. When the cursor turns into a hand, drag the toolbar to the right or the left until the rest of the buttons appear.

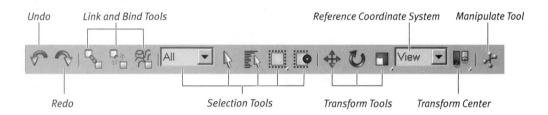

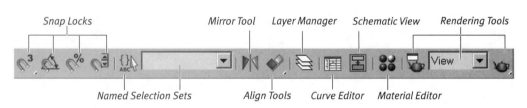

Figure 1.22 The Main toolbar contains the most commonly used tools.

SPECIAL CONTROLS

The viewports

The viewports are the four main viewing areas in the center of the interface (**Figure 1.23**). Viewports can be resized by dragging the borders between two viewports or by dragging the intersection of all four viewports. Right-click a viewport boundary and choose Reset to reset the layout.

Chapter 3, "Viewport Navigation and Display," explains in detail how to work with viewports and viewport controls.

SPECIAL CONTROLS

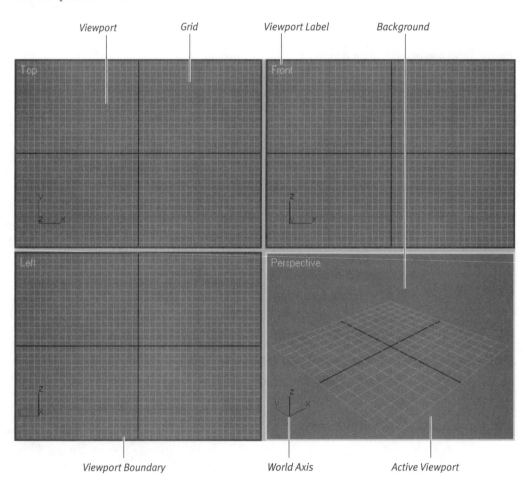

Viewport   *Grid*   *Viewport Label*   *Background*

Viewport Boundary   *World Axis*   *Active Viewport*

Figure 1.23 Viewports display the scene from different angles.

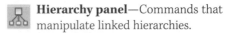

Figure 1.24 3ds max has six command panels of related tools. Click a tab to bring the panel that you want to the foreground.

The command panels

The command panels give you access to the majority of modeling and animation commands. They also provide display controls and an assortment of utilities. You access command panels by clicking tabs at the top of each panel (**Figure 1.24**). Long command panels can be expanded horizontally to form two or more columns by dragging their edges left or right.

The six command panels contain:

Create panel—Commands that create objects.

Modify panel—Commands that reshape objects.

Hierarchy panel—Commands that manipulate linked hierarchies.

Motion panel—Commands that control motion.

Display panel—Commands that control the display of objects.

Utilities panel—Commands for a miscellaneous assortment of tasks.

The status bar controls

The area at the bottom of the interface contains the status bar controls, including command prompts, status information, animation controls, time controls, and viewport controls (**Figure 1.25**). It also includes the MAXScript Mini Listener for scripting commands.

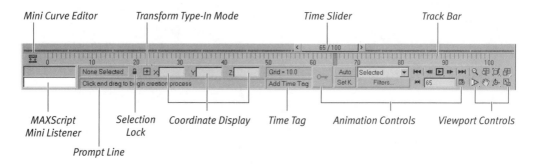

Figure 1.25 The status bar controls include status display, viewport display, animation controls, and time controls.

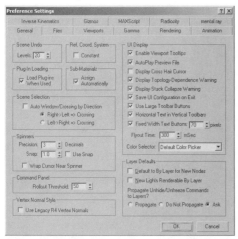

Figure 1.26 The Preference Settings dialog box allows you to set preferences for program features and file management.

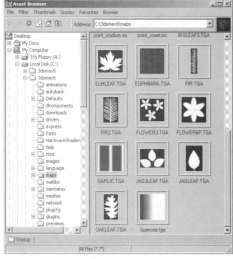

Figure 1.27 Use the Asset Manager to browse external files and to drag elements into your scene.

Additional features

3ds max has a large number of utilities, modules, and dialog boxes. Among them, three stand out as being particularly useful:

◆ The **Preference Settings** dialog box (**Figure 1.26**) contains global settings for numerous features and file management options. You access this dialog box from the Customize menu.

◆ The **Asset Browser** (**Figure 1.27**) allows you to browse for image files and scene files. Use the Asset Browser, which can be found in the Utilities command panel, to drag files directly into your scene.

continued next page

SPECIAL CONTROLS

◆ The **Object Properties** dialog box
(**Figure 1.28**) allows you to access and
manipulate essential object settings.
Access this dialog box by right-clicking a
selected object and choosing Properties
from the menu.

Other useful features include:

◆ The **Viewport Configuration** dialog
box (covered in Chapter 3, "Viewport
Navigation and Display")

◆ The **Viewport Background** dialog box
(Chapter 3)

◆ The **Selection Floater** and the **Display
Floater** (Chapter 4, "Object Selection
and Display")

◆ The **Transform Type-In** dialog box
(Chapter 5, "Transforms")

◆ The **Track View** module (Chapter 7,
"Animation")

◆ The **Light Lister** dialog box (Chapter 11,
"Lights")

◆ The **Material Editor**, **Material/Map
Browser**, and **Material/Map Navigator**
(Chapter 13, "Materials")

◆ The **Environment and Effects** dialog
box (Chapter 14, "Maps")

◆ The **Render Scene** dialog box (Chapter
15, "Rendering")

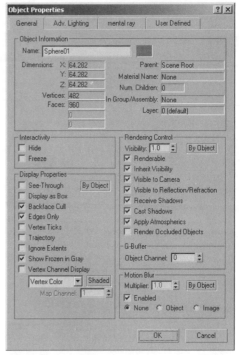

Figure 1.28 The Object Properties dialog box displays
parameters of selected objects.

Figure 1.29 The File menu contains commands for managing files.

Managing Files

When you first initialize the program, it displays a new untitled scene. At this point, you can either start building a new scene or build upon an existing file.

Building a scene generally starts by setting preferences and creating objects, which is covered in Chapter 2, "Creating Objects." If you want to save your scene or work with a previously saved file, you need to know some basic operations:

◆ Open a scene (Ctrl + O)

◆ Open a new scene (Ctrl + N)

◆ Open a recent scene

◆ Play an animation (/)

◆ Save a scene (Ctrl + S)

◆ Save selected objects in the scene

◆ Reset the program

◆ Merge objects into your scene

◆ Replace objects in your scene

◆ Hold the scene in a special Hold file (Alt + Ctrl + H)

◆ Fetch the scene from the Hold file (Alt + Ctrl + F)

◆ Import a scene from a different format

◆ Export a scene to a different format

◆ View an image file

◆ Configure paths

◆ Archive the scene

◆ Exit the program

Most of these file management operations are found in the File menu (**Figure 1.29**).

Now, take a step-by-step look at these operations. If you have never used 3ds max before, you can practice the tasks in the sequence that follows.

MANAGING FILES

The native file format for 3ds max scenes is called a max file. The three-letter extension for scene files is .max.

To open a scene:

1. Choose File > Open.

    The Open File dialog box appears. It opens to the 3dsmax6\scenes directory by default.

2. Navigate to the max scene file you want to open and click the name of the file.

    A thumbnail image of the scene appears in the dialog box (**Figure 1.30**).

3. Click Open.

    The file opens. The layout of the viewports changes to match the layout that was saved with the scene file. The objects in the scene are displayed in the viewports (**Figure 1.31**).

    If the file you are opening was saved with an earlier version of the program, you will be prompted to resave the file.

✔ Tips

■ To reopen a scene that was opened just recently, choose File > Open Recent.

■ 3ds max opens only one scene file at a time. If you have enough RAM and graphics card memory, and you are using the Heidi software display driver or an OpenGL display driver, you can run multiple sessions of the program and open a different scene file in each.

■ The New command saves settings from the previously loaded scene and places them in a new, untitled scene. You are also given the option of keeping objects and their hierarchy of links.

Figure 1.30 The Open File dialog box opens to the 3dsmax6\scenes directory by default. The thumbnail in the Open File dialog box displays the contents of the selected scene file.

Figure 1.31 When you open a scene file, the contents of the file are displayed in the viewports.

Figure 1.32 The scene opens to the first frame of the animation.

Figure 1.33 The animation controls work just like a VCR.

Figure 1.34 When the animation plays back, the dragon flies across the scene.

If a scene file contains an animation track, you can play it back in the viewports. The controls governing animation playback are similar to those of a VCR.

To play an animation:

1. Open an animated scene file (**Figure 1.32**).

2. ▶ Click Play Animation (**Figure 1.33**).
   The animation plays back in the current viewport (**Figure 1.34**).

✔ Tips

- The keyboard shortcut for playing an animation and stopping it is the / key.

- Go to Start displays the first frame of the animation. The keyboard shortcut is the Home key.

- Go to End displays the last frame of the animation. The keyboard shortcut is the End key.

- The Next Frame button advances the animation by one frame.

- The Previous Frame button moves the animation back one frame.

MANAGING FILES

The File menu offers a quick way to view image files, including both still images and animations.

To view an image file:

1. Choose File > View Image File.

2. Navigate to the image you want to view. Then click the file to highlight it.

   Images may be found in the 3dsmax6\images folder (**Figure 1.35**).

3. Click View (if you want to view the image and keep surfing).

   or

   Click Open (if you want to open the image and close the dialog box).

   The image file appears on your screen (**Figure 1.36**).

Figure 1.35 The View File dialog box displays information about viewable image files.

Figure 1.36 The image file that you select appears in a special window called the rendered frame window.

Managing Files

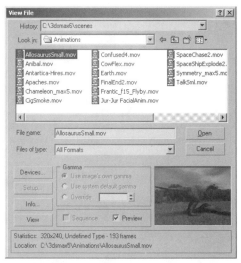

Figure 1.37 Select the animation you want to play.

Figure 1.38 Playing back an animation in the QuickTime movie player.

To view an animation file:

1. Choose File > View Image File.

2. Navigate to the animation you want to view, and highlight the file.

   Animations may be found in the 3dsmax6\Animations folder (**Figure 1.37**).

3. Click View (if you want to view the animation and keep surfing).

   or

   Click Open (if you want to open the animation and close the dialog box).

   A movie player appears on your screen (**Figure 1.38**). If it is an animation file, it opens in Windows Media Player or QuickTime Player, or whatever program is associated with that file type.

✔ Tips

- You can also view image files from the Asset Manager, the Material Editor, and the rendered frame window.

- To associate a file with a program in Windows, open a window in Windows Explorer and choose Tools > Folder Options. Click the File Types tab, and navigate to the file type you want to associate. Highlight the file, and click Change. Then choose a program, and click OK.

MANAGING FILES

To save a scene:

1. Choose File > Save.

   If you are saving a previously saved scene, the file is saved.

   If the scene has never been saved and named before, the Save File As dialog box appears (**Figure 1.39**).

2. Navigate to the folder where you want to save the file.

3. Type a name for your scene in the File name field (**Figure 1.40**).

4. Click Save.

   The file is saved under the new file name. A snapshot of the active viewport (the one with the yellow border) is saved as the thumbnail image for the new file.

If you want to save the scene under a different name, use the Save As command.

To save as:

1. Choose File > Save As.

2. Follow steps 2 through 4 for saving a scene.

✔ Tips

- 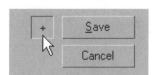 To increment a file name by +01, click the plus sign (+) in the Save File As dialog box (**Figure 1.41**).

- To save off a copy of the scene so that you can refer to it later, choose File > Save Copy As. The program will suggest a file name that is incremented by +01, or you can give the file a different name.

- To increment a file automatically when saving, choose Customize > Preferences and click the Files tab. Then check Increment on Save (**Figure 1.42**).

- To save selected objects in your scene to a new file, choose File > Save Selected.

Figure 1.39 You save new or renamed scene files using the Save File As dialog box.

Figure 1.40 Rename scene files using the Save File As dialog box.

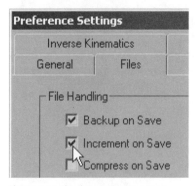

Figure 1.41 Click the plus sign to increment the filename by 01.

Preference Settings

Inverse Kinematics

General   Files

File Handling

☑ Backup on Save

☑ Increment on Save

☐ Compress on Save

Figure 1.42 Check Increment on Save to make the program automatically increment the file each time you save.

MANAGING FILES

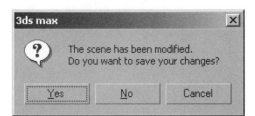

Figure 1.43 This dialog box gives you the opportunity to save changes.

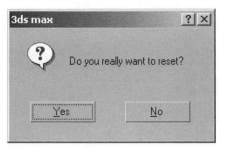

Figure 1.44 Last chance!

The Reset command returns the program to its initial state. All objects, hierarchy, animation data, and materials are eliminated. A new, untitled scene is displayed using the default viewport layout.

To reset the program:

1. Choose File > Reset.

   If you have not saved all of your changes, you will be prompted to do so (**Figure 1.43**). Then you will be asked if you want to reset the program (**Figure 1.44**).

2. Click Yes.

   The original settings are restored.

✔ Tip

- If the layout of the interface has been changed, the Reset command will not restore the original layout. Instead, choose Customize > Revert to Startup Layout.

To exit the program:

1. Choose File > Exit.

2. If necessary, save changes to the current file.

   The program window closes and the program quits.

✔ Tip

- To quit the program, you can also close the program window.

By merging files, you can bring objects into your current scene from other scene files, along with their materials and animation data. This allows you to develop parts of your scene in different files and then combine them into a single scene.

To merge an object into a scene:

1. Choose File > Reset.

   or

   Open a scene file (**Figure 1.45**).

2. Choose File > Merge.

3. Select and open the file that contains the objects you want to merge into the scene file you opened in step 1.

   The Merge dialog box appears with a list of objects in the scene file.

4. Select the object you want to merge (**Figure 1.46**). Then click OK.

   The object appears in the scene. White lines drawn around the edges of the object indicate that it is selected (**Figure 1.47**). To deselect the object, press the Ctrl key and click the object.

✔ Tip

■ If the object has the same name as an object that is already in the scene, you will be prompted to change the name of the object before merging it, to skip merging the object, or to delete the old object in your current file (**Figure 1.48**). A similar prompt appears when you merge materials that have duplicate names.

   Because the program permits duplicate naming, it does not require that you change duplicate names before merging objects or materials that have the same name. However, it is a good practice to give each object or material a unique name so you can locate it easily later when your scene gets more complex.

Figure 1.45 Dragon_Character_Rig.max before merging it with another file.

Figure 1.46 In the Merge dialog box, choose the objects that you want to add to your scene.

Figure 1.47 The scene after merging in the object.

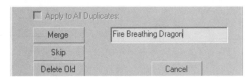

Figure 1.48 Changing the name of a duplicate object.

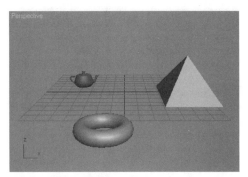

Figure 1.49 The initial scene file contains a teapot, a torus, and a pyramid.

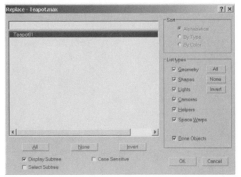

Figure 1.50 In the second scene file, the only object with the same name is the teapot.

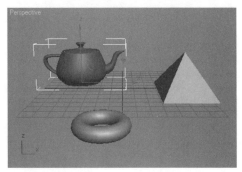

Figure 1.51 After replacing the teapot object, the new teapot is selected.

Using the Replace command, you can substitute an object in your scene with another object with the same name that is saved in another scene. The substitute object takes on the properties and animation data of the object it replaces. This allows you to animate your scene faster by using simple objects and then substituting complex objects later when you have finished developing them.

To replace an object in a scene:

1. Open a scene file (**Figure 1.49**).

2. Choose File > Replace.

3. In the Replace File dialog box, open the scene that has the object you want to substitute into your file. If the scene does not have an object with the same name as an object in your current scene, you will not be able to access the file.

4. Select the objects you want to import as replacements.
   The Replace dialog box appears (**Figure 1.50**).

5. Click Yes to replace materials along with the objects, or click No to bring in objects only. If in doubt, choose No.
   The replacement objects appear in the scene (**Figure 1.51**).

MANAGING FILES

25

Use the Import and Export commands to exchange geometry with other 3D modeling programs. You can also import .AI files from Adobe Illustrator.

Exporting files causes 3ds max to translate the native .max scene information into universal 3D file formats such as .3DS or .DXF. Because these universal files are usually less robust, some of the scene information may change or disappear. 3ds max usually warns you of such changes, while preserving the most important information.

To import a file:

1. Choose File > Import.

   The Select File to Import dialog box appears.

2. Select a file format from the Files of type menu (**Figure 1.52**).

3. Double-click the name of the file you want to import.

4. If the 3DS Import dialog box appears, choose Completely Replace Current Scene and check Convert Units.

5. Click OK to accept the default settings. The imported file appears on the screen (**Figure 1.53**).

To export a file:

1. Choose File > Export. The Select File to Export dialog box appears.

2. Select an export file format from the Save as type menu (**Figure 1.54**).

3. Choose a directory to hold the exported file.

4. Name the file, and click Save.

3D Studio Mesh (*.3DS,*.PRJ)
Adobe Illustrator (*.AI)
AutoCAD Drawing (*.DWG,*.DXF)
IGES (*.IGE,*.IGS,*.IGES)
Lightscape (*.LS,*.VW,*.LP)
3D Studio Shape (*.SHP)
StereoLitho (*.STL)
VRML (*.WRL,*.WRZ)
VIZ Material XML Import (*.XML)

Figure 1.52 When you import a file, start by choosing a file type from the Select File to Import dialog box.

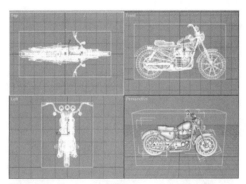

Figure 1.53 The imported files appear in the 3ds max viewports.

3D Studio (*.3DS)
Adobe Illustrator (*.AI)
ASCII Scene Export (*.ASE)
Lightscape Material (*.ATR)
Lightscape Blocks (*.BLK)
Lightscape Parameter (*.DF)
AutoCAD (*.DWG)
AutoCAD (*.DXF)
IGES (*.IGS)

Figure 1.54 When you export a file, you select a file and an export file format.

Figure 1.55 The file before you make any changes.

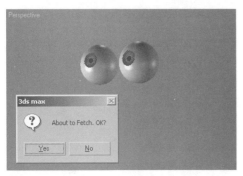

Figure 1.56 Click Yes to restore the original file.

Figure 1.57 The restored hold file.

If you want to try out some changes that you are not sure you will like, you can back up your scene to a temporary file called a **hold file**. This file is named maxhold.max, and it is saved in the autoback directory. To restore the contents of the hold file to the current scene, you use the Fetch command.

To hold a file:

1. Open a scene file (**Figure 1.55**).

2. Choose Edit > Hold.

   The scene is backed up to the Autoback directory. You can now try out changes to your scene.

To fetch a file:

1. Choose Edit > Fetch.

2. In the About to Fetch. OK? dialog box, click Yes (**Figure 1.56**).

   The program restores the hold file to the current scene (**Figure 1.57**).

✔ Tip

- Remember that fetching a file overwrites the current scene without saving changes. If you want to save changes, save the file before you choose Fetch.

   The hold file in the Autoback directory remains intact until it is overwritten by the next Hold command. I have at times saved myself a good deal of heartache by recovering lost work from this file.

MANAGING FILES

File paths cause the program to look for certain types of files in designated locations on your system or network. For example, if you are working on a project, you can configure the program to look in the project scene folder for scene files, and the project map folder for map files. If more than one person is working on the project, you can make the files available across a network.

To configure a file path:

1. Choose Customize > Configure Paths.

   The Configure Paths dialog box appears (**Figure 1.58**).

2. Select a file type and click Modify.

3. In the Choose Directory for dialog box, navigate to a folder or click Create New Folder and open the new folder.

4. Click Use Path.

5. Click OK.

   The program goes to the designated folder whenever you attempt to open a file of that type. If the path is a scene file path, the program will begin saving scene files to the newly designated folder, instead of to the default 3dsmax6\scenes folder.

Most file types only have one path, but bitmaps can have multiple paths, which 3ds max searches in this order:

1. The path of the image file last loaded.

2. The folder of the current scene.

3. The subfolders below the current scene.

4. The paths listed in the External Files tab panel of the Configure Paths dialog box, starting at the top of the list (**Figure 1.59**).

If a bitmap that has been used in the scene is not available along any of the paths listed, you will be prompted to locate it.

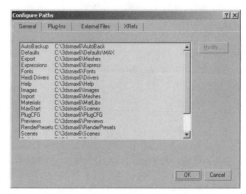

Figure 1.58 The Configure Paths dialog box tells the program where to find different types of files.

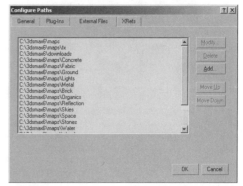

Figure 1.59 The External Files panel allows you to add a sequence of paths for finding bitmaps.

The 3dsmax.ini file

File pathnames are stored in 3dsmax.ini, located in the main 3dsmax directory. The .INI file is an ASCII text file that contains all the settings that the program reads upon initialization. If you want, you can open and edit this file directly with a text editor, such as Notepad. If you delete the file, the program will create a new .INI file the next time it boots using the default pathnames and preferences.

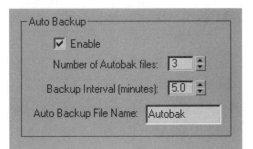

Figure 1.60 The Auto Backup area of the Files panel of the Preference Settings dialog box. These settings govern saving, backing up, and archiving files.

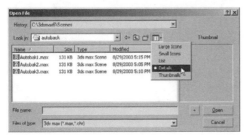

Figure 1.61 When restoring a scene file from the Autoback directory, click Details to see which file was modified the most recently.

Backup File Naming

The automatic backup process saves a limited number of backup files at set intervals of time. 3ds max automatically names the files Autobak1.max, Autobak2.max, Autobak3.max, and so on to AutobakN.max, where N is the maximum number of backup files you have set the program to save. When the number of backup files exceeds the maximum, the backup process saves over the oldest file starting with Autobak1.max.

Backing up files is crucial to the success of any project. Besides saving files manually, you can set a preference to back up files automatically.

To back up files automatically:

1. Choose Customize > Preferences.

2. In the Preference Settings dialog box, click the Files tab.

3. In the Auto Backup area, be sure that Enable is checked (**Figure 1.60**).

4. Enter the maximum number of backup files to maintain, or use the default of three files.

5. Enter the backup interval in minutes, or use the default of five minutes.

6. Click OK.

To recover a file from automatic backup:

1. Choose File > Open.

2. Navigate to the 3dsmax6\Autoback folder.

3. Click the View Menu icon and choose Details icon in the upper-right corner of the dialog box.

   The modification dates of the Auto Backup files appear (**Figure 1.61**).

4. Open the most recently modified file.

5. Choose File > Save As. Navigate to the scenes folder and rename your file.

✔ Tip

■ To back up your file every time you use Save, choose Customize > Preferences > Files > Backup on Save. Your file will be saved to a nonincrementing file in the Autoback folder called MaxBack.bak.

MANAGING FILES

The Archive command gathers all the bitmaps that you used in a scene and archives them with the scene into a ZIP file.

To archive a scene:

1. Open the scene file you want to archive.

2. Choose File > Archive > Archive.
   The File Archive dialog box appears.

3. Navigate to the folder where you want to save the archive. If you want to give the archive a different name than the name of your scene file, enter the new name in the File name field (**Figure 1.62**).

4. Click Save.
   A log window appears briefly and then disappears. The scene and any bitmaps used in the scene are zipped up and saved in the folder you designated (**Figure 1.63**). A file called Maxfiles. txt is also created and added to the archive. This file contains a list of all the files in the archive and their original pathnames (**Figure 1.64**).

To open an archived scene:

1. Using a decompression program such as WinZip, extract the archived files to a folder.

2. Choose File > Open.

3. Navigate to the scene file and click Open.
   The scene opens. If a bitmap is not in its original location, you will be prompted to browse for the missing file (**Figure 1.65**). If this happens, browse to the bitmap in the extracted archive, or move the bitmap to the location shown in the Missing External Files dialog box. Then choose File > Open Recent to reopen the scene.

Figure 1.62 Navigate to the folder where you want to save the archive.

Figure 1.63 Viewing the archive files in WinZip before extracting them to a folder.

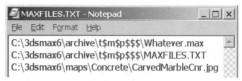

Figure 1.64 Viewing the list of files and pathnames stored in the Maxfiles.txt file.

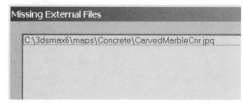

Figure 1.65 The Missing External Files prompts you to browse for any bitmaps that the program cannot find.

CREATING OBJECTS

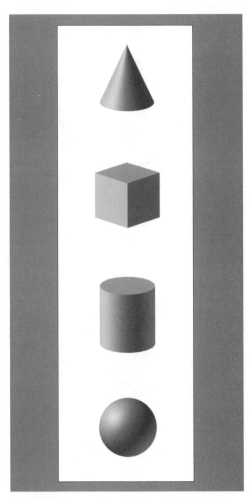

Everything in nature can be represented as a combination of geometric forms. As the painter Paul Cézanne once wrote, "Treat nature in terms of the cylinder, the sphere, the cone; everything in proper perspective." He also is reported to have said, "One must first of all study geometric forms: the cone, the cube, the cylinder, the sphere."

Today, 3D artists use geometric forms called **objects** to create and animate entire worlds. Starting with the cone, the cube, the cylinder, and the sphere (**Figure 2.1**), you can combine and manipulate basic objects to create highly complex and realistic scenes.

This chapter explains how to create mesh objects and shape splines, which are the basic building blocks of 3D scenes. You will also learn how to create helper objects to assist you in placing objects in your scene. In later chapters, you will learn to create lights and cameras, and to create compound objects by combining objects together.

Figure 2.1 The cone, the cube, the cylinder, and the sphere are basic objects in 3ds max.

About Creating Objects

3ds max is written in an **object-oriented** programming language called C++. This means that the type of object you create and the current status of that object determine which commands may next be applied. If a command may not be applied to an object, it becomes unavailable, until the object changes to an appropriate state.

When you create an object in 3ds max, it is automatically assigned a name, a color, a position, an orientation, a pivot point, an axis tripod, display properties, and rendering properties. If an object can be rendered to an image output file, a white **bounding box** appears at the dimensional extents of the object when it is selected (**Figure 2.2**).

As you place objects in a scene, the viewports display them from different angles. The Front, Left, and Top viewports always view objects from the front, left, and top of the world. By default, objects in these views are displayed in **wireframe**. In contrast, the Perspective viewport can display an object from any angle. By default it looks at the scene from in front and a little above, and draws objects using a smooth shaded mode of display (**Figure 2.3**).

The grids that you see in the viewports are all part of the **home grid**. The home grid provides construction planes for creating objects. What this means is that objects automatically sit on top of the grid when they are created. Because the grids of the home grid are perpendicular to one another, objects created in different viewports may orient in different directions (**Figure 2.4**).

For more information on navigating viewports and viewport modes of display, see Chapter 3, "Viewport Navigation and Display."

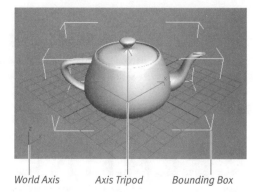

World Axis   Axis Tripod   Bounding Box

Figure 2.2 The axis tripod and bounding box indicate that the object is selected. The origin of the axis tripod is located at the pivot point of the object; the bounding box is drawn at the object's extents.

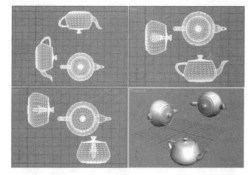

Figure 2.3 Viewing a scene from four different angles. Three of the views are displayed in wireframe; the Perspective view is shaded.

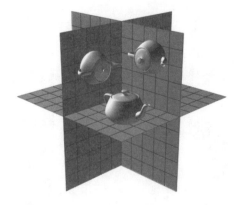

Figure 2.4 The home grid consists of three intersecting grids. Creating objects on different grids results in different orientations.

Figure 2.5 The Create command panel contains all of the object creation commands.

Figure 2.6
The Create menu contains shortcuts to most of the object creation commands in the Create panel.

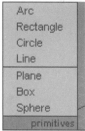

Figure 2.7 The primitives quad menu contains shortcuts to commands for creating the most commonly used primitives.

Most objects that you create in 3ds max start out as **parametric objects**. Parametric objects are mathematically defined forms that you give exact size and proportion by assigning numerical values called **parameters**. Simple parametric objects that define basic geometric forms are known as **parametric primitives**, or simply **primitives**.

Non-parametric objects are created by converting them from parametric objects or by building them from smaller components. Rather than being defined by mathematical equations, non-parametric objects are defined by explicit descriptions of each of their parts. Most non-parametric objects include built-in commands for editing their structures. Such objects are called **editable objects** in 3ds max.

All commands for creating objects are found in the tab panels and drop-down menus of the Create command panel (**Figure 2.5**). For your convenience, 3ds max provides shortcuts to some of these commands:

◆ **Create menu** (**Figure 2.6**). Organized by object type, contains shortcuts to nearly all of the object creation commands in a series of flyout menus.

◆ **Primitives quad menu** (**Figure 2.7**). Contains shortcuts to the most commonly created primitives. Access this menu by Ctrl + right-clicking in any viewport.

◆ **Reactor panel**. Contains advanced objects for simulating complex physical phenomena (**Figure 2.8**). Found on the left-hand side of the user interface, this panel may be dragged out by its upper edge and closed when not in use.

Figure 2.8 The Reactor panel contains shortcuts to commands for creating simulations of physical phenomena.

The click and drag method is highly intuitive.

To create an object by clicking and dragging:

1. In the Create panel, click the button for the object you want to create. The creation rollouts for the object appear (**Figure 2.9**).

2. Choose an option from the Creation Method rollout, or simply use the default.

3. In the Perspective viewport, click and drag across the grid to create the base of the object. Release the mouse button when the base is the right size (**Figure 2.10**).

4. If the object is not complete, move and click to set other parameters as needed.

5. Adjust the parameters by entering new values in the Parameters rollout or by dragging the spinners next to parameter input fields (**Figure 2.11**).

   The object updates in the viewport interactively (**Figure 2.12**).

6. Right-click in any viewport to exit object-creation mode.

The Utah Teapot

Students often ask me why the Teapot object is included among the Standard Primitives. After all, how many forms are based on teapots? It all started in the 1970s at the University of Utah when a computer graphics researcher named Martin Newell created an elegant wireframe model of a teapot. His colleague, James Blinn, used the teapot to experiment with methods of surface rendering. Soon, so many people were making reflecting teapots that the "Utah Teapot" became immortalized as a symbol of the field.

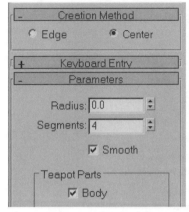

Figure 2.9 The teapot creation rollout.

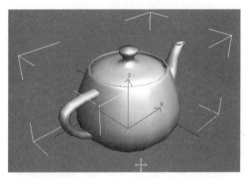

Figure 2.10 The quickest way to create a mesh object is to click and drag.

Figure 2.11 Dragging a spinner.

Figure 2.12 Increasing the value of the Radius parameter increases the size of the teapot.

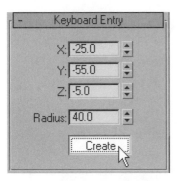

Figure 2.13 After entering the location and dimensions of an object, click Create.

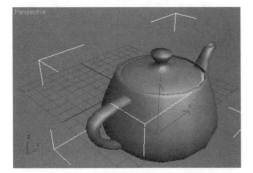

Figure 2.14 Increasing the number of segments makes the teapot object appear smoother.

Figure 2.15 You make variations on a theme by changing settings before you click Create.

The keyboard-entry method aids precision.

To create an object using the keyboard-entry method:

1. Activate the Perspective viewport.

2. In the Create panel, click on the button for the object you want to create.

3. Open the Keyboard Entry rollout, and enter the dimensions of the object.

   If you want to position the object in a place other than the origin, enter location coordinates for X, Y, and Z as well.

4. Click Create (**Figure 2.13**).

5. Adjust the creation parameters in the Parameters rollout of the Create panel or the Modify panel (**Figure 2.14**).

✔ Tip

- You can create as many objects as you like by clicking the Create button repeatedly. Or you can change the settings a little each time to get variations on a theme (**Figure 2.15**).

Disappearing Parameters

Beginners are often surprised when their creation parameters disappear. This usually happens when they click in a viewport and inadvertently start creating another object.

As long as a newly created object remains selected, its parameters will appear in the Create panel. Once the object is deselected, you access its parameters in the Modify panel. To do so, click the Modify tab and then click the object to reselect it. The creation parameters reappear. Now you can adjust them as much as you like.

ABOUT CREATING OBJECTS

3ds max automatically assigns names to objects based on the object type and the order in which it was created. For example, the first, second, and third sphere that you create will be named Sphere01, Sphere02, and Sphere03. After you create your objects, it is helpful if you assign more descriptive names so you can find them easily when your scene gets more complex.

3ds max also assigns colors to objects as you create them. By default, color assignment is random, but you can change the color of objects after they are created, or set an option so that all objects are assigned the same color.

To assign a name and a color to an object:

1. Create an object, or select an existing object by clicking on it.

2. In the Create panel, highlight the name of the object in the Name and Color rollout (**Figure 2.16**).

3. Enter a new name (**Figure 2.17**).

4. Click on the color swatch located just to the right of the name field.

   The Object Color dialog box appears (**Figure 2.18**).

5. Click on a swatch to pick color, and click OK.

   The object changes to the new shade.

✔ Tips

- To assign the same color to objects as you create them, uncheck Assign Random Colors in the Object Color dialog box.

- To assign the same color to existing objects, click and drag a selection region around them before picking a color (**Figure 2.19**). Note that you cannot assign a name to a multiple selection.

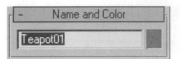

Figure 2.16 Highlighting the name of the object.

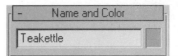

Figure 2.17 Entering a new name.

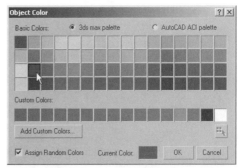

Figure 2.18 Picking a color from the Object Color dialog box.

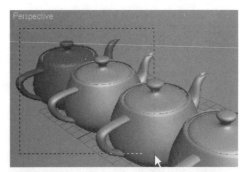

Figure 2.19 Selecting a group of objects by dragging a selection window around them.

ABOUT CREATING OBJECTS

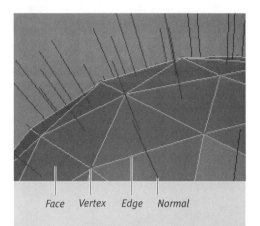

Face   Vertex   Edge   Normal

Mesh Concepts

There are three components of a mesh:

 Vertices are point locations in space.

 Edges are lines that connect vertices.

 Faces are triangular surfaces bound by 3 edges and 3 vertices.

Surface normals are vectors that stick straight up from the center of each face. Called *normals* for short, they determine which side of the face is rendered.

Smoothing (below) creates gradations of value across mesh surfaces by averaging the intensity of light between vertices. The more vertices that are present, the subtler the gradations will be, and the smoother the mesh surface will appear.

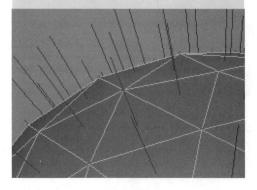

Creating Mesh Objects

Mesh primitives come in two varieties: **Standard Primitives**, which include basic geometric forms, and **Extended Primitives**, which include more complex objects. By clicking on different object types, you can quickly create objects from predefined forms.

In the next few pages, I'll show you how to intuitively create objects using the click and drag method. After you master this simple technique, try creating a few objects with the keyboard entry method to see what this approach has to offer.

Creating Standard Primitives

There are ten Standard Primitives in 3ds max 6: the Box, Cone, Sphere, GeoSphere, Cylinder, Tube, Torus, Pyramid, Teapot, and Plane (**Figure 2.20**).

Standard Primitives are found in the Geometry branch of the Create panel, which is "on deck" when you start the program (**Figure 2.21**). Shortcuts to these commands are located in the Create menu.

Shortcuts to the most commonly used primitives are found in the primitives quad menu, as described on page 33.

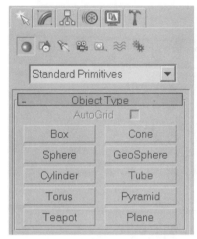

Figure 2.21 Standard Primitives are located in the Geometry branch of the Create panel.

Figure 2.20 Standard Primitives are used to make basic geometric forms.

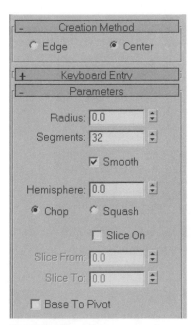

Figure 2.22 The main parameter of a Sphere is its Radius.

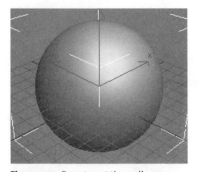

Figure 2.23 Drag to set the radius.

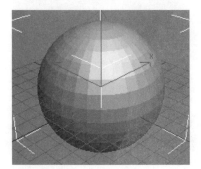

Figure 2.24 You unsmooth a sphere by unchecking the Smooth parameter.

To create a standard sphere:

1. In the Create panel, click Sphere.

   The Sphere creation rollout appears (**Figure 2.22**).

2. In the Perspective viewport, click and drag a sphere of any size (**Figure 2.23**).

3. Release the mouse button to set the radius.

✔ Tips

- To make a sphere sit on top of the grid, check Base to Pivot. This moves the pivot point of the object to its base.

- To make a radial object, such as a sphere, geosphere, cylinder, or cone, appear smoother, increase the Sides parameter. To unsmooth a radial object, so it appears faceted, uncheck Smooth (**Figure 2.24**).

Low-Poly Objects

Low-polygon count objects, or "low-poly objects," are the lifeblood of interactive applications like 3D games. Because they have fewer faces, low-poly objects can be redrawn more quickly than other objects.

With a GeoSphere, you can easily create low-poly spheres, such as a tetrahedra, octahedra, or icosahedra (above).

To find out how many faces there are in an object, select the object, and press 7. This toggles the display of the Polygon Counter, which appears in the upper-left corner of the active viewport.

CREATING MESH OBJECTS

Square objects, such as planes, boxes, and pyramids, use a click-drag sequence to define the base. An additional move and click action defines the height of a box or pyramid.

To create a box:

1. In the Create panel, click Box.

   The Box creation rollout appears (**Figure 2.25**).

2. In the Perspective viewport, click and drag across the grid to form the base of the box.

3. Release the mouse button to set the length and width of the box (**Figure 2.26**).

4. Without clicking, move the cursor upward in the viewport.

5. Click to set the height (**Figure 2.27**).

✔ Tips

■ Planes are simple to create. You just click and drag to set the length and width, as in step 2.

■ To create a box that hangs below the grid plane, move the cursor downward in step 4.

■ To create a box with equal sides, choose Cube in the Creation Method rollout.

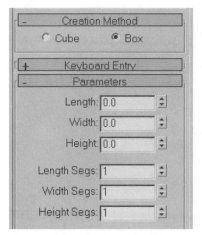

Figure 2.25 A box has inputs for length, width, and height.

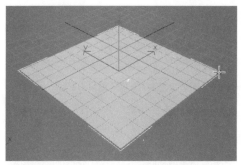

Figure 2.26 Drag to set the length and width.

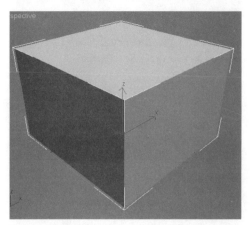

Figure 2.27 Move and click to set the height.

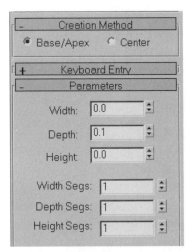

Figure 2.28 A pyramid has width and depth as well as height.

To create a pyramid:

1. In the Create panel, click Pyramid.

   The Pyramid creation rollout appears (**Figure 2.28**).

2. In the Perspective viewport, click and drag across the grid to form the base of the pyramid.

3. Release the mouse button to set the width and depth of the base (**Figure 2.29**).

4. Without clicking, move the cursor upward in the viewport.

5. Click to set the height (**Figure 2.30**).

✔ Tips

- To create a square base for a box, plane, or pyramid, hold down the Ctrl key as you drag out the base. In this method, the first click sets the center of the base, and dragging causes the base to grow equally in all directions.

- To increase the number of divisions in a box, plane, or pyramid, increase the segment parameter values.

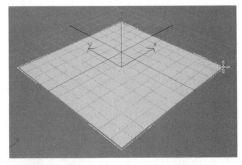

Figure 2.29 Drag to set the base of the pyramid.

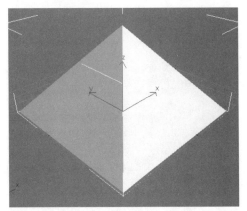

Figure 2.30 Move and click to set the height.

Cylinders, cones, torii, and tubes each have a radius and a height. Cones, torii, and tubes also have a second radius.

To create a cylinder:

1. In the Create panel, click Cylinder.

   The Cylinder creation rollout appears (**Figure 2.31**).

2. In the Perspective viewport, click and drag the base of the cylinder.

3. Release the mouse button to set the base radius (**Figure 2.32**).

4. Without clicking, move the cursor up in the viewport.

5. Click to set the height (**Figure 2.33**).

✔ Tip

■ To slice a radial object like you slice an apple, check Slice. Then set the beginning and end of the slice in degrees of arc by entering Slice From and Slice To values.

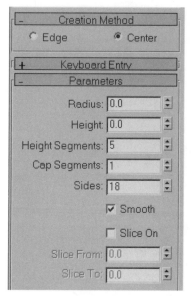

Figure 2.31 A cylinder has a radius and a height. It can also be sliced.

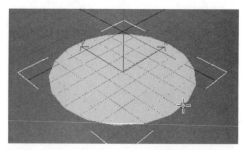

Figure 2.32 Drag outward to set the radius.

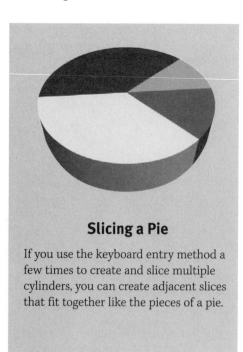

Slicing a Pie

If you use the keyboard entry method a few times to create and slice multiple cylinders, you can create adjacent slices that fit together like the pieces of a pie.

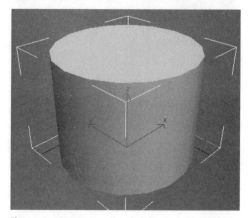

Figure 2.33 Drag upward and click to set the height.

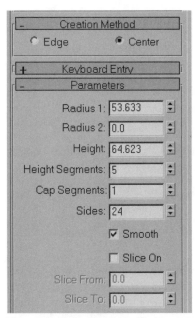

Figure 2.34 A cone has two radii.

A cone is created in the same manner as a cylinder, with two additional steps at the end.

To create a cone:

1. In the Create panel, click Cone.

   The Cone creation rollout appears (**Figure 2.34**).

2. In the Perspective viewport, click and drag the base of the cone.

3. Release the mouse button to set the base radius (**Figure 2.35**).

4. Without clicking, move the cursor up in the viewport.

5. Click to set the height (**Figure 2.36**).

6. Without clicking, move the cursor down to establish the radius for the top.

   If you want to close up the point at the top of the cone, drag downward from the top until it closes up.

7. Click to set the radius of the top (**Figure 2.37**).

✔ Tip

■ You can make the radius of the top wider than the radius of the base by dragging upward in the viewport in step 6.

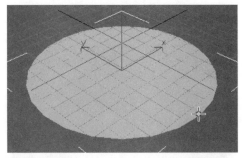

Figure 2.35 Drag outward to set the radius of the base.

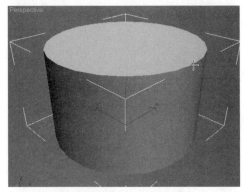

Figure 2.36 Drag upward to set the height.

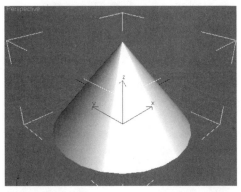

Figure 2.37 Move down and click to complete the top.

The second radius of a torus defines the thickness of its cross section.

To create a torus:

1. In the Create panel, click Torus.

   The Torus creation rollout appears (**Figure 2.38**).

2. In the Perspective viewport, place the cursor where you want the center of the torus to be. Then click and drag outward.

3. Release the mouse button to set the first radius (**Figure 2.39**).

4. Without clicking, move the cursor back toward the center of the torus.

5. Click to set the second radius (**Figure 2.40**).

   This sets the thickness of the torus.

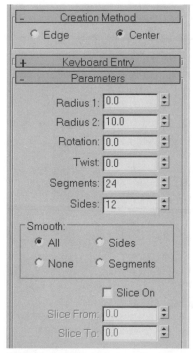

Figure 2.38 A torus has two radii.

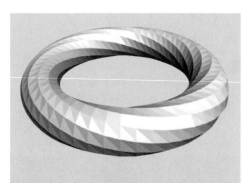

Fun with Parameters

If you take a closer look at some of the object creation parameters, you will find that you can make a lot of interesting variations on a theme. For instance, this torus was created by setting Twist to 360, Segments to 54, and Smooth to None.

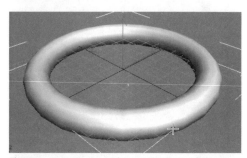

Figure 2.39 Drag outward to set the first radius.

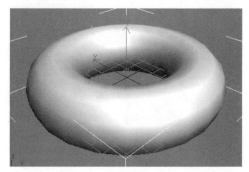

Figure 2.40 Drag inward to set the second radius.

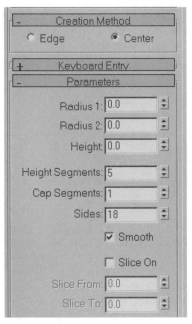

Figure 2.41 A tube has two radii and height.

A tube has an inner and outer radius, as well as a height.

To create a tube:

1. In the Create panel, click Tube.

   The Tube creation rollout appears (**Figure 2.41**).

2. In the Perspective viewport, place the cursor where you want the center of the tube to be. Then click and drag outward.

3. Release the mouse button to set the first radius (**Figure 2.42**).

   This will be the outer wall of the tube.

4. Without clicking, move the cursor back toward the center of the tube.

5. Click to set the second radius (**Figure 2.43**).

   This defines the inner wall of the tube.

6. Move the cursor up in the viewport. Then click to set the height (**Figure 2.44**).

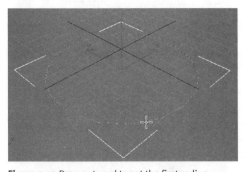

Figure 2.42 Drag outward to set the first radius.

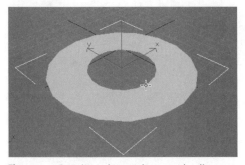

Figure 2.43 Drag inward to set the second radius.

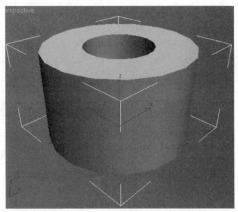

Figure 2.44 The completed tube.

Creating Extended Primitives

Extended Primitives are more complex objects that take a little more work to create than Standard Primitives. Available objects include the ChamferBox, ChamferCyl, OilTank, Capsule, Spindle, Gengon, Prism, L-Ext, C-Ext, Hedra, Torus Knot, RingWave, and Hose (**Figure 2.45**).

Like Standard Primitives, each of these objects has its own characteristic set of parameters. Because they are more complex, Extended Primitives have more parameters.

Extended Primitives are found in the drop-down menu of the Geometry category (**Figure 2.46**). Shortcuts to these commands are found in the Create menu.

Figure 2.46 Extended Primitives are found in the Geometry drop-down menu.

Figure 2.45 Extended Primitives have more specialized forms.

CREATING MESH OBJECTS

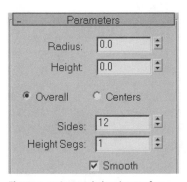

Figure 2.47 A capsule has inputs for radius and height.

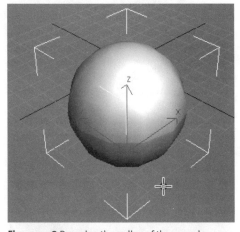

Figure 2.48 Dragging the radius of the capsule.

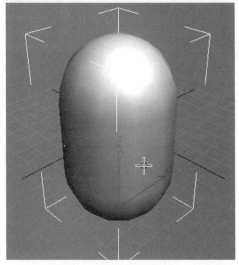

Figure 2.49 Setting the capsule's height.

To create an extended primitive:

1. Open the drop-down menu of the Geometry branch of the Create panel. Then choose Extended Primitives.

   A menu of Extended Primitives appears in the Object Type rollout (**Figure 2.46**).

2. Click the name of an Extended Primitive.

   The parameters for that object appear in the Create panel (**Figure 2.47**).

3. In the Perspective viewport, click and drag the radius or base (**Figure 2.48**).

4. Move the cursor up or down in the viewport and then click to set the height (**Figure 2.49**).

5. Keep moving and clicking the cursor to set additional parameters, such as length, width, height, radius, fillet, cap height, segments, slices, or sides (**Figure 2.50**).

6. Adjust the dimensions of your object in the Parameters rollout. Remember, if the object becomes deselected, you re-access its parameters in the Modify panel.

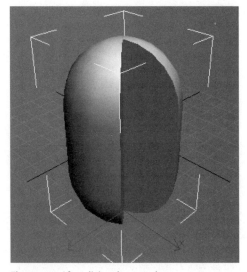

Figure 2.50 After slicing the capsule.

A spindle is like a capsule with pointed ends called **caps**. You adjust the slope, or "pointiness," of the caps by adjusting their height.

To create a spindle:

1. In the Create panel, click Capsule.
   The Capsule rollout appears (**Figure 2.51**).

2. In the Perspective viewport, click and drag the radius of the capsule (**Figure 2.52**).

3. Move the cursor, and click to set the height (**Figure 2.53**).

4. Move the cursor up again, and click to set the cap height (**Figure 2.54**).
   The caps become more pointy or flat.

✔ Tips

- The Blend parameter (not shown) allows you to soften the edges of the cap.

- The oil tank is a variation on the spindle that has rounded ends like a capsule.

- As with any radial object, adding more sides to the spindle, capsule, or oil tank makes them look rounder and smoother.

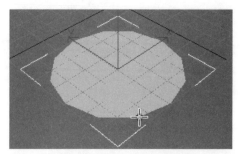

Figure 2.52 Dragging the radius of a spindle.

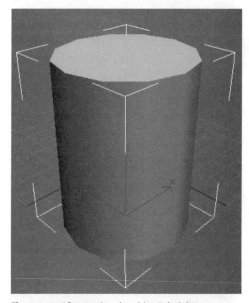

Figure 2.53 After setting the object's height.

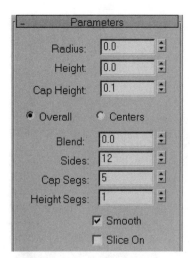

Figure 2.51 A spindle has inputs for radius, height, and cap height.

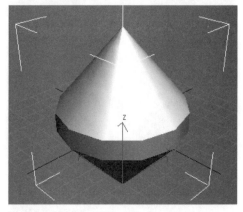

Figure 2.54 Click again to set the cap height.

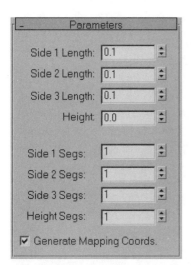

Figure 2.55 A prism has height and length settings for each side.

The Prism is a triangle projected into three dimensions.

To create a Prism:

1. In the Create panel, click Prism.
   The Prism rollout appears (**Figure 2.55**).

2. In the Perspective viewport, click and drag to set the length of the first side of the prism (**Figure 2.56**).

3. Move the cursor and click to set the apex and complete the base (**Figure 2.57**). This sets the length of sides 2 and 3.

4. Move the cursor and click to set the height (**Figure 2.58**).

✔ Tip

- Hold down the Ctrl key during step 3 to create an equilateral base.

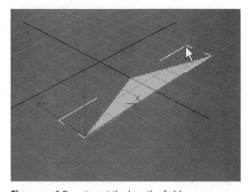

Figure 2.56 Drag to set the length of side 1.

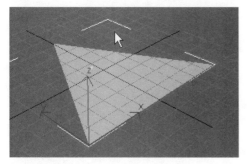

Figure 2.57 Move and click to set the apex.

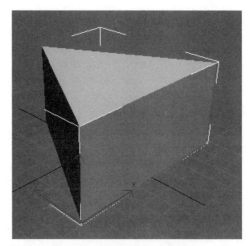

Figure 2.58 Move and click to set the height.

A ChamferBox is a box with filed edges, or **fillets**. It is a useful replacement for the standard box because most real-world objects have rounded edges and corners.

To create a ChamferBox:

1. In the Extended Primitives Object Type rollout, click ChamferBox.

   The ChamferBox creation rollout appears (**Figure 2.59**).

2. In the Perspective viewport, click and drag the base (**Figure 2.60**).

3. Release the mouse button to set the base length and width.

4. Move the cursor upward, and click to set the height (**Figure 2.61**).

5. Move the cursor up again, and click to set the fillet (**Figure 2.62**).

✔ Tips

■ Unchecking the Smooth parameter reveals the structure of a fillet.

■ To refine the appearance of a fillet, increase the Fillet Segs value. This makes the chamfered edges look smoother.

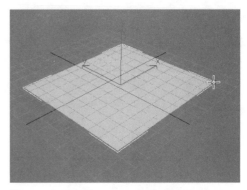

Figure 2.60 First, drag to create the base.

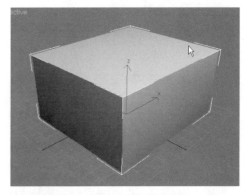

Figure 2.61 Next, click to set the height.

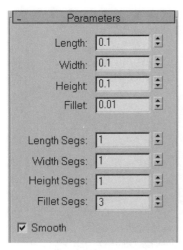

Figure 2.59 A ChamferBox has inputs for length, width, and height as well as fillet.

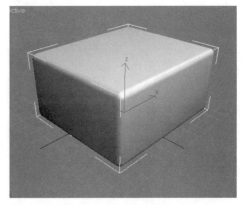

Figure 2.62 Click again to set the fillet.

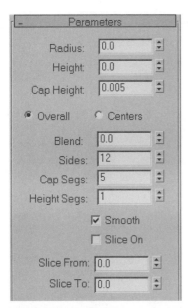

Figure 2.63 A ChamferCyl has inputs for radius, height, and fillet.

A ChamferCyl is a cylinder with fillets. Use this object instead of a cylinder to create more realistic-looking forms.

To create a ChamferCyl:

1. In the Extended Primitives Object Type rollout, click ChamferCyl.

   The ChamferCyl creation rollout appears (**Figure 2.63**).

2. In the Perspective viewport, click and drag the radius of the ChamferCyl (**Figure 2.64**).

3. Release the mouse button to set the base length and width.

4. Move the cursor, and click to set the height (**Figure 2.65**).

5. Move the cursor up again, and click to set the fillet (**Figure 2.66**).

✔ Tip

■ A gengon is a polygon with an adjustable number of sides that has been projected into three dimensions. It is closely related to the ChamferCyl, but instead of having fillets along its top and bottom edges, the gengon has fillets along its sides.

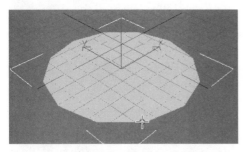

Figure 2.64 First, drag to create the radius.

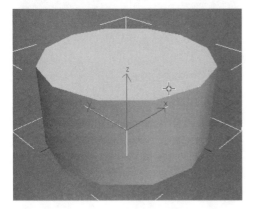

Figure 2.65 Next, click to set the height.

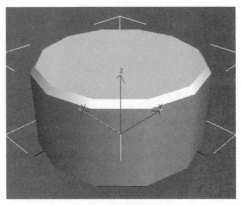

Figure 2.66 Click again to set the fillet.

CREATING MESH OBJECTS

An L-Ext looks like two walls that come together in a corner. You set the thickness, or width, of the walls after you establish the length and height.

To create an L-Ext:

1. In the Create panel, click L-Ext.

   The L-Ext creation rollout appears (**Figure 2.67**).

2. In the Perspective viewport, click and drag to create the base of the L-Ext (**Figure 2.68**).

3. Release the mouse button to set the length of the back, side, and front.

   The initial width, or thickness, of the walls is set by default.

4. Move the cursor up, and click to set the height (**Figure 2.69**).

5. Move the cursor up, and click to set the thickness of the walls (**Figure 2.70**).

✔ Tip

- To constrain the base of the L-Ext to sides of equal length, hold down the Ctrl key as you drag the base.

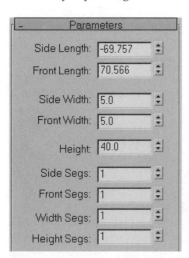

Figure 2.67 An L-Ext has length and width inputs for two sides.

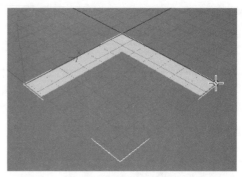

Figure 2.68 Dragging the base of the L-Ext.

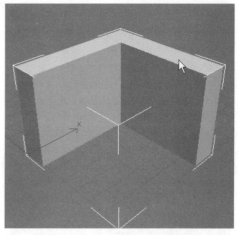

Figure 2.69 Move and click to set the height.

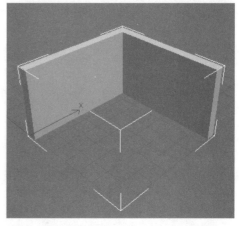

Figure 2.70 Move and click to set the thickness.

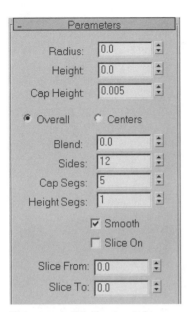

Figure 2.71 An C-Ext has inputs for three sides.

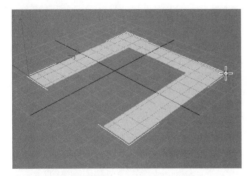

Figure 2.72 Dragging the base of the L-Ext.

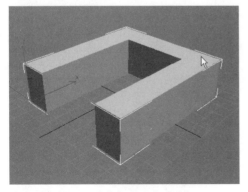

Figure 2.73 Move and click to set the height.

A C-Ext looks like an office cubicle. Like its sibling, the L-Ext, you set the thickness, or width, of the walls after you establish the length and height.

To create a C-Ext:

1. In the Create panel, click C-Ext.

   The C-Ext creation rollout appears (**Figure 2.71**).

2. In the Perspective viewport, click and drag to create the base of the C-Ext (**Figure 2.72**).

3. Release the mouse button to set the length of the back, side, and front of the base.

   The initial width, or thickness, of the walls is assigned by default.

4. Move the cursor up, and click to set the height (**Figure 2.73**).

5. Move the cursor up, and click to set the thickness of the walls.

   The three sides all adopt the same width (**Figure 2.74**).

✔ Tip

- To constrain the base of the C-Ext to sides of equal length, hold down the Ctrl key as you drag the base.

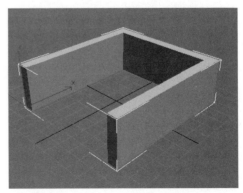

Figure 2.74 Move and click to set the thickness.

Torus Knots look better if you create them in an orthogonal viewport, such as the Top viewport.

To create a Torus Knot:

1. In the Create panel, click Torus Knot. The Torus Knot creation rollout appears (**Figure 2.75**).

2. In the Front viewport, position the cursor where you want the center of the torus knot to be. Then click and drag outward.

   A three-lobed knot appears as you drag.

3. Release the mouse button to set the radius of the base (**Figure 2.76**).

4. Slowly move the cursor up or down to establish the cross-section radius.

5. Click to set the radius of the cross section. To change the view to shaded mode, press F3 (**Figure 2.77**). Press F3 again to return to wireframe mode.

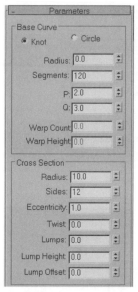

Figure 2.75 The dimensions of a Torus Knot include a base radius and a cross-section radius.

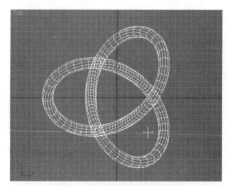

Figure 2.76 Drag to set the first radius.

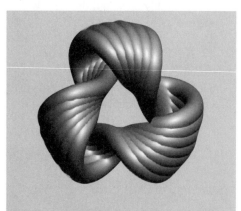

Tying the Knot

In a Torus Knot, P controls the number of times the strands of the knot wind around its center. Q controls the number of times the strands cycle up and down. If the ratio of P and Q are uneven, the results can be strange and beautiful.

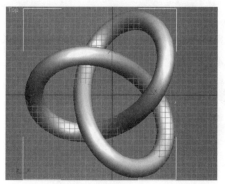

Figure 2.77 After setting the cross-section radius.

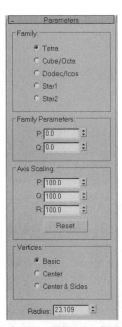

Figure 2.78 There are five Hedra "families."

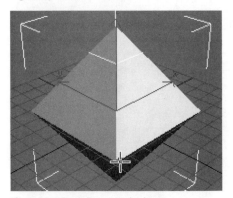

Figure 2.79 Dragging a tetrahedron.

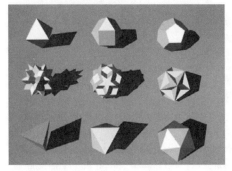

Figure 2.80 Examples of each of the Hedra families.

Hedra have variable numbers of sides and shapes that are primarily determined by their family type. They are the only mesh objects that do not have a keyboard-entry method.

To create a hedron:

1. In the Create panel, click Hedra.

   The Hedra creation rollout appears (**Figure 2.78**).

2. In the Perspective viewport, click and drag a hedron (**Figure 2.79**).

3. Release the mouse button to set the radius.

4. Select a family in the Parameters rollout.

   The hedron dramatically changes form (**Figure 2.80**).

The Many Headed Hedra

For Hedra, P and Q Family Parameters control the dimensions of rectangles that intersect more complex shapes. Axis scaling causes axes to protrude or intrude from different groups of shapes. Above, a Star1 hedra with the P Family Parameter set to .38, Q Family Parameter set to .62, and P Axis Scaling set to 75%.

A RingWave is a special-purpose object that has animation controls built into it. By animating the ring to ripple and expand, you can create the effect of a shock wave.

To create a RingWave:

1. In the Create panel, click RingWave.

   The RingWave creation rollout appears (**Figure 2.81**).

2. In the Perspective viewport, place the cursor where you want the center of the RingWave to be. Then click and drag outward from the center.

3. Release the mouse button to set the radius.

4. Move the cursor and click to set the ring width (**Figure 2.82**).

5.  Click Play Animation to play back the default animation.

   The inner ring of the RingWave ripples in and out from the center of the object.

6. Increase the Height if you want to give the RingWave some thickness.

   To make the RingWave expand over time, choose Grow and Stay in the RingWave Timing area.

   To make the outer edge of the RingWave ripple like the inner ring, set Outer Edge Breakup to On. Then copy the Inner Edge Breakup settings to their corresponding parameters in the Outer Edge Breakup area (**Figure 2.83**).

✔ Tips

■ A complete description of the RingWave settings may be found in the help files.

■ For more information about animating scenes, see Chapter 7, "Animation."

Figure 2.81 A RingWave has a radius and a width.

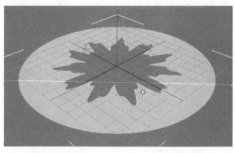

Figure 2.82 Setting the width of the RingWave.

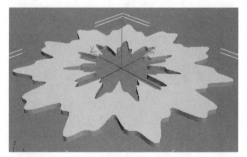

Figure 2.83 After breaking up the outer edge and adding some height to the RingWave.

CREATING MESH OBJECTS

Figure 2.84 A Hose can be free standing or bound to two other objects.

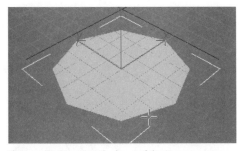

Figure 2.85 Dragging the base of the Hose.

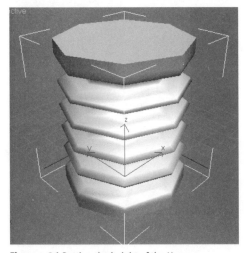

Figure 2.86 Setting the height of the Hose.

A Hose is a flexible object designed for simulating the action of a spring. You can also use it to create a variety of forms.

To create a Hose:

1. In the Create panel, click Hose.

   The Hose creation rollout appears (**Figure 2.84**).

2. In the Perspective viewport, click and drag the base of the hose.

3. Release the mouse button to set the radius of the base (**Figure 2.85**).

4. Move the cursor upward in the viewport. Then click to set the height (**Figure 2.86**).

5. In the Hose Shape area, adjust the shape of the hose by choosing Round, Rectangular, or D-Section hose.

   Additional parameters for dimension and orientation become enabled.

6. Adjust the radius, sides, width, depth, fillet, segments, and rotation as needed.

Spring Has Sprung

A Hose has built-in animation parameters to make it expand and contract over time. Below, a D-Section Hose springs upward. For more information, go to "Hose" in the help files and see Chapter 7, "Animation."

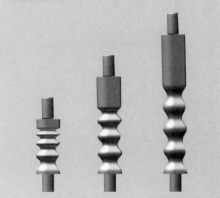

Creating Shape Splines

Splines are linear objects that can be curved. 3ds max provides two types of splines: **Shapes** are simple splines that you use to create flying logos, low-polygon models, architectural elements, and motion paths; **NURBS**, or non-uniform rational B-splines, have advanced curvature controls suitable for modeling complex organic forms. The topic of NURBS is beyond the scope of this book.

3ds max 6 provides 11 shape primitives: the Line, Circle, Arc, NGon, Text, Section, Rectangle, Ellipse, Donut, Star, and Helix (**Figure 2.87**). The Shapes menu is found in the Shapes branch of the Geometry category (**Figure 2.88**). Shortcuts to the Shape commands are found in the Create menu.

Figure 2.88 The Shapes menu contains 11 different object types.

Figure 2.87 Shape splines are composed of open and closed shapes.

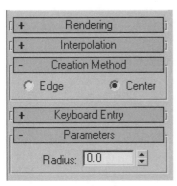

Figure 2.89 A Circle has only one parameter.

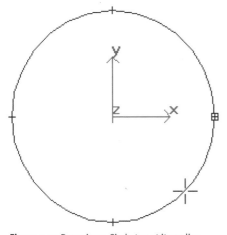

Figure 2.90 Dragging a Circle to set its radius.

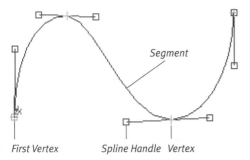

First Vertex   Spline Handle Vertex

Figure 2.91 Shapes are made up of vertices, segments, and splines. Controls, like these Bézier spline handles, determine the curvature of each segment.

To create a shape:

1. Open the Shapes branch of the Create panel, and choose a shape.

   The creation rollout of the shape appears (**Figure 2.89**).

2. In the Creation Method rollout, choose a creation option, or use the default.

3. In the Top viewport, position the cursor where you want to start the object. Then click and drag to set the first parameter.

   For a Circle, you simply define its radius (**Figure 2.90**).

4. Move and click the mouse to set additional parameters as needed.

5. Adjust the parameters in the Create panel or the Modify panel.

About Shapes

Shapes are made up of three sub-object components: **vertices**, which are point locations in space; **segments**, which are straight or curved lines; and **splines**, which are made from a sequence of vertices that are connected by segments. Controls located at each vertex determine the curvature of adjacent segments (**Figure 2.91**).

As with mesh objects, shapes can be created by dragging or from the keyboard. Because most shapes initially lie flat on the grid, it is usually easier to create them in the Top viewport where you can look straight down at them.

Compound shapes are two or more shapes joined together as a single object.

To create a compound shape:

1. Create a shape.

2. Uncheck Start New Shape at the top of the Object Type rollout (**Figure 2.92**).

3. Create any additional shapes that you want to include in the compound objects.

   As you complete each shape, it is added to the compound shape (**Figure 2.93**).

4. When you want to go back to creating separate shapes, check Start New Shape.

✔ Tips

■ Shapes are non-rendering by default. This means that when you render a view, spline shapes are not drawn. To make a spline object visible during rendering, open the Rendering rollout and check Renderable. Then and set the thickness of the rendered spline in pixels (**Figure 2.94**).

■ To make a spline shape curve more smoothly, open the Interpolation rollout and increase the number of steps. This increases the number of divisions between vertices. You can also check Adaptive to make the program do this automatically.

Figure 2.92 Uncheck Start New Shape to begin creating a compound shape.

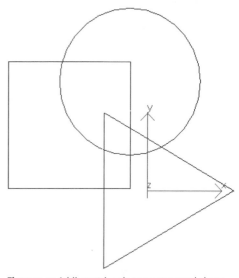

Figure 2.93 Adding a triangle to a compound shape.

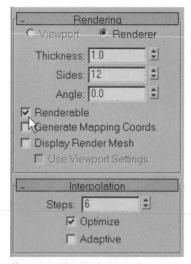

Figure 2.94 The Rendering and Interpolation rollouts allow you to make shapes renderable and control their smoothness.

Spline Origins

The term "spline" dates back to the 18th century, when shipbuilders and architects used a long, thin strip of wood or metal called a **spline** to create curved lines. This helped them to build large curved surfaces, such as the hulls of boats.

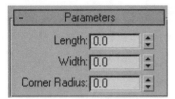

Figure 2.95 A Rectangle has inputs for length, width, and corner radius.

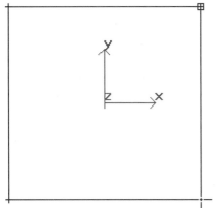

Figure 2.96 Drag a rectangle to set its length and width.

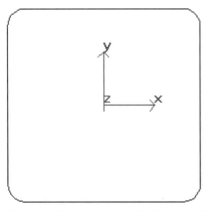

Figure 2.97 You make a rectangle with rounded corners by increasing the Corner Radius parameter.

The Rectangle is created by dragging its length and width in a single click-and-drag sequence. Ellipses are made in a similar fashion; the only difference is the edges are round.

To create a Rectangle:

1. In the Create panel, click Rectangle. The Rectangle rollout appears (**Figure 2.95**).

2. Choose the Edge creation method in the rollout.

3. In the Top viewport, click and drag the Rectangle diagonally from one corner to another (**Figure 2.96**).

4. Release the mouse button when the rectangle is the right size.

✔ Tip

■ To round the corners of a Rectangle, increase the Corner Radius parameter (**Figure 2.97**).

CREATING SHAPE SPLINES

NGons are regular polygons of up to 100 sides. You adjust the number of sides of an NGon after you create the basic shape.

To create an NGon:

1. In the Create panel, click NGon.

   The NGon creation rollout appears (**Figure 2.98**).

2. In the Parameters rollout, set the number of sides that you want the NGon to be, or accept the default setting of 6 sides.

   This also sets the number of vertices.

3. In the Parameters rollout, choose Inscribed or Circumscribed.

   Inscribed means that the radius of the NGon will be measured by the radius of the smallest circle that the NGon can fit inside of.

   Circumscribed means that the radius of the NGon will be measured by the largest circle that can fit inside the NGon.

4. In the Top viewport, position the cursor where you want the center of the NGon to be. Then click and drag outward to make the NGon.

   A regular polygon appears in the viewport (**Figure 2.99**).

5. Release the mouse button to set the radius.

✔ Tips

- To create an equilateral triangle, set the sides parameter to 3.

- Check Circular to create a circle that has an adjustable number of vertices. This is useful for making loft and morph objects, as described in Chapter 10, "Compound Objects."

- You can create a snowflake by setting the Radius and Corner Radius parameters to extremely high values (**Figure 2.100**).

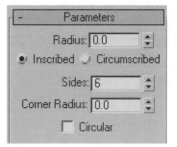

Figure 2.98 An NGon forms a regular polygon of up to 100 sides.

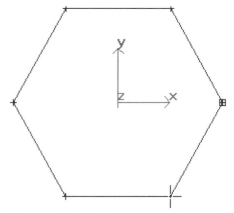

Figure 2.99 Dragging an NGon in the Top viewport. The default number of sides is six.

Figure 2.100 An NGon with Radius = 60, Sides = 12, and Corner Radius = 1152.

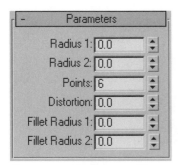

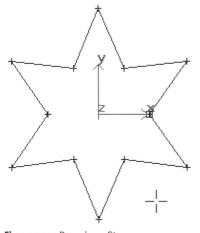

Figure 2.101 A Star has two radii, two fillet radii, and up to 100 points.

Stars have two radii that define a perimeter of anywhere from 3 to 100 points.

To create a Star:

1. In the Create panel, click Star.

   The Star creation rollout appears (**Figure 2.101**).

2. In the Top viewport, position the cursor where you want the center of the Star to be. Then click and drag outward (**Figure 2.102**).

3. Release the mouse button to set the first radius.

4. Move and click to set the second radius (**Figure 2.103**).

5. In the Parameters rollout, adjust the number of points as needed.

✔ Tips

- You can fillet the points of a Star to round them off or distort them to make them twist (**Figure 2.104**).

- If you can make a Star, you can easily make a Donut, which is simply two concentric circles.

Figure 2.102 Dragging a Star.

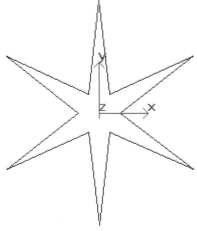

Figure 2.103 Setting the second radius alters the shape of the Star considerably.

Figure 2.104 After filleting, distorting, and changing the number of points.

Lines are non-parametric objects. You create them by defining the location of their vertices.

To create a Line:

1. In the Create panel, click Line.

   The Line creation rollout appears (**Figure 2.105**).

2. Set the first vertex point by clicking in the Top viewport.

3. Move the cursor to a new position, and click to set the next vertex (**Figure 2.106**).

4. Continue creating vertex points until the Line is complete (**Figure 2.107**).

5. Right-click to end the line.

✔ Tips

■ To create a closed shape from line segments, set the last point on top of the first point. When prompted, click Yes to close the spline.

■ To create a curved line, set Drag Type Smooth or Bézier in the Creation Method rollout. Then click and drag to create smooth or Bézier vertex points (**Figure 2.108**).

■ Bézier points are particularly hard to control during the line creation process. For better results, start with all Corner points, convert them to Bézier points *en masse*, and then adjust them, as shown on the next two pages.

Figure 2.105 Different types of vertex points can be used to create a line.

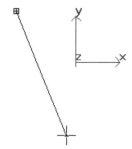

Figure 2.106 Click to set the second vertex point.

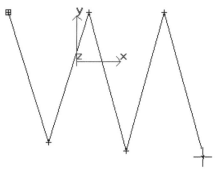

Figure 2.107 Create a zigzag line by moving and clicking in a zigzag pattern.

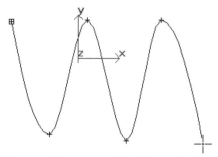

Figure 2.108 Create a wavy line after setting Initial Type and Drag Type to Smooth.

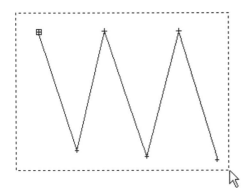

Figure 2.109 Drag a selection region around the points you want to convert.

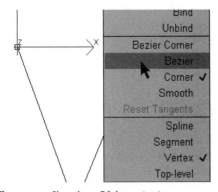

Figure 2.110 Choosing a Bézier vertex type.

To smooth a Line, you convert its vertex points. Creating an angular line and then smoothing it makes curves easier to control.

To convert vertex points:

1. Select a Line.

2. Open the Modify panel.

3. In the Selection rollout, click the Vertex button.

4. Click on the point you want to convert. To convert multiple points at once, drag a selection region around them (**Figure 2.109**).

5. Right-click on a selected point.

6. In the Tools1 quad menu, choose Bézier Corner, Bézier, or Smooth (**Figure 2.110**).

   The vertex points convert to the new type. The corners of the Line become curved (**Figure 2.111**).

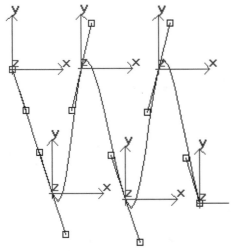

Figure 2.111 The result is a curved Bézier line.

Because Lines are non-parametric objects, you adjust each vertex individually.

To adjust a Line:

1. Select a Line.

2. Open the Modify panel.

3. In the Selection rollout, click the Vertex button.

   The Vertex button turns yellow. The program shifts to vertex sub-object mode. This allows you to edit the line at the vertex level of definition.

4. Choose the Select and Move tool from the Main toolbar.

5. Adjust vertex points by dragging them (**Figure 2.112**).

6. To adjust the curvature of a Bézier point, drag its handles (**Figure 2.113**).

7. When you are done, click the Vertex button again to exit sub-object mode.

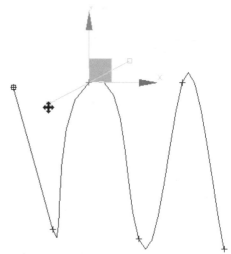

Figure 2.112 Using the Move tool to adjust a vertex point.

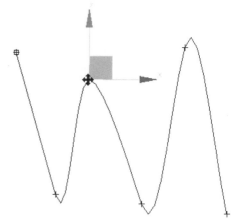

Figure 2.113 Using the Move tool to drag a Bézier handle.

CREATING SHAPE SPLINES

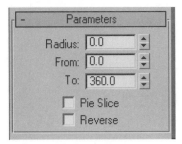

Figure 2.114 An Arc has inputs for radius and degrees of Arc.

Figure 2.115 Set the end point of the Arc.

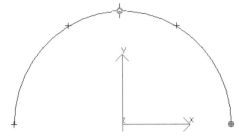

Figure 2.116 Set the curvature of the Arc.

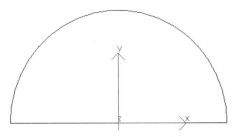

Figure 2.117 Check the Pie Slice parameter to create a closed shape like a slice of pie.

You create Arcs by defining their endpoints and defining the shape of the curve between them.

To create an Arc:

1. In the Create panel, click Arc.
   The Arc creation rollout appears (**Figure 2.114**).

2. Make sure that End-End-Middle is selected in the Creation Method rollout.

3. In the Top viewport, position the cursor where you want the Arc to begin.

4. Click and drag from the beginning point to the end point.
   The click sets the beginning point; releasing the mouse button sets the end point. It still looks like a straight line (**Figure 2.115**).

5. Without clicking, slowly move the cursor along the line toward the middle of the Arc.

6. Move the cursor to either side of the line.
   The Arc appears to stick to the cursor (**Figure 2.116**).

7. Click to set the curvature of the Arc.

✔ Tips

■ To create a closed form called a pie slice, check the Pie Slice parameter (**Figure 2.117**).

■ The Center-End-End creation method allows you to establish a center point and radius before drawing the Arc around the center.

CREATING SHAPE SPLINES

The Helix is the only spline that has three-dimensional creation parameters. It is usually easier to create Helices in Perspective viewports.

To create a Helix:

1. In the Create panel, click Helix.

   The Helix creation rollout appears (**Figure 2.118**).

2. In the Perspective viewport, click and drag the base of the Helix. Release the mouse button to set the first radius (**Figure 2.119**).

3. Move the cursor upward, and then click to set the height (**Figure 2.120**).

4. Move the cursor up or down in the viewport, and click to set the second radius.

5. Enter the number of turns and the bias amount to give your Helix its final shape (**Figure 2.121**).

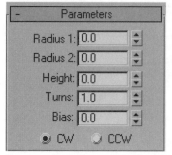

Figure 2.118 A Helix has two radii and a height.

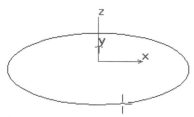

Figure 2.119 Set the first radius of a Helix.

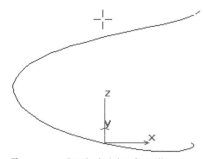

Figure 2.120 Set the height of a Helix.

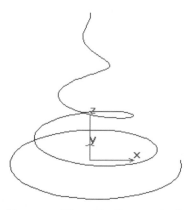

Figure 2.121 After setting the second radius, the number of turns, and the bias.

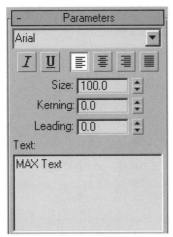

Figure 2.122 Text objects have different fonts and styles.

Figure 2.123 The default text appears in the view.

Lightweaver

Figure 2.124 Changing the default text gives immediate results.

Lightweaver

Figure 2.125 After changing the font to Georgia Italic.

Lightweaver

Figure 2.126 Applying an Extrude modifier fills in the text and gives it depth.

To create text:

1. In the Create panel, click Text.
   The Text creation rollout appears (**Figure 2.122**).

2. Click in the center of the Front viewport.
   The words MAX Text fill the viewport (**Figure 2.123**). This is the default text.

3. In the Text input field, highlight the default text. Then type in the text you want.
   The text replaces the default text (**Figure 2.124**).

4. Adjust the size of the text.
   To center the text in the viewport, click the Zoom Extents button in the lower-right corner of the interface.

5. Choose a font from the drop-down list.
   The text changes to the new font (**Figure 2.125**).

6. *I* Click the *I* button to italicize text.
   U Click the U button to underline it.

7. Use these text controls to align the text:

Left	Center	Right	Justify

8. To increase the amount of space between letters, increase the Kerning amount.
   To increase the amount of space between lines of text, increase the Leading value.

✔ Tips

■ The default setting for the number of steps in a text object is 6. Usually this is more than you need. If your scene is acting sluggish, try reducing the steps.

■ Apply an Extrude modifier to make it appear solid or three-dimensional (**Figure 2.126**). (See Chapter 6, "Modifying Objects.")

CREATING SHAPE SPLINES

A section is a plane that slices the objects it intersects into cross-section shapes.

To create a section:

1. In the Perspective viewport, create a mesh object whose base intersects the home grid, such as a sphere or a torus knot.

2. In the Create panel, click the Shapes button. Then click Section.

   The Section creation rollout appears (**Figure 2.127**).

3. In the Perspective or Top viewport, click and drag a section of any size.

   A yellow line appears where the section bisects the object (**Figure 2.128**).

4. In the section Parameters rollout, click Create Shape.

   The Name Section Shape dialog box appears (**Figure 2.129**).

5. Click OK to accept the default name or type a new name.

   A cross section of the object is created.

✔ Tip

■ To get a better look at the cross-section shape, select and delete the mesh object (**Figure 2.130**).

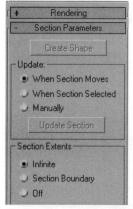

Figure 2.127 A section can have infinite extents.

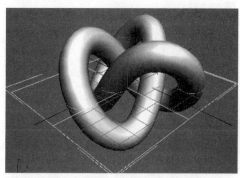

Figure 2.128 Dragging a section causes a yellow line to appear at the "waterline" of the torus knot.

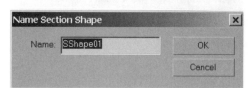

Figure 2.129 Clicking Create Shape brings up the Name Section Shape dialog box.

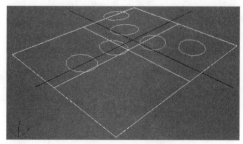

Figure 2.130 The resulting cross-section shape.

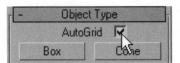

Figure 2.131 AutoGrid is located at the top of the Object Type menu.

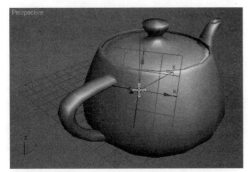

Figure 2.132 Click and hold to see the orientation of the AutoGrid.

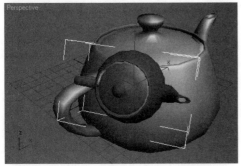

Figure 2.133 Drag to create the object on top of the AutoGrid.

Precision Aids

When you want to create objects to precise specifications, you can customize your units of measurement, grid spacing, and cursor snaps. You can also create custom grids to use as alternative construction planes.

If you want to create objects that align to the surfaces of other objects, you use an AutoGrid. This feature allows you to place a temporary construction grid on the surface of an object, aligned to the surface normal under your cursor.

To create objects on an AutoGrid:

1. In the Create panel, turn on the AutoGrid feature in the Object Type roll-out (**Figure 2.131**).

2. Move the cursor over the surface of a mesh object. Then click and hold to check the orientation of the grid (**Figure 2.132**).

3. When the grid is aligned properly, drag to create the object.

   The object is created on top of the AutoGrid (**Figure 2.133**).

   If no object is present under the cursor, the object will align itself to the home grid.

✔ Tip

- You can also turn on AutoGrid from the Extras toolbar. This and other toolbars are accessed by right-clicking on any blank gray area of the Main toolbar.

PRECISION AIDS

When you want to create a series of objects on a construction plane other than the home grid, you use a helper grid.

To create a helper grid:

1. 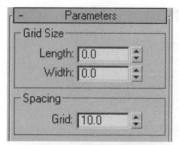 In the Create panel, open the Helpers rollout by clicking the Helpers icon.

2. In the Helpers subpanel, click Grid.

   The Grid creation rollout appears (**Figure 2.134**).

3. In any viewport, click and drag to create a grid (**Figure 2.135**).

4. Choose the Select and Rotate tool from the Main toolbar.

5. In the status bar controls, orient the grid by dragging the X, Y, and/or Z spinners.

6. Right-click the grid object, and choose Activate Grid (**Figure 2.136**).

   The grid object becomes active, and grid line subdivisions appear. The home grid becomes inactive, and grid line subdivisions disappear.

7. Create some objects.

   The objects appear on the construction plane defined by the grid (**Figure 2.137**).

8. When you are done, click the grid to select it and then right-click. Then choose Activate HomeGrid from the quad menu.

   The helper grid becomes inactive and the home grid becomes active.

✔ Tips

■ To make user grids activate automatically upon creation, choose Customize > Grid and Snap Settings > User Grids. Then check Activate Grids When Created.

■ Another way to create a grid object is by holding down the Alt key when creating an AutoGrid. Use this method when you want to align a user grid to an object.

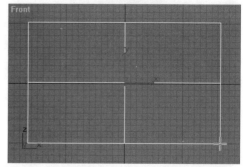

Figure 2.134 A Grid defines a new construction plane.

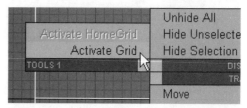

Figure 2.135 The XY plane of the grid aligns to the home grid of the viewport in which you are working.

Figure 2.136 Activate the grid using the Tools 1 right-click quad menu.

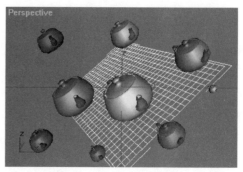

Figure 2.137 Created objects lie on the grid.

PRECISION AIDS

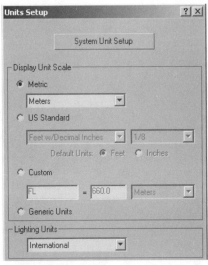

Figure 2.138 Setting the scene units to meters.

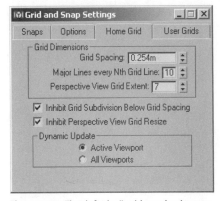

Figure 2.139 The default 1" grid spacing is now measured in meters.

Figure 2.140 Change the grid spacing to match a whole unit of measure.

By default, 3ds max measures space in generic units of measurement equivalent to inches. But if you want to build a house or a highway, you may want to use an exact system of measurement, such as feet and inches or kilometers.

To set units of measure:

1. Choose Customize > Units Setup.

   The Units Setup dialog box appears.

2. In the Display Unit Scale area, choose a unit of measurement: Metric, US Standard, Custom, or Generic Units (**Figure 2.138**).

3. Click OK.

   Once you set the units of measurement, you will want to set the spacing of the grid to match.

To set grid spacing:

1. Choose Customize > Grid and Snap Settings, and click on the Home Grid tab (**Figure 2.139**).

2. In the Grid Spacing input field, enter the grid spacing you prefer.

   The grid spacing changes to the unit of measure (**Figure 2.140**).

PRECISION AIDS

Use 3D Snap when you want to create objects to exact dimensions using the click and drag method.

To use 3D Snap to snap to the grid:

1. 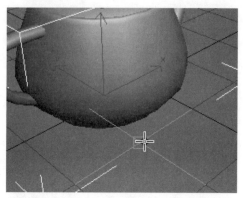 Click the 3D Snap tool in the Main toolbar.

2. Create an object by dragging.

   As you drag the base of the object, the cursor jumps to points of grid intersection, and a blue square appears at the tip of the cursor (**Figure 2.141**).

   In setting the height of an object, the cursor snaps to an interval equivalent to the space between grid lines.

3. When you are done, turn off 3D Snap by clicking the 3D Snap button. You can also toggle the Snap tool by pressing the S key.

You can snap to other targets besides grid points. This feature comes in handy when you need to create exact arrangements of objects (**Figure 2.142**). For more information on snaps and their settings, see Chapter 5, "Transforms."

Figure 2.141 Snapping the corner of an object to a grid point during object creation.

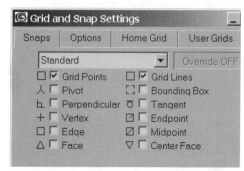

Figure 2.142 The Grid and Snap Settings dialog box allows you to set up to 12 different snap targets.

PRECISION AIDS

VIEWPORT NAVIGATION AND DISPLAY

Figure 3.1 Navigating 3D space is a lot like flying.

Navigating 3D space is a lot like flying. You can wheel around, fly in fast and low, or fly up high for a bird's eye view. If you have ever played 3D games, you know how exhilarating it is to fly.

To be the master of this 3D universe, you need to get your bearings and learn how to operate the controls. Once you learn how the universe is laid out, you will teleport from place to place to see how things look from different perspectives. You will also learn how to customize the cockpit and change the display resolution of the window (**Figure 3.1**).

Getting Your Bearings

In this section, we take a page out of your old planar geometry textbook and expand it to the third dimension.

In 2D space, any two lines that intersect define the surface of a plane. To locate any position in space, all you need to know is how far along each line you must travel from their intersection.

To define 3D space, all you need to do is introduce a third line that does not lie on the plane of the first two. To locate a position in 3D space, you need to measure distance along three lines instead of two.

In planar geometry, the lines that define space are called the **X** and **Y axes**. The point where they intersect is called the **origin**. The coordinates of the origin are (0,0) (**Figure 3.2**).

In 3D geometry, the third line is called the **Z axis**, and it intersects the other two axes at the origin. Together, the X, Y, and Z axes are called the world axes. The origin of the world axes is located at (0,0,0) (**Figure 3.3**).

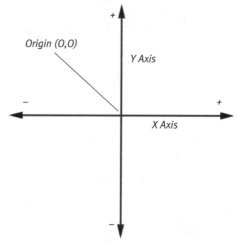

Figure 3.2 Rectangular coordinates measure space using perpendicular axes that meet at the origin.

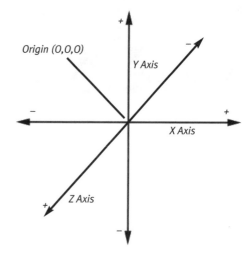

Figure 3.3 Adding the Z axis to rectangular coordinates makes it possible to measure depth.

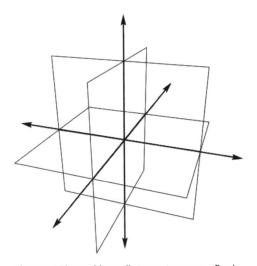

Figure 3.4 The world coordinate system uses a fixed system of reference to define world space.

When the X, Y, and Z axes are assigned to a fixed position and orientation in space, they define an absolute frame of reference called the **world coordinate system**. This system keeps track of all objects in space relative to the world axes (**Figure 3.4**).

When axes are tied to an object instead of being fixed in space, they define a **local coordinate system**. This relative frame of reference keeps track of individual objects as they change position, orientation, and scale relative to their local axes (**Figure 3.5**).

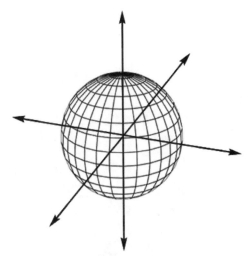

Figure 3.5 The local coordinate system uses a relative system of reference to define object space.

Putting It in Perspective

The axes of the world coordinate system define three planes: the XY, YZ, and ZX planes. When you divide these planes at regular intervals, they form three perpendicular grids that intersect at the origin. Together, these three grids make up the home grid. In 3ds max, only one part of the home grid is shown in each viewport: the grid that defines the construction plane for creating objects in that viewport (**Figure 3.6**).

For the purposes of viewing and navigating space, 3ds max defines six views that squarely face the origin from six directions: Front, Back, Left, Right, Top, and Bottom. These directions are called **orthogonal views** because they face the planes of the world coordinate system and the home grid perpendicularly (**Figure 3.7**). They are also a type of axonometric view because they use parallel projection to draw the scene.

If you rotate an orthogonal view, it turns into a User view. A User view is a user-defined axonometric view that looks at a scene from any direction, rather than from one of the six fixed directions assigned to orthogonal views.

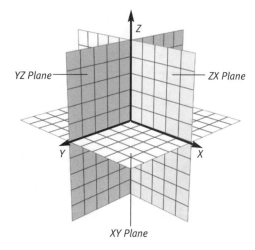

Figure 3.6 The home grid is made of three intersecting grids that are aligned to the XY, YZ, and ZX planes of the world coordinate system.

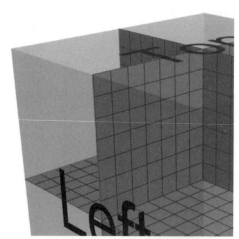

Figure 3.7 The orthogonal views face the origin from six fixed directions to help you keep track of your orientation in space.

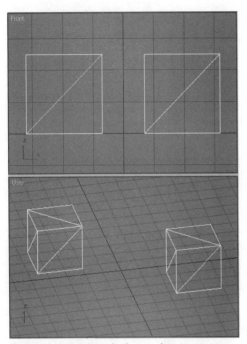

Because parallel projection systems draw objects without any foreshortening, objects in orthogonal and User views always appear true to size, no matter how far away they are from the viewer. In addition, parallel lines always appear to be parallel no matter how far they project into space (**Figure 3.8**).

In contrast, perspective views such as Perspective, Camera, and Light views use **perspective projection** to draw the scene. Objects in perspective views appear to get smaller as they recede in the distance, and parallel lines appear to converge as they move further into space (**Figure 3.9**).

Figure 3.8 In axonometric views, cubes appear true to size. Parallel lines remain parallel no matter how far the project in space.

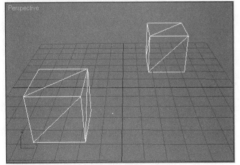

Figure 3.9 The same cubes in the perspective views appear to get smaller as they recede. Parallel lines converge as they get farther away.

PUTTING IT IN PERSPECTIVE

Customizing Viewports

You need to view a scene from at least three directions in order to understand where you are in space. In 3ds max, you can view a scene from up to four directions at once by assigning different views to each of the viewports (**Figure 3.10**). To look at the details of a scene, you maximize a viewport to fill the display. You can also change the layout and proportions of the viewports.

Elements that are common to all viewports include a grid for navigation, a label for identification, a world axis for orientation, a boundary to delimit the view, and a background that goes behind the scene (**Figure 3.11**). To customize these elements, you can turn them on or off, or you can change their colors.

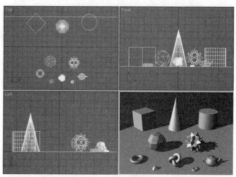

Figure 3.10 The viewports can show up to four views at once.

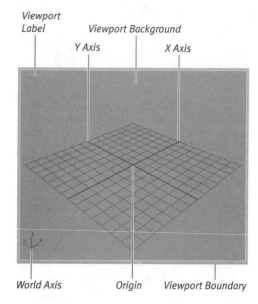

Figure 3.11 Viewport elements may be customized.

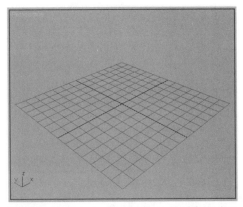

Figure 3.12 An inactive viewport has a black boundary around it.

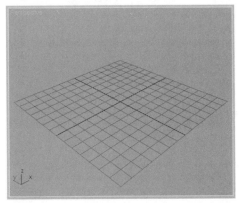

Figure 3.13 The viewport boundary turns yellow when the viewport is active.

In order to work in a viewport, you must first select it, or **activate** it. Activating a viewport tells the program which viewport to redraw, and it establishes an orientation for creating, manipulating, and rendering objects. One viewport is always active, and only one can be active at a time.

To activate a viewport:

◆ Right-click in a viewport that has a black boundary and is therefore inactive (**Figure 3.12**).

The viewport activates, and the boundary of the viewport turns yellow (**Figure 3.13**).

✔ Tips

■ Left-clicking also activates viewports, but it can cause you to lose a selection.

■ Right-clicking in an active viewport brings up context-sensitive menus.

■ ActiveShade viewports are the exception to the rule: Right-clicking in an inactive viewport brings up quad menus, so use left-clicking to activate them instead. Your selection will not be affected.

CUSTOMIZING VIEWPORTS

Once a viewport is active, you can change the view of the scene that it displays. The view that is displayed in an active viewport is called the active view.

To change a view:

1. Press V on your keyboard.

   The Viewports menu appears (**Figure 3.14**).

2. Choose a view from the menu.

   The viewport display changes to show the view you selected.

✔ Tips

■ Press Shift + Z to undo a view change. Press Shift + Y to redo a view change.

■ To reorient a Perspective view, first open the Display panel and hide all the objects. Click Zoom Extents. Then unhide all the objects. (In Chapter 4, "Object Selection and Display," see the section "Hiding Objects.")

Most view-change commands have keyboard shortcuts, as summarized in **Table 3.1**.

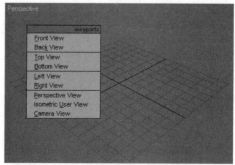

Figure 3.14 You use the Viewports menu to change views.

Table 3.1

Keyboard Shortcuts for Changing Views	
SHORTCUT	**NAME**
F	Front View
V + K	Back View
V + R	Right View
L	Left View
T	Top View
B	Bottom View
P	Perspective User View
U	Isometric User View
C	Camera View
Shift + 4	Spotlight/Directional Light View
G	Hide Grids Toggle
Alt + W	Maximize Viewport Toggle
D	Disable Viewport
Shift + Z	Undo Viewport Operation
Shift + Y	Redo Viewport Operation
Alt + B	Viewport Background Dialog
Alt+Shift+Ctrl+B	Update Background Image
Ctrl + X	Expert Mode
`(Accent Grave)	Redraw All Views

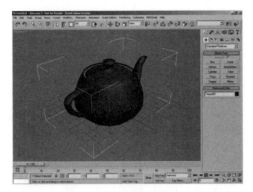

Figure 3.15 Clicking the Min/Max Toggle enlarges the viewport to fit the entire display area.

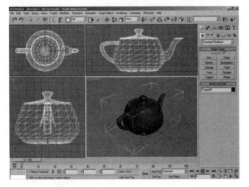

Figure 3.16 Clicking the Min/Max Toggle a second time returns the viewports to the previous layout.

The Min/Max Toggle button toggles the display between the current viewport layout and a single viewport that expands to fill the entire display area. Use this feature whenever you want to view your scene on a grand scale.

To maximize a viewport:

◆ Click the Min/Max Toggle button.

The active viewport enlarges to fill the display area (**Figure 3.15**).

If a viewport is already maximized, clicking the Min/Max Toggle button returns the display to the original layout.

To minimize a viewport:

◆ Click the Min/Max Toggle button.

The viewports are redrawn using the current layout (**Figure 3.16**).

✔ Tip

■ The keyboard shortcut for the Min/Max Toggle button is Alt + W.

To turn the grid display off and on:

1. Right-click on the viewport label, and choose Show Grid (**Figure 3.17**).

   The grid display turns off (**Figure 3.18**).

2. To turn the grid display back on, repeat step 1.

✔ Tips

■ Press G to toggle the grid display from the keyboard.

■ If pressing G does not toggle the grid display, make sure that the keyboard shortcuts are set to DefaultUI.kbd. To do so, choose Customize > Customize User Interface, and click the Keyboard tab. Then click Load and select DefaultUI.kbd from the list of shortcut files.

To turn the world axis off and on:

1. Choose Customize > Preferences.

2. In the Preference Settings dialog box, click the Viewports tab.

3. In the Viewport Parameters group, uncheck Display World Axis (**Figure 3.19**).

4. Close the Preference Settings dialog box. The world axis disappears (**Figure 3.20**).

✔ Tip

■ To turn the world axis back on, reopen the Preference Settings dialog box and check Display World Axis.

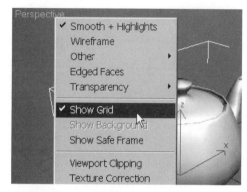

Figure 3.17 Turning off the grid display.

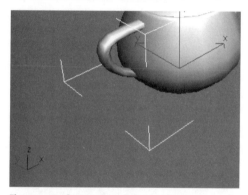

Figure 3.18 After turning off the grid display.

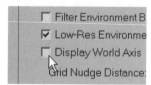

Figure 3.19 Uncheck Display World Axis.

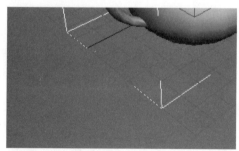

Figure 3.20 The World Axis no longer appears in this or any other viewport.

Figure 3.21 Access the Viewport Configuration dialog box from the viewport menu.

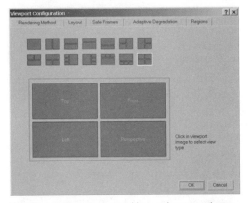

Figure 3.22 The Layout panel has 14 layout options.

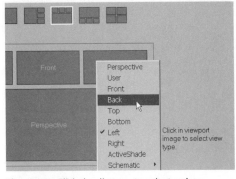

Figure 3.23 Click the diagram to select a view.

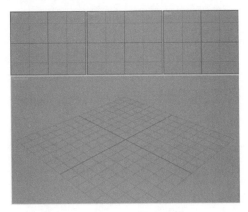

Figure 3.24 The new layout is displayed.

Changing the viewport layout changes the viewports to one of 14 preset arrangements. It also allows you to change the views that they display.

To change the layout of the viewports:

1. Right-click on any viewport label, and choose Configure (**Figure 3.21**).

2. In the Viewport Configuration dialog box, click on the Layout tab.
   The Layout panel appears (**Figure 3.22**).

3. Click in a layout at the top of the panel.
   A diagram that previews the new layout appears in the lower part of the panel.

4. Click in the diagram to assign views to each viewport (**Figure 3.23**).

5. Click OK.
   The new layout appears (**Figure 3.24**).

CUSTOMIZING VIEWPORTS

To change the proportions of the viewports interactively:

1. 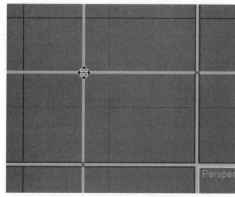 Choose the Select Object tool from the main toolbar.

2. Move the cursor over the border between two viewports, or in the center of the viewports where the corners meet.

   The cursor changes to a double or quadruple arrow.

3. Click and drag the viewport boundaries to a different position (**Figure 3.25**).

   The viewports redraw with the new proportions (**Figure 3.26**).

✔ Tip

■ To clear the contents of a viewport, choose File > Reset. This clears the contents of the viewport and opens a new scene without any objects in it. For more information, see Chapter 1, "Getting Started."

Figure 3.25 Dragging the boundaries between viewports gives your layout new proportions.

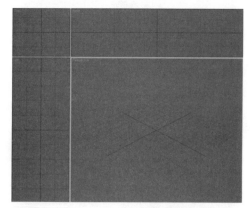

Figure 3.26 After dragging the boundaries, a new layout is displayed.

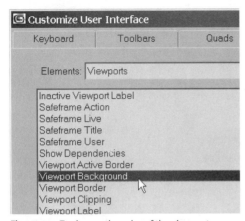

Figure 3.27 To change the color of the viewport background, choose Viewport Background from the Viewport Elements menu.

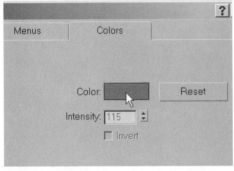

Figure 3.28 Click the color swatch to bring up the Color Selector dialog box. Note Reset button at right.

To customize viewport colors:

1. Choose Customize > Customize User Interface.

2. In the Customize User Interface dialog box, click the Colors tab.

3. In the Elements drop-down menu, choose Viewports.

4. In the scrolling window, choose the viewport element you would like to change (**Figure 3.27**). Then click the color swatch at right (**Figure 3.28**). The Color Selector dialog box appears.

5. Click on the color palette to select a Hue. Then drag the Whiteness slider to choose a value. You can also use the RGB or HSV settings at right (**Figure 3.29**).

6. Click Apply Colors Now to see the result. If you do not like the result, choose a new color and click the Reset button. Then click Apply Colors Now.

7. Choose a new viewport element and repeat steps 6 and 7 until you are satisfied with your viewport colors.

8. Close the Color Selector and the Customize User Interface dialog boxes. The new color scheme is displayed. To revert to the original colors, choose Customize > Revert to Startup Layout.

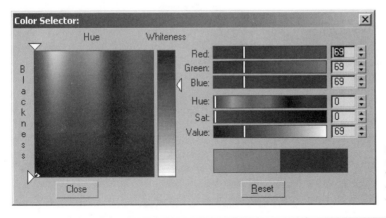

Figure 3.29 Using the Hue and Whiteness sliders to pick a color from the palette.

CUSTOMIZING VIEWPORTS

To place an image in a background:

1. Activate the viewport that you want to place a background image in.

2. Choose Views > Viewport Background.

   or

   Press Alt + B.

3. In the Viewport Background dialog box, click the Files button (**Figure 3.30**).

4. In the Select Background Image dialog box, navigate to the image you want to place in the background.

5. Select the image, and click Open.

6. In the Viewport Background dialog box, check Display Background.

7. In the Aspect Ratio group, decide if you want to match the image to the dimensions of the viewport or the output size specified in the Render Scene dialog box, or keep the proportions of the bitmap true to size (**Figure 3.31**).

8. Click OK.

   The image appears in the background of the viewport (**Figure 3.32**).

✔ Tips

- To toggle a background image on or off, right-click the viewport label and choose Show Background (**Figure 3.33**).

- Viewport background images and colors do not render to output files unless they have been assigned to the rendering environment. You will find these settings under Render > Environment. For more information, see Chapter 15, "Rendering."

- Pressing ` (accent grave) on your keyboard makes the interactive renderer redraw the viewports.

Figure 3.30 Clicking the Files button to access the Select Background Image dialog box.

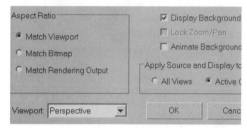

Figure 3.31 These options will display the image so it fits the dimensions of the Perspective viewport.

Figure 3.32 The image appears in the background. Note that the grid display has been turned off.

Figure 3.33 Toggle the background image display using the Viewport right-click menu.

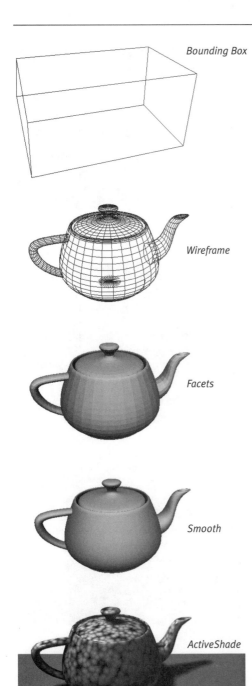

Bounding Box

Wireframe

Facets

Smooth

ActiveShade

Figure 3.34 Levels of viewport display resolution.

Viewport Resolution

A renderer is a software "engine" that draws images to a display device, such as your screen. The amount of information that a renderer draws is called resolution.

3ds max employs two different rendering engines for drawing scenes in the viewports: the fast, interactive viewport renderer and the high-resolution ActiveShade renderer.

The interactive viewport renderer can be set to different levels of resolution. Low-resolution display modes are good for editing objects and navigating complex scenes. High-resolution display modes are good for evaluating lighting and materials.

The interactive viewport renderer has four basic modes of display. From the lowest level of resolution to the highest, they include:

◆ **Bounding Box**—Renders objects as wireframe boxes. The boxes are drawn at the extents of the object.

◆ **Wireframe**—Renders mesh surfaces by tracing the edges of their polygons.

◆ **Facets**—Renders polygons by shading each one uniformly so that edges remain visible, like the facets of a gem.

◆ **Smooth**—Renders gradations of lighting and surface texture by averaging shading across edges.

The ActiveShade renderer uses the 3ds max scanline renderer to render a high-resolution image in two passes. The first pass stores pixel color information in a buffer. This is called the **initialization pass**. The second pass updates the buffer by adding lights, cast shadows, and material texture data. This is called the **update pass**. The result is a high-resolution rendering that can be updated interactively (**Figure 3.34**).

Viewports that display objects in ActiveShade mode are called **ActiveShade viewports**. Because ActiveShade viewports do not update geometry in real time, you cannot use them to fly through scenes.

To change viewport resolution:

1. Right-click on the viewport label.

2. Choose a display mode from the menu (**Figure 3.35**).

   Objects in the viewport are rendered at the new resolution (**Figure 3.36**).

✔ Tips

- The Edged Faces display option adds edges to any smooth or faceted display (**Figure 3.37**).

- The Edged Faces Toggle keyboard shortcut is F4.

- The Wireframe/Smooth + Highlights Toggle keyboard shortcut is F3.

- By default, 3ds max reduces the display resolution of your scene when the playback speed exceeds the speed at which your system can redraw. If you prefer to maintain a high-resolution display, choose Views > Adaptive Degradation Toggle, or press O on the keyboard.

- You can set keyboard shortcuts for display and other commands by choosing Customize > Customize User Interface > Keyboard from the main menu.

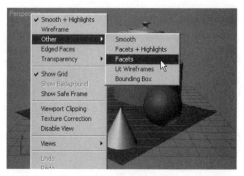

Figure 3.35 Choosing Facets display from the viewport menu.

Figure 3.36 The viewport display changes to facets.

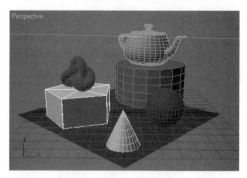

Figure 3.37 After turning on Edged Faces.

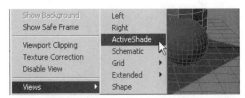

Figure 3.38 Choose ActiveShade from the Views menu.

Figure 3.39 The viewport is rendered at higher resolution. The render background is black by default.

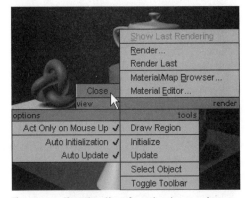

Figure 3.40 Choosing Close from the view quad menu.

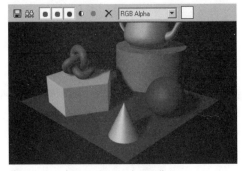

Figure 3.41 After turning on the toolbar.

ActiveShade is found on the Views menu, but it is really a high-resolution mode of display. As such, it takes a little bit longer to render than a simple screen redraw.

To change views to ActiveShade:

1. Right-click on the viewport label, and choose Views.

   The Views menu pops out.

2. Select ActiveShade (**Figure 3.38**).

   The viewport is redrawn at a higher level of display resolution. Viewport UI elements are replaced by the environment background color, which is black by default (**Figure 3.39**).

   To redraw the rest of the viewports, click in an inactive viewport and press ` (the accent grave key).

You "close" an ActiveShade viewport to restore it to its previous mode of display.

To close an ActiveShade viewport:

1. Right-click in the viewport.

2. Choose Close from the View quad menu (**Figure 3.40**).

   The ActiveShade viewport returns to its previous mode of display.

✔ Tips

- To toggle the ActiveShade viewport toolbar on and off, choose Toggle Toolbar in the ActiveShade viewport right-click menu, or press the Spacebar (**Figure 3.41**).

- To save the image, click the Save Bitmap icon in the toolbar. You will be prompted to choose a name, location, and type for the file.

- To zoom and scroll the image, use the following keyboard shortcuts:

   Ctrl + left-click to zoom in
   Ctrl + right-click to zoom out
   Roll the wheel to zoom in and out
   Alt + right-click to sample colors

VIEWPORT RESOLUTION

Navigating Viewports

Viewport navigation buttons allow you to fly through scenes by manipulating viewports. Each of the four sets of viewport navigation buttons appears automatically to match the view in the active viewport:

Figure 3.42 Axonometric Viewport controls navigate axonometric views.

- ◆ Axonometric Viewport controls allow you to navigate viewports that display Front, Back, Left, Right, Top, Bottom, or User views (**Figure 3.42**).

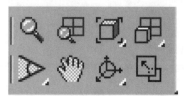

Figure 3.43 Perspective Viewport controls navigate Perspective views.

- ◆ Perspective Viewport controls allow you to navigate viewports that display Perspective views (**Figure 3.43**).

- ◆ Camera Viewport controls manipulate Cameras and navigate Camera viewports (**Figure 3.44**).

Figure 3.44 Camera Viewport controls manipulate cameras and navigate camera views.

- ◆ Light Viewport controls manipulate spotlights and directional lights and navigate views from those lights (**Figure 3.45**).

(See Chapter 11, "Lights," and Chapter 12, "Cameras," for more information about the controls for Camera and Light viewports.)

Figure 3.45 Light Viewport controls manipulate spotlights and directional lights and navigate their views.

Table 3.2 outlines the function of the viewport control buttons available for Axonometric and Perspective viewports.

Table 3.2

Keyboard Shortcuts and Buttons for Navigating Viewports

SHORTCUT	BUTTON	NAME	DESCRIPTION
Alt + Z		Zoom Mode	Zooms in or out of a viewport at cursor
assignable		Zoom All Mode	Zooms in or out of all viewports at cursor
Alt + Ctrl + Z		Zoom Extents	Centers all objects in the viewport
assignable		Zoom Extents Selected	Centers selected objects in the viewport
Shift + Ctrl + Z		Zoom Extents All	Centers all objects in all viewports
Z		Zoom Extents All Selected	Centers selected objects in all viewports
Ctrl + W		Zoom Region Mode	Enlarges selected area to fill the viewport
assignable		Field-of-View Mode	Changes the angle of the Perspective view
Ctrl + P		Pan View	Moves the view parallel to the view plane
Alt+Middle		Arc Rotate	Rotates the viewport Mouse Button around the center of the view
Alt + W		Min/Max Toggle	Toggles the viewport display between the viewport layout and a full-screen display of the active viewport
Alt + Q		Isolate Selection	Hides unselected objects and centers selected objects in the viewport
Ctrl + X		Expert Mode (toggle)	Hides/Unhides toolbars and command panels
[		Zoom Viewport In	Zooms into center of viewport
]		Zoom Viewport Out	Zooms out of center of viewport

NAVIGATING VIEWPORTS

Panning viewports

Panning allows you to see beyond the edges of the current view by moving viewports across the scene parallel to the view plane (the plane of the screen).

To pan a viewport:

1. Click on the Pan tool.
   The Pan cursor appears.

2. Drag the pan cursor across a viewport (**Figure 3.46**).

   The viewport moves across the scene (**Figure 3.47**).

✔ Tips

- Holding down the Ctrl key speeds up panning. Pressing Alt slows it down.

- The IntelliMouse wheel zooms the viewport when you are in Pan mode.

- The keyboard shortcut to enable the Pan tool is Ctrl + P.

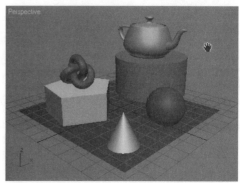

Figure 3.46 Placing the hand-shaped Pan tool in the viewport.

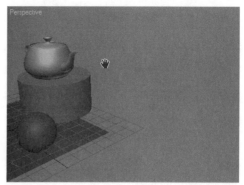

Figure 3.47 Dragging the Pan tool moves the viewport across a scene.

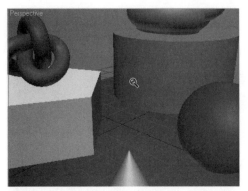

Figure 3.48 Dragging the Zoom tool up increases the viewport magnification.

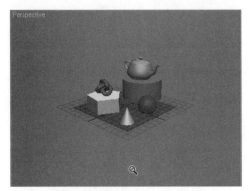

Figure 3.49 Dragging the Zoom tool down decreases the viewport magnification.

Zooming viewports

Zooming moves viewports closer or farther away from a scene so you can examine details or see the big picture.

By default, orthographic viewports, such as the Front viewport, zoom around the cursor. Perspective viewports zoom around the center of the view.

To zoom a viewport:

1. Click on the Zoom tool.
The Zoom cursor appears.

2. Click and slowly drag up or down in a viewport.

The viewport zooms in as you drag up (**Figure 3.48**) and out as you drag down (**Figure 3.49**).

✔ Tips

- To undo a zoom, choose Views > Undo View Change, or press Shift + Z. To redo a view change, choose Views > Redo View Change, or press Shift + Y.

- Holding down the Ctrl key speeds up zooming. Pressing Alt slows it down.

- To zoom in and out around the cursor using the keyboard, press the bracket keys, [and], respectively. If you have a mouse with a wheel, such as an IntelliMouse, you can use the wheel to zoom.

The Zoom All command zooms the scene in all viewports as you drag.

To zoom all viewports:

1. 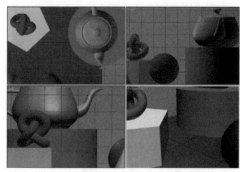 Click on the Zoom All tool.
    The Zoom All cursor appears.

2. Drag up or down in any viewport.
    All the viewports zoom at once
    (**Figure 3.50**).

✔ Tip

■ To make an Orthographic viewport zoom around the center of the view, choose Customize > Preferences > Viewports > Mouse Controls, and uncheck Zoom About Mouse Point (Orthographic).

Figure 3.50 Zoom All magnifies all four viewports at once.

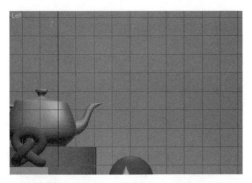

Figure 3.51 Here, objects in a scene do not fit neatly in the viewports.

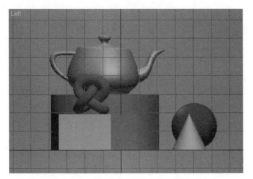

Figure 3.52 Zoom Extents makes the scene fit in the active viewport.

Zoom Extents centers the scene in the active viewport. Use it when you want to get the big picture on how your scene is developing.

To zoom extents:

1. Activate a viewport in which the objects have been panned away from the center (**Figure 3.51**).

2. Click Zoom Extents. The scene is centered in the viewport (**Figure 3.52**).

✔ Tip

■ To make Zoom Extents ignore certain objects, such as lights that are far from the center of your scene, select the objects and then check Ignore Extents in the Display Properties rollout of the Display command panel.

Zoom Extents Selected centers the current selection in the active viewport. Use it to focus in on your work.

To zoom extents selected:

1. Select an object by clicking it with the Select Object tool (**Figure 3.53**).

   or

   Select multiple objects by holding down the Ctrl key while clicking each one with the Select Object tool.

2. Choose Zoom Extents Selected from the Zoom Extents flyout.

   The active viewport changes its view to frame the object in the viewport (**Figure 3.54**).

The Zoom Extents All command centers the scene in all viewports at the same time. Use it whenever you need to reorganize your views.

To zoom extents all:

1. Choose Zoom Extents All from the Zoom Extents flyout.

   The object becomes centered in all the viewports (**Figure 3.55**).

✔ Tips

■ To center a viewport around the cursor, press I.

■ The keyboard shortcut for Zoom Extents All is Shift + Ctrl + Z.

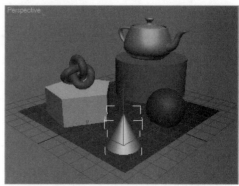

Figure 3.53 Select the object you want to zoom in on.

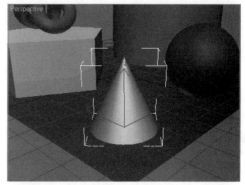

Figure 3.54 After you select one or more objects in the scene, click Zoom Extents Selected to zoom in on your selection.

Figure 3.55 Zoom Extents All instantly centers objects in all of the viewports at once.

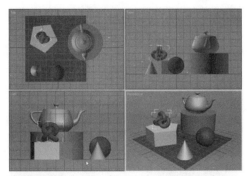

Figure 3.56 Select the object you want to zoom in on.

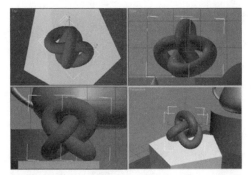

Figure 3.57 After clicking Zoom Extents All Selected, the selected objects become centered in all viewports.

Zoom Extents All Selected centers the current selection in all viewports at the same time. Use it to see your work from all sides.

To zoom extents all selected:

1. Select one or more objects (**Figure 3.56**).

2. Choose Zoom Extents All Selected from the Zoom Extents All flyout. All viewports zoom up to the objects that you have selected (**Figure 3.57**).

✔ Tips

■ To zoom to the extents of multiple objects in all viewports, select all the objects, and then click on Zoom Extents All Selected.

■ The keyboard shortcut for Zoom Extents All Selected is Z.

■ To prevent an inactive viewport from redrawing when you click Zoom All or Zoom Extents All, press D to disable the view. To re-enable the view, press D again.

NAVIGATING VIEWPORTS

The Isolate tool zooms to the extent of the current selection and hides all other objects. This comes in handy when you want to work without distraction.

To isolate an object:

1. 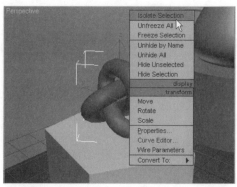 Select an object.

2. Right-click on the object.

   The Display quad menu appears.

3. In the Display quad menu, choose Isolate Selection (**Figure 3.58**).

   The object becomes centered in the viewport, and all other objects are hidden from view (**Figure 3.59**). The Isolated floater appears.

4. When you have finished with operations that require the object to be isolated, click Exit Isolation Mode.

✔ Tips

- You can also isolate a selected object by choosing Tools > Isolate Selection.

- The keyboard shortcut for the Isolate Tool is Alt + Q.

Figure 3.58 You find the Isolate Selection command by opening an object's menu; hold down the Ctrl key while you right-click the object.

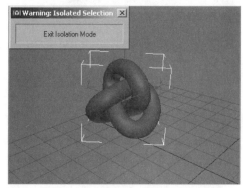

Figure 3.59 When you isolate an object, the Isolated floater appears; use it to exit isolation mode.

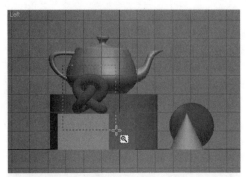

Figure 3.60 Drag to select a region for zooming in an axonometric view.

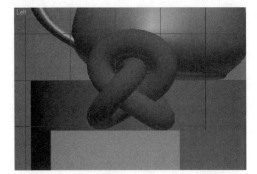

Figure 3.61 The result of zooming the region.

Region Zoom enlarges an area to fill the viewport. Use it for working on the details of your models.

To zoom a region:

1. Click on the Region Zoom tool. The Region Zoom cursor appears.

2. Drag a region in the viewport (**Figure 3.60**).

   When you release the mouse button, the viewport zooms in on the selected region (**Figure 3.61**).

✔ Tips

- In the Perspective Viewport controls, the Region Zoom tool flies out from the Field-of-View tool.

  To use Region Zoom in a Perspective view, change the Perspective view to a User view by pressing U. After you are finished, press P to restore the Perspective view.

- The keyboard shortcut to enable the Region Zoom tool is Ctrl + W.

The Field-of-View tool zooms and changes perspective at the same time. This tool is only available in Perspective viewports and Camera viewports.

To change the field of view:

1. Activate a Perspective viewport or a Camera viewport (**Figure 3.62**).

2. Click on the Field-of-View tool. The Field-of-View tool appears.

3. Drag the Field-of-View cursor up or down in the Perspective viewport.

   The viewport changes magnification and perspective (**Figure 3.63**).

✔ Tips

■ To undo a Field-of-View change, choose Views > Undo View Change, or press Shift + Z. To redo a viewport change, choose Views > Redo View Change, or press Shift + Y.

■ You can assign a keyboard shortcut to Field-of-View in the Customize User Interface dialog box by choosing Customize > Customize User Interface > Keyboards tab panel.

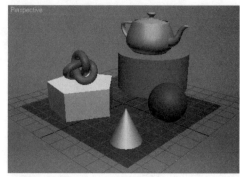

Figure 3.62 The Perspective viewport before using the Field-of-View tool.

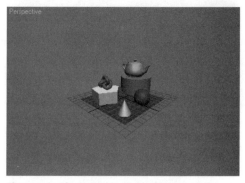

Figure 3.63 After using the Field-of-View tool, the viewport display changes magnification and perspective.

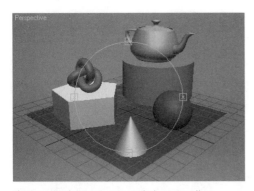

Figure 3.64 The Arc Rotate tool places a yellow navigation circle in the viewport.

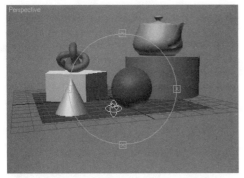

Figure 3.65 Rotate the viewport by dragging in the circle.

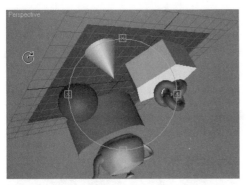

Figure 3.66 Rotating the viewport by dragging around the outside of the circle causes the viewport to spin parallel to the viewplane.

Rotating viewports

The Arc Rotate command orbits a viewport around its center so you can see your objects from different sides.

To rotate around a scene:

1. Click on the Arc Rotate tool. A yellow circle appears in the active viewport. Four square handles are positioned around it (**Figure 3.64**).

2. Drag across the inside of the circle. The viewport orbits around the center of the view in a motion similar to that of a track ball (**Figure 3.65**).

3. Drag around the outside of the circle. The viewport rotates around the center of the view and parallel to the screen, or **viewplane**, like a disk spinning upon a platter (**Figure 3.66**).

✔ Tips

- Drag the handles of the Arc Rotate circle to rotate the view vertically or horizontally.

- Rotating an Orthogonal view changes that view to a User view.

Arc Rotate Selected rotates a viewport around a selection so you can freely review your work from all sides.

To rotate a viewport around a selection:

1. [icon] Select one or more objects.

2. [icon] Optional: Click on Zoom Extents Selected.

   The viewport zooms in on the selection (**Figure 3.67**).

3. [icon] Choose Arc Rotate Selected from the Arc Rotate flyout.

4. Drag across the inside of the circle.
   The viewport rotates around the object (**Figure 3.68**).

5. Drag around the outside of the circle.
   The viewport rotates around the object and parallel to the screen (**Figure 3.69**).

✔ Tips

■ The keyboard shortcut to enable the Arc Rotate tool is Ctrl + R.

■ [icon] Arc Rotate Sub-Object works the same way as Arc Rotate Selected, except it rotates the view around a selection of sub-object components.

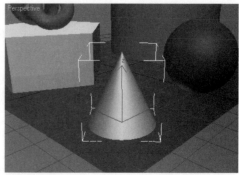

Figure 3.67 Usually you will want to zoom in on your selection first.

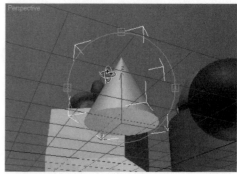

Figure 3.68 Rotating around the selection. Note that the object stays centered in the viewport.

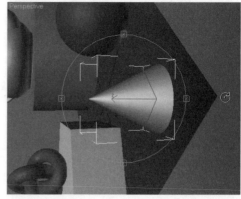

Figure 3.69 Dragging around the outside of the circle causes the viewport to spin around the selection parallel to the viewplane.

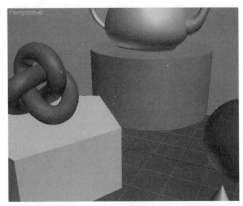

Figure 3.70 After zooming, panning, and rotating a view, it has a unique viewpoint on the scene.

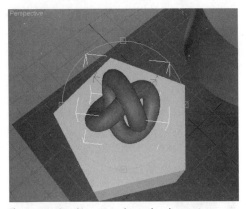

Figure 3.71 Continue to navigate the viewport.

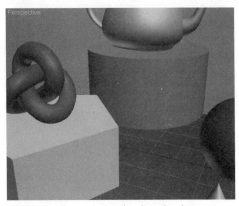

Figure 3.72 After restoring the view, the viewport returns to its previously saved viewpoint.

Saving Views

After you pan, zoom, rotate, or change a field of view to get the exact view of the scene that you want, how do you save your place?

The Save Active View command saves the active view to an internal buffer that is specifically reserved for that view type. Because this buffer is saved with the scene, you can restore saved views even after you close and reopen the scene.

To save a view:

1. Navigate a viewport to a point of view that you would like to save (**Figure 3.70**).

2. Choose Views > Save Active ... View, where ... is the name of the view.

   The active view is saved.

To restore a view:

1. Activate a viewport the contains a view that has been saved (**Figure 3.71**).

2. Choose Views > Restore Active ... View, where ... is the name of the view.

   The saved view is redrawn in the active viewport (**Figure 3.72**).

✔ Tips

- The Disable command prevents a viewport from redrawing while you are working in other viewports. The keyboard shortcut for the Disable command is D.

- To undo a view change, press Shift + Z. To redo a view change, press Shift + Y.

- 3ds max 6 saves up to 500 view changes. The default setting is 20. To change this setting, choose Customize > Preferences. In the General tab panel, use the spinner to adjust the Scene Undo level.

NAVIGATING VIEWPORTS

Test Rendering

For general production purposes, 3ds max uses the scanline renderer, which renders high-resolution images line by line. For your convenience, the default Quick Render settings create a single 640 × 480 pixel image that you can use to test your scene.

For more information on rendering, see Chapter 15, "Rendering."

There are two Quick Render options:

◆   **Quick Render (Production)** uses the scanline render to draw the active viewport in a floating window called a **rendered frame window**. After rendering, the image will not update.

◆   **Quick Render (Active Shade)** uses the ActiveShade renderer to draw the active viewport in a floating window called an **ActiveShade window**. Like the ActiveShade viewport, the image updates whenever you make changes to lighting or materials.

To make a test rendering:

1. Activate a viewport. Then navigate it to the point of view you want to render (**Figure 3.73**).

2.   From the Main toolbar, click Quick Render (Production).

   The Rendering dialog box displays the progress of the rendering (**Figure 3.74**).

   The viewport is rendered line by line in a rendered frame window (**Figure 3.75**).

✔ Tips

■   To save the image, click the Save Bitmap icon in the toolbar. You will be prompted to choose a name, location, and type for the file.

■ To zoom and scroll the image, use the following keyboard shortcuts:

   Ctrl + left-click to zoom in
   Ctrl + right-click to zoom out
   Roll wheel to zoom in and out
   Alt + right-click to sample colors

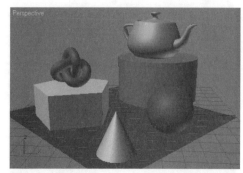

Figure 3.73 Navigate the viewport to the point of view you want to render.

Figure 3.74 The Rendering dialog box shows the progress of your rendering.

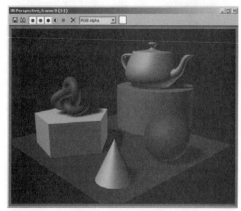

Figure 3.75 The rendered frame window displays the final image that you can save to disk.

OBJECT SELECTION AND DISPLAY

Figure 4.1 Selection allows you to apply commands to objects. Top: In wireframe views, objects turn white when they are selected. Middle: In shaded views, the corners of the bounding boxes appear. Bottom: Selection does not affect rendered images.

To apply commands to an object, you must first select it (**Figure 4.1**). Selection tells the program which sorts of commands may be applied, based on the object type. Only those commands that can be applied to the object in its current state are enabled. Commands that cannot be applied are grayed out.

In previous chapters, you learned how to select an object by clicking it with the Select Object tool. You also found out how to select multiple objects by Ctrl + clicking. In this chapter, you will learn more about selecting multiple objects and how to save selections in sets and groups.

At the end of the chapter, you will learn how to control most aspects of object display, including how to hide and freeze objects so that they cannot be accidentally selected.

Selecting Objects

The most basic way to select objects is by clicking them. When you select an object by clicking, other objects become deselected, unless you hold down the Ctrl key while you click.

To select an object by clicking:

1. Choose the Select Object tool from the Main toolbar, if it is not already in use.

2. Move the cursor over an object.

3. Click on the object.

   The object is selected, replacing the previous selection (**Figure 4.2**).

To add an object to a selection:

1. Choose the Select Object tool.

2. Hold down the Ctrl key, and click on an object.

   The object is added to the current selection (**Figure 4.3**).

3. Repeat step 2 until you have selected all the objects you want.

To subtract an object from a selection:

1. Choose the Select Object tool.

2. Hold down the Alt key, and click on an object.

   The object is subtracted from the current selection (**Figure 4.4**).

3. Repeat step 2 until you have deselected all the objects you want to subtract from the selection.

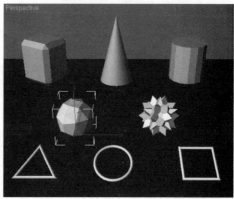

Figure 4.2 The corners of the bounding box indicate that the GeoSphere is selected.

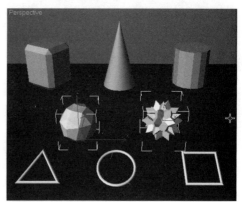

Figure 4.3 After adding the hedra to the selection.

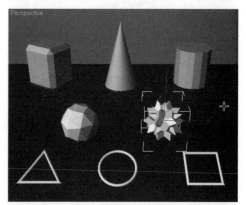

Figure 4.4 After subtracting the GeoSphere from the selection.

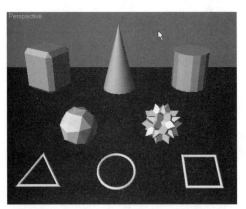

Figure 4.5 Click in the background to deselect objects.

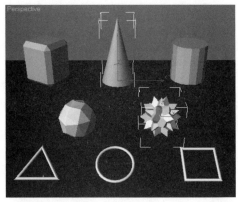

Figure 4.6 Select the objects that you want to exclude from the selection.

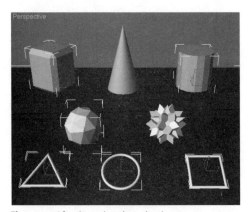

Figure 4.7 After inverting the selection.

To deselect all objects:

1. Choose the Select Object tool.

2. Click the background of one of the viewports (**Figure 4.5**).

   or

   Press Ctrl + D.

   All of the objects become deselected.

Locking a selection prevents objects from being deselected accidentally.

To lock a selection:

1. Make a selection of objects.

2. Click the Selection Lock toggle in the Status Bar Controls.

   or

   Press the Spacebar.

   The objects stay selected, no matter where else you click in the viewports.

To unlock a selection:

1. Click the Selection Lock Toggle in the Status Bar Controls.

   or

2. Press the Spacebar.

   Now the objects can be deselected.

Inverting deselects the current selection of objects, and selects everything else in the scene.

To invert a selection:

1. Make a selection (**Figure 4.6**).

2. Choose Edit > Select Invert.

   or

   Press Ctrl + I.

   The selection is inverted so that everything except the objects you selected in step 1 are now selected (**Figure 4.7**).

SELECTING OBJECTS

Region Selection

Region selection is the fastest way to select multiple objects. You simply click and drag a window around the objects you want to select. When you release the mouse button, every object inside the window is selected, no matter how far away it is in space.

3ds max 6 provides four methods of region selection (**Figure 4.8**):

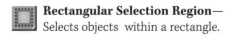 **Rectangular Selection Region—** Selects objects within a rectangle.

Circular Selection Region—Selects objects within a circle.

Fence Selection Region—Selects objects within a polygon that you define.

Lasso Selection Region—Selects objects within a freehand shape.

In addition, there are two settings for region selection that determine which objects will be included in the selection. These settings are controlled by a single button in the main toolbar called the Window/Crossing toggle:

Crossing Selection—Selects all objects enclosed by the window and all objects that the window crosses. This is the default.

Window Selection—Selects only those objects that are completely enclosed by the window. Objects crossed by the window are ignored.

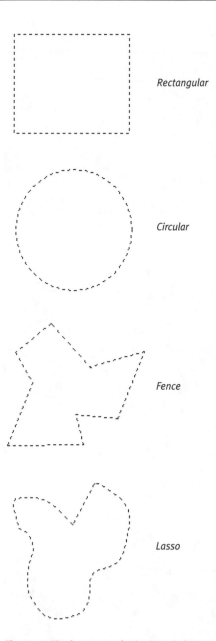

Rectangular

Circular

Fence

Lasso

Figure 4.8 The four types of selection windows.

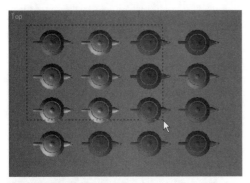

Figure 4.9 Dragging a rectangular selection region around and across some objects.

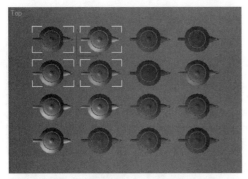

Figure 4.10 The window selection includes only the objects that were fully enclosed by the rectangle.

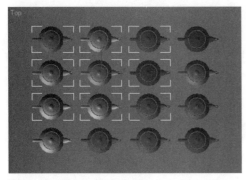

Figure 4.11 The crossing selection includes everything that was enclosed or touched by the rectangle.

You will no doubt be familiar with rectangular selection from using it in other programs. The window and crossing settings may be a bit new.

To make a rectangular selection:

1. Choose Select Object and Rectangular Selection.

2. Choose Window Selection or Crossing Selection from the Window/Crossing toggle.

3. Drag a rectangle around the objects you want to select (**Figure 4.9**).

4. Release the mouse.

   If you chose Window Selection, only the objects that are completely enclosed by the rectangle are selected (**Figure 4.10**).

   If you chose Crossing Selection, the objects that are both enclosed and crossed by the rectangle are selected (**Figure 4.11**).

✔ Tips

■ To add objects to a selection, hold down the Ctrl key and drag a region around the objects you want to add.

■ To subtract objects from a selection, hold down the Alt key and drag a region around the objects you want to subtract.

REGION SELECTION

111

Circle Selection Region is often used for editing radial objects, such as spheres, cylinders, and cones.

To make a circle selection:

1. Choose Circle Selection Region from the Selection Region flyout.

2. Optional: Choose Window Selection.

3. Place the cursor where you want the center of the selection to be. Then click and drag a circle until it encloses all the objects you want to select (**Figure 4.12**).

4. Release the mouse button.

The objects enclosed within the circle are selected (**Figure 4.13**).

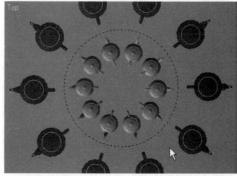

Figure 4.12 Dragging a circular selection region within a radial arrangement of objects.

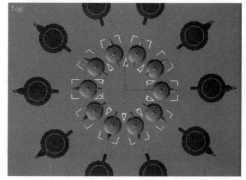

Figure 4.13 The resulting selection covers a circular area.

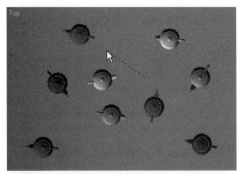

Figure 4.14 Start the fence with a click-drag action.

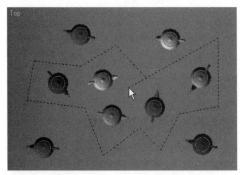

Figure 4.15 Double-click to complete the fence.

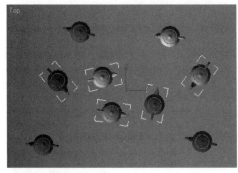

Figure 4.16 All the objects that were enclosed within the fence are selected.

Fence Selection Region allows you to select objects with an open or closed polygon region. Use this method when you need to make a selection within a more jumbled arrangement of objects.

To make a fence selection:

1. Choose Fence Selection Region from the Selection Region flyout.

2. Optional: Choose Window Selection Region.

3. Place the cursor next to the objects you want to select. Click and drag to create the first side of the region (**Figure 4.14**).

4. Click to set the second point of the region.

5. Move and click the mouse to set more points, until the fence encloses all the objects you want to select (**Figure 4.15**).

6. Double-click the mouse button.
   The objects inside the fence are selected (**Figure 4.16**).

✔ Tip

- Right-clicking during Fence Selection Region releases the fence and ends the selection process.

Lasso Selection Region allows you to drag an irregular selection region with a single click. Use this as an alternative to the Fence Selection method.

To make a lasso selection:

1. Choose Lasso Selection Region from the Selection Region flyout.

2. Optional: Choose Window Selection Region.

3. Place the cursor next to the sub-objects you want to select. Click and drag a lasso around all the objects you want to select (**Figure 4.17**).

4. Release the mouse button.

   The objects enclosed within the lasso are selected (**Figure 4.18**).

✔ Tip

- Right-clicking during Lasso Selection Region releases the lasso and ends the selection process.

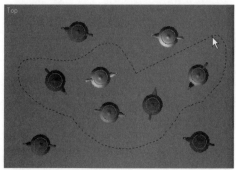

Figure 4.17 Dragging the lasso around the objects.

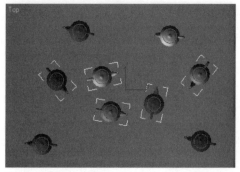

Figure 4.18 All the objects that you surrounded with the lasso are selected.

Figure 4.19 By default, the Select Objects dialog box lists all objects in the scene that are not hidden.

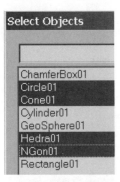

Figure 4.20 Choose the objects you want to select.

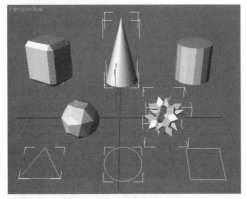

Figure 4.21 The resulting selection.

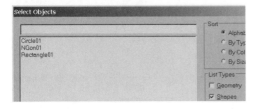

Selecting by Name

If you give objects meaningful names, you can more easily select them from a list. This is especially useful when scenes contain a large number of objects.

You can select one or more objects by name, or you can select a named set of objects.

To select objects by name:

1. Click the Select by Name button.

   or

   Press the H key.

   The Select Objects dialog box appears with a list of all selectable objects in the scene (**Figure 4.19**).

2. Click to highlight the names of the objects you want to select (**Figure 4.20**).

3. Click Select.

   The objects are selected (**Figure 4.21**).

✔ Tips

- You can double-click an object in the list of names to select it and close the Select Objects dialog box.

- If you have a lot of objects to choose from, you may want to switch to a different sorting order or filter the list of names (**Figure 4.22**).

- To bring up a selection list floater that stays open while you work, choose Tools > Selection Floater.

Figure 4.22 When you uncheck an object type, the objects of that type disappear from the list. Here, the mesh objects disappear when you uncheck Geometry, leaving only three spline objects on the list.

To easily select multiple objects, you use named selection sets.

To create a named selection set:

1. Select the objects you want to assign to the set (**Figure 4.23**).

2. In the Selection Sets toolbar, enter a name for the set in the Named Selection Sets field (**Figure 4.24**).

3. Press Enter to save the set.

To select a named selection set:

◆ Choose a named selection set from the Named Selection Set drop-down list in the Main toolbar (**Figure 4.25**) or from the Selection Sets drop-down list in the Select Objects dialog box (**Figure 4.26**).

To edit a named selection set:

1. From the menu bar, choose Edit > Edit Named Selection Sets.

2. In the Named Selection Sets dialog box, click the name of a set.

3. Using the button icons at the top of the dialog box, choose to (**Figure 4.27**):

Create New Set—Create a new set from selected objects. If no objects are selected, creates an empty set.

Remove—Deletes a set or removes selected objects from a set.

Add Selected Objects—Adds selected objects to a set.

Subtract Selected Objects—Subtracts selected objects from a set.

Select Objects in Set—Selects all the objects in a set.

Select Objects By Name—Opens the Select Objects dialog box.

Highlight Selected Objects—Highlights the name of selected objects and the name of the set.

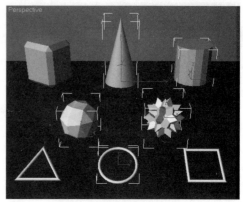

Figure 4.23 Select objects for the set.

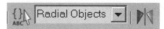

Figure 4.24 Type a name in the Named Selection Sets input field.

Figure 4.25 The selection set appears in the Named Selection Sets drop-down list.

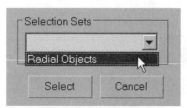

Figure 4.26 You can choose a selection set from the drop-down list in the Select Objects dialog box.

Figure 4.27 In the Named Selection Sets dialog box, you can create, select, or delete named selection sets and manipulate their contents.

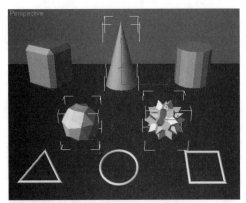

Figure 4.28 Select some objects to group.

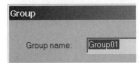

Figure 4.29 The Group dialog box allows you to enter a new group name.

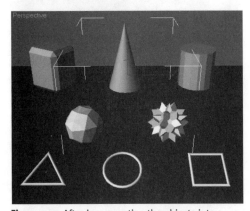

Figure 4.30 After incorporating the objects into a group, they share a single bounding box.

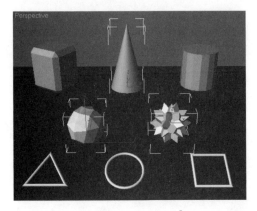

Grouping Objects

Grouping combines objects into a single unit called a group. You can select, transform, modify, and animate groups as if they were a single object. Objects in the group cannot be selected individually unless you open the group or dissolve it.

If you want to work with the objects together only part of the time and expect to select individual objects the rest of the time, create a named selection set, as described previously, instead of making a group.

To create a group:

1.  Select some objects (**Figure 4.28**).

2. Choose Group > Group.
   The Group dialog box appears (**Figure 4.29**).

3. Name the group, or accept the default name, Group01.

4. Click OK.
   The group is formed from the selected objects (**Figure 4.30**).
   In the command panel, the name of the group appears in boldface. In the Select Objects dialog box, the name of the group appears in brackets.

To dissolve a group:

1. Select a group.

2. Choose Group > Ungroup.
   The objects are ungrouped (**Figure 4.31**).

Figure 4.31 After ungrouping a group of objects, the objects can be selected individually.

You open a group to manipulate its contents. When you are done, you close the group.

To open a group:

1. 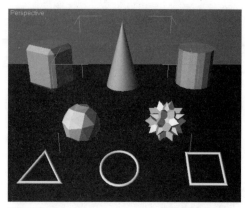 Select a group.

Figure 4.32 A pink bounding box appears when the group opens.

2. Choose Group > Open.

   A pink bounding box appears around the group, indicating that the group is open (**Figure 4.32**). You can now select and manipulate individual members of the group.

To close a group:

1. Select a member of an open group by clicking on its pink bounding box.

2. Choose Group > Close.

   The pink bounding box disappears, and the group closes (**Figure 4.33**). Individual group members can no longer be selected.

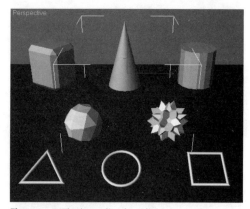
Figure 4.33 The bounding box disappears when the group closes.

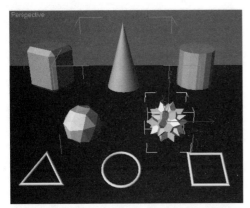

Figure 4.34 Select the object you want to remove from the group.

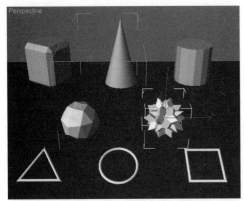

Figure 4.35 The group is reduced to two objects. The detached object can now be selected individually.

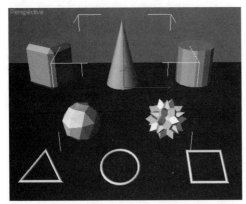

Figure 4.36 After attaching an object to a group, the object becomes part of the group.

As with named selection sets, you can add and subtract objects from a group after the group has been created.

To subtract an object from a group:

1. Open the group.

2. Select the object you want to detach (**Figure 4.34**).

3. Choose Group > Detach.
   The object is subtracted from the group (**Figure 4.35**).

To add an object to a group:

1. Select an object.

2. Choose Group > Attach.

3. Click a group.
   The object is added to the group (**Figure 4.36**).

✔ Tip

■ You can add an object to an open or closed group. The example in Figure 4.36 uses a closed group.

Nesting places one group inside of another. This gives you a convenient way to organize complex scenes.

To nest groups:

1. 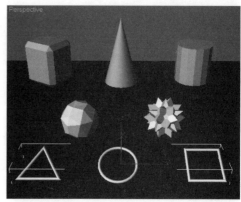 Select a group (**Figure 4.37**).

2. Choose Group > Attach.

3. Click another group.

   The second group nests inside the first (**Figure 4.38**).

The explode command ungroups all nested groups at once.

To explode groups:

1. Select a group.

2. Choose Group > Explode.

   All the objects that were grouped can now be selected individually (**Figure 4.39**).

Figure 4.37 Click on any member of a group to select the entire group.

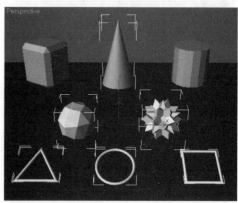

Figure 4.38 After nesting the group of shapes inside the group of mesh objects.

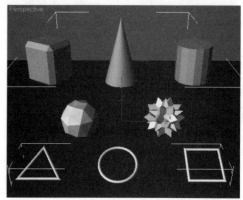

Figure 4.39 Exploding a nested group leaves former group members individually selected.

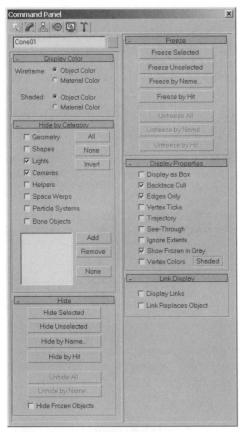

Figure 4.40 You control object display in the Display command panel.

Figure 4.41 The Display Properties group of the Object Properties dialog box is nearly identical to the Display Properties rollout in the Display panel.

Changing Object Display

In 3ds max, you control the display of an object individually or for an entire viewport. In this section, you will find out how to change the object display by manipulating the properties of the individual object. For information on how to change the viewport display, see Chapter 3, "Viewport Navigation and Display."

The commands in the Display panel control the display and selectability of objects and their components (**Figure 4.40**).

To help you distinguish between objects, the radio buttons in the Display Color rollout allow you to switch between the colors of the objects that you assign in the Name and Color rollout and the colors of the materials that you assign to them.

To help prevent unintended changes, the hide and freeze commands make objects temporarily unselectable. In addition, the hide command temporarily halts the display of objects in the viewports.

Any changes that you make to objects in the Display panel are reflected in the Object Properties dialog box, and vice versa (**Figure 4.41**). The Object Properties dialog box contains all the same display commands except hiding and freezing by category. To access the Object Properties dialog box, choose Edit > Object Properties, or right-click on a selection and choose Properties from the Transform menu.

To call up a floating dialog box of display commands, choose Tools > Display Floater.

Display property commands affect how viewports display objects (**Figure 4.42**):

- **Display as Box**—Displays an object in box mode, even when the viewport display is set to a higher level of resolution. Use this for any high-poly object that slows down viewport navigation.

- **Backface Cull**—Hides the display of the inside of a wireframe object. Uncheck this box when you want to see the entire structure.

- **Edges Only**—Hides the common edge between pairs of **coplanar** faces, which are adjacent faces that form a polygon. Uncheck this box to see the true number of faces that make up a mesh surface.

- **Vertex Ticks**—Displays vertices as small or large dots, depending on the preference you set in the Viewports panel of the Preference Settings dialog box.

- **Trajectory**—Displays the animation path of an object.

- **See-Through**—Causes a smooth shaded object to appear transparent. Affects viewport but not rendered output.

- **Ignore Extents**—Causes the Zoom Extents command to disregard the object.

- **Show Frozen in Gray**—Causes objects to turn gray when they are frozen.

- **Vertex Colors**—Displays Vertex colors that have been assigned during sub-object editing (see Chapter 8). May be displayed with or without surface shading.

Finally, the link display commands control the display of hierarchical links between objects. For more information on linking, see Chapter 7, "Animation."

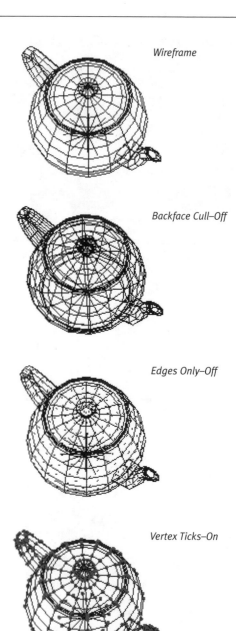

Wireframe

Backface Cull–Off

Edges Only–Off

Vertex Ticks–On

Figure 4.42 A teapot displayed on a white background using different wireframe display options.

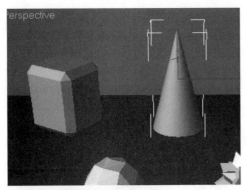

Figure 4.43 Select an object to hide.

Figure 4.44
The Hide rollout
contains
commands for
hiding and
unhiding objects.

Figure 4.45 After hiding the selected object.

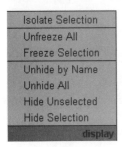

Figure 4.46 The Display
quad menu contains
shortcuts to the Hide and
Freeze commands.

Hiding Objects

Hiding objects helps you to manage complex scenes by simplifying the viewport display and speeding up redraw time. Hidden objects disappear from view and cannot be selected until they are unhidden.

To hide an object:

1. Select an object that you want to hide (**Figure 4.43**).

2. Open the Display command panel (**Figure 4.44**).

3. Open the Hide rollout.

4. Click Hide Selected.

   or

   Select Hide from the display quad menu. The object disappears from view (**Figure 4.45**).

✔ Tips

■ Hide Unselected hides unselected objects.

■ Hide by Name allows you to select objects from a filtered list.

■ Hide by Hit allows you to hide objects by clicking on them.

■ Frozen objects cannot be hidden unless you enable Hide Frozen Objects.

■ The right-click Display quad menu contains many of the Hide and Freeze commands (**Figure 4.46**).

CHANGING OBJECT DISPLAY

To unhide an object:

1. Click Unhide by Name.

   or

   Select Unhide from the display quad menu.

   A list of all the hidden objects appears (**Figure 4.47**).

2.  Select the object that you want to unhide.

3. Click OK.

   The object reappears (**Figure 4.48**).

To unhide all objects:

◆ In the Hide rollout, click Unhide All.

   All the hidden objects reappear.

The Hide by Category rollout allows you to hide objects according to type. I often hide lights and cameras when I am not working on them so I can zoom to the extents of a scene more closely. Another good use for this set of commands is for hiding helper objects and for hiding objects that have been used in building compound objects.

To hide an object by category:

1. In the Display panel, open the Hide by Category rollout (**Figure 4.49**).

2. Place a check in the boxes next to the types of objects you would like to hide.

   The objects disappear.

✔ Tip

■ To unhide objects by category, uncheck the object types you want to make visible.

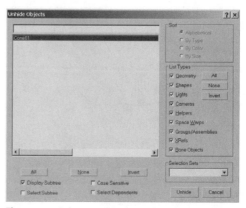

Figure 4.47 Select an object to unhide in the Unhide Objects dialog box.

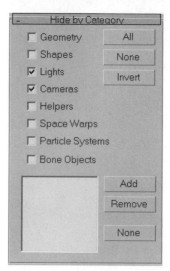

Figure 4.48 After unhiding the object.

Figure 4.49 You hide objects according to type in the Hide by Category rollout.

CHANGING OBJECT DISPLAY

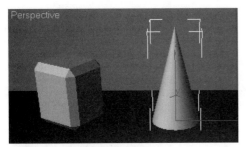

Figure 4.50 Select an object to freeze.

Figure 4.51 The Freeze rollout contains commands that make objects unselectable.

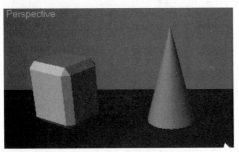

Figure 4.52 The frozen object turns dark gray.

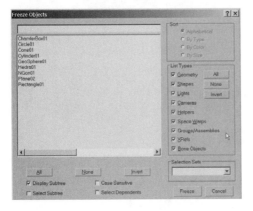

Figure 4.53 You can select objects to freeze in the Freeze Objects dialog box.

Freezing Objects

Freezing prevents objects from being manipulated without hiding them from view. When objects are frozen, they turn dark gray and cannot be selected until they are unfrozen.

To freeze an object:

1. Select an object (**Figure 4.50**).

2. Open the Display command panel.

3. Open the Freeze rollout.
   The Freeze rollout appears (**Figure 4.51**).

4. In the Freeze rollout, click Freeze Selected.
   or
   Select Freeze from the display quad menu.
   The object freezes (**Figure 4.52**).

✔ Tips

- Freeze Unselected freezes all visible objects that are unselected and unfrozen.

- Freeze by Name brings up a list of unhidden and unfrozen objects to freeze (**Figure 4.53**).

- Freeze by Hit allows you to freeze objects by clicking on them.

- If you do not want an object to turn gray when you freeze it, first select the object and uncheck Show Frozen in Gray in the Display Properties rollout.

CHANGING OBJECT DISPLAY

To unfreeze objects:

1. Click Unfreeze by Name.

   or

   Choose Unfreeze from the display quad menu.

   A list of all the frozen objects appears (**Figure 4.54**).

2. 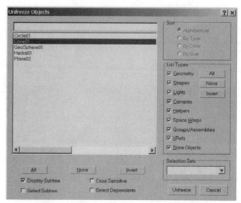 Select the objects that you want to unfreeze.

3. Click OK.

   The objects become unfrozen (**Figure 4.55**).

To unfreeze all objects:

◆ In the Freeze rollout, click Unfreeze All.

   or

   Choose Unfreeze All from the display quad menu.

   All the frozen objects become unfrozen.

✔ Tip

■ Unfreeze by Hit allows you to unfreeze objects by clicking on them.

Figure 4.54 Select an object to unfreeze in the Unfreeze Objects dialog box.

Figure 4.55 The unfrozen object returns to its original color and can now be selected.

TRANSFORMS

Figure 5.1 From top to bottom: translation along a diagonal line, rotation around the tip of the spout, scaling from large to small, reflection from side to side.

Transforms are the most basic commands for animating objects. With transforms, you make objects bounce, squash, spin, and fly. They are also essential for modeling surface details, placing objects in a scene, creating clones, and composing arrays.

Transforms are based on a class of mathematical functions called **affine transformations.** These functions change the coordinates of geometry objects with minimum distortion by keeping parallel sides of objects parallel.

Basic transformations include:

◆ **Translation**—Moving along a straight line

◆ **Rotation**—Revolving around a point

◆ **Scaling**—Enlarging or reducing

◆ **Reflection**—Mirroring

Figure 5.1 illustrates the results of applying translation, rotation, and scaling to a teapot. In 3ds max, these transformations are called the **Move**, **Rotate**, and **Scale** transforms.

In this chapter, to show the before-and-after view of transforms, two views of an object appear in some figures. The transparent image represents the object before transformation; the opaque image represents the results of the transform.

Transform Tools

The three basic transforms are move, rotate, and scale. These transforms change the position, orientation, and scale of objects with respect to a system of reference:

 Select and Move—Repositions objects by translating in an axis or plane.

 Select and Rotate—Reorients objects by spinning them around a point.

 Select and Scale Tools— Expand or shrink objects toward or away from a point.

Because of their central importance, most of the transform tools are located in the Transform toolbar. Additional tools are located in the Axis Constraints toolbar and the Extras toolbar (**Figure 5.2**). The Tools menu and Transform quad menu also provide access to transform tools (**Figure 5.3**).

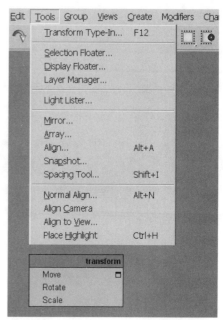

Figure 5.3 The Tools menu and Transform quad menu also provide access to transform tools.

Figure 5.2 Transform tools appear in the Transform toolbar, Extras toolbar, and Axis Constraints toolbar.

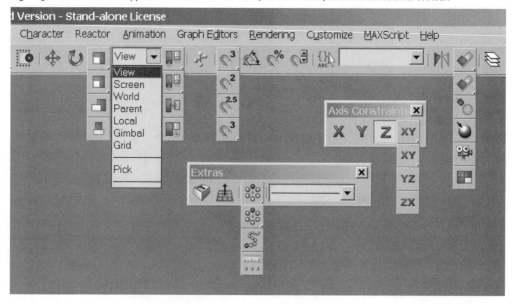

Table 5.1

Keyboard Shortcuts and Buttons for Transforms

Shortcut	Button	Name
W		Move Mode
E		Rotate Mode
R		Scale Cycle
F12		Transform Type-In Dialog
F5		Restrict to X
F6		Restrict to Y
F7		Restrict to Z
F8		Restrict to Plane Cycle
X		Transform Gizmo Toggle
=		Transform Gizmo Size Up
-		Transform Gizmo Size Down
S		Snap Toggle
A		Angle Snap Toggle
Shift + Ctrl + P		Snap Percent Toggle
assignable		Spinner Snap Toggle
assignable		Mirror Tool
assignable		Array
assignable		Snapshot
Shift + I		Spacing Tool
Alt + A		Align
Alt + N		Normal Align
Ctrl + H		Place Highlight
assignable		Align Camera
assignable		Align to View

To modulate and combine the effects of the three basic transforms, 3ds max provides you with the following tools:

Axis Constraints—Restrict the direction of transforms to selected axes of the current system of reference.

Transform Gizmos—Change axis constraints on the fly as you perform transforms (see "Transform Gizmos" later in the chapter).

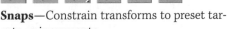

Reference Coordinate Systems—Assign a system of reference for computing the distance, direction, and scale of transforms.

Transform Centers—Set the centers of rotation and scaling for Rotate and Scale transforms.

Snaps—Constrain transforms to preset targets or increments.

Mirror and Array Tools—Create, transform, and arrange object clones.

Align Tools—Line up objects to the viewplane or to other objects.

Table 5.1 lists all the transform tools and their shortcuts.

Axis constraints limit the direction in which a transform may be applied to a single axis or to a plane that is defined by two axes. Once assigned, axis constraints "stick" to a transform until a new constraint is assigned.

To constrain a transform using the Axis Constraints toolbar:

1. 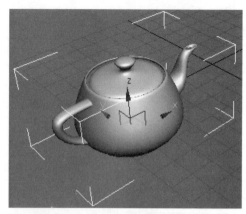 Choose a transform tool from the Main toolbar.

2. Select an object by clicking on it.

   A transform gizmo appears at the object's pivot point (**Figure 5.4**).

3. Lock the selection by clicking the Selection Lock Toggle.

4. Right-click on the edge of any toolbar so that the toolbar menu appears. Then choose Axis Constraints (**Figure 5.5**).

5. In the Axis Constraints toolbar, click the Restrict Axis button for the direction you want to constrain the transform.

6. Click and drag in different directions anywhere in the viewport. Be careful not to click on the transform gizmo, as this may reset the constraints.

   The transform is limited to the axis or plane that you constrained it to (**Figure 5.6**).

7. Unlock the selection by clicking the Selection Lock Toggle again.

✔ Tips

- The shortcuts for axis constraints are:

  F5—Restrict to X

  F6—Restrict to Y

  F7—Restrict to Z

  F8—Cycles through the Restrict to XY, Restrict to YZ, and Restrict to ZX planes

- To lock or unlock a selection from the keyboard, press the Spacebar.

Figure 5.4 A Move transform gizmo at the pivot point of a teapot. The transform is currently constrained to the plane that is defined by the X and Y axes.

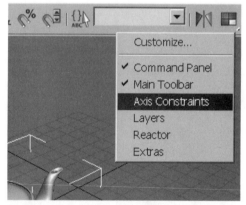

Figure 5.5 After right-clicking on the edge of a toolbar, choose Axis Constraints from the toolbar menu.

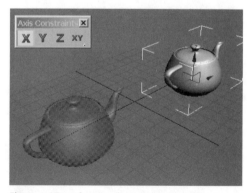

Figure 5.6 Transforming the teapot with a Move transform in the positive direction of the X axis.

TRANSFORM TOOLS

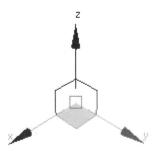

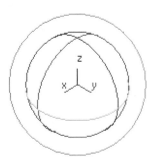

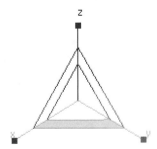

Figure 5.7 From top to bottom: a Move transform gizmo, a Rotate transform gizmo, and a Scale transform gizmo.

Transform Gizmos

Transform gizmos allow you to assign constraints at the same time that you apply transforms. Like the axis constraints that you set in the Axis Constraints toolbar, transform gizmo constraints "stick" to a transform until you assign new constraints.

You assign a constraint to a transform gizmo by clicking one of its handles (**Figure 5.7**). These handles are color coded to indicate the direction of constraint: red for the X axis, blue for the Y axis, and green the Z axis. To assign a constraint at the same time that you apply a transform, you click and drag the handle that corresponds to the constraint.

The Move transform gizmo contains seven handles: three for moving along the X, Y, or Z axes; three for moving along the XY, YZ, and ZY planes; and one for moving parallel to the screen. This last handle, called the screen handle, is turned off by default. When it is enabled, the handle appears as a small gray box at the base of the gizmo.

The Rotate transform gizmo consists of five handles that encircle the point of rotation, and an axis tripod at the center. Red, green, and blue handles constrain the transform to rotation around the X, Y, and Z axes. To rotate an object freely or parallel to the screen, you use the medium and light gray handles that lie parallel to the screen.

The Scale transform gizmo includes seven handles. Boxes at the ends of the axes serve as handles for single axis constraints. Parallel lines that connect each pair of axes are handles for dual axis constraints. To constrain a scale transform to all three axes so that an object scales uniformly in all directions, you use the triangular handle in the middle of the scale gizmo.

The size of a gizmo can be adjusted by pressing the "=" key (to enlarge it) and the "-" sign (to decrease it). To toggle the display of a gizmo on or off, press X.

Move transforms change the position of objects.

To move an object:

1. Choose the Select and Move tool from the Main toolbar.

2. Click an object to select it.

   The Move transform gizmo appears.

3. Position the cursor over the handle that corresponds to the direction you want to move the object. For single axis constraints, click the tip or the shaft of the X, Y, or Z axis handles (**Figure 5.8**). For planar constraints, click the lines that form a square at the base of the XY, YZ, or ZX axes (**Figure 5.9**).

   The handle turns yellow.

4. Click and drag the handle along the axis or plane.

   The object moves, following the handle.

5. Release the handle by releasing the mouse button.

   The handle remains yellow to let you know that the constraint is still in effect.

6. To move an object parallel to the screen, choose
   Customize > Preferences > Gizmos.
   In the Center Box Handle area of the Move Gizmo settings, check Move in Screen Space. Then drag the screen handle (**Figure 5.10**).

   The screen handle turns yellow and the object moves parallel to the screen. When you release the mouse button, the handle turns gray, and the previous constraint is reassigned.

✔ Tip

- The keyboard shortcut for the Move tool is W.

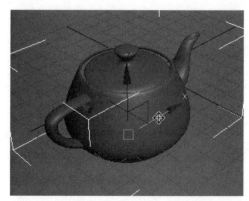

Figure 5.8 Using the Move transform gizmo to restrict move transforms to the Z axis. Axis handles and their labels turn yellow when activated.

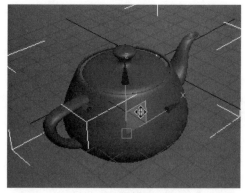

Figure 5.9 Using the Move transform gizmo to restrict move transforms to the ZX plane. Like the handles of the axis constraints, the square defined by the planar handle turns yellow when activated.

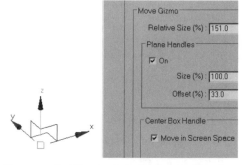

Figure 5.10 Enabling the center box handle. Dragging the handle at the base of the Move transform gizmo moves objects parallel to the screen.

TRANSFORM GIZMOS

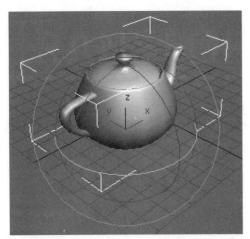

Figure 5.11 The Rotate transform gizmo encircles the pivot point of the teapot.

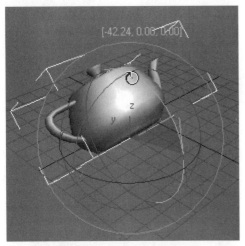

Figure 5.12 Rotating a teapot in X. The pie slice shows the amount of rotation. The numerical readout gives the same information in degrees of arc.

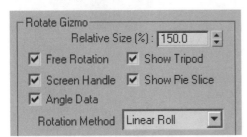

Figure 5.13 You customize a gizmo in the Gizmo tab panel of the Preference Settings dialog box.

Rotate transforms change the orientation of objects.

To rotate an object:

1. Choose the Select and Rotate tool from the Main toolbar.

2. Click on an object to select it.

   The Rotate transform gizmo appears (**Figure 5.11**).

3. Position the cursor over the handle that corresponds to the direction you want to rotate the object.

   The handle turns yellow.

4. Click and drag the handle along its edge. For free rotation, drag in any direction.

   The object rotates. A short tangent line appears at the point that you clicked, indicating the direction you should drag the handle. If you are using the X, Y, or Z constraints, a sweeping pie slice appears inside the handle, and angle data appears above the gizmo (**Figure 5.12**).

5. Release the mouse button.

   The angle data and pie slice disappear. The handle remains yellow to let you know that the constraint is still in effect.

✔ Tips

- To customize a gizmo, choose Customize > Preferences > Gizmos (**Figure 5.13**).

- By default, an object's center of rotation or scaling is its pivot point, located at the origin of its local axes.

- For multiple selected objects, the default center is the geometric center of the entire selection—that is, the average of all their pivot points.

- The keyboard shortcut for the Rotate tool is E.

TRANSFORM GIZMOS

Scale transforms change the size and proportions of objects. Scale tools include:

Select and Uniform Scale—Selects and scales objects equally in all three axes, regardless of constraints.

Select and Non-Uniform Scale—Selects and scales an object in one or two axes, resulting in a change in the object's proportions.

Select and Squash—Selects and scales objects in one or two axes and inversely scales objects in the remaining axes, so that the proportions of the object change but its volume does not (**Figure 5.14**).

To scale an object:

1. Choose a scale tool from the scale flyout.

2. Select an object by clicking on it.

   The Scale transform gizmo appears.

3. Position the cursor over the handle that corresponds to the direction you want to scale the object. To proportionally scale the object, place the cursor over the center of the scale gizmo. To disproportionately scale the object, place the cursor over one side of the gizmo or over an axis (**Figure 5.15**).

   The handle turns yellow.

4. Drag toward or away from the center of the gizmo.

   The handle stretches or shrinks as the object scales up or down (**Figure 5.16**).

5. Release the mouse button.

   The gizmo resets.

✔ Tip

- The keyboard shortcut for the scale tool is R. Pressing R repeatedly cycles through the Scale tools.

Figure 5.14 Clockwise from upper left: uniform scaling, non-uniform scaling, and squashing a teapot.

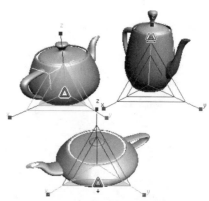

Figure 5.15 Scale transform gizmos for the teapots above.

Figure 5.16 Squashing in X and Y results in a proportional reduction in Z.

TRANSFORM GIZMOS

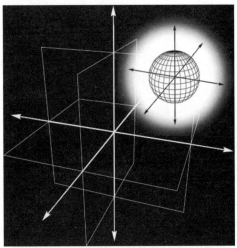

Figure 5.17 Black: World coordinates define world space. White: An object's coordinates define object space.

Table 5.2

How They Line Up	
Screen	X and Y are parallel to the display screen; Z is perpendicular to the screen.
World	X, Y, and Z align to the world coordinate system.
View	Combination of Screen and World. X and Y lie on the visible grid plane of the active view; Z is perpendicular to the grid.
Parent	X, Y, and Z align to the local coordinates of an object's parent. If the object is not linked to a parent, it is a child of the world and uses world coordinates.
Local or Gimbal	X, Y, and Z align to the local coordinates of an object.
Grid	X, Y, and Z align to the coordinate system of the active grid.
Pick	X, Y, and Z align to the local coordinate system of any object in the scene that you pick.

Advanced Controls

Now that you have learned the basics of performing transforms, here are some more advanced ways to control them.

Systems of Reference

Systems of reference govern the orientation of the transform axes. Transform centers set the point of origination to either the origin of the current system of reference or to the individual or collective centers of the objects that are being transformed.

The system of reference that is assigned to a transform defines the origin and the potential direction of that transform. The coordinate system that you choose "sticks" to the transform that you assign it to until you choose another system.

Chapter 3, "Viewpoint Navigation and Display," reviewed two systems of reference: the absolute, fixed system of reference called the **world coordinate system** and the relative system of reference of object space called the **local coordinate system** (**Figure 5.17**).

A third system of reference called the **screen coordinate system** is based on the plane of the monitor screen. Because screen coordinates relate to the position of the viewer, they are easy to understand: the Y axis goes up and down; the X axis moves from left to right; and the Z axis moves in and out, perpendicular to the screen.

3ds max uses a combination of local, world, and screen coordinates to provide you with a reference system for every occasion. The default system is **View**. View coordinates use screen coordinates in Orthogonal views, and world coordinates in Perspective views. In all views, the X and Y axes are marked by the darkest horizontal and vertical grid lines, while the Z axis sticks up at a perpendicular angle, invisible to the viewer.

In addition to the world, local, screen, and view coordinates, you can use the coordinates of one object to provide a system of reference for the coordinates of another object. To find out how the different coordinate systems compare, see **Table 5.2** on the previous page.

To select a coordinate system:

1.  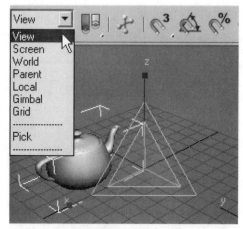 Choose a transform tool from the Transform toolbar.

2. Open the Reference Coordinate System drop-down list (**Figure 5.18**).

3. Choose a new coordinate system from the list.

   The coordinate system is assigned to the current Move, Rotate, or Scale transform. The **axis tripods** and the transform gizmos of the selected objects align themselves to the new coordinate system (**Figure 5.19**).

✔ Tip

- Most of the time, you can use the default View coordinate system with satisfactory results. Later on, when you are animating and editing objects, you will make more use of the other coordinate systems.

Figure 5.18 The Reference Coordinate System drop-down list allows you to choose a system of reference for the current transform.

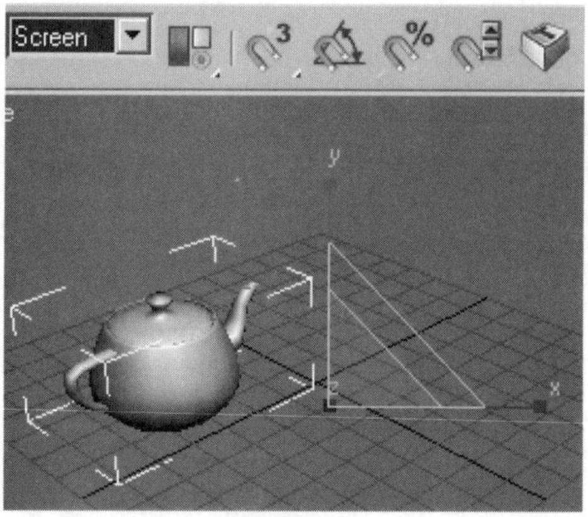

Figure 5.19 After changing the system of reference to Screen, the transform gizmo aligns to the screen.

ADVANCED CONTROLS

Tracking Transforms

3ds max uses a constantly updating matrix to keep track of transforms with respect to local and world coordinate systems. Only the net effect of transforms—i.e., the current position, orientation, and scale of the object—is preserved. Compare this to modifiers, which tracks the history of changes in an ordered list that can be edited later.

Transform Centers

Transform centers provide alternative points of origination for Rotate and Scale transforms. By default, transforms are applied to the pivot point of each object. If more than one object is selected, the transform is applied to the geometric center of the selection. Transform centers do not affect move transforms.

The available settings are:

Use Selection Center—Assigns the center of rotation or scaling to be the geometric center of a selection. This is the default setting for multiple object selections.

Use Pivot Point Center—Assigns the center of rotation or scaling to the pivot point of each selected object. This is the default setting for single object selections.

Use Transform Coordinate Center—Assigns the center of rotation or scaling to the origin of the current system of reference.

ADVANCED CONTROLS

To select a transform center:

1.  Choose a rotate or scale transform from the Transform toolbar.

2. From the Transform Center flyout in the Transform toolbar, choose a transform center.

3. **View** ▼ If you chose Use Transform Coordinate Center in step 2, then choose a system of reference from the Reference Coordinate System drop-down list.

   The transform center is assigned to the current transform. Axis tripods and **transform gizmos** update to show the position and orientation of the transform center you have selected (**Figure 5.20**).

✔ Tips

- The combination of Use Transform Coordinate Center and the Pick coordinate system allows you to pick another object to use as the center of rotation or scaling.

- When you choose Use Pivot Point Center, by default only one transform gizmo appears, even if multiple objects are selected. To turn on multiple gizmos, choose Customize > Preferences > Gizmos and check Allow Multiple Gizmos. Now gizmos will appear at the center of each selected object.

- To transform an object's pivot point, open the Adjust Pivot rollout in the Hierarchy panel and click Affect Pivot Only.

Figure 5.20 Top: rotation around a selection center. Middle: rotation around individual pivot points. Bottom: rotation around a transform center.

ADVANCED CONTROLS

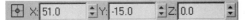

Figure 5.21 The coordinate display allows you to type in transforms when a transform tool is selected.

Figure 5.22 The object moves to the exact coordinates that you entered, regardless of axis constraints.

Precision Aids

When you need to transform objects with precision, you use **transform type-ins** or **snaps**. Transform type-ins execute transforms using numerically precise coordinates or coordinate offsets. Snaps constrain transforms to precise increments or to certain types of targets.

Transform type-ins offer two options for transforming objects relative to the current system of reference:

 Absolute Mode transforms objects to exact coordinates.

 Offset Mode transforms objects by incremental amounts.

There are two ways to perform transform type-ins: from the status bar or in the floating Transform Type-In dialog box. Both methods have equal capabilities, so use whichever method is most convenient for you.

To type-in a transform from the status bar:

1. Choose a transform tool from the Transform toolbar.

2. Select an object.

3. In the center of the status bar (just below the viewports), choose a transform type-in mode.

4. In the coordinate display area just to the right, enter the absolute or offset amounts by typing in the input fields or dragging the spinners next to them (**Figure 5.21**).

   The selection is transformed (**Figure 5.22**). For uniform scales, the amount applies equally to all three axes.

To type-in a transform using the Transform Type-In dialog box:

1. Choose a transform tool from the Transform toolbar.

2. Select an object.

3. Choose Tools > Transform Type-In.

   or

   Right-click on the transform tool.

   The Transform Type-In dialog box for the current transform appears.

4. In the Transform Type-In dialog box, enter absolute coordinates or offset amounts by typing in the input fields or dragging the spinners next to them (**Figure 5.23**).

   The selection is transformed by the precise amount that you entered (**Figure 5.24**).

✔ Tips

- The keyboard shortcut for opening the Transform Type-In dialog box is F12.

- Transform type-ins override snap locks and axis constraints.

- To set a spinner to its minimum value, right-click on the spinner.

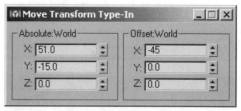

Figure 5.23 The Transform Type-In dialog box provides another way to enter transform amounts.

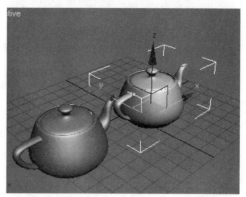

Figure 5.24 After offsetting the position of the teapot 45 units in the negative X direction.

PRECISION AIDS

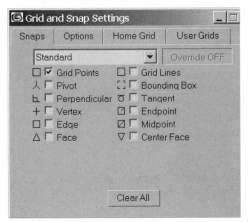

Figure 5.25 You set options for grids and snaps in the Grid and Snap Settings dialog box.

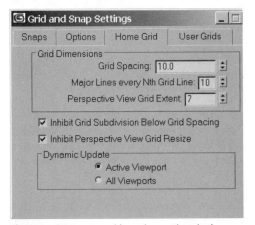

Figure 5.26 You enter grid spacing settings in the Home Grid panel.

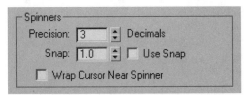

Figure 5.27 You enter spinner snap settings in the Spinners group of the Preference Settings dialog box General panel.

Snaps constrain transforms to preset intervals or targets. Snap locks, the buttons that turn snaps on and off, are found on the Main toolbar.

   2D, 2.5D, and 3D Snaps constrain Move transforms to targets on a grid, object components, or to relative distances.

 Angle Snap constrains Rotate transforms to increments of degrees of arc.

 Percent Snap constrains Scale transforms to a percentage of the size of an object.

 Spinner Snap constrains spinners to incremental or decremental amounts.

To configure snap settings:

1. Choose Customize > Grid and Snap Settings.

   or

   Right-click on any snap lock except Spinner Snap.

   The Grid and Snap Settings dialog box appears (**Figure 5.25**).

2. Open the panel you want to access.

3. Set the options you want by checking boxes or entering values (**Figure 5.26**).

4. Choose Customize > Preferences.

   or

   Right-click on the Spinner Snap lock.

   The Preference Settings dialog box appears.

5. In the General panel, enter the settings you want for spinner precision, spinner snap, and spinner wrap (**Figure 5.27**).

6. Click OK or close the dialog box.

✔ Tip

■ The Shift + right-click menu allows you to configure snaps and certain snap options on the fly.

PRECISION AIDS

You use snaps to constrain Move transforms to preset targets. Snap targets include grid points, grid lines, bounding boxes, pivot points, perpendiculars, tangents, and sub-object components.

To set snap targets:

1. Choose Customize > Grid and Snap Settings.

   or

   Right-click on any snap tool.

   The Grid and Snap Settings dialog box appears.

2. Open the Snaps panel (**Figure 5.28**).

3. Click Clear All to clear all the check boxes.

4. Check the snap targets you want to use (**Figure 5.29**).

5. Close the dialog box.

   The next time you snap a cursor to a target, the cursor will change to the snap icon that matches that target (**Figure 5.30**).

To snap a move in any direction:

1. 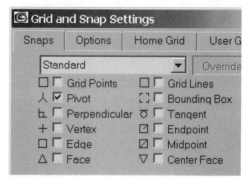 Choose the Select and Move tool from the Main toolbar.

2. Choose 3D Snap from the Snap Toggle flyout.

3. Move an object.

   The object snaps from one target to another as you move it (**Figure 5.31**).

✔ Tips

■ You increase the strength of a snap—the distance a cursor jumps to its target—in the Options panel of the Grid and Snap Settings dialog box.

■ The keyboard shortcut for the Snap Toggle is S.

Figure 5.28 You set snap targets in the Snaps panel. Snap icons are located to the left of the snap targets.

Figure 5.29 Setting the snap target to Pivot will snap the cursor to the pivot points of objects.

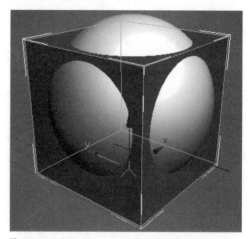

Figure 5.30 Snapping a sphere to the pivot point of a box. The Pivot snap icon and bounding box of the target object light up blue.

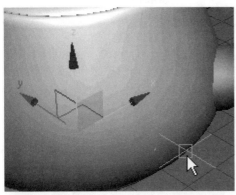

Figure 5.31 Snapping a move to grid intersections. A snap icon appears when an intersection is crossed.

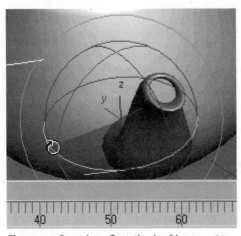

Figure 5.32 Snapping a Z rotation in 5° increments.

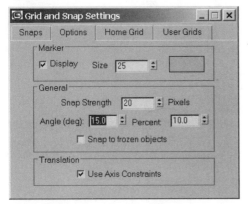

Figure 5.33 Changing the angle snap increment to 15°.

Angle snaps constrain rotations to degree increments. The default increment is 5°.

To snap a rotation:

1. Choose the Select and Rotate tool from the Transform toolbar.

2. Turn on Angle Snap by clicking Angle Snap in the Transform toolbar.

3. Rotate an object.

   The object snaps to degree increments as it rotates (**Figure 5.32**).

To set angle snap increments:

1. Open the Options panel of the Grid and Snap Settings dialog box.

2. Set the Angle value in degrees (**Figure 5.33**).

3. Close the dialog box.

✔ Tip

- Press A to turn angle snaps on and off.

Percent snaps constrain scales to percentage increments. The default increment is 10%.

To snap a scale:

1. 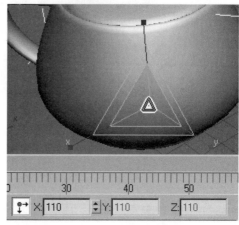 Choose the Select and Uniform Scale tool from the Transform toolbar.

2. Turn on Percent Snap by clicking on the Percent Snap button in the Transform toolbar.

3. Scale an object.

   The object snaps to percentage increments as it scales (**Figure 5.34**).

To set percent snap increments:

1. Open the Options panel of the Grid and Snap Settings dialog box.

2. Enter a new percentage in the Percent field (**Figure 5.35**).

3. Close the dialog box.

✔ Tip

■ Press Shift + Ctrl + P to turn percent snaps on and off.

Figure 5.34 Snapping a uniform scale by 10%.

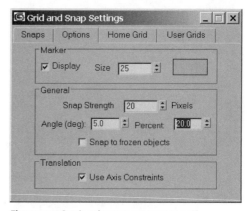

Figure 5.35 Setting the percent snap to 20%.

Cloning

A **clone** is a duplicate object. With cloning, you can create thronging multitudes that line up in precise formations (**Figure 5.36**).

There are three types of clones that you can create: a **copy**, an **instance,** or a **reference**. In order to know which one to choose, you first need to learn a little more about objects.

To 3ds max, objects are a stream of data. Every time you apply a command to an object, it changes the object's data stream. Commands that affect object data include creation parameters, modifiers, transforms, space warps, and object properties. (For more information on modifiers and object data flow, see Chapter 6, "Modifying Objects.")

When you clone an object, you duplicate its data stream, including all the commands that have been applied to it. But there are exceptions. Some clone types refer to the original modifiers instead of referring to independent duplicates. If original or cloned objects refer to the same modifiers, they are influenced by them simultaneously. This is what allows us to animate objects in unison.

A **copy** is independent of the original object. Use copies to create duplicate objects that you want to animate individually.

An **instance** shares all of its modifiers with the original object and all other instances. Any modifier you apply to the original object applies to its instances, and vice versa. Use instances to create and animate flocks of birds, swarms of bees, schools of fish, etc.

A **reference** shares its initial modifiers with the original object, but it can also be assigned its own separate modifiers. Use references to create variations on a theme: birds that veer from a flock, bees that split from a swarm, or fish that pause to look at the camera.

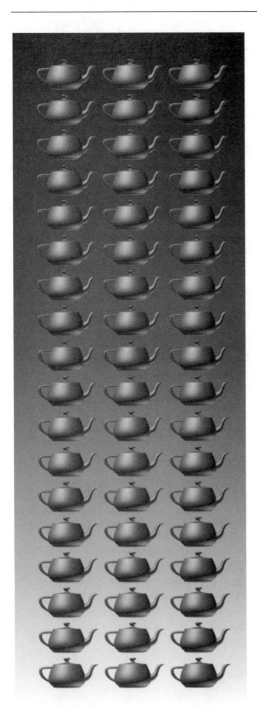

Figure 5.36 Cloning creates exact duplicates that can be precisely placed.

The simplest way to make a clone is to use the Edit > Clone command. This method creates a clone in the same place as the original object.

To clone an object:

1. Select an object (**Figure 5.37**).

2. Choose Edit > Clone.

   The Clone Options dialog box appears (**Figure 5.38**).

3. Choose a clone type, or accept the default, which is Copy.

4. Enter a name or accept the default. The default name is the name of the original object plus a numerical suffix that has been incremented by +01.

5. Click OK.

   The clone is created. It occupies the same spot as the original. To see the clone, move it away from the original (**Figure 5.39**).

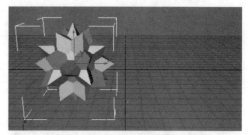

Figure 5.37 Select the object you want to clone.

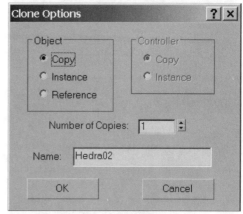

Figure 5.38 The Clone Options dialog box allows you to choose a clone type and name the clone.

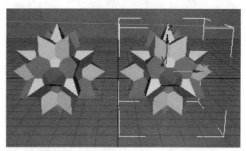

Figure 5.39 After moving the clone, you see it is an exact duplicate of the original.

CLONING

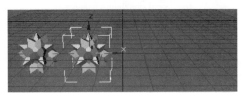

Figure 5.40 Shift-cloning an object using the Move tool.

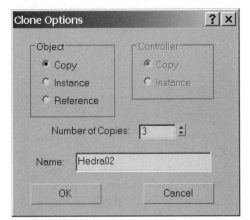

Figure 5.41 In the Clone Options dialog box, you enter the number of clones you want to create.

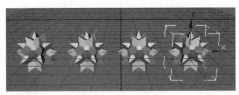

Figure 5.42 The resulting clones of a Move transform are always spaced an even distance apart.

You can create multiple clones if you hold down the Shift key before transforming an object. This is known as Shift-cloning.

If you use the Move tool for Shift-cloning objects, the clones will automatically be spaced the exact same distance apart.

To create multiple clones:

1. Choose the Move tool from the Transform toolbar.

2. Select an object.

3. Hold down the Shift key.

4. Move the object by dragging it.

    A second object is dragged out of the first one (**Figure 5.40**), and the Clone Options dialog box appears. This time there is place to enter the number of copies (**Figure 5.41**).

5. Enter a value for Number of copies.

6. Click OK.

    The clones appear. Each one is moved incrementally from the original object (**Figure 5.42**).

✔ Tip

■ To Shift-clone an object in place so that the clones completely overlap the original, click the object instead of dragging it.

CLONING

Using Advanced Transforms

The Mirror, Array, and Align commands apply a combination of Move, Rotate, and Scale transforms to objects and their clones.

The Mirror tool reflects an object along one or two of its axes.

To mirror an object:

1. Select an object.

2. From the Transform toolbar, choose the Mirror tool.

   or

   Choose Tools > Mirror.

   The Mirror dialog box appears (**Figure 5.43**).

3. Choose a mirror axis, or use the default.

4. Choose a clone type, or choose No Clone to mirror the original object.

   A mirrored object is created.

5. Enter an Offset value to specify how far away the mirrored object will be.

   The object is offset in the direction of the mirror axis (**Figure 5.44**).

✔ Tips

- If you use the Offset spinner, holding down the Ctrl key will visibly accelerate the rate at which the object offsets.

- To create a symmetrical pattern, create an object and mirror it. Then select the object and its clone and mirror them together (**Figure 5.45**).

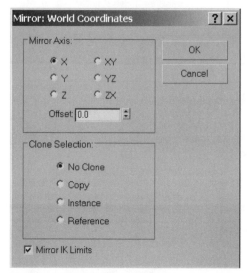

Figure 5.43 In the Mirror dialog box, you choose the axes of reflection and the clone type.

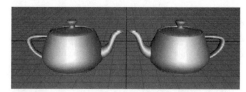

Figure 5.44 The result of mirroring an object and offsetting its clone in X.

Figure 5.45 By selecting and mirroring objects repeatedly, you can create repeating patterns.

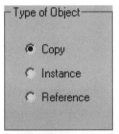

Figure 5.46 Choose a clone type in the Type of Object group.

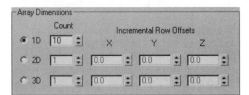

Figure 5.47 In the Array Dimension group, you set the number of dimensions you want in the array and the number of objects in each dimension.

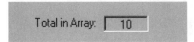

Figure 5.48 The Total in Array value is the number of objects that will appear in the final array.

The Array tool creates an array of clones by transforming them in up to three dimensions. The Array tool is found in the Transform toolbar.

The Array dialog box includes the following:

◆ **Type of Object group**—Allows you to choose a clone type of copy, instance, or reference (**Figure 5.46**).

◆ **Array Dimensions group**—Allows you to choose the number of dimensions you want in your array and the number of objects you want in each dimension of the array. The Incremental Row Offsets set the amount of space you will have between each row (**Figure 5.47**).

◆ **Total in Array indicator**—Indicates the total number of objects in the final array. Calculated by multiplying together the number of objects in each dimension (**Figure 5.48**).

◆ **Array Transformation group**—Indicates the current system of reference and allows you to set incremental or total amounts for each transform. You click the left arrows if you want to enter incremental amounts; click the right arrows if you want to enter the total amounts. The Re-Orient parameter causes clones to follow the direction of a rotation when it is checked. When the Uniform parameter is checked, Y and Z scaling are disabled and the X scale value is applied to all axes (**Figure 5.49**).

USING ADVANCED TRANSFORMS

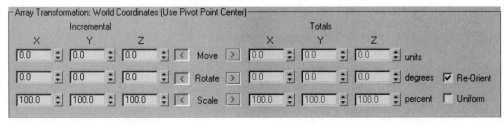

Figure 5.49 The Array Transformation group allows you to configure transforms you will use in the array.

A grid array is a two-dimensional array of objects arranged in rows and columns. A lattice array adds the dimension of height.

To create a grid array:

1. 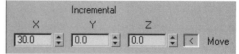 Select an object.

2. From the Transform toolbar, choose a reference coordinate system and a transform center.

3. From the Transform toolbar, choose the Array tool.

   or

   Choose Tools > Array.

4. In the Type of Object group, choose a clone type.

5. In the Array Dimensions group, choose 2D.

6. In the 1D Count field, enter the number of clones you want in each row.

7. In the 2D Count field, enter the number of clones you want in each column.

8. In the Array Transformation group, enter incremental or total amounts for each transform you want to perform on the clones. For a simple grid without rotation or scaling, just enter a Move value for X to space apart the columns (**Figure 5.50**).

9. In the Y input field of the 2D Incremental Row Offsets, enter the amount of space you want between each row (**Figure 5.51**).

10. Click OK to create the array.

    The grid array appears (**Figure 5.52**).

To create a lattice array:

1. Follow steps 1–9 for creating a grid array.

2. In the Array Dimensions dialog box, choose 3D Count.

3. In the Count field, enter the number of clones for the vertical dimension. Then enter the offset amount in the Z field.

4. Click OK to create the array (**Figure 5.53**).

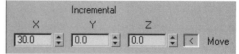

Side tab: **USING ADVANCED TRANSFORMS**

Figure 5.50 This setting will move the columns of the grid apart 30 units.

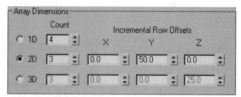
Figure 5.51 Entering a Y offset amount moves the rows apart. The values for a 3D array are grayed out.

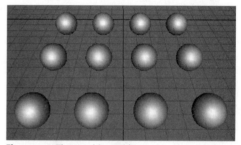
Figure 5.52 The resulting grid array.

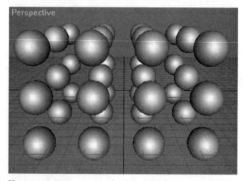
Figure 5.53 You create a lattice array by entering 3D parameter values.

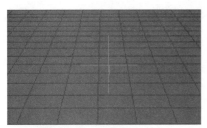

Figure 5.54 Create a Point helper object to serve as the center of rotation.

Figure 5.55 Setting the 1D Count to create a 12-object array.

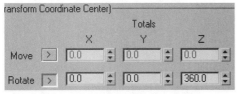

Figure 5.56 A total of 360° creates a circular array.

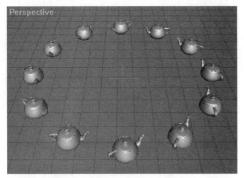

Figure 5.57 The resulting circular array. Notice that the teapots all follow the direction of rotation.

A circular array is a one-dimensional array of clones arranged in a circle.

To create a circular array:

1. In the Create panel, open the Helpers sub-panel.

2. In the Object Type rollout, click Point.

3. In any viewport, click the spot that you want to be the center of the array.

   A Point helper object appears (**Figure 5.54**).

4. Create or position the first object in the array. The distance between this object and the Point object will define the radius of the array.

5. From the Transform Center drop-down menu, choose Use Transform Coordinate Center.

6. From the Reference Coordinate System drop-down menu, choose Pick. Then click the Point object.

7. From the Transform toolbar, choose the Array tool.

   or

   Choose Tools > Array.

8. In the Array dialog box, choose a clone type in the Type of Object group.

9. In the Array Dimensions group, choose 1D. Then enter the Count value for the number of objects you want to have in the array (**Figure 5.55**).

10. In the Array Transformation group, click the right arrow next to the word Rotate. Then enter Z = 360 degrees (**Figure 5.56**).

11. Enter any other transformations you want to add, if needed. Then click OK to create the array (**Figure 5.57**).

USING ADVANCED TRANSFORMS

151

To create a spiral array:

1.  Follow steps 1–10 for creating a circular array. (If you completed step 11, see the tip below.)

2. Adjust the number of objects in the array by changing the 1D Count parameter (**Figure 5.58**).

3. Multiply the Z rotation amount by the number of turns you want in the spiral. Then change the Z rotation amount to this value (**Figure 5.59**).

4. Enter a Z Move value to set the height increment or total height of the array (**Figure 5.60**).

5. Click OK.

   A spiral array appears, beginning with the original object (**Figure 5.61**).

✔ Tip

■  To adjust an array that you just created, press Ctrl + Z or click the Undo button. Then click the Array button. Your last settings are preserved, so you can adjust them for a new array.

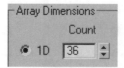

Figure 5.58 Changing the number of objects to 36.

Figure 5.59 A total rotation of 1080° will cause the array to spiral three times.

Figure 5.60 This sets the height increment to 25 units.

Figure 5.61 The resulting spiral array, as seen in an ActiveShade View.

Figure 5.62 You see what an object's animation path looks like when you turn on its trajectory.

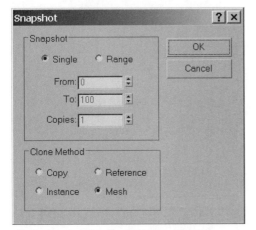

Figure 5.63 The Snapshot dialog box allows you to choose the number and type of clones you will create in a snapshot array.

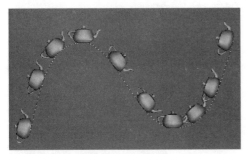

Figure 5.64 The clones in the snapshot array follow the object's trajectory. The distribution of the clones is directly dependent on the number of copies chosen.

The Snapshot tool creates clones by taking "multiple exposures" of an object over time. If the object is animated to move through space, the clones will be distributed along its trajectory. (For more information on animation, see Chapter 7, "Animation.")

To create a snapshot array:

1. Select an animated object.

2. Right-click on the object, and choose Properties from the quad menu.

3. In the Object Properties dialog box, turn on Trajectory.

   The trajectory of the object appears (**Figure 5.62**).

4. Choose Snapshot from the Array flyout in the Axis Transform toolbar.

   or

   Choose Tools > Snapshot.

5. In the Snapshot dialog box, choose Range and enter the number of copies you want to create (**Figure 5.63**).

6. In the Clone Method group, choose a clone type or accept the default (Mesh). (Note: Mesh clones are mesh object copies of an original object that may or may not be a mesh object.)

7. Click OK.

   A snapshot array appears along the trajectory of the original object (**Figure 5.64**).

✔ Tip

■ The Snapshot command does not count the original object as part of the array. Instead, it creates a copy of the object in the exact same location. Compare this to the Array tool, which includes the original object as part of the final array.

The Spacing tool creates arrays by distributing clones along a path, not unlike the Snapshot array (**Figure 5.65**). The main difference is that the Spacing tool has more parameters for arranging clones and does not use movement to determine spacing. The Spacing tool also does not offer the mesh clone type.

The main parameters of the Spacing tool are:

◆ **Count**—Sets the number of clones.

◆ **Spacing**—Sets the distance between clones.

◆ **Start Offset**—Determines how far away from the starting point the first clone will appear.

◆ **End Offset**—Determines how far away from the end point the last clone will appear.

As you check and uncheck parameters, the drop-down list below updates to reflect the current combination. You can also lock the offset values. If you choose a setting from the drop-down list, it will automatically check or lock your parameters (**Figure 5.66**).

In the Context group, you specify how you want to measure distance between the clones: from center to center or edge to edge. By default, clones in the array will "follow" the path, meaning they align to the direction of the path. But if you uncheck Follow in the Context menu, they will orient in the same direction as the original object (**Figure 5.67**).

When you use the Spacing tool to distribute clones along an existing spline path, the first vertex of a spline is always used to set the start point for spacing. (To learn how to change the first vertex of a spline, see Chapter 8, "Editing Meshes and Polymeshes.")

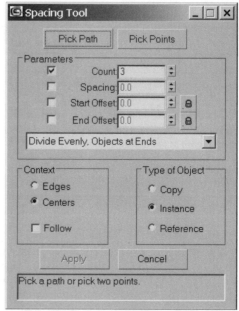

Figure 5.65 The Spacing tool creates an array by distributing clones along a path.

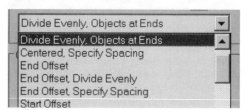

Figure 5.66 The Parameters drop-down list both reflects and affects parameter settings.

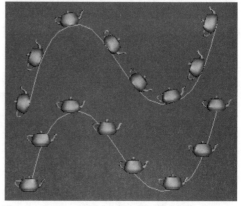

Figure 5.67 Clones follow the path by default, but you can also orient them in the same direction.

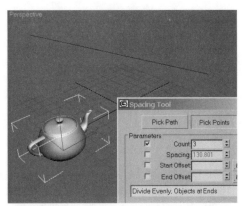

Figure 5.68 Click points in a viewport to define a path.

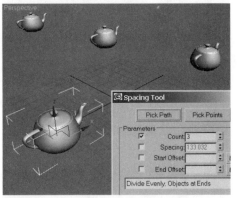

Figure 5.69 Three clones appear by default.

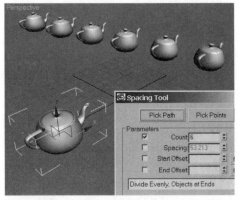

Figure 5.70 Setting the number of clones in the Count field automatically updates the number of clones in the array.

To distribute objects along a path:

1. Select an object.

2. In the Transform toolbar, choose the Spacing tool from the Array flyout.

   or

   Choose Tools > Spacing Tool.

   The Spacing Tool dialog box appears.

3. In the Type of Object area, select a clone type.

4. In the Context area, choose a spacing option.

5. Click Pick Path, and then click a spline to use as a path.

   or

   Click Pick Points. Then click two different locations in a viewport to define a path (**Figure 5.68**).

   Three clones appear along the path from the start to end (**Figure 5.69**).

6. In the Count field, set the number of clones that you want in the array (**Figure 5.70**).

   As you change the Count, the number of clones updates in the viewports, and the Spacing parameter updates interactively.

7. If you want to offset the clones from the end of the path, check Start Offset and End Offset. Then type in start and end offset values.

8. When you are satisfied with the array, click Apply and close the dialog box.

✔ Tips

- The Spacing tool does not count the original object as part of the array.

- The keyboard shortcut for opening the Spacing Tool dialog box is Shift + I.

155

The Align tool uses transforms to align the position, orientation, or scale of one or more objects to another object.

To align objects:

1. Select the object you want to align. This becomes the current object (**Figure 5.71**).

2. From the Transform toolbar, choose the Align tool from the Align flyout.

   or

   Choose Tools > Align.

3. Click the object you want to align to. This becomes the target object.

   The Align Selection dialog box appears.

4. Accept the default alignment reference point—the center of each object—or choose another option for each object.

   Minimum and Maximum refer to opposite edges of the object's bounding box.

5. Check the position, orientation, and scale of each axis in the target object to which you want to align the current object (**Figure 5.72**).

   As you check each axis, the current object aligns with that axis of the target object (**Figure 5.73**).

6. Click Apply to apply the alignment and reset the parameters.

7. Click OK when the alignment is complete.

✔ Tip

■ The keyboard shortcut for aligning selected objects is Alt + A. When you click a target object, the Align dialog box appears.

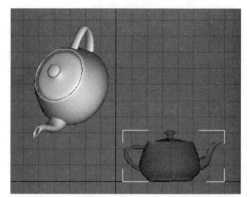

Figure 5.71 Select the object you want to align.

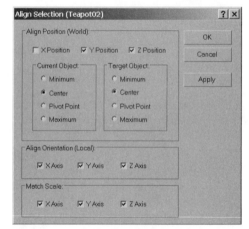

Figure 5.72 Aligning the position, orientation, and scale of the teapots.

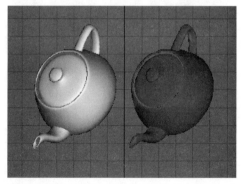

Figure 5.73 The teapots are aligned in all ways except the X position.

USING ADVANCED TRANSFORMS

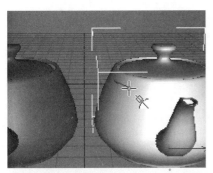

Figure 5.74 When you click on the first object, a blue surface normal appears.

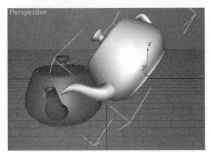

Figure 5.75 The normal of the first object aligns to the normal of the second object.

Figure 5.76 In the Normal Align dialog box, you set position and rotation offsets for the normal aligned objects.

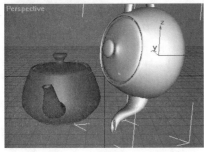

Figure 5.77 After offsetting and rotating an object along its surface normal.

Normal vectors project perpendicularly from the center of each face so the program knows which side to render. When you align the normal of one face to the normal of another, they align so that the faces just touch.

To align objects to normals:

1. Select an object.

2. Choose the Normal Align tool from the Align flyout.

    or

    Choose Tools > Normal Align.

3. Click and hold on surface of the object. A blue surface normal appears at the crosshairs of the cursor (**Figure 5.74**).

4. Drag the cursor across the surface of the object until the blue surface normal projects from the face you want to align. Then release the mouse button.

5. Click and hold on another second object. A green surface normal appears at the crosshairs of the cursor.

6. Drag the cursor across the surface of the object until the green surface normal projects from the face you want to align. Then release the mouse button.

    The blue surface normal of the first object aligns to the green surface normal of the second object (**Figure 5.75**). The Normal Align dialog box appears.

7. In the Normal Align dialog box, enter a Position Offset value if you want to move the first object toward or away from the second object. To rotate the object around the aligned normals, enter a Rotation Offset value. Check Flip Normal if you want to flip the object upside down. Then click OK (**Figure 5.76**).

8. Click OK to complete the alignment (**Figure 5.77**).

✔ Tips

- The keyboard shortcut for the Normal Align tool is Alt + N.

- 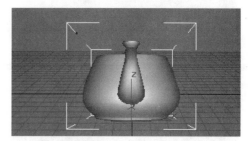 Use the Place Highlight tool in the Align flyout to align a selected light to a surface normal by clicking the surface of an object. The keyboard shortcut for the Place Highlight tool is Ctrl + H.

- 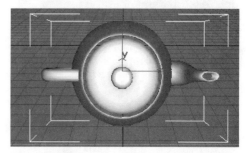 Use the Align Camera tool in the Align flyout to align a selected camera to the surface normal of an object by clicking the surface of the object.

The Align to View tool in the Align flyout aligns an object to the screen coordinates of the active view using the object's pivot point center and local axes for reference.

To align an object to a view:

1. Select an object.

2. Choose the Align to View tool from the Align flyout. The Align to View dialog box appears (**Figure 5.78**). The object aligns the currently selected axis in the Align to View dialog box to the active view (**Figure 5.79**).

3. Change the axis of alignment, if necessary, in the Align to View dialog box (**Figure 5.80**).

4. To flip an object 180° in the axis of alignment, check Flip in the dialog box (**Figure 5.81**).

5. Click OK.

Figure 5.78 The Align to View dialog box aligns objects to the viewplane of the active view.

Figure 5.79 The object aligns to the viewport.

Figure 5.80 When you change the axis of alignment, the object immediately reorients in the direction of the axis.

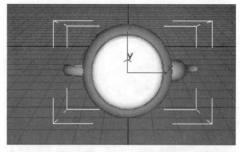

Figure 5.81 Check Flip to reverse the alignment 180°.

USING ADVANCED TRANSFORMS

MODIFYING OBJECTS

Figure 6.1 A box that has been tapered and twisted.

Figure 6.2 This is how the modifiers that were applied to the box appear in the modifier stack.

Modifiers change the structure and appearance of objects. With the dozens of modifiers that ship with 3ds max 6, you can bend, twist, taper, ripple, wave, lathe, and extrude objects (**Figure 6.1**). Objects can be squeezed, sliced, stretched, or smoothed. You can even turn them inside out.

Like transforms, multiple modifiers can be applied in succession to obtain cumulative results. As you apply a succession of modifiers, they are tracked in an ordered list that stays with the object they modify. This list, or history, of modifiers is called the **modifier stack (Figure 6.2)**.

Every time you apply a modifier, the object data is modified and passed up the modifier stack. Because the modifiers in the stack are completely accessible, you can adjust their parameters as often as you like. You can also turn off, rearrange, or remove modifiers from the stack. This flexibility gives the modifier stack its power for modeling, mapping, and animating objects.

Using Modifiers

You access modifier commands from the Modifiers menu and the Modify command panel. Commands that cannot be applied to the current selection are made unavailable.

The Modifiers menu organizes commands by function into a series of flyout menus (**Figure 6.3**).

The Modify command panel lists commands in a drop-down menu or in menus of buttons (**Figure 6.4**). Features of the Modify panel include:

Name and Color Rollout—Input fields for changing the name and color of objects.

Modifier List—A drop-down menu of all the modifiers that can be applied to the current selection (**Figure 6.5**).

Modifier Button Sets—Collections of buttons that apply modifiers to objects. Button sets are turned off by default.

Stack Display—Lists all the modifiers in the stack of the current selection.

 Lightbulb icons in the stack turn the modifiers on and off.

Stack Tools—Button-driven commands that control the modifier stack. They include:

 Pin Stack—Locks the modifier stack to the current selection

 Show End Result On/Off Toggle—Previews the effects of the modifier stack on an object. Modifiers below the current stack selection are ignored.

 Make Unique—Converts instanced modifiers into modifier copies.

 Remove Modifier from the Stack— Deletes the current modifier from the stack. Also unbinds space warps.

Configure Modifier Button Sets— Allows you to create and display modifier button sets (**Figure 6.4**).

Figure 6.3 The modifiers in the Modifiers menu are organized by function.

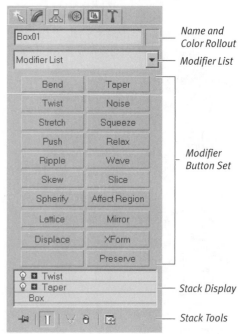

Figure 6.4 The Modify command panel with a modifier button set displayed.

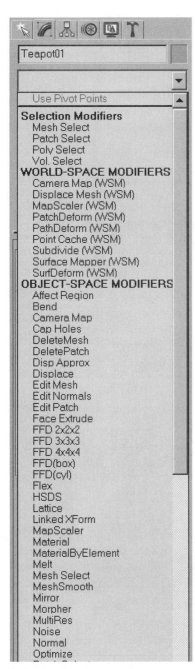

Figure 6.5 Left: The Modifier List contains all the modifiers that 3ds max 6 offers. In the default display setting, modifiers that reference world space are listed separately from modifiers that reference object space.

Right: When Show All Sets in List is enabled, the commands in the Modifier List are grouped into sets according to function and made available in the Configure Modifier Sets list for display as button sets.

Modifier button sets place selections of related modifiers at your fingertips.

To turn on a modifier button set:

1.  Open the Modify panel.

Figure 6.6 Turn on the button display.

2. Click Configure Modifier Sets.

3. In the pop-up menu, click Show Buttons (**Figure 6.6**).

4. Click Configure Modifier Sets again.

5. In the pop-up menu, choose a button set (**Figure 6.7**).

    The button set that you chose appears in the Modify panel. Modifiers that can be applied to the current selection are enabled. Modifiers that cannot be applied to the current selection are grayed out (**Figure 6.8**).

✔ Tips

■ To change button sets, follow steps 1 through 4, and pick another button set.

■ To arrange the modifiers in the Modifier list by button sets, click Configure Modifier Sets and check Show All Sets in List.

■ To turn off the button set display, click Configure Modifier Sets and uncheck Show Buttons.

Figure 6.7 Choose a button set.

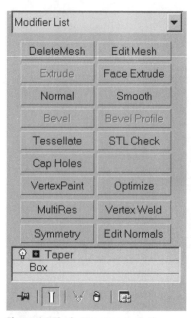

Figure 6.8 The buttons appear in the Modify panel.

USING MODIFIERS

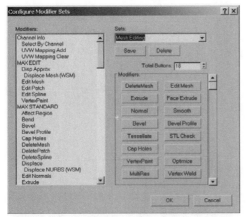

Figure 6.9 Choose a button set.

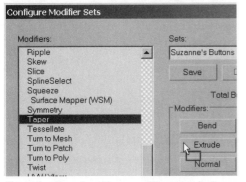

Figure 6.10 Dragging a Taper modifier onto a button.

Figure 6.11 After turning on the display of the completed custom button set.

Custom button sets place your favorite modifiers at your fingertips. Button sets are written to the max .ini file so they will be available for subsequent work sessions.

To create a custom button set:

1. Open the Modify panel.

2. Click Configure Modifier Sets.

3. In the pop-up menu, choose Configure Modifier Sets.

   The Configure Modifier Sets dialog box appears (**Figure 6.9**).

4. In the Sets drop-down menu, highlight the name of the current button set. Then type in a new set name. If you are working on a shared system, you might want to use your own name, as in "Suzanne's Buttons." Then click Save.

5. Set the number of buttons that you want to have in your set.

6. Drag the names of the modifiers that you find most useful from the list at left onto the buttons (**Figure 6.10**).

7. Click OK.

   The button set is created. The contents of the button set are written to the 3dsmax .ini file so that they will be available for future use.

8. Use Configure Modifier Sets to display your custom button set in the Modifier panel (**Figure 6.11**).

To apply a modifier to an object:

1. 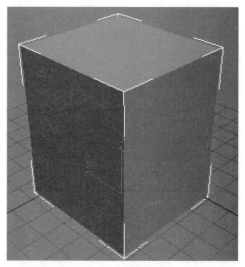 Select an object (**Figure 6.12**).

2. Open the Modify panel.

3. Choose a modifier from the Modifier List drop-down menu.

   or

   Click a modifier button in the Modifier panel.

   or

   Choose a modifier from the Modifiers menu.

   or

   Drag the name of a modifier from the Modifier List to the object.

   The modifier is applied to the object. In the Modify panel, the name of the modifier appears in the stack display and its parameters appear below (**Figure 6.13**).

4. Adjust the parameters of the modifier until the object looks the way you want it (**Figure 6.14**).

✔ Tips

- You can select multiple objects and apply a modifier to all of them at once.

- To undo the application of a modifier, press Ctrl + Z.

- Sometimes a modifier seems to have no effect upon an object. Or, the object may appear to contort rather than deform smoothly. This may be because the object needs a more detailed structure in order to be flexible. For more information, see "Deformation Modifiers" and "Spline Modifiers" later in this chapter.

Figure 6.12 Select an object to modify.

Figure 6.13 After you choose a modifier, it is added to the modifier stack.

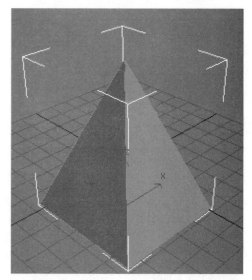

Figure 6.14 The appearance of the object is modified.

USING MODIFIERS

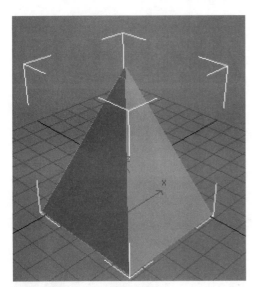

Figure 6.15 Select a modified object.

Figure 6.16 Choose a modifier from the Modifier List.

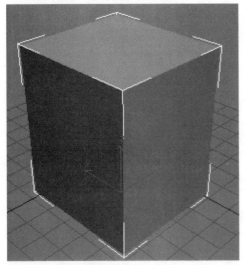

Figure 6.17 After removing the modifier, its effect upon the object ceases.

To remove a modifier from an object:

1. Select an object (**Figure 6.15**).

2. Select the modifier you want to remove by clicking its name in the stack display (**Figure 6.16**).

3. Click Remove Modifier from the Stack.

   The modifier is removed from the stack. Its effect upon the object ceases (**Figure 6.17**).

✔ Tips

- You can also remove a modifier from the stack by right-clicking on the modifier and choosing Delete from the menu.

- To turn off a modifier without removing it from the stack, click the lightbulb icon next to the modifier in the stack display.

- To turn the modifier back on, click the darkened lightbulb.

Deformation Modifiers

Deformation modifiers, also known as geometric modifiers, deform the surface geometry of objects. Deformation modifiers have two components: the **modifier gizmo**, which is a wireframe device that shows how a modifier acts on the object it is applied to, and the **modifier center**, which is an axis tripod in the center of the gizmo that determines the direction that the modifier parameters are applied (**Figure 6.18**). By default, the axes of the modifier align to the local axes of the object it modifies.

When you change the parameters of the modifier, the modifier gizmo changes shape. This in turn alters the shape of the object it modifies (**Figure 6.19**). (Modifier gizmos should not be confused with transform gizmos, which are discussed in Chapter 5, "Transforms.")

Another way to affect the action of a modifier is by selecting its gizmo or center in the stack display and applying a transform to it. Changing the position, orientation, or scale of a modifier component can have a profound effect on the modified object (**Figure 6.20**).

Deformation modifiers are usually applied to geometry objects, but you can also apply them to shape splines and NURBS. To affect splines that are flat, you need to be sure to align the modifier to the axes of the plane in which the spline is lying.

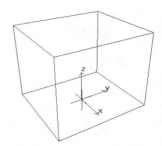

Figure 6.18 A modifier gizmo is a wireframe device that transfers the parameters of a modifier to an object. The modifier center lies within it.

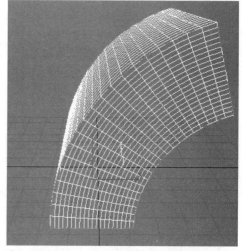

Figure 6.19 The shape of this Bend modifier gizmo aligns to the contours of the box that it modifies.

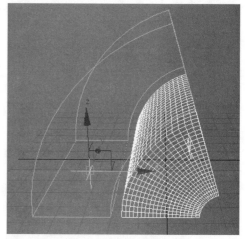

Figure 6.20 Moving the Bend gizmo changes the effect that the Bend modifier has on the box.

DEFORMATION MODIFIERS

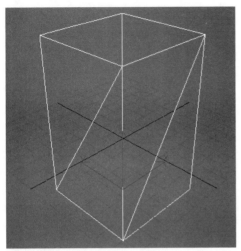

Figure 6.21 A basic box has one segment per side.

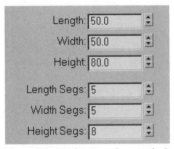

Figure 6.22 You increase the complexity of a box by increasing its segments.

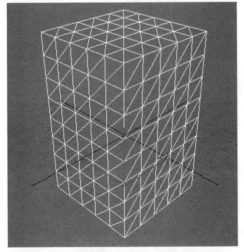

Figure 6.23 After increasing the box's complexity.

Mesh objects deform by bending at their vertices, much like bones bending at joints. To deform objects smoothly, you usually need to increase the number of segments that subdivide the surface of a mesh so that it can bend in smaller increments at each vertex. This is called increasing the density, or complexity, of a mesh.

If you are not sure how many segments you will need, a good rule of thumb for straight-sided objects is 1 segment for every 10 units of measure. Complex deformations, such as Noise, which can displace a surface many times within a small area, may require many times that amount.

To increase the complexity of a mesh object:

1. Select a mesh object (**Figure 6.21**).

2. Open the Modify panel.

3. If the object has already been modified, choose the name of the primitive from the bottom of the stack display.

   The creation parameters of the object appear in the Modify panel (**Figure 6.22**).

4. Increase the number of segments or sides in the direction that you plan to deform.

   The surface of the mesh subdivides into more faces, edges, and vertices, making the mesh appear denser (**Figure 6.23**).

✔ Tip

- To increase the complexity of an editable mesh that has no parameters to manipulate, see "To Tessellate a mesh" and "To MeshSmooth a mesh" later in this chapter under the heading, "Subdividing Surfaces."

The Bend modifier deforms an object by curving it along one of its axes.

To bend an object:

1. Select an object (**Figure 6.24**). Make sure the object has enough structural complexity to be able to bend.

2. Open the Modify panel.

3. Click the Bend button.

   or

   Choose Bend from the modifier list.

   The Parameters rollout appears in the Modify panel (**Figure 6.25**).

4. Choose a Bend axis.

   In 3ds max, the Bend axis is the axis of the object that bends, rather than being the axis that the object bends around. By default, the bend axis aligns to the local axes of the object. This will change if the modifier gizmo is rotated.

5. Enter an Angle value in degrees, or drag the Angle spinner.

   The gizmo and the object bend by the number of degrees that you entered (**Figure 6.26**). If the object does not bend smoothly, increase its complexity along the axis that is being bent.

✔ Tips

- Changing the Direction parameter causes bend action to veer off course from the direction of the bend axis.

- Check Limit Effect and enter a value to constrain the modifier to the upper or lower part of the object.

- If an object seems to lean or buckle or otherwise resists your attempts to deform it, try increasing the complexity of the mesh.

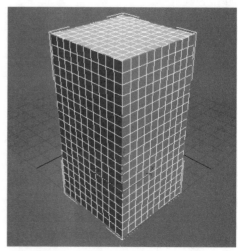

Figure 6.24 Selecting a box to bend.

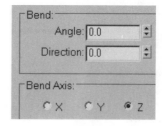

Figure 6.25 The Parameters rollout allows you to set the direction and degree of curvature.

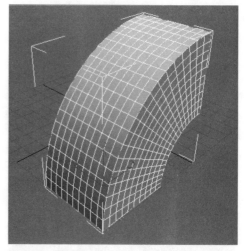

Figure 6.26 Bending the box in its Z axis.

DEFORMATION MODIFIERS

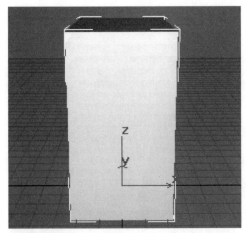

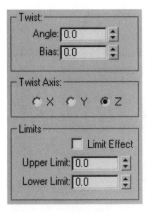

Figure 6.27 Select an object to twist.

Figure 6.28
The Parameters
rollout allows
you to set the
bias and degree
of twisting.

The Twist modifier causes an object to corkscrew along a central axis.

To twist an object:

1. Select an object (**Figure 6.27**).

2. Open the Modify panel.

3. Apply a Twist modifier.
   The Parameters rollout appears (**Figure 6.28**).

4. Choose a Twist axis for the gizmo.

5. Enter an Angle value in degrees, or drag the Angle spinner.
   The gizmo twists, and the object follows (**Figure 6.29**). If the object does not follow the gizmo smoothly, increase the density of its mesh along the axis that is being twisted.

✔ Tips

- Bias causes the object to twist more at one end of an axis than the other, like the Bias parameter of the Helix primitive.

- Check Limit Effect and enter a value to constrain the modifier to the upper or lower part of the object.

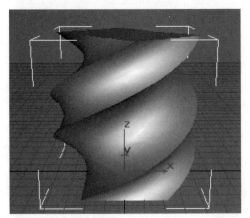

Figure 6.29 Twisting the box in its Z axis.

DEFORMATION MODIFIERS

The Taper modifier tapers the sides of an object toward or away from a central axis.

To taper an object:

1. Select an object (**Figure 6.30**).

2. Apply a Taper modifier.

   The Parameters rollout appears (**Figure 6.31**).

3. Choose a Primary Taper Axis.

   This sets the gizmos central axis of tapering.

4. Choose an Effect Taper Axis for the effect of the Taper gizmo.

   This determines which sides of the gizmo and object taper. Tapering is always symmetrical in the effect axis.

5. Enter an amount between -10 and 10, or drag the Amount spinner.

   The gizmo and the object taper together (**Figure 6.32**).

✔ Tips

- Enter a Curve value if you want to make the sides of the object curve as they taper.

- Check Symmetry if you want the taper to be symmetrical on both sides of the primary axis.

- Remember that you can animate nearly any parameter in 3ds max. For practice, animate each of these basic deformation modifiers by changing their parameters over time (see Chapter 7, "Animation").

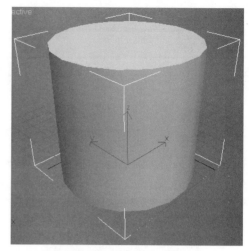

Figure 6.30 Selecting a cylinder to taper.

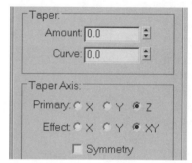

Figure 6.31 The Parameters rollout allows you to taper an object in one or two axes.

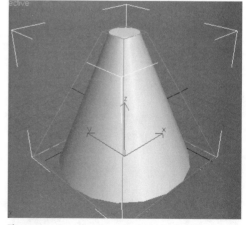

Figure 6.32 Tapering the cylinder in its Z axis.

DEFORMATION MODIFIERS

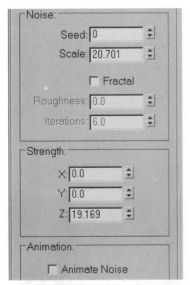

Figure 6.33 The Parameters rollout allows you to vary the direction and strength of the noise.

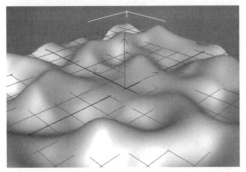

Figure 6.34 Noise randomly displacing the surface of a plane.

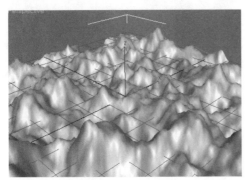

Figure 6.35 Fractal settings increase the roughness of the noise.

The random displacement of Noise is very important because most surfaces in nature are irregular. On a small scale, the Noise modifier introduces texture to pristine 3d surfaces which makes them look more real. On a large scale, Noise creates great surface contours for landscapes. Use it for rocks, hills, mountains, oceans, moons, asteroids, and alien planets.

To apply noise to a surface:

1. Select an object, such as a plane.

2. In the Modify panel, increase the number of segments so that the mesh becomes quite dense.

3. Apply a Noise modifier.
    The Parameters rollout appears (**Figure 6.33**).

4. Set Scale to a number between 10 and 20.

5. Gradually increase the Strength of the noise. For flat surfaces, such as planes, you need only increase strength in the direction that is perpendicular to the surface—usually the Z axis.

    The vertices of the mesh are displaced above and below the mesh surface in a random pattern (**Figure 6.34**). If the surface becomes too choppy, increase the number of segments in the base object until the surface looks smooth.

6. For a more varigated surface, check Fractal. Then increase the roughness and number of iterations (**Figure 6.35**).

✔ Tips

- Setting the viewport display mode to Wireframe or Edged Faces makes it easier to see the density of your mesh.

- Check Animate Noise to automatically animate noise. Adjust the animation by changing its Frequency and Phase values.

- Texture maps also have noise settings that disturb the pattern of the map. By combining a Noise modifier with a noisy map, you can create realistic effects.

DEFORMATION MODIFIERS

Free-form deformation (FFD) modifiers deform objects using a lattice of control points instead of a gizmo. The more control points in the lattice, the better you can articulate the deformation.

There are five types of free-form deformation modifiers. FFD (2x2x2) has 8 control points. FFD (3x3x3) and FFD (4x4x4) have 27 and 64 control points. FFD(box) and FFD(cyl) allow you to set the number of control points.

To freely deform an object:

1. Select a Mesh object.

2. Apply an FFD modifier. Choose from FFD (2x2x2), FFD (3x3x3), FFD (4x4x4), FFD (box), or FFD (cyl).

   The FFD Parameters rollout for that modifier appears (**Figure 6.36**).

   A lattice of control points appears around the object (**Figure 6.37**).

3. Click Conform to Shape.

4. In the stack display, access the sub-object components of the modifier by clicking the plus sign next to its name. Then select Control Points from the rollout (**Figure 6.38**).

5. Select and transform the control points of the lattice.

   Each control point deforms the part of the object that is closest to it (**Figure 6.39**).

✔ Tip

■ Locking the control points makes them easier to transform and prevents them from being accidentally deselected. Remember to unlock them when you want to choose different control points.

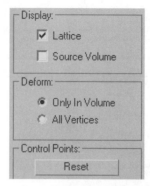

Figure 6.36 The upper portion of an FFD Parameters rollout allows you to control the display and action of an FFD modifier.

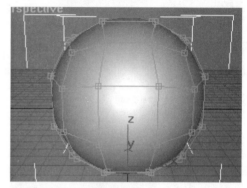

Figure 6.37 A free-form deformation lattice of control points conforming to a sphere.

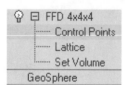

Figure 6.38 Select the Control Points sub-object in the stack display.

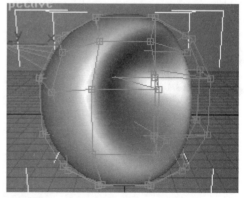

Figure 6.39 The result of moving a single control point back through a GeoSphere.

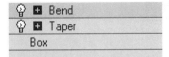

Figure 6.40 The new modifier appears at the top of the stack.

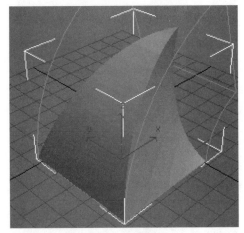

Figure 6.41 Bending the tapered box along its Z axis.

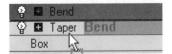

Figure 6.42 Dragging the Bend modifier to the bottom of the stack.

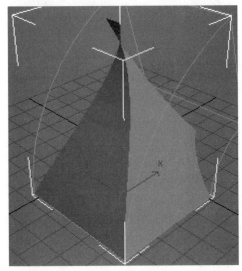

Figure 6.43 The result of rearranging the modifiers.

Using Multiple Modifiers

Now that you have applied a few modifiers, you can start combining them to create more advanced effects.

The effect that modifiers have on an object depends upon the order in which they are evaluated. By clicking and dragging modifiers, you can rearrange modifiers in the stack so that they are evaluated in a different order. This may produce markedly different results, especially if one of the modifiers affects the object asymmetrically.

To apply multiple modifiers to an object:

1. Select a modified object.

2. Apply a modifier to the object.

   The modifier is placed at the top of the stack, where it is evaluated last (**Figure 6.40**). The display of the object is updated in the viewport (**Figure 6.41**).

✔ Tip

- If you want max to put your modifier somewhere else in the stack, select the modifier just below where you want the new modifier to be placed, and then apply the modifier.

To rearrange a modifier stack:

1. Select a modified object.

2. Open the Modify panel.

3. In the stack display, click the modifier you want to move, and drag it to a new location in the stack (**Figure 6.42**).

   The modifier stack rearranges. The object in the viewport updates to reflect the new order of evaluation (**Figure 6.43**).

Using the drag method, you can copy modifiers from one object to another. If you want to copy an entire stack, it is easier to use the Copy and Paste commands.

To copy a modifier stack:

1. Select a modified object (**Figure 6.44**).

2. Open the Modify panel.

3. In the stack display, click the modifier at the top of the stack. Then hold down the Shift key and click the modifier at the bottom of the stack.

   The entire Modify stack is selected.

4. Right-click on the selected modifiers, and choose Copy from the right-click menu (**Figure 6.45**).

5. Select the object that you want to paste the modifier stack onto.

6. In the stack display of that object, click just below the point where you want to insert the modifier. If the object does not have any modifiers in the stack, select the base creation object.

7. Right-click and choose Paste.

   The modifiers are applied to the object (**Figure 6.46**).

✔ Tips

- Shift-dragging cuts a modifier from one object and pastes it onto another.

- Ctrl-dragging instances a modifier before applying it to another object, so that any changes you make to one modifier are replicated in the other.

- Use Make Unique stack to turn an instanced modifier into a copy.

- Pasting a modifier onto an incompatible object type has no effect on the object.

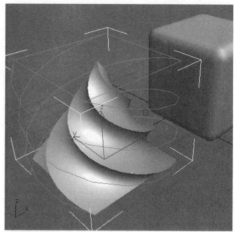

Figure 6.44 Selecting a box that has been modified.

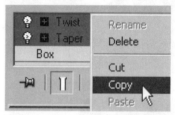

Figure 6.45 Copying the entire stack.

Figure 6.46 The result of pasting the Twist and Taper modifiers from the box onto a ChamferBox.

Figure 6.47 Right-click in the stack display and choose Collapse All.

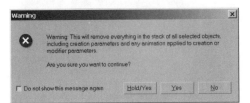

Figure 6.48 The Warning dialog box warns you of the consequences of collapsing the stack and gives you the option of holding the scene.

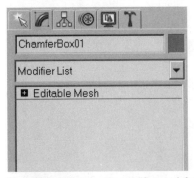

Figure 6.49 Collapsing the modifier stack freezes all the modifier parameters at their current state and converts the object to an editable mesh.

When you are satisfied with the changes you have made to your object, you can choose to collapse the modifier stack.

Collapsing the modifier stack converts an object to an editable object and eliminates its modifier stack. Like taking a snapshot, collapsing the stack records the state of an object at a single moment in time. This stabilizes the object and saves memory because the program does not need to keep evaluating old parameters.

Because collapsing the stack eliminates creation parameters, make sure your object has enough segments, sides, and good basic proportions before you proceed.

To collapse a modifier stack:

1. Select a modified object.

2. Open the Modify panel.

3. In the stack display, right-click in the stack view window and choose Collapse All (**Figure 6.47**).

   A warning appears to let you know that collapsing the stack removes all parameters (**Figure 6.48**).

4. Click Yes to collapse everything.

   or

   Click Hold/Yes if you want to save the scene in the maxhold.mx file before collapsing the stack.

5. Click OK.

   All modifiers, their parameters, and the original creation parameters are collapsed. The object is converted to an editable mesh (**Figure 6.49**).

Subdividing Surfaces

You control the surface complexity of a mesh primitive by adjusting its segments and sides parameters. Once a primitive has been converted to an editable object, however, these creation parameters disappear.

Tessellate increases the complexity of a mesh by subdividing edges and faces.

To Tessellate a mesh:

1. Select a mesh object.

2. Apply a Tessellate modifier.

   The Parameters rollout appears (**Figure 6.50**).

   The complexity of the object increases automatically (**Figure 6.51**).

3. Try both the Edge and Face-Center options to see which one makes the object look better.

4. Increase the Iterations value to further increase the complexity of the mesh (**Figure 6.52**).

✔ Tips

- Face-center divisions work better on objects with planar surfaces, such as boxes.

- To tessellate a limited surface area, select the area at the Face level using Mesh Select before applying the Tessellate modifier.

Figure 6.50 The Parameters rollout offers two ways to increase mesh density.

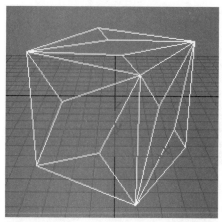

Figure 6.51 A box after one iteration of tessellation.

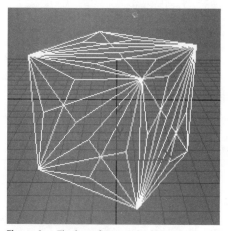

Figure 6.52 The box after a second iteration.

SUBDIVIDING SURFACES

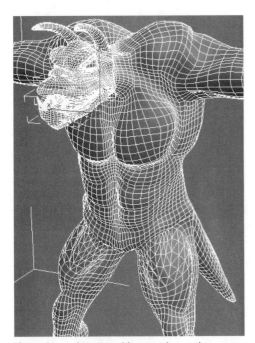

Figure 6.53 A character with a complex mesh.

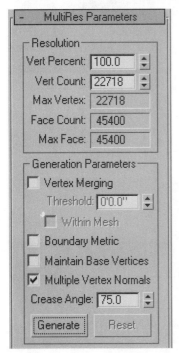

Figure 6.54 After you click Generate, the Resolution parameters become available.

When you work with complex models, the memory overhead needed for rendering can slow down your system significantly. The MultiRes modifier optimizes mesh structure by progressively eliminating coplanar faces.

To optimize a mesh:

1. Select a complex object (**Figure 6.53**).

2. Apply a MultiRes modifier. The MultiRes Parameters rollout appears.

3. In the Generation Parameters group, click the Generate button.

   The mesh is initialized. The Resolution inputs become available (**Figure 6.54**).

4. Slowly decrease the Vert Percent or Vert Count spinners until the mesh begins to lose its smoothness.

   The number of faces decreases, reducing the complexity of the mesh (**Figure 6.55**).

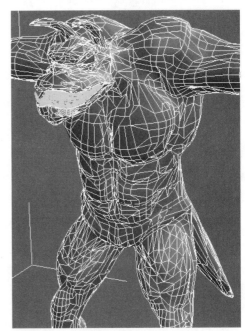

Figure 6.55 After simplifying the body mesh to 33% of the original number of vertices.

SUBDIVIDING SURFACES

177

MeshSmooth increases the complexity of a mesh by adding an extra face for every vertex and edge in the mesh.

To MeshSmooth a mesh:

1. Select an object (**Figure 6.56**).

2. Apply a MeshSmooth modifier. The MeshSmooth rollouts appear (**Figure 6.57**).

   The object is automatically smoothed using the default parameters (**Figure 6.58**).

3. Slowly increase the Iterations value. This increases the overall number of divisions in the mesh.

4. Reduce the Smoothness value to optimize the mesh.

✔ Tips

- The Subdivision Method is set to NURMS by default. NURMS stands for Non-Uniform Rational MeshSmooth, a humorous play on the term NURBS. For complete instructions on how to use the weighted control mesh and the other MeshSmooth types, see the online help files.

- To avoid severely deforming objects with planar surfaces, make sure that the mesh has a reasonable number of divisions on each side before you apply MeshSmooth.

- MeshSmooth can be used as a modeling tool because it rounds off corners and edges at the same time. Starting with rough, blocky forms, you can quickly create birds, fish, monsters, and spaceships. Try combining MeshSmooth with the Extrude modifier to convert splines to rounded forms.

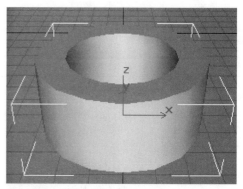

Figure 6.56 Selecting a tube.

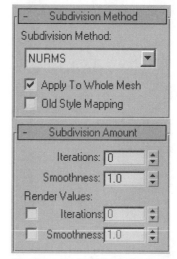

Figure 6.57 The MeshSmooth rollout. As with the Tessellate modifier, you increase the MeshSmooth effect by increasing the number of iterations.

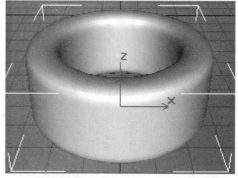

Figure 6.58 After MeshSmoothing the tube. Note the rounded edges.

Figure 6.59 The more directly a surface normal points toward the light, the brighter its face is shaded by the program.

Figure 6.60 This Teapot object has two smoothing groups which are distributed throughout the teapot. One group has been smoothed; the other has not.

Rendering Modifiers

Rendering is the process by which a 3D program draws an image of a 3D scene. There are a number of variables it must take into account: the point of view; the system of projection; the position of objects; lighting; object properties such as color and visibility; the mode of display; and so on.

To speed up rendering, 3ds max shades only the outside surfaces of objects unless you set it to do otherwise. This means that each face is shaded only on one side—the side that the surface normal projects from. By comparing the angle of a normal to the source of light, the program determines how much intensity, or brightness, of light it should use to render each individual face (**Figure 6.59**).

In faceted shading modes, faces stand out distinctly on curved surfaces because each face is rendered with a different intensity. In smooth shading modes, faces blend together in a smooth gradient because the program averages the intensity values between normals. With the Smooth modifier, you can set smoothing for an entire object, or for discrete selections of faces (**Figure 6.60**).

The Normal modifier allows you to invert, or **flip**, surface normals, so that the inside of a surface is shaded instead of the outside.

To flip the normals of an object:

1. Select an object (**Figure 6.61**).

2. Apply a Normal modifier. The Parameters rollout appears (**Figure 6.62**).

3. Check Flip Normals.

   The surface normals of the faces are flipped. The opposite sides of the faces are rendered (**Figure 6.63**).

Sometimes normals get flipped accidentally, such as when you import an object into 3ds max. You should suspect flipped normals whenever you see triangular holes in the surface of an object.

To unify normals:

1. Select an object that you suspect has flipped normals.

2. Apply a Normal modifier.

3. Check Unify Normals.

   The flipped normals are restored to their original orientation, so that the surface of the object appears continuous (**Figure 6.64**).

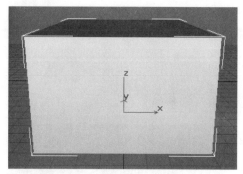

Figure 6.61 Select an object that you want to turn inside out.

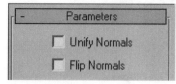

Figure 6.62 The Parameters rollout has just two parameters.

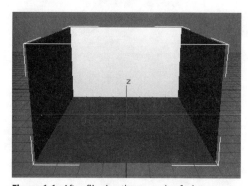

Figure 6.63 After flipping the normals of a box.

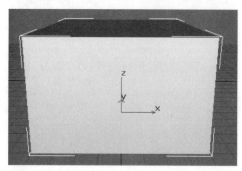

Figure 6.64 Unifying the normals of the box returns them to their original orientation.

RENDERING MODIFIERS

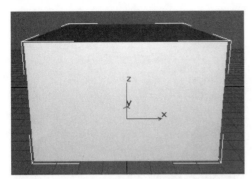

Figure 6.65 Select an object that has faces you want to flip.

Figure 6.66 The Surface Properties rollout contains an option for flipping normals interactively.

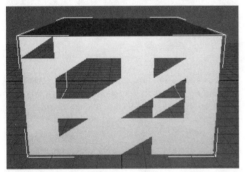

Figure 6.67 The result of flipping the normals of a selected faces in a box.

There are two ways you can flip normals of individual faces: by applying a Normal modifier to a selection of faces, or by clicking faces with Flip Normal mode enabled. The advantage of using Flip Normal mode is that you can see the results update in the viewport as you work.

To flip normals of individual faces:

1. 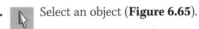 Select an object (**Figure 6.65**).

2. 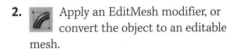 Apply an EditMesh modifier, or convert the object to an editable mesh.

3. Enable Face or Polygon level selection.

4. Open the Surface Properties rollout, and click Flip Normal Mode (**Figure 6.66**).

5. Click the faces that you want to flip. The faces flip interactively (**Figure 6.67**).

The STL-Check and Cap Holes modifiers find and fix actual holes in your mesh.

To fix holes in a mesh:

1. Select an object that has holes in it. For practice, try creating a lidless teapot by unchecking the Lid element.

2. Apply an STL Check modifier. The Parameters rollout appears (**Figure 6.68**).

3. In the Errors group, check Open Edge. Then check Select Edges.

4. Check the box next to Check.

   The open edges become selected and turn red, indicating they are next to an open area (**Figure 6.69**).

5. Apply a Cap Holes modifier. The holes are covered with new faces (**Figure 6.70**).

   Note: The new faces may not be visible, but you can see the difference in the face count by viewing the object information in the Object Properties dialog box before and after applying the modifier.

✔ Tip

■ Use this combination of modifiers to fix holes in preparation for Boolean operations. (For information on Boolean operations, see Chapter 10, "Compound Objects.")

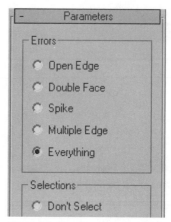

Figure 6.68 The Parameters rollout gives you different options for checking the structural integrity of a mesh.

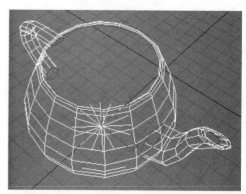

Figure 6.69 The STL-Check modifier selects open edges, which turn red. This teapot displays open edges around the lid, rim, spout, and handle.

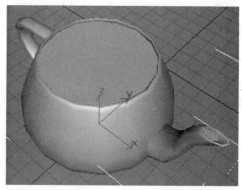

Figure 6.70 Applying a Cap Holes modifier automatically builds a cap on the openings of a teapot.

Figure 6.71 The Smoothing Groups rollout parameters allow you to smooth faces in numbered groups or to smooth an entire object.

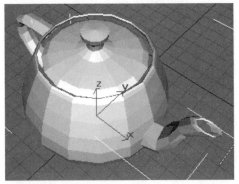

Figure 6.72 When you first apply a Smooth modifier, it turns off smoothing for the object.

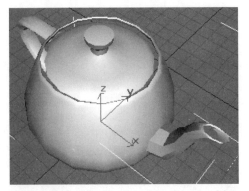

Figure 6.73 After checking Auto Smooth, some of the edges are smoothed.

You can smooth an object in its entirety, or you can smooth discrete selections of faces. For mesh primitives, you control smoothing for the entire object by checking or unchecking the Smooth creation parameter. Editable objects do not give you this option, so you must use a Smooth modifier instead.

To smooth an object:

1. Select a mesh object.

2. Apply a MeshSmooth modifier.

   The Parameters rollout appears (**Figure 6.71**). The object becomes unsmoothed (**Figure 6.72**).

3. Check Auto Smooth.

   The faces that meet at an angle that is less than the Threshold parameter are smoothed (**Figure 6.73**).

4. Increase the Threshold value until all the edges are smoothed.

   or

   Uncheck Auto Smooth and click button number 1 in the Smoothing Groups area.

   All the faces in the object are assigned to the same smoothing group. The entire object becomes smoothed (**Figure 6.74**).

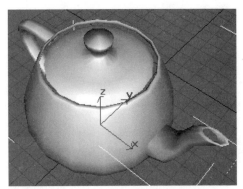

Figure 6.74 After increasing the smoothing threshold to 180°, all the edges in the object are smoothed.

Creating Creases

Another use for the Smooth modifier is for creating creases. By assigning adjacent selections of faces to different smoothing groups, you can keep the program from smoothing the edges between them.

For the convenience of selecting and smoothing faces within the same modifier, apply an Edit Mesh modifier or convert the object to an editable mesh. Then enable Face or Polygon level selection and use the Surface Properties rollout to access smoothing commands (**Figure 6.75**).

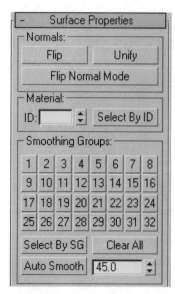

Figure 6.75 The Surface Properties rollout allows you to smooth selections of faces, as well as to select faces by smoothing group.

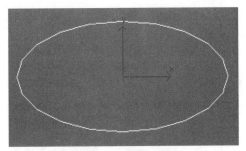

Figure 6.76 Selecting an ellipse to interpolate.

Figure 6.77 The Interpolation rollout allows you to adjust the number of points that lie between vertices.

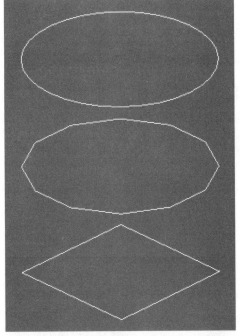

Figure 6.78 Top: After setting the Steps to 7, the edge of the ellipse appears smooth. Middle: After setting the Steps to 1, the ellipse turns into a flattened oxagon. Bottom: At Interpolation = 0, the ellipse looks like a diamond.

Spline Modifiers

Splines are often modified to create custom geometry objects using the Extrude, Lathe, and Bevel modifiers. Splines are also used for creating such compound objects as lofts and terrains, which are explained in Chapter 10. However you decide to use them later on, the number of vertex points on the original splines have a crucial effect on the appearance and polygon count of the final output.

To adjust the complexity of a spline:

1. Select a spline (**Figure 6.76**). It doesn't matter if the spline is a primitive or an editable spline. Both may be adjusted in the same fashion.

2. Open the Modify panel.

3. Open the Interpolation rollout (**Figure 6.77**).

4. Adjust the number of steps by dragging on the Steps spinner.

   The spline increases or decreases in complexity. If you make a curved spline more complex, the curves will take on a smoother appearance. If you make a curved spline less complex, the curves will take on a more angular appearance (**Figure 6.78**).

✔ Tip

- To make highly specific adjustments to the complexity of a spline, use the Refine, Insert, Chamfer, Fillet, Weld, Delete, or Fuse commands of the Edit Spline modifier and editable splines, as explained in Chapter 9, "Editing Shapes."

SPLINE MODIFIERS

The Extrude modifier generates a mesh object by extruding a spline in a straight line along its Z axis.

To extrude a spline:

1. Select a spline object (**Figure 6.79**).

2. Apply an Extrude modifier.

   The Parameters rollout appears (**Figure 6.80**).

3. Enter an Amount value.

   The spline is extruded. If the spline is a closed shape, then a cap of faces is built in the enclosed area by default (**Figure 6.81**).

✔ Tips

- To increase the complexity of the output object, increase the Segments parameter.

- To create patches or NURBS objects, choose Patch or NURBS in the Output area.

- To extrude a spline along the path of another spline, see "Lofting Objects" in Chapter 10.

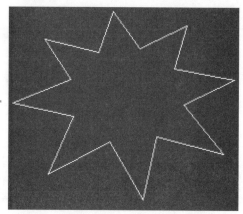

Figure 6.79 Selecting a star shape to extrude.

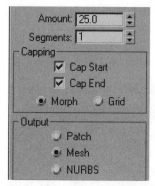

Figure 6.80 The Parameters rollout has settings for the amount of extrusion, as well as the number of segments that will be built on the sides.

Figure 6.81 The extruded star has three dimensions.

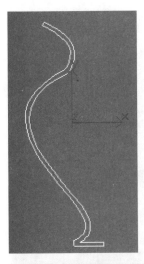

Figure 6.82 Select a spline to lathe. This spline has been doubled using the Outline command in the Edit Spline modifier. (For more information on spline editing commands, see Chapter 9, "Editing Shapes.")

Figure 6.83 You can lathe a spline along different axes.

The Lathe modifier generates a mesh object by revolving a spline on an axis.

To lathe a spline:

1. Select a spline (**Figure 6.82**).

2. Apply a Lathe modifier.
   The Parameters rollout appears (**Figure 6.83**).
   The spline is lathed along its central Y axis.

3. Adjust the axis of revolution as needed.
   To use a different axis of revolution, click X or Z in the Direction group.
   To align the axis of revolution to the minimum, center, or maximum extents of the object, click Min, Center, or Max in the Align group (**Figure 6.84**).
   To make the axis of revolution able to be moved freely, click Lathe in the stack display and then click the Axis sub-object.

✔ Tips

- Check Flip Normals if the object appears inside out.

- To outline a shape spline, as in this example, see "To outline a spline" in Chapter 9.

- To lathe an object less than 360 degrees, decrease the Degrees parameter.

- To change the complexity of the lathed object, adjust the Segments parameter.

- Check Weld Core to weld coincident vertices along the axis of revolution. Uncheck this box if you are creating morph targets so you can control the number of vertices that are generated. (See Chapter 10 for more information on morphing.)

Figure 6.84 After clicking the Max button, the axis of rotation aligns to the right side of the shape.

The Bevel modifier extrudes a spline using different widths to bevel the edges.

To bevel text:

1. Select a Text Spline object (**Figure 6.85**).

2. Apply a Bevel modifier.

   The Parameters and Bevel Values rollouts appear (**Figure 6.86**). The text is capped.

3. In the Bevel Values rollout, enter a value for the Start Outline, or leave the value at 0.

   The starting width of the outline is set.

4. Set the Height and Outline values for Level 1.

   Height sets the initial extrusion amount, and Outline sets the bevel amount (**Figure 6.87**).

5. Set the Height and Outline values for Level 2 and, if needed, Level 3.

   Setting values for each level causes additional extrusion and beveling to be added to the text (**Figure 6.88**).

✔ Tips

- In the Parameters rollout, check Smooth Across Levels to smooth the edges of the levels.

- Bevel works best if spline angles are greater than 90°. More acute angles may overlap nearby edges when they are extruded and beveled. To prevent this from happening, check Keep Lines From Crossing in the Parameters rollout.

- Bevel Profile is a related modifier that extrudes a spline using a second spline to define the outline of the beveled edge.

Figure 6.85 Text shapes can be extruded and beveled.

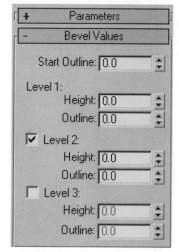

Figure 6.86 The Bevel Values rollout allows you to set multiple bevels.

Figure 6.87 After setting the initial extrusion and bevel amounts.

Figure 6.88 Rendered output of a two-level bevel.

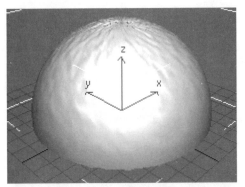

Figure 6.89 This hemisphere has a Noise modifier added to it to suggest the texture of ice cream.

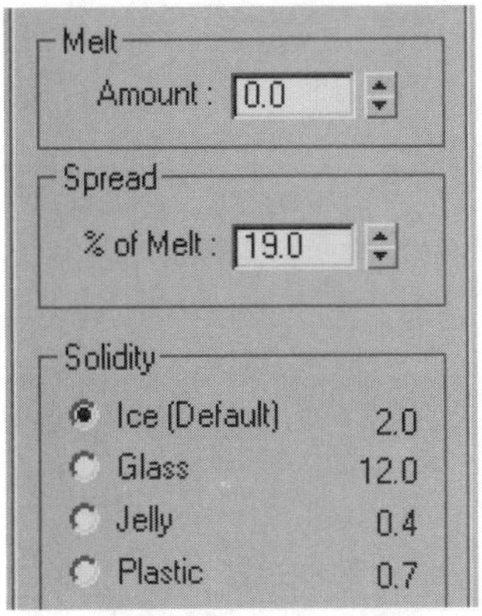

Figure 6.90 The Melt parameters control the deformation of the object.

Figure 6.91 Moving the time slider to frame 100.

Figure 6.92 Playing back the melt animation.

Animating with Modifiers

This section previews some animation techniques using modifiers. Along the way, you will learn how to create **keyframes** and move your scene display through time.

Animation concepts such as keyframes are explained more fully in Chapter 7, "Animation." Briefly, if you think of an animation as a videotape that plays back frames of scene images over time, a keyframe is a point in the tape where the contents of the scene begin to change. The container that stores the change data is called a **key**. The rest of the frames interpolate between keyframes.

Melt collapses an object along an axis, giving it the appearance of melting.

To melt an object:

1.  ▮ Select an object (**Figure 6.89**).

2.  ▮ Apply a Melt modifier.

   The Melt parameters appear (**Figure 6.90**).

3.  Auto Key Click the Auto Key button in the animation controls.

   This allows keyframes to be created automatically.

4. Drag the time slider (the bar just below the viewport that reads 0/100) all the way to the right so that it reads 100/100 (**Figure 6.91**).

5. Increase the Melt Amount so that the object flattens and spreads out.

6.  ▶ Click Play animation.

   The animation plays back in the active viewport. The object melts over the course of 100 frames, which is about 3 seconds by default (**Figure 6.92**).

189

Ripple and Wave create wave patterns like ripples on water and shock waves in space. Because their parameters are exactly the same, only one modifier—Ripple—is shown here.

To create a ripple effect:

1. Select an object, such as a plane.

2. In the Modify panel, increase the number of segments so that the mesh becomes quite dense: about 20 segments for every 100 units of measure.

3. Apply a Ripple modifier.
   The Parameters rollout appears (**Figure 6.93**).

4. Adjust Amplitude 1 to set the height of the ripples in one direction. Then adjust Amplitude 2 to set the height in the other direction. You will probably want to start with equal heights for both directions (**Figure 6.94**).

5. Adjust the Wave Length to set the distance between waves.

6. Click Auto Key. Then slide the time slider all the way to the right.

7. Set the Phase and Decay parameters. Setting Phase to a negative number will cause the ripples to expand outward. Decay causes the ripples to smooth out over time (**Figure 6.95**).

8. Click Auto Key to turn off automatic keyframing.

9. Click Play. The plane ripples like the surface of a lake (**Figure 6.96**).

✔ Tip

- If you click Open Mini Curve Editor, a trackbar with keyframe editing features pops up along the bottom of the viewport area. Have a look around to see what your animation is made of.

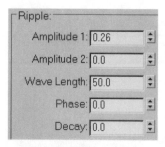

Figure 6.93 The Parameters rollout has amplitude settings for both the X and Y directions.

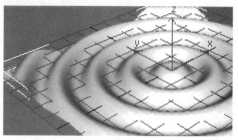

Figure 6.94 Rippling the Plane object with both amplitude settings.

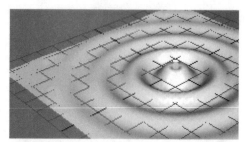

Figure 6.95 Decay causes the ripple effect to fall off from the center.

Figure 6.96 A rendered image of the rippled plane.

ANIMATING WITH MODIFIERS

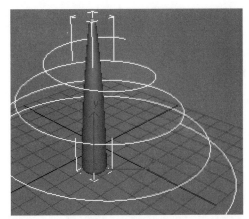

Figure 6.97 Choosing a ChamferCyl to deform along a helix.

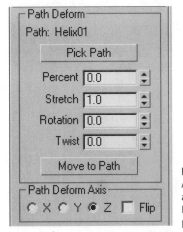

Figure 6.98 After picking a path in the PathDeform parameters.

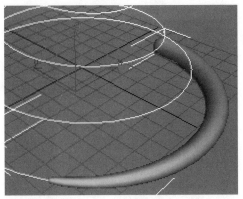

Figure 6.99 Deforming an object along a path.

PathDeform deforms an object as it moves along a spline path of your choosing. Use this as quick way to create an animation, or simply use it as a modeling tool.

To deform an object along a path:

1. Select an object (**Figure 6.97**).

2. Apply a PathDeform(WSM) modifier.

3. In the PathDeform parameters, click Pick Path (**Figure 6.98**). Then click the path you want the object to follow.

4. Click Move to Path.

   The object moves to the path. To stretch the object along the path, increase the Stretch parameter (**Figure 6.99**).

   If necessary, increase the complexity of the mesh so that the object stays smooth.

5. To animate the object along the path, turn on Auto Key mode.

6. Move the time slider to frame 100.

7. Set Percent to 100.

8. Play the animation.

   The object deforms as it follows the contours of the path from beginning to end.

✔ Tips

- If you increase the Percent parameter past 100, the object will continue past the end of the path as if it were following a straight line.

- To use a PathDeform modifier as a modeling tool, leave out steps 5 through 8.

- To change the orientation of the object to the path, click the Path Deform Axis radio buttons. Checking the Flip option inverts the object along the current axis.

ANIMATING WITH MODIFIERS

Using XForm Modifiers

XForm modifiers provide a container for transforms so you can put them in the modifier stack.

Normally, 3ds max evaluates transforms after modifiers, even if the transforms have been applied first. The XForm modifier gives you control over the order of evaluation by allowing you to place transforms anywhere in the modifier stack. When you remove an XForm modifier, the transforms that it contains are removed as well.

The XForm modifier has no parameters. The only inputs are the transforms you apply.

To animate a transform using an XForm modifier:

1. Select an object.

2. Apply an XForm modifier. The XForm modifier has no parameters (**Figure 6.100**).

3. Click Auto Key.

4. Slide the time slider to a new position.

5. Move, rotate, or scale the object.

   A key is placed in the animation track at the current frame. The object transforms are contained in the XForm modifier (**Figure 6.101**).

6. Play the animation. The object transforms over time (**Figure 6.102**).

✔ Tips

- Moving the modifier center moves the center of rotation and scaling.

- A Linked XForm modifier causes an object to inherit the transforms of the object to which it is linked. For more information, see Chapter 7, "Animation."

Figure 6.100 The XForm modifier has a gizmo and center, but no parameters.

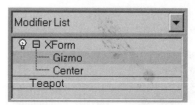

Figure 6.101 The XForm modifier stores the transform in its gizmo.

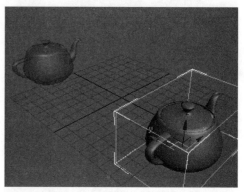

Figure 6.102 Playing back the transform animation.

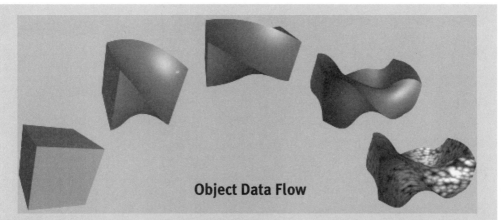

Object Data Flow

As you may recall from Chapter 2, 3ds max is written in an object-oriented program called C++. When you create an object in 3ds max, you are actually creating a set of data based on a pre-defined data type. As you apply different kinds of commands to an object, its data is updated as it passes from one command subroutine to another. The result is a change in the appearance or behavior of your object.

3ds max evaluates commands according to three criteria: the order of application, the order within a list or stack, and the order of **object data flow**. Of these, object data flow has the highest priority.

Because the order of evaluation can differ from the order in which commands are applied, you sometimes get surprising results. For example, if you apply a Bend modifier after a Scale transform, the Bend modifier will be evaluated first. But if you put the Scale transform in an XForm modifier, the Scale will be evaluated first, producing a markedly different result.

For best results, if you model or animate with Scale transforms, place them in the modifier stack with an XForm modifier.

3ds max object data flow causes the program to evaluate commands in the following order:

1. The Master Object. This includes the object type, which defines the basic structure and parameters of an object, as well as the position and orientation of the object's local coordinate system in world space.

2. Modifiers change an object's data with respect to its local coordinate system, often deforming the shape of an object. They are stored as part of the object's definition in an ordered list called a modifier stack.

3. Transforms change the position, orientation, and scale of objects. Transform data is stored in a constantly updating matrix that does not keep track of the command history.

4. Space Warps cause objects that are bound to them to deform in world space. Used to simulate forcefields and other environmental effects, space warps are placed at the top of the modifier stack.

5. Object Properties include the name, color, material assignments, display properties, and rendering properties of an object. Because they are evaluated last, object properties are not affected by other commands.

ANIMATION

Figure 7.1 Animation brings a scene to life.

Animation introduces the concept of time. We recognize time is passing by observing changes in our world: sunlight moving through the clouds, a beating heart, a ticking clock, bodies dancing to a beat, the steady rhythm of machines, rivers flowing to the sea, the silent turning of the stars. We also draw conclusions about the passage of time by comparing experience to memory: white hair, a wrinkled brow, an empty glass, an empty house. Time can make the world empty or full, high or low, light or dark, loud or soft, near or far, old or new.

According to Webster, the word "animation" is based on the Latin verb **animare**, which means, to give life to. This chapter tells you how to bring objects to life by making them change over time (**Figure 7.1**).

Applying traditional animation principles such as anticipation, squash and stretch, overlapping action, exaggeration, and follow-through can infuse your scenes with humor and bring them to life. An excellent reference to get you started is **The Illusion of Life: Disney Animation**, by Frank Thomas and Ollie Johnston (Hyperion, 1995).

Moving Through Time

When you hit the play button on your VCR, it plays back a series of images in rapid succession. As you watch, each image persists in your visual cortex until the next image takes its place. This creates an illusion of continuous change that we call the **persistence of vision (Figure 7.2)**.

In animation, the sequence of images that you play back are called **frames**. In 3ds max, you view frames in the viewports by changing the display of a scene over time.

By default, the length of a scene is set to 100 frames. When open a scene in 3ds max, the display is always set to the first frame.

Figure 7.2 Persistence of vision makes change between similar images appear continuous.

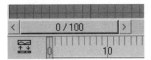

Figure 7.3 The readout on the time slider displays 0/100, indicating that frame 0 is displayed.

Figure 7.4 The dragon flies across the viewport at frame 26 of 60.

Figure 7.5 Click Play Animation in the animation controls.

To move a scene through time:

1. Locate the time slider in the status bar controls underneath the viewports.

   The time slider reads 0/100 (**Figure 7.3**).

2. Open an animation file.

   The time slider readout changes from 01/100 to 0/60 because the animation in this scene file is 60 frames long.

3. Slowly drag the time slider all the way to the right.

   The dragon flies across the viewport as the scene display moves forward in time. The frame readout on the time slider increments from 0/60 to 60/60 (**Figure 7.4**).

4. Slowly drag the time slider all the way to the left.

   The scene display moves backwards in time. The readout on the time slider decrements from 60/60 to 0/60.

5. "Scrub" the time slider by moving it back and forth in its channel.

   The dragon flies back and forth across your scene as you move through time.

6. Click Play Animation, or press the / key to see the dragon fly in real time (**Figure 7.5**).

✔ Tip

■ The animation playback controls work like VCR controls. They also allow you to step through keyframes. See Chapter 1, "Getting Started," for more information about these controls.

Configuring Time

Time is surprisingly flexible. It can move fast or slow, speed up or slow down, or appear to be standing still. When you are immersed in work that you love, the hours fly by in the blink of an eye. When you are feeling blue, time crawls as slowly as the hands of a clock. To a child, a year lasts an eternity. But to an elder, years collapse into moments, like dewdrops suspended in a spider's web.

3ds max gives you the ability to manipulate time, and conduct the mysterious rites of relativity. Using the Time Configuration dialog box, you make frames run faster, or slow down to only a few frames per second. You can also make an animation last longer or shorter, and you can even scale time to change the speed of action and the timing of events (**Figure 7.6**).

The frame rate of an animation determines how fast new frames will appear when you play back an animation from a rendered output file. Higher frame rates produce smoother animations and yield larger files. Lower frame rates produce choppier animations and yield smaller files.

You pick a frame rate based on the purpose of your animation. Standard frame rates include:

◆ **NTSC Video**—30 frames per second (fps). Set by the National Television Standards Committee, NTSC is the standard used in the Americas and Japan. Good for playing back animations on your hard drive. This is the default setting.

◆ **PAL Video**—25 fps. PAL, or Phase Alternation Line, is the standard used for European television.

◆ **Film**—24 fps. This is the standard for making movies in the film industry.

◆ **Custom**—Allows you to set the frame rate to a number you enter.

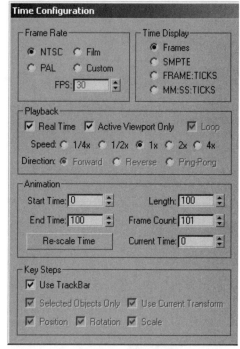

Figure 7.6 Using the Time Configuration dialog box, you can vary the timing and length of your animation.

Figure 7.7 Setting the frame rate to 30 frames per second.

To set the frame rate of an animation:

1. ![icon] Click Time Configuration.
   The Time Configuration dialog box appears.

2. In the Frame Rate group, choose a standard frame rate, or choose Custom (**Figure 7.7**).

3. If you chose Custom, enter a frame rate in the FPS entry field.

4. Click OK.
   The number of frames changes so that the playback time remains the same.

✔ Tips

- Right-clicking on any of the animation playback buttons also brings up the Time Configuration dialog box.

- If you want to make your file smaller, try 15 fps, a rate that initially became popular for multimedia CD-ROMs. For Web sites, try 12 or 8 fps to decrease download time over the Internet.

Time Codes

A time code is a system of measuring and displaying time. 3ds max 6 offers four time code options:

- **Frames**—Measures time by frame number. The default.

- **SMPTE**—Measures time in minutes, seconds, and frames. SMPTE is the Society of Motion Picture Technical Engineers.

- **FRAME:TICKS**—Measures time in frames and ticks.

- **MM:SS:TICKS**—Measures time in minutes, seconds, and ticks.

CONFIGURING TIME

The number of frames in an animation, along with the frame rate, determines how long an animation will last. By default, a rendered animation plays back at a rate of 30 fps. This means that a 300-frame animation will last 10 seconds.

To set the length of an animation:

1.  Click Time Configuration.

2. In the Animation group, enter the length (**Figure 7.8**).

   The length of the animation changes to the number of frames that you set. The readout on the time slider updates to reflect the number of frames in the animation (**Figure 7.9**).

✔ Tip

■ 3ds max measures time internally using a very small unit called a **tick**. A tick is 1/4800th of a second, which at 30 frames per second equals 1/160th of a frame.

By changing the time display in the Time Configuration dialog box, you can view the animation in terms of frames and ticks, minutes and seconds, or minutes, seconds, and ticks.

Figure 7.8 Setting the length to 300 frames.

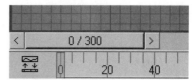

Figure 7.9 The time display on the time slider updates whenever you reconfigure time.

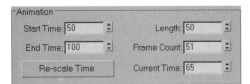

Figure 7.10 Entering a new start time sets the beginning point of the active time segment.

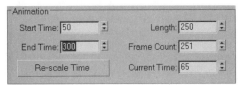

Figure 7.11 Entering a new end time sets the end point of the active time segment.

Figure 7.12 The time display on the time slider updates.

The **active time segment** is the period of time that is displayed on the time slider and in the viewports. By default, the active time segment is set to the start and end point of the animation. Changing the start and end times of the active time segment lets you zero in on the part of the animation where you want to work. The rest of the animation remains intact and out of view.

To specify an active time segment:

1. Open the Time Configuration dialog box.

2. In the Animation group, enter a Start Time value (**Figure 7.10**).

   The new start time becomes the first frame of the active time segment.

3. In the Animation group, enter an End Time value (**Figure 7.11**).

   The new end time becomes the last frame of the active time segment.

4. Click OK.

   The range of the active time segment changes. The change is reflected in the time slider, which shows a different start frame and length (**Figure 7.12**).

The Time Configuration dialog box allows you to control animation playback in the viewports, so that time appears to move faster, slower, or even backwards.

Slowing the playback of an existing animation helps you see how it was created.

To play an animation slowly:

1. Open an animation file.

2. Click Time Configuration.

3. In the Playback group, click 1/2x or 1/4x (**Figure 7.13**).

4. Close the dialog box.

5. Click Play Animation.

   The animation plays back at half speed or quarter speed.

✔ Tips

- To play back an animation at double speed or quadruple speed, set playback to 2x or 4x.

- Unchecking Active Viewport Only enables animation playback in all viewports.

- To play back an animation in reverse, uncheck Real Time and select Reverse. To play back an animation in alternating forward and reverse, uncheck Real Time and select Ping-Pong (**Figure 7.14**).

Figure 7.13 Changing animation playback speed for the viewports does not affect playback in the rendered output file.

Figure 7.14 Choosing Ping-Pong causes playback to alternate directions in the viewports only.

Table 7.1

Keyboard Shortcuts and Buttons for Animation		
SHORTCUT	**BUTTON**	**NAME**
Home	⏮	Go to Start
End	⏭	Go to End
. (period)		Next Frame
, (comma)		Previous Frame
		Key Mode toggle
assignable		Next Key
assignable		Previous Key
N	Auto Key	Auto Key Mode toggle
'	Set Key	Set Key Mode toggle
K		Set Keys
/		Play Animation
/		Play Selected
/		Stop Animation
\		Sound toggle
assignable		Time Configuration dialog box
		Expand Track Bar

CONFIGURING TIME

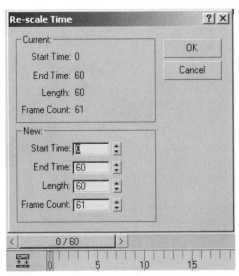

Figure 7.16 The Re-scale Time dialog box allows you to proportionally add and subtract tweens to make animation proceed slower or faster.

Figure 7.17 After rescaling the length to 30.

Adaptive Degradation

Adaptive degradation is a feature that reduces viewport display resolution in order to maintain animation playback speed. You will notice adaptive degradation kick in if you play an animation with more polygons than your graphics card can handle in real time. If you prefer to play your animation at full resolution and don't mind seeing your animation slow down, you can raise the level of degradation in the Adaptive Degradation panel of the Viewport Configuration dialog box (**Figure 7.15**). To toggle adaptive degradation override off and on, choose Views > Adaptive Degradation Toggle or press O.

Rescaling time changes the timing of an animation. If time is scaled up, the timing of the animation slows down. If time is scaled down, the timing of the animation speeds up.

Compare rescaling time, which changes the actual rendered output of an animation, to changing the playback rate, which affects playback in the viewports only.

To rescale time:

1. Open an animation file.

2. Click Time Configuration.

3. In the Animation group, click the button that says Re-scale Time.

   The Re-scale Time dialog box appears (**Figure 7.16**).

4. Enter a new Length value and click OK.

   The number of frames displayed in the track bar and time slider change accordingly (**Figure 7.17**).

5. Click OK to close the Time Configuration dialog box.

6. Click Play Animation.

   The animation plays back at a different speed.

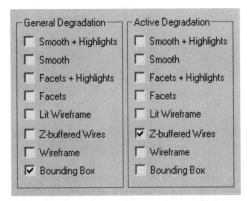

Figure 7.15 Adaptive degradation reduces viewport resolution for faster playback but does not affect rendered output.

Keyframing

3D animation derives many of its terms and techniques from traditional animation methods, like the ones developed at Walt Disney Studios. In traditional cel animation, a head animator draws key poses, or **keyframes,** to show the high point of an action. Junior animators draw the frames in between, or **tweens**, that make the action appear to flow smoothly.

In 3D animation, you create keyframes by changing object or scene data over time (**Figure 7.18**). **Animation controllers** store these settings in **animation keys,** and act as your team of junior animators by instantly interpolating the values of the tweens.

In 3ds max 6, keyframing tools are found in the status bar controls (**Figure 7.19**), the Motion command panel (**Figure 7.20**), and the Track View.

The Auto Key button makes keyframing easy. You just click the button, move the time slider, and transform your scene. Keyframes are created automatically.

The Set Key mode provides an alternate way to set keys that is especially suited to character animation. For more information, look up "Set Key" in the User Reference.

Figure 7.18 Keyframes from the Dragon animation. 3ds max calculates tweens by interpolating the values between the frames.

Figure 7.19 Animation tools in the status bar area allow you to create, move, and delete keys.

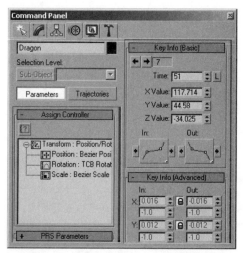

Figure 7.20 You assign motion controllers and manipulate trajectories and keys in the Motion command panel.

KEYFRAMING

Figure 7.21 Red indicates that the program is in animation mode.

Figure 7.22 Turning on the object's trajectory.

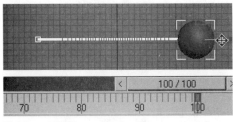

Figure 7.23 Making a change at frame 100 sets keys at frame 0 and frame 100. A red and white trajectory shows the path of the object's movement.

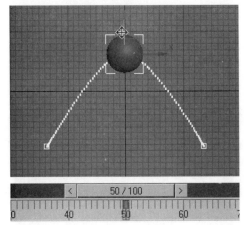

Figure 7.24 Setting a key at frame 50. Because the default controller for a Move transform is a Bézier controller, the trajectory smoothes out between keys.

You can keyframe virtually any parameter in 3ds max. In Chapter 6, "Modifying Objects," you keyframed the parameters of some modifiers. This time, try creating action by keyframing transforms.

To keyframe a transform:

1. Drag the time slider all the way to the left.

2. **Auto Key** Click Auto Key.

   The Auto Key button, time slider channel, and the active viewport boundary turn red (**Figure 7.21**).

3. Select an object.

4. Place the object where you want it to be at the beginning of the animation.

5. Turn on the display of the object's trajectory in the Display panel or Object Properties dialog box (**Figure 7.22**).

6. Drag the time slider to the right.

7. Transform the object in some way (**Figure 7.23**).

   A key is set in the track bar at frame 0 and at the current frame. These frames have now turned into keyframes.

8. Scrub the time slider a few times to get a rough sense of the animation.

9. Create additional keyframes by moving the time slider and making more changes (**Figure 7.24**).

10. Click Play Animation.

    The animation plays back all frames in the sequence. The object follows the trajectory from beginning to end.

11. **Auto Key** Turn off Auto Key mode, or like the sorcerer's apprentice, you may get results you did not intend.

KEYFRAMING

205

One of the main ways to change an animation is by adjusting its keyframes. This alters the values that are stored in the animation keys.

To adjust a keyframe:

1. ▷ Select an animated object.

   The animation keys of the object appear in the track bar.

2. ▣ Turn on the Auto Key button.

3. ▐◀▶▌ Click the Key Mode Toggle.

4. ◀▌ ▐▶ Click Next Key or Previous Key until the time slider ...aches the keyframe you want to adjust.

5. ✛ ⟳ ▣ Transform or modify the object in some way.
   The values stored in the animation keys are adjusted. If the object is animated to move through space, the trajectory of the object adjusts as well (**Figure 7.25**).

6. ▶ Click Play Animation.

   The animation plays back in the viewport, reflecting the adjustments you made.

7. Repeat steps 4 through 6 until all the keyframes are set the way you want.

✔ Tips

■ ▐▶ ◀▐ To step through the animation one frame at a time, click Next Frame or Previous Frame.

■ You can move the time slider to a specific frame by entering the frame number in the animation controls (**Figure 7.26**).

■ Another way to adjust keyframes is by changing key values in the X, Y, or Z Key Properties dialog box (**Figure 7.27**). To access it, right-click on the key and choose the key controller from the list at the top of the pop-up menu.

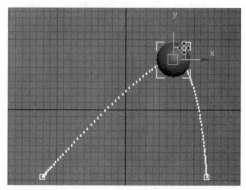

Figure 7.25 Adjusting a motion key adjusts the trajectory of an object.

Figure 7.26 Entering a frame number moves the time slider to that frame.

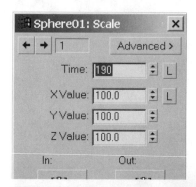

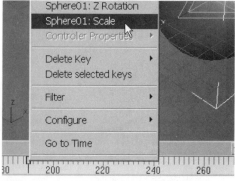

Figure 7.27 Above: In a Key Properties dialog box, you can adjust the value of the key and the rate at which this value may change. Below: You access a Key Properties dialog box by selecting it from the right-click menu of an animation key.

KEYFRAMING

Figure 7.28 The Trajectories rollout of the Motion panel is where you adjust trajectories and their keys.

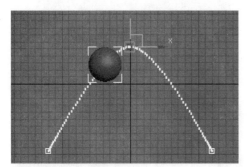

Figure 7.29 Select a key in the trajectory.

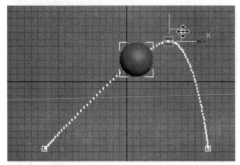

Figure 7.30 Moving the key deforms the trajectory.

You can adjust a trajectory interactively in the viewports.

To adjust a trajectory:

1. Choose the Select and Move tool from the Transform toolbar.

2. Select an object that has a trajectory, such as an object that has been animated with a Move transform.

3. Open the Motion panel.

4. Click the Trajectories button.
   The Trajectories rollout and the trajectory of the object appears.

5. Click the Sub-Object button to enable access to the object's keys (**Figure 7.28**).

6. Select a key in the trajectory (**Figure 7.29**).

7. Move the key.
   The trajectory deforms to follow the key (**Figure 7.30**).

8. Play the animation to see the results.
   The animation plays back in the viewports, following the new shape of the trajectory.

✔ Tip

■ Each white dot on the red line of the trajectory represents the location of a single frame. The farther apart the dots are, the faster the object will move as it follows that part of the trajectory. The closer together the dots are, the slower the progress of the object will be. To affect the spacing of frames, and therefore the acceleration of an object along its trajectory, see "To assign a Bézier tangent type" later in this chapter.

KEYFRAMING

To get a better idea of what you have created, you render a preview animation.

You can render an entire active time segment or any range of frames that you specify. Take advantage of the Range and Preview options to test-render different parts of your animation.

To render a preview animation:

1. Choose Animation > Make Preview.

   The Make Preview dialog box appears (**Figure 7.31**).

2. Set the Preview Range, Frame Rate, and Image Size parameters, or accept the defaults.

3. Click Create. If necessary, choose a compression option.

   The preview window replaces the viewports. The preview renders in the center of the window (**Figure 7.32**).

   In the status bar, the progress of the rendering is displayed.

4. When the preview has finished rendering, the Windows Media Player appears. It automatically plays back the preview (**Figure 7.33**).

✔ Tip

- Previews are named _scene.avi and saved in the 3dsmax6/Previews folder by default. Use the Animation > Rename Preview command if you want to save the preview to a new file that will not be saved over.

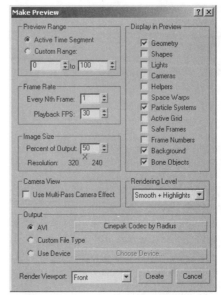

Figure 7.31 Use Make Preview to quickly produce a test rendering of your animation.

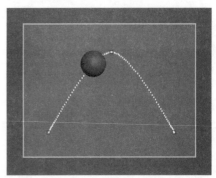

Figure 7.32 You can see the preview as it renders frame by frame in the preview window.

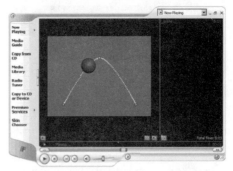

Figure 7.33 3ds max uses the Windows Media Player to play back the preview.

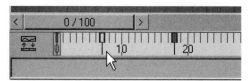

Figure 7.34 Select a key in the track bar.

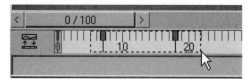

Figure 7.35 Dragging a selection region around multiple keys.

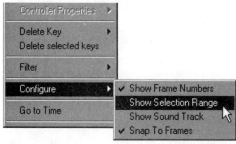

Figure 7.36 The Configure pop-up menu allows you to set different display options for the track bar.

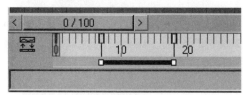

Figure 7.37 The selection range bar extends from the first key to the last key in your selection.

Working with Keys

Animation keys are the values of animated parameters or transforms at keyframes. By manipulating keys, you adjust the timing, duration, and repetition of your animation.

There are three ways you can work with keys: in the track bar, in the Motion panel, and in the Track View module. The easiest way to work with keys is in the track bar.

To select a key:

1. In the track bar, make sure that an animated object is selected. Then click the animation key that you want to select.

    The key and the track bar turn white (**Figure 7.34**).

2. To add to your selection, Ctrl + click additional keys or drag a selection region around them (**Figure 7.35**).

✔ Tips

- To subtract a key from a selection, Alt + click on the key.

- To see the range of your selection, right-click in the track bar and choose Configure > Show Selection Range (**Figure 7.36**). A black bar appears at the bottom of the track bar to indicate the range between the keys (**Figure 7.37**).

- To filter keys in the track bar so that only parametric animation keys appear, right-click the track bar and choose Filter > Object from the pop-up menu.

- To filter keys in the track bar so that only transform animation keys appear, right-click the track bar and choose Filter > All Transform Keys from the pop-up menu.

Moving keys in the track bar adjusts the timing of an animation. Moving keys closer together speeds up the animation. Moving keys farther apart makes the animation run slower.

To move a key:

1. Select a key by clicking it.

2. Drag the key to the left or right.

   As you drag the key, a small line marks the original location of the key until the mouse button is released. The prompt line displays the old frame number of the key, the new frame number, and the number of frames moved (**Figure 7.38**).

   If the object displays a trajectory, the trajectory will deform if you move a position key (**Figure 7.39**).

✔ Tips

■ To move multiple keys, select the keys you want to move and drag any one of them. If the selection range bar is displayed, you can move your selection by dragging the range bar (**Figure 7.40**).

■ You can also move keys by using the Key Properties dialog box (**Figure 7.41**). To access this dialog box, right-click on one of the object's keys and choose a key type from the top of the pop-up menu.

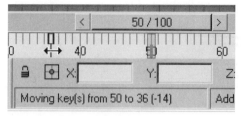

Figure 7.38 Drag a key in the track bar.

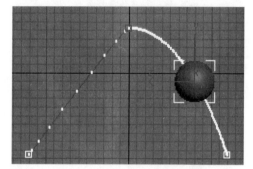

Figure 7.39 Moving a position key deforms the trajectory of an object.

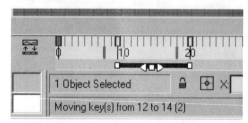

Figure 7.40 Dragging a selection range bar moves the keys in the selection.

Figure 7.41 You can change the position of a key in time in the Key Properties dialog box.

WORKING WITH KEYS

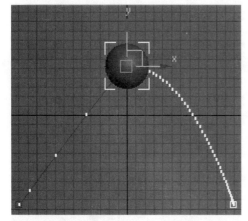

Figure 7.42 Dragging a clone from an original key.

Figure 7.43 A trajectory deforms in response to cloning a key.

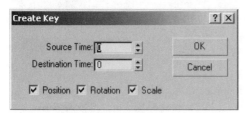

Figure 7.44 The Create Key dialog box allows you to clone keys to exact frame locations.

Cloning animation keys allows you to copy a portion of your animation and move it forward or backward in time.

If you clone an animation key and place it next to the original key, the animation will pause between the two keys.

If you select and clone a group of keys, the animation of the entire group will be repeated.

To clone a key:

1. Select a key in the track bar.

2. Hold down the Shift key, and drag the key to a new location.

   A copy of the key is placed at the new location (**Figure 7.42**).

   If a trajectory is displayed, it will deform accordingly (**Figure 7.43**).

3. To clone multiple keys, make a multiple selection and then Shift-drag them.

✔ Tip

- You can also clone keys by right-clicking the time slider to open the Create Key dialog box. There you select a key from one position (the source time) and copy it to another position (the destination time) (**Figure 7.44**).

Deleting keys removes animation data from objects.

To delete a key:

1. Select a key in the track bar (**Figure 7.45**).

2. Press the Delete key.

   The animation at that keyframe is removed from the object. The trajectory of the object adjusts accordingly (**Figure 7.46**).

Deleting all keys in the track bar removes all animation data from an object, so that the animation of the object ceases altogether.

To delete all keys:

1. Drag a selection region around all the keys in the track bar.

2. Press the Delete key.

   All animation data is removed from the object.

✔ Tips

- To delete all animation keys from a single frame, right-click on a key at that frame. Then choose Delete Key > All from the right-click menu (**Figure 7.47**).

- You can also add, move, clone, and delete keys in the Track View and in the expanded track bar (**Figure 7.48**).

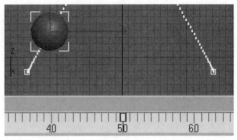

Figure 7.45 Selecting a key in the track bar.

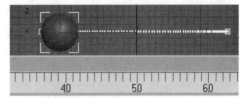

Figure 7.46 The trajectory after deleting the key.

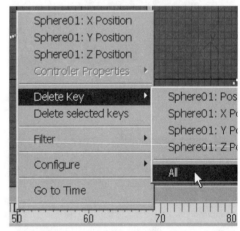

Figure 7.47 You can delete all the animation keys at a single frame using the track bar right-click menu.

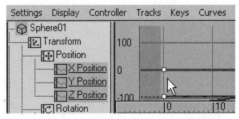

Figure 7.48 Selecting a key in the expanded track bar.

Working with Controllers

Animation controllers are plug-in programs that handle all animation tasks in 3ds max. Controllers generally fall into two categories. **Key controllers** store key values and use them to interpolate tween values. **Parametric controllers** store values that are generated by procedures and convert values from outside inputs, such as sound files.

3ds max keeps track of the values generated by each controller in separate animation tracks. The master dialog box for viewing animation tracks and their assigned controllers is called the **Track View**.

The Track View is divided into two windows. On the left, the Controller window displays a list of all the available tracks in the scene and any controllers that have been assigned to them. On the right, the Edit window displays a timeline of animation.

The Edit window has two modes of display. In **Dope Sheet** mode, it displays tracks as a sequence of keys laid out in a spreadsheet over time. In **Curve Editor** mode, it displays tracks as function curves that chart animation values over time. For the sake of simplicity, I'll refer to the Track View and its two modes of operation as if it were two separate modules called the Dope Sheet and the Curve Editor (**Figure 7.49**).

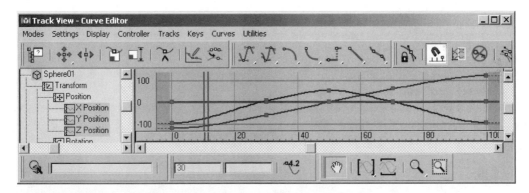

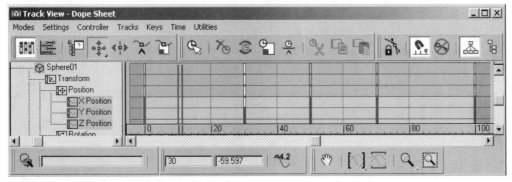

Figure 7.49 The Track View allows you to assign all animation controllers and perform operations on both controllers and keys. Top: The Curve Editor displays keys and their function curves. Bottom: The Dope Sheet displays keys in a spreadsheet.

Motion controllers are an important subset of key controllers that handle position, rotation, and scale animations.

You assign controllers in the Motion panel, the Curve Editor, or in the Mini Curve Editor, which is a miniature version of the Curve Editor accessible from the track bar.

The Motion panel is limited to motion controllers and does not display their function curves. Because of its simplicity, the Motion panel is often easier to use.

To assign a controller in the Motion panel:

1. Select an animated object (**Figure 7.50**).

2. 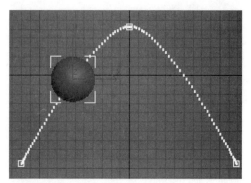 Open the Motion panel.

3. Click the Parameters button. Then open the Assign Controller rollout.

   A list of tracks and their animation controllers appears in the rollout. Currently animated tracks are selected. Clicking the "+" sign next to a track reveals a hierarchy of tracks below it (**Figure 7.51**).

4. Select an animation track.

5. 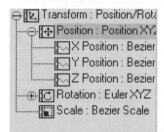 Click Assign Controller.
   The Assign Controller dialog box appears (**Figure 7.52**).

6. Select a controller, and click OK.

   The controller is assigned to the track. The trajectory of the object updates to show its effect (**Figure 7.53**).

7. 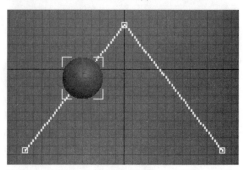 Click Play to see the result.

✔ Tips

- You can also assign controllers from the Animation menu in the Menu bar.

- Press Ctrl + Z to undo an assignment.

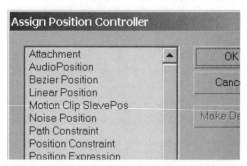

Figure 7.50 An object and its trajectory with a Bézier controller assigned.

Figure 7.51 The Transform track of the Parameters rollout includes Position, Rotation, and Scale tracks.

Figure 7.52 The Assign Controller dialog box presents all the controllers that can be applied to a track.

Figure 7.53 After assigning a Linear position controller to the object, the trajectory straightens between keys.

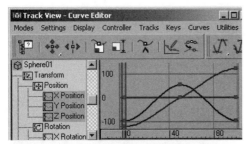

Figure 7.54 For the bouncing ball, the Z function slopes up and down, the X function increases steadily, and the Y function stays the same.

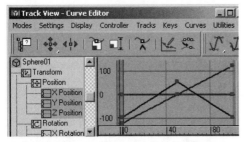

Figure 7.55 After assigning a Linear position controller to the ball, the function curve graphs its steady, linear movement.

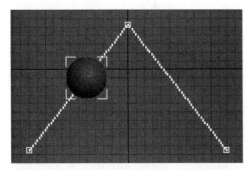

Figure 7.56 The trajectory straightens in response.

Using the Curve Editor or the Mini Curve Editor, you can assign controllers to any animation track in the scene.

To assign a controller in the Curve Editor or the Mini Curve Editor:

1. Select an animated object.

2. From the main menu, choose Graph Editors > Track View - Curve Editor or click Open Mini Curve Editor.

   In the Controller window, the selected tracks are highlighted in yellow. Their function curves appear at right in the Edit window. X values appear in red, Y in green, and Z in blue (**Figure 7.54**).

3. From the Controller window, select an animation track.

4. Choose Controller > Assign.

   The Assign Controller dialog box appears.

5. Select a controller, and click OK.

   The controller is assigned to the track. The function curve updates to show the effect of the controller (**Figure 7.55**). The trajectory of the object updates accordingly (**Figure 7.56**).

6. Close the window by clicking the close box, or, in the track bar, by clicking the Close button in the toolbar.

✔ Tips

■ You can apply controllers to more than one track at a time. Ctrl-click to add to or subtract from your selection.

■ To access navigation tools in the track bar, right-click on the menu bar and choose Load Layout > Default.

■ If you find the track bar Edit window too small to work in, click on the menu bar and drag it free of the status bar. Then drag the edges of the module to enlarge it.

WORKING WITH CONTROLLERS

If you want to create an animation sequence that cycles beyond the range of its keys, you change the Parameter Curves Out-of-Range:

Constant—Plays the animation once. Holds the value of keys constant before and after the sequence.

Cycle—Repeats the animation sequence indefinitely.

Loop—Repeats the animation sequence indefinitely and smoothly interpolates between cycles.

Ping Pong—Repeats the animation sequence backward and forward.

Linear—Linearly projects an animation so that it continues at a constant speed before or after the sequence.

Relative Repeat—Repeats the animation sequence and offsets repetitions so that they build on each other.

To cycle an animation:

1. Select an animated object, such as a ball bouncing once over the course of 30 frames (**Figure 7.57**).

2. Right-click on the object, and choose Curve Editor.

3. Choose Controller > Out-of-Range Types.

4. Choose a pattern by clicking its graph. To make a ball bounce repeatedly, choose Relative Repeat (**Figure 7.58**). Then click OK.

   The function curve and trajectory repeat the pattern (**Figure 7.59**).

5. Play the animation to see the result.

✔ Tip

- When you change any part of an animation cycle, the changes are repeated throughout the pattern.

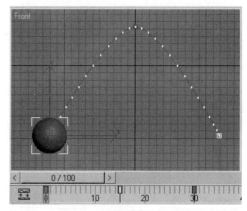

Figure 7.57 The object after animating a single cycle in the animation.

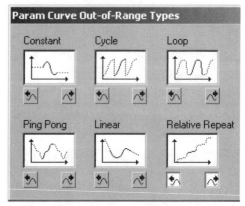

Figure 7.58 Choosing an animation pattern.

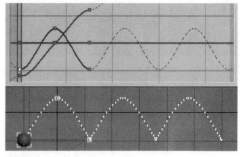

Figure 7.59 The function curve loops or cycles, depending on the pattern you chose.

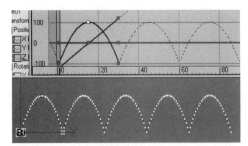

Figure 7.60 Top: The function curve of a bouncing ball appears in the Edit window of the Curve Editor. Below: In the viewport, the trajectory of the ball imitates the function curve.

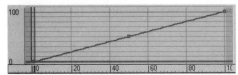

Figure 7.61 The ease curve slopes in a straight line from 0 to 100% at frame 100.

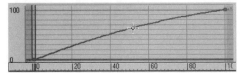

Figure 7.62 It doesn't take much to ease an animation.

Figure 7.63 The frame ticks gather toward the peaks of the trajectory, easing the speed of the ball near the top of each bounce.

Ease curves control the rate of acceleration of an animation sequence by scaling time—that is, by spacing frames farther apart or closer together along the function curve.

To ease an animation:

1. Right-click on an animated object and choose Curve Editor.

   The object's function curves appear in the Edit window (**Figure 7.60**).

2. Select a track.

3. Choose Curves > Apply—Ease Curve.

   An ease curve is applied to the track.

4. Click the "+" sign next to the track. Then select the Ease Curve track below.

   The ease curve appears in the Edit window (**Figure 7.61**).

5. Select the key in the middle of the ease curve. Then drag it slightly upward to make the ball decelerate over the course of the animation (**Figure 7.62**).

   The animation is eased (**Figure 7.63**).

6. To remove an ease curve, select the track and choose Curves > Remove.

✔ Tips

- Multipliers increase the values of animation data throughout a function curve. To apply a multiplier curve, choose Curves > Apply—Multiplier Curve.

- To scale the value of a selection of keys, click the Scale Values button and then drag the keys.

- To add a key to a function curve, select the Add Keys button and then click the function curve. To delete a key, select the key and press Delete.

- You can also add, scale, and delete keys in the Dope Sheet.

Bézier Controllers

Objects usually speed up or slow down gradually as they start, stop, or change direction. Abrupt acceleration or braking usually indicates extreme agitation, a collision, or mechanical motion.

Bézier controllers allow you to control the rate of change by adjusting the shape of function curves as they pass through each key. Using one of seven tangent types, you can create rapid acceleration, leisurely deceleration, sudden change, or steady progress. Bézier controllers are the default controllers for most tracks in 3ds max.

You assign a Bézier tangent type to a Bézier controller from any key properties dialog box or from the Curve Editor toolbar. Different tangent types may be assigned to affect the function curve as it approaches a key (going "In") or departs a key (going "Out").

Table 7.2

Track View Navigation Tools		
	TOOL	DESCRIPTION
	Pan	Pans the Edit window
	Zoom Horizontal Extents	Scales and centers horizontally
	Zoom Horizontal Extents keys	Scales and centers Keys horizontally
	Zoom Extents Values	Scales and centers the function curve vertically
	Zoom	Scales around the center of the window
	Zoom Time	Scales horizontally
	Zoom Values	Scales vertically
	Zoom Region	Scales a window that you drag

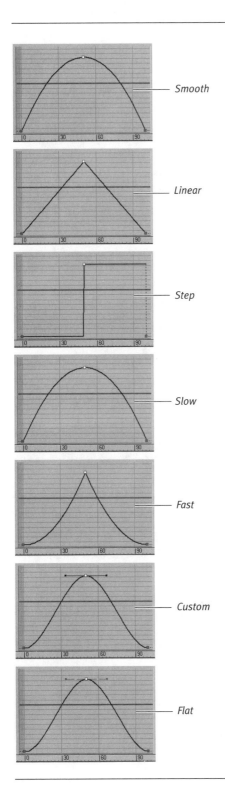

Smooth

Linear

Step

Slow

Fast

Custom

Flat

The seven basic tangent types are listed below. Curve Editor buttons for assigning tangent types to the In and Out parameter of each key precede each type (**Figure 7.64**):

Smooth—Interpolates tween values using a smooth curve, so that change takes place gradually through the key. Use smooth tangent types to smooth out the motion of lights and cameras.

Linear—Interpolates tween values using a straight line, so that change progresses steadily from one key to another. Use linear tangent types to create robot-like movements or anything that takes place at a constant pace.

Step—Interpolates tween values using a step function so change occurs abruptly at a key. Use the step tangent type to switch on a light or crash a car.

Slow—Interpolates tween values using a cubic Bézier curve, so the animation slows down as it approaches a key and speeds up after it departs.

Fast—Interpolates tween values using a cubic Bézier curve, so the animation speeds up as it approaches a key and slows down after it departs.

Custom—Interpolates tween values using an adjustable spline curve that initially appears smooth. Comes with Bézier handles that you can drag to create a curve with sharper angles.

Flat—Interpolates tween values using a smooth curve, so that change takes place gradually through the key. Avoids the problem of overshooting, which is sometimes associated with Smooth tangent types. This is the default for PRS (position, rotation, scale) controllers.

Figure 7.64 After assigning a single Bézier tangent type to the In and Out directions of a Bézier key.

BÉZIER CONTROLLERS

To assign a Bézier tangent type:

1. Select an animated object.

2. 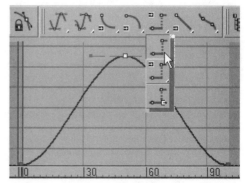 Open the Mini Curve Editor or the Curve Editor.

3. In the Controller list, select a track that has a Bézier controller assigned to it, or assign a Bézier controller to it.

4. In the Edit window, select a key by clicking on it.

5. In the toolbar, click a tangent button. Use the flyouts to select tangent types that affect the function curve as it approaches or departs from a key, as indicated by arrows on the buttons pointing right or left (**Figure 7.65**).

   Depending on the tangent type you chose, the function curve changes shape (**Figure 7.66**).

   If you changed the shape of a position function curve, the shape of the object's trajectory and the distribution of frame ticks along the trajectory also change. Note that the position of the key remains the same (**Figure 7.67**).

✔ Tips

- You can also assign tangent types in the Key Properties dialog box, which is available by right-clicking on a key in the Track View or Mini Curve Editor. A similar interface is available in the Key Info (Basic) rollout of the Modify panel (**Figure 7.68**).

- To assign a precise value to a key, highlight the current value in the status bar or the Key Properties dialog box, and type in the new value.

- To assign an exact frame number to a key, highlight the current time in the status bar or the key properties dialog box, and type in the new frame number.

Figure 7.65 Assigning a Step tangent type to the In parameter of the key.

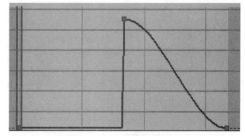

Figure 7.66 The function curve to the left of the key changes shape.

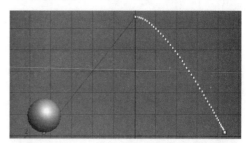

Figure 7.67 The trajectory changes shape as well.

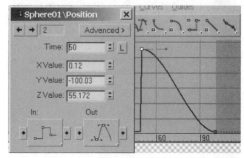

Figure 7.68 You can also change tangent types in the Key Properties dialog box.

BÉZIER CONTROLLERS

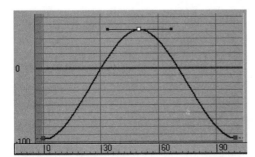

Figure 7.69 When you assign a Custom tangent type, Bézier handles become available.

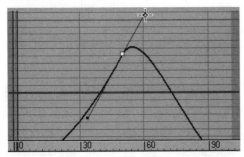

Figure 7.70 Bézier handles allow you to change the shape of a function curve as it passes through a key.

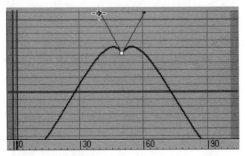

Figure 7.71 When you press Shift, the Bézier handles move independently.

The Bézier Custom tangent type allows you to precisely adjust function curves as they approach to and depart from animation keys.

To adjust a function curve:

1. Open the Mini Curve Editor or the Curve Editor.

2. In the Controller window, select an animation track that has a Bézier controller assigned to it.

3. Use the track view navigation tools to zoom to the extents of the selected track's function curve.

4. In the toolbar, choose the Move Keys button. Then select the key you want to adjust in the Edit window.

5. In the toolbar, choose Set Tangents to Custom.

   Bézier handles appear on the key (**Figure 7.69**).

6. Zoom into the key. Then adjust the function curve by clicking and dragging the Bézier handles of the key.

   The handles move like a seesaw. The function curve changes shape so that it is always tangent to the handles (**Figure 7.70**).

7. To release the handles from each other, press the Shift key as you drag on one of them.

   Now you can make the function curve come to a point at the key (**Figure 7.71**).

8. Play the animation to see the results.

✔ Tip

- If the Flat tangent type is assigned, you do not need to change it to Custom in order to make it adjustable. Just drag the gray Bézier handles of the key, and the tangent type will change to Custom automatically.

Adding Sound

Sound adds a whole new dimension to animation. Using the Track View, you can add a sound track by importing an external sound file. When you play back the animation, the sound track plays with it. This opens up the possibility of driving your animations with sound. By combining a sound track with audio controllers that you apply to the position, rotation, or scale tracks, you can make your objects dance to music.

To add a sound track:

1. 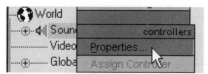 Open the Mini Curve Editor or the Curve Editor.

2. Select the Sound track from the top of the scene hierarchy.

3. Right-click on Sound, and choose Properties (**Figure 7.72**).

4. In the Sound Options dialog box, click Choose Sound (**Figure 7.73**).

5. In the Open Sound dialog box, navigate to a .WAV, .AU, or .AVI file on your hard drive or network (**Figure 7.74**). Then click OK and OK to close both dialog boxes.

6. Click the plus sign (+) next to the Sound track and select the Waveform track (**Figure 7.75**).
   If the sound track is in stereo, two waves appear. If the sound track is in mono, just one wave appears.

7. Play the animation to hear the results. If you cannot hear any sound, be sure to check the volume.

✔ Tip

■ To display the sound wave in the track bar, right-click on the track bar, and choose Configure > Show Sound Track (**Figure 7.76**).

Figure 7.72 Choose Properties from the Sound right-click menu.

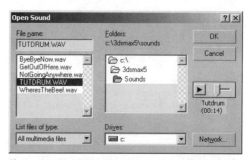

Figure 7.73 Choose a sound file in the Sound Options dialog box.

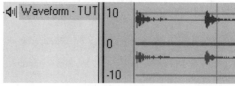

Figure 7.74 The Open Sound dialog box allows you to import a .WAV file or an .AVI file that has an audio stream from anywhere in your network.

Figure 7.75 The Waveform track displaying a stereo sound track in two waves: one blue and the other red.

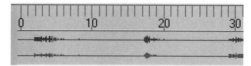

Figure 7.76 After turning on a stereo sound track display in the track bar.

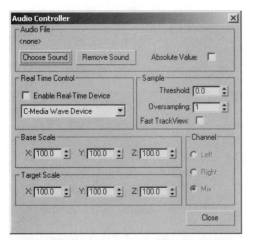

Figure 7.77 In the Audio Controller dialog box, click Choose Sound to control an animation track with an external sound file.

Figure 7.78 Choose the same sound that is in the sound track.

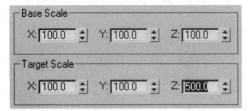

Figure 7.79 These settings mean the object will stay the same size during silence, but grow up to five times its height at peak amplitude.

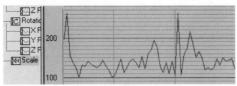

Figure 7.80 The waveform of the sound appears in the scale track.

Audio controllers convert the amplitude of sound waves from .AVI and .WAV files into scale values for X, Y, and Z. Use them to make objects dance to music, or to lip-synch a character to the sound of its voice.

To animate objects with sound:

1. Apply an Audio controller to an animation track, such as the scale track.

2. In the Audio Controller dialog box, click Choose Sound (**Figure 7.77**).

3. Choose a sound file. Use the same sound that is in the sound track if you want the object to dance to the tune. Then click OK (**Figure 7.78**).

4. In the Audio Controller dialog box, set the Base Scale parameters. This sets the state of the object at zero amplitude (when there is no sound).

5. Set the Target Scale Parameters of the object. This sets the state of the object at maximum amplitude (at peak volume) (**Figure 7.79**).

6. Close the dialog box. The sound wave appears in the track (**Figure 7.80**).

7. To see how the sound animates your object, click Play. To change the sound, right-click on the sound track and choose Properties. This brings up the Audio Controller dialog box again.

✔ Tips

- To provoke a stronger response to the sound, check Absolute Value. This ensures that the target values are reached at the maximum amplitude of the wave, rather than at the *potential* maximum amplitude of the wave.

- To set a lower limit of response, increase the Threshold value. To smooth the sound wave, increase Oversampling.

- You can also assign an audio controller to a track from the Motion panel.

ADDING SOUND

The Noise controllers produce random values using fractal-based functions. Use noise to create random changes of motion and color.

You adjust the Noise controller by changing the seed value, frequency, roughness, strength, and ramp in and out parameters.

To animate objects with noise:

1. Apply a Noise controller to an animation track, such as the scale track.

   The Noise Controller dialog box appears (**Figure 7.81**).

2. ▶ Play the animation to see the results.

   If you applied the controller to the scale track, the object shivers and shakes.

3. In the Noise Controller dialog box, adjust the shape of the noise graph by adjusting the seed value, frequency, roughness, strength, and ramp in and out parameters.

   To make the Noise smoother, uncheck Fractal Noise.

   To make the Noise affect a single direction, set two of the three X, Y, and Z Strength parameters to 0.

   To make the Noise ramp in and out slowly, increase the Ramp in and Ramp out values (**Figure 7.82**).

4. ▶ Play the animation.

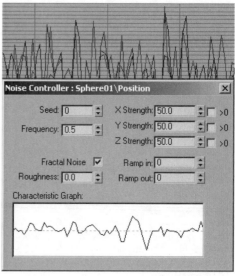

Figure 7.81 The Noise Controller dialog box allows you to make random changes to an animation track.

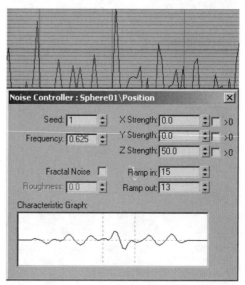

Figure 7.82 These settings will make the Noise gradually affect the Z direction and then taper off.

Figure 7.83 After adding Line01 as a path.

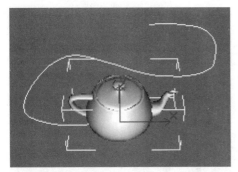

Figure 7.84 Adding a path causes the object to move to the first vertex of the spline. To reverse the order of vertices, see Chapter 8, "Editing Meshes and Polymeshes."

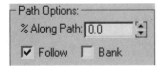

Figure 7.85 Check Follow to make the object orient along the length of the path.

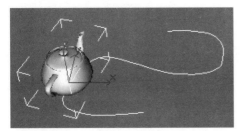

Figure 7.86 The object follows the path when you play the animation.

Constraining Animations

Animation constraints are animation controllers that constrain transform animations with respect to one or more target objects. Because they are based on the motion of another object, you can work with the simpler interface of the Motion panel.

The Path constraint restricts an object to move along a path.

To assign a path constraint:

1. In the Parameters rollout of the Motion panel, assign a Path Constraint to the position track of an object.

2. In the Parameters rollout, click Add Path. Then pick an open or closed spline.

   The spline appears in the list of target paths (**Figure 7.83**). The object moves to the first vertex of the spline (**Figure 7.84**).

3. To make an object orient in the direction of the path, click Follow (**Figure 7.85**).

4. Play the animation. The object follows the path from beginning to end (**Figure 7.86**).

✔ Tips

- If you want to make your object bank like a racecar through three-dimensional curves, click Bank.

- To change the beginning and end point of the animation, turn on the Auto Key button and adjust the % Along Path amount.

- If you add multiple paths, the object will move between the paths. To make an object move closer to a path, select the path and increase the Weight value.

- To make an animation deform like an eel as it follows a path, use a PathDeform modifier instead of a Path constraint.

CONSTRAINING ANIMATIONS

225

The LookAt constraint causes an object to keep facing another object, no matter where the objects move in relation to each other. This can be used not only for geometry, but also for lights and cameras that follow objects through a scene.

To assign a LookAt constraint:

1. In the Parameters rollout of the Motion panel, assign a LookAt Constraint to the rotation track of an object.

2. In the LookAt Constraint rollout, click Add LookAt Target. Then pick a target object (**Figure 7.87**).

   The object rotates to face the target object.

3. Play the animation.

   The object faces the target, no matter where the objects are positioned in space relative to each other (**Figure 7.88**).

✔ Tip

■ To change the axis of orientation of the object, choose an axis in the Select LookAt Axis group.

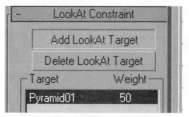

Figure 7.87 After picking Pyramid01 to be a LookAt target.

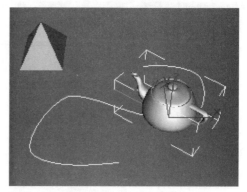

Figure 7.88 The teapot faces the pyramid no matter where it moves along the path.

CONSTRAINING ANIMATIONS

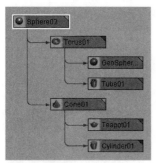

Figure 7.89 A linked hierarchy in the Schematic View displaying one grandparent, two parents, and four children.

Object Family Trees

Objects in linked hierarchies are referred to as if they are members of a family or parts of a tree:

◆ **Child**—An object that has been linked to another object.

◆ **Parent**—The object to which a child object is linked. Each child can have only one parent, but a parent object can have multiple children.

◆ **Grandparent**—The parent of a parent.

◆ **Ancestor**—The parent and all of a parent's parents.

◆ **Grandchild**—The child of a child.

◆ **Descendant**—The child and all of a child's children.

◆ **Root**—An object at the top of a hierarchy.

◆ **Scene**—The root of an object that is not linked to a parent.

◆ **Leaf**—An object at the end of a hierarchy.

◆ **Branch**—The path through a hierarchy from an ancestor to a leaf.

Linking Objects

To increase the possibilities of transform animation, you can create a one-way link between objects so that one object passes its transforms onto the other. The **child** object that inherits the transforms will then move, rotate, or scale in the same way as the **parent**.

By linking a series of objects together, you can create a branching tree structure called a **linked hierarchy**. This allows you to create sophisticated animation sequences involving multiple objects and complex motions.

The Schematic View is a module that allows you to view and modify linked hierarchies (**Figure 7.89**). It is accessed from the Editors toolbar and from the Graph Editors menu.

The Select and Link tool links the pivot point of a child object to the pivot point of its parent. When linked, the child inherits the transforms of the parent. You cannot link a parent to its child.

To link an object:

1. Choose Select and Link from the main toolbar.

2. Click an object.
   This will be the child object.

3. Drag to a second object. When the link cursor appears, release the mouse button (**Figure 7.90**).
   The second object (the parent) flashes, indicating that the objects are linked.

4. Test the link by transforming the parent object in some way.
   The child follows the parent (**Figure 7.91**).

5. Exit Select and Link mode by clicking the Select Object button.

✔ Tips

- To select a parent from a list, press H on your keyboard (**Figure 7.92**).

- If you need an additional pivot point for your animation sequence, create a dummy object from the Helpers menu to serve as a stand in. Dummy objects are non-rendering wireframe boxes that are often used for animating lights and cameras. They can also serve as proxies for more complex objects that you replace them with later (**Figure 7.93**).

The Unlink Selection tool halts the flow of transform data from parent to child.

To unlink an object:

1. Select a child object.

2. Choose Unlink Selection from the Link/Unlink toolbar.

3. Click the child object.
   The child object unlinks from its parent.

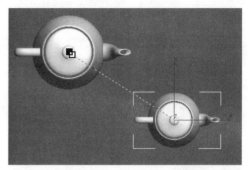

Figure 7.90 Linking the small teapot to the large one.

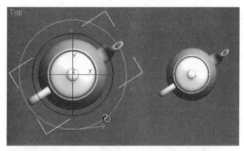

Figure 7.91 Rotating the parent object causes the child to rotate with it.

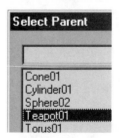

Figure 7.92 The Select Parent dialog allows you to pick a parent by name. The rest of the dialog box looks just like the Select Object dialog box, except the Select button says Link instead of Select.

Figure 7.93 A dummy object (foreground) can be used for an additional pivot point or as a substitute for a more complex object.

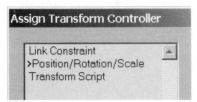

Figure 7.94 Assigning a Link constraint to the transform controller.

Figure 7.95 After you link the object to the world, set the Start Time to frame –1.

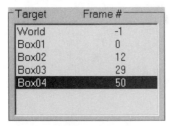

Figure 7.96 After linking the object to four boxes at frames 0, 12, 29, and 50.

Figure 7.97 The object is passed from one swinging box to another. Here at frame 45, Box02 is about to pass the sphere to Box03.

Using a Link Constraint, you can make a child object switch links to different parent objects over time. This causes the child to inherit the transforms of each parent in sequence.

To animate link inheritance:

1. Select an object.

2. Open the Motion panel.

3. Open the Assign Controller rollout, and highlight the Transform controller.

4. Click Assign Controller and choose Link Constraint (**Figure 7.94**).

5. Move the time slider to frame 0.

6. In the Link Params rollout, click Link to World. Then change the Start Time to -1. This keeps the object from moving when you assign the first new link (**Figure 7.95**).

7. Move the time slider to frame 0.

8. Click Add Link. Then pick a target object to transfer link inheritance to.

9. Move the time slider to the point in the animation where you want to switch links.

10. Repeat steps 8 and 9 until you have added all the target objects you want (**Figure 7.96**).

11. Play the animation.
    As the animation plays back, the object changes links. The parent objects pass their transform animations to the child object (**Figure 7.97**).

✔ Tips

- To adjust the timing of link transfers, move the time slider to the frame number in question. Then highlight a target object and drag the Start Time spinner.

- To delete a link, highlight the linked object in the target display and click Delete Link.

EDITING MESHES AND POLYMESHES

Figure 8.1 3D medical illustration requires highly detailed editing work.

Mesh editing is essential for character modeling, 3D medical illustration, or any other application that requires precision modeling (**Figure 8.1**). With this in mind, 3ds max 6 provides you with an abundant supply of tools for modeling mesh and poly objects at the smallest level of detail.

Before you begin, it is important to evaluate the level of detail that you need. Will the work be visible when you play the animation? Will it be obscured by shadow? Lost in the distance? If so, you might want to concentrate on the larger issues of scene composition—materials, lighting, and timing—or on editing just those objects that appear prominently in the scene.

Mesh Sub-Object Selection

Sub-objects are the components of an object. Mesh objects have five types of sub-objects (**Figure 8.2**):

Vertex—A point location in space, defined by XYZ coordinates.

Edge—A straight line that connects two vertices.

Face—A triangular surface bounded by three vertices and three edges that connect the vertices.

Polygon—A closed sequence of three or more edges connected by a surface.

Element—A discrete set of contiguous faces that share vertices with all of their neighbors.

You **edit** an object by selecting its sub-object components and manipulating them with modifiers, transforms, and edit commands. To make sub-object components selectable, you apply a sub-object modifier to the object, or convert it to a non-parametric object called an **editable object**. These editable objects include editable meshes, editable polys, editable patches, and editable splines.

Converting an object to an editable object of any type preserves it in its current state by changing it from a parametric object to an explicit description of sub-object components. Changes that you have made to the object are "frozen" because its creation parameters and modifiers are discarded.

The method that you use to make sub-objects selectable depends on what you plan to do with the object. If you need an object that has as little memory overhead as possible, you convert it to an editable object. If you will need to adjust or animate its creation parameters, you use a select or edit modifier.

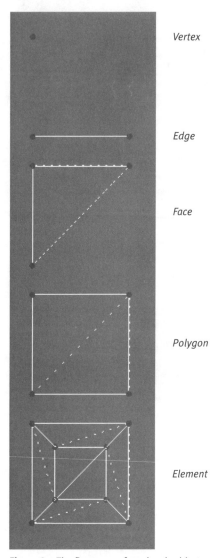

Figure 8.2 The five types of mesh sub-objects.

Figure 8.3 Convert an object to an editable mesh in the Transform quad menu.

Figure 8.4 In the Modify panel, the editable mesh replaces the original object type in the modifier stack.

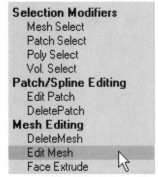

Figure 8.5 Choose a Select or Edit modifier from the Modifier drop-down list.

Figure 8.6 The modifier appears above the object in the stack display.

To convert a mesh object to an editable mesh:

1. Select a mesh object.

2. Right-click on the object.

3. In the Transform quad menu, roll the cursor over Convert To. Then choose Convert to Editable Mesh from the pop-up menu (**Figure 8.3**).

   The object is converted to an editable mesh (**Figure 8.4**). It is now selectable at a sub-object level.

✔ Tip

- You can also convert mesh objects to editable meshes by right-clicking on the name of the object in the modifier stack display and choosing Convert To: Editable Mesh.

Mesh Select, Volume Select, and Edit Mesh modifiers make mesh sub-objects selectable while preserving their creation parameters. In addition, Edit Mesh allows you to apply edit commands to the sub-objects you select. These commands are identical to the commands in an editable mesh. The only difference is that creation parameters and modifiers are preserved.

To apply a mesh sub-object modifier:

1. Select an object.

2. Open the Modify panel.

3. Apply a Mesh Select, Volume Select, or Edit Mesh modifier (**Figure 8.5**).

   The mesh sub-object modifier is applied to the object (**Figure 8.6**). It is now selectable at the mesh sub-object levels.

Once you convert an object to an editable mesh, or apply a mesh sub-object modifier to it, you can make a sub-object selection (**Figure 8.7**). Different selections can exist simultaneously on each sub-object level.

Methods of sub-object selection include:

◆ Clicking

◆ Dragging a selection region

◆ Choosing a named selection set that you created from a previous selection

As with object selection, you can:

◆ Add to a sub-object selection by holding down the Ctrl key

◆ Subtract from a selection by holding down the Alt key

◆ Lock and unlock sub-object selections

◆ Invert sub-object selections

In addition, you can:

◆ Cycle through sub-object selection levels by pressing the Insert key

◆ Import a selection from another level using the Mesh Select modifier

Region selection is especially well suited to mesh sub-object selection because of the density of most meshes. By drawing rectangular, circular, fence, or lasso selection regions, you can define sub-object selection with great precision.

Sub-object selection can be performed only when the Modify panel is open and a level of sub-object selection is chosen. When you are in a sub-object selection mode, object selection in the viewport is disabled.

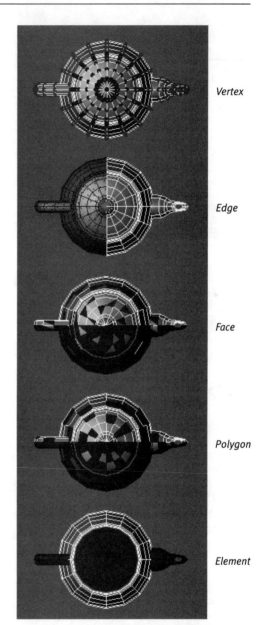

Vertex

Edge

Face

Polygon

Element

Figure 8.7 Poly sub-object selections created at each of the five levels of selection.

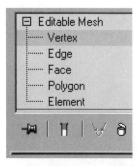

Figure 8.8 Enabling vertex-level selection.

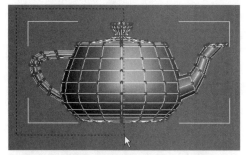

Figure 8.9 Selecting vertices with a rectangular selection region. Note that vertex ticks are visible.

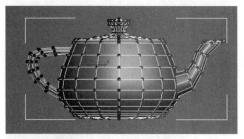

Figure 8.10 The selected vertices turn red.

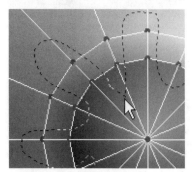

Figure 8.11 Drag a lasso to create an irregular selection region.

To select vertices:

1. Select a mesh object.

2. Optional: Enable Edged Faces or Wireframe viewport display.

3. Open the Modify panel.

4. Convert the mesh object to an editable mesh or apply an Edit Mesh modifier to it.

5. In the stack display, click the plus (+) sign next to the mesh sub-object modifier or the editable mesh. Then choose Vertex from the drop-down list.

   or

   Click the Vertex button in the Selection rollout (**Figure 8.8**).

   or

   Right-click in a viewport and choose Vertex from the tools 1 quad menu.

   The Vertex button turns yellow. Commands that can be applied at the vertex level become available below.

   In the viewports, blue vertices appear on the surface of the mesh object.

6. Ctrl + click or drag a selection region around the vertices you want to select (**Figure 8.9**).

   The vertices turn red, indicating that they are selected (**Figure 8.10**).

✔ Tips

- Check Ignore Backfacing to prevent vertices on the far side of a mesh object from being selected.

- Lasso and fence selection are great for making precise selections of vertices (**Figure 8.11**).

- Circle selection is a great way to select sub-objects in radial objects.

To select edges:

1. Select a mesh object.

2. Optional: Enable Edged Faces or Wireframe viewport display.

3. Open the Modify panel.

4. Convert the mesh object to an editable mesh, or apply an Edit Mesh modifier to it.

5. In the stack display, click the plus (+) sign next to the mesh sub-object modifier or the editable mesh. Then choose Edge from the drop-down list.

    or

    Click the Edge object button in the Selection rollout (**Figure 8.12**).

    or

    Right-click in a viewport and choose Edge from the tools 1 quad menu.

    The edge type becomes highlighted.

    Commands that can be applied at the edge level become available below.

6. Ctrl + click or drag a selection region around the edges you want to select (**Figure 8.13**).

    The selected edges turn red (**Figure 8.14**).

✔ Tips

- Check Ignore Backfacing to prevent edge selection on the far side of a mesh.

- Check By Vertex to select adjacent edges and faces when you click a vertex.

- To verify the continuity of a mesh surface before performing a Boolean operation, enable Edge level selection and click Select Open Edges (**Figure 8.15**).

- You can import a selection from another sub-object level using the commands in the Get from Other Levels group of the Mesh Select modifier.

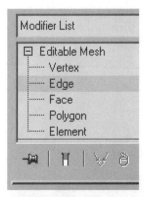

Figure 8.12 Enabling edge-level selection.

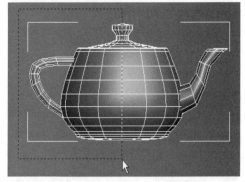

Figure 8.13 Selecting edges with a rectangular selection region.

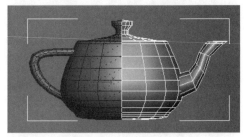

Figure 8.14 The selected edges turn red.

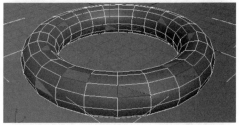

Figure 8.15 After checking for open edges, the edges around the holes in this mesh are selected in red.

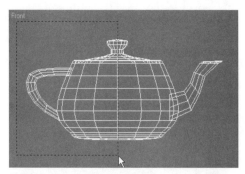

Figure 8.16 Drag a selection region around the faces you want to select.

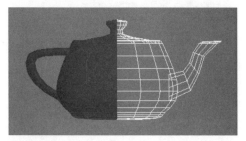

Figure 8.17 The selected faces turn red and become shaded.

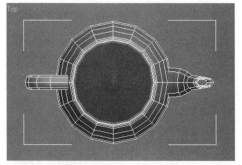

Figure 8.18 After clicking the lid of the teapot with element selection enabled.

To select faces:

1. Select a mesh object.

2. Optional: Enable Edged Faces or Wireframe viewport display.

3. Open the Modify panel.

4. Convert the object to an editable mesh, or apply an Edit Mesh modifier to it.

5. In the stack display, click the plus (+) sign next to the mesh sub-object modifier or the editable mesh. Then choose Face from the drop-down list.

   or

   Click the Face button in the Selection rollout.

   or

   Right-click in a viewport and choose Face from the tools 1 quad menu.

   The face button turns yellow. Commands that can be applied at the face level become available below.

6. Ctrl + click or drag a selection region around the faces you want to select (**Figure 8.16**).

   The selected faces turn red. If you are working in wireframe mode, the faces also become shaded (**Figure 8.17**).

✔ Tips

- Check Ignore Backfacing to prevent face selection on the far side of a mesh.

- Polygon selection selects coplanar pairs of faces.

- Element are sets of polygons and faces (**Figure 8.18**). Selecting an object at the element level also selects it at the face and polygon level.

- Faces and polygons are often easier to select using Windows selection.

MESH SUB-OBJECT SELECTION

Use Volume Select to select vertices or faces within a three-dimensional area.

To select a mesh within a volume:

1. 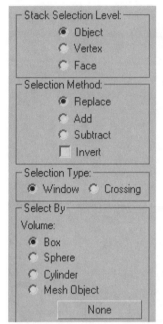 Select a mesh object.

2. Open the Modify panel.

3. Choose Vol. Select from the Modifier drop-down list.

   The Volume Select modifier is applied to the object (**Figure 8.19**).

4. In the Stack Selection Level group, choose Object, Vertex, or Face.

5. Choose a selection method and a selection type, or use the defaults.

6. In the Select By group, choose a volume type. If you choose Mesh Object, click the None button. Then pick a mesh object to define the extents of the selection.

   The Volume Select modifier gizmo changes to match the type of volume you choose.

7. In the modifier stack display, click the plus (+) sign next to Vol. Select. Then click Gizmo (**Figure 8.20**).

   If you choose Vertex or Face, a vertex or polygon icon appears in the stack display.

8. Use the Move tool to position the gizmo so that it encloses the vertices or faces you want to select.

   The sub-objects enclosed within the volume are selected (**Figure 8.21**).

✔ Tips

■ To fit, center, or reset the gizmo, click the Fit, Center, and Reset buttons in the Alignment group.

■ If you apply a Volume Select modifier to a spline object, it will convert the spline object to a mesh object.

Figure 8.19 The Parameters rollout for the Volume Select modifier.

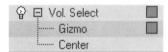

Figure 8.20 Click the plus sign to access the Gizmo and Center of the Volume Select modifier. Note the polygon icon at the right, which indicates that face selection is active.

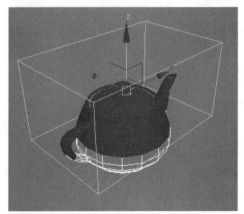

Figure 8.21 The sub-objects enclosed by the volume are selected.

Figure 8.22 A circle of vertices are selected on a sphere.

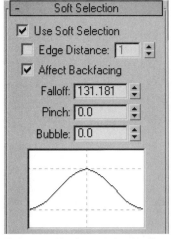

Figure 8.23 Check Use Soft Selection and drag the falloff spinner.

Figure 8.24 The colors of the vertices change from warm to cool to indicate the degree of selection.

Soft selections gradually fall off beyond the bounds of the original selection. This allows you to make changes to an object that gradually diminish over distance.

To soft select a mesh:

1. Make a vertex-level sub-object selection using any method (**Figure 8.22**).

2. Open the Soft Selection rollout.

3. Check Use Soft Selection. Then drag the Falloff spinner to adjust the degree of selection (**Figure 8.23**).

   The sub-objects in range of the soft selection change colors from red to orange to yellow to blue as you increase the falloff value. Red indicates the hottest selection where commands will be applied at full intensity; blue indicates the coolest selection where the effect of commands will have no effect (**Figure 8.24**).

✔ Tips

- The Pinch and Bubble parameters affect the intensity of selection according to the Soft Selection graph. For an example of how these parameters affect a sub-object transform, see "To move a vertex" in the next section.

- You can see falloff only at the vertex level, but with the select modifiers, you can get around this by using Get Vertex Selection to import the selection into another level. You can also soft-select sub-objects at the edge and face levels and import them to the vertex level to see the selection falloff.

MESH SUB-OBJECT SELECTION

Transforming Mesh Sub-Objects

You transform mesh sub-objects to shape the details of your model. Because mesh structure is defined primarily by vertices, sub-object transforms are mostly applied at the vertex level.

Like sub-object selections, sub-object transforms are performed exclusively in the Modify panel. There are three ways to do this (**Figure 8.25**):

◆ **Make a sub-object selection with a Mesh Select modifier, and then apply an XForm modifier.** When you apply your transforms, the XForm modifier will apply them to the sub-object selection. Use this option for animating sub-objects with transforms.

◆ **Make a sub-object selection within an editable object, and then transform the selection.** Use this option for sculpting structural details.

◆ **Make a sub-object selection with an Edit modifier and then apply a transform.** This option is used for modeling the details of objects when you want the operation to be reversible and you have plenty of RAM.

Figure 8.25 You can raise the lid of a teapot with a move transform after you select it at the element sub-object level.

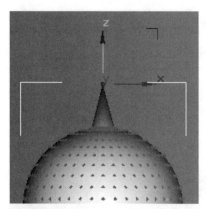

Figure 8.26 Selecting a vertex at the top of the sphere.

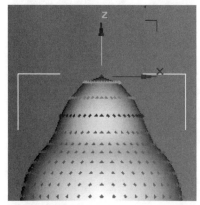

Figure 8.27 Applying a Move transform to the sub-object selection.

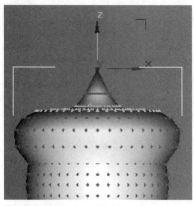

Figure 8.28 Pinch and Bubble alter the distribution of soft selection.

The Move tool is your primary tool for editing and animating vertices.

To move a vertex:

1. Select a vertex.

2. Optional: Apply a soft selection to the surrounding vertices.

3. If you used one of the select modifiers, apply an XForm modifier to the object.

4. Choose a reference coordinate system and an axis restriction. Note: You might find the Local Z axis to be a useful choice.

5. Optional: Lock the selection.

6. Move the selection (**Figure 8.26**).

   If you used a soft selection, the surface of the object will deform smoothly through the volume of the selection (**Figure 8.27**).

✔ Tips

- Changing the Pinch and Bubble parameters alters the distribution of soft selection intensity. This in turn changes how subsequent commands are interpreted (**Figure 8.28**).

- To transform a selection of vertices in the local axis of the object, rather than the local axis of each sub-object, make the selection and change the reference coordinate system to Pick. Then pick the object you are working on. This works around the problem of having multiple local axis tripods being active and obscuring your work.

Rotating a vertex rearranges the faces and edges that adjoin it, but does not deform the mesh surface unless you apply a soft selection.

To rotate a vertex:

1. 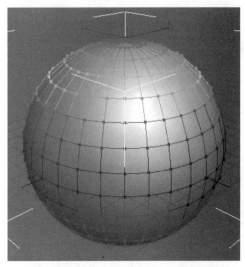 Select a vertex (**Figure 8.29**).

2. Apply a soft selection to the surrounding vertices.

3. If you used one of the select modifiers, apply an XForm modifier to the object.

4. Choose a reference coordinate system and an axis restriction.

5. Optional: Lock the selection.

6. Rotate the selection.

   The surface of the object deforms smoothly around the turning vertex (**Figure 8.30**).

Figure 8.29 Selecting a vertex at the top of a sphere. A soft selection has been applied.

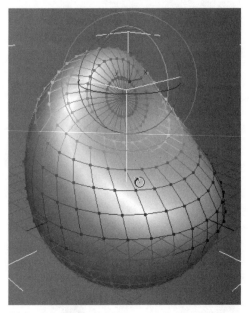

Figure 8.30 Rotating a single vertex deforms the top half of the object.

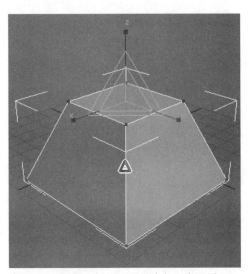

Figure 8.31 Scaling down vertices brings them closer together to achieve a taper effect.

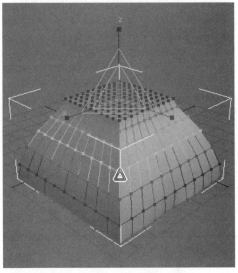

Figure 8.32 Scaling the top of a box with soft selection and additional segmentation adds a curve to the taper action.

Scaling vertices is a common way of making vertices move closer together or farther apart.

To scale vertices:

1. Select one or more vertices.

2. Optional: Apply a soft selection to the surrounding vertices.

3. If you used one of the select modifiers, apply an XForm modifier to the object.

4. Choose a reference coordinate system and an axis restriction, if you intend to use a non-uniform scale or squash.

5. Optional: Lock the selection.

6. Scale the selection.

The vertices move closer or farther apart (**Figure 8.31**).

If you used a soft selection, you can make the sides of a mesh curve inward or outward (**Figure 8.32**).

Modifying Mesh Sub-Objects

Mesh sub-object selections are preserved in the modifier stack. When a mesh sub-object level is enabled, the sub-object selection saved at that level is passed up the modifier stack. If you change the level of selection, the selection made at that level will be passed along instead.

If you want to make a new sub-object selection at any level without losing the old selection, you simply apply another selection modifier and make a new selection.

To apply a modifier to a mesh sub-object selection:

1. Make a sub-object selection using Mesh Select or Volume Select.

2. Apply a modifier.

3. Adjust the parameters of the modifier. The modifier is applied to the sub-object selection (**Figure 8.33**).

✔ Tip

■ Using soft selection gives you a second option for controlling the curvature of a Taper modifier (**Figure 8.34**).

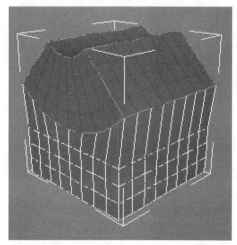

Figure 8.33 After applying a Bend modifier just to the upper half of a box.

Figure 8.34 This vase was created from a tube using a Taper modifier and soft selection.

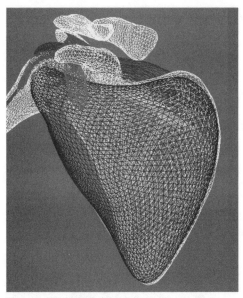

Figure 8.35 A high mesh density is often necessary for organic modeling.

Editing Mesh Objects

To make a mesh object editable, you apply an Edit Mesh modifier or you convert the object to an editable mesh.

The advantage of using Edit modifiers is that they are flexible and non-destructive. With Edit modifiers, you apply a series of commands, save off clones, and then reverse the effect of the modifier by removing it from the stack. The disadvantage is that Edit modifiers add memory and computational overhead to your scene because they keep track of every command.

In comparison, editable meshes are more stable and have less overhead because they do not track commands in a modifier stack. For complex objects, this can significantly speed up editing operations (**Figure 8.35**). The disadvantage of editable meshes is that you cannot undo them after closing a file.

As a beginner, you may find Edit modifiers to be more forgiving. As you develop your skills and begin making more complex scenes, you will probably want to switch to editable meshes.

Mesh objects can be edited at the vertex, edge, face, polygon, element, and object levels. When you choose a selection level, the editing commands for that level become available in the Modify panel. They also become available in the Tools 1 and Tools 2 quad menus (**Figure 8.36**).

| Ignore Backfacing |
| View Align |
| Make Planar |
| Turn Edges Mode |
| Flip Normals Mode |
| Divide Edges |
| Divide Polygons |
| Cut Polygons |
| Element |
| Polygon |
| Face |
| Edge |
| Vertex ✓ |
| Top-level |
| tools 1 |
| tools 2 |
| Create Polygons |
| Attach |
| Detach |
| Bevel Polygon |
| Extrude Polygons |
| Extrude Edge |
| Chamfer Edge |
| Chamfer Vertex |
| Break Vertices |
| Target Weld |

Figure 8.36 The right-click quad menus of an editable mesh contains two menus of mesh-editing commands. These menus only become available when the Modify panel is open.

The Attach, Delete, Remove Isolated Vertices, View Align, Grid Align, Make Planar, and Collapse commands can be used at every level of selection. Other commands are specific to certain levels (**Figure 8.37**):

Vertex editing commands control the smallest details of mesh structure. Commands include Create, Detach, Break, Weld, and Edit Vertex Colors Tools.

Edge editing commands affect the interstices of a mesh. Level-specific commands include Divide, Turn, Extrude, Chamfer, Slice, Cut, Split, and Visibility.

Face editing commands change the rendering properties of a mesh, including shading, smoothing, visibility, material assignments, and structure. Level-specific commands include Create, Detach, Divide, Extrude, Bevel, Slice, Cut, Split, Weld, Tessellate, Explode, Flip, Unify, Smooth, Material ID, and Edit Vertex Colors Tools.

Polygon editing commands affect coplanar pairs of faces. Polygon commands are the same as face-editing commands.

Element editing commands alter discrete collections of faces. Element commands are the same as face- and polygon-editing commands.

Object editing commands act upon the entire mesh. They are used primarily for attaching objects and controlling surface subdivision during displacement mapping (editable meshes only). The object level is the only level that allows you to attach multiple objects from a list.

Note: You can exit most editable mesh command modes, such as Extrude and Chamfer, by right-clicking in the active viewport.

Table 8.1 shows the availability of editing commands at each sub-object level.

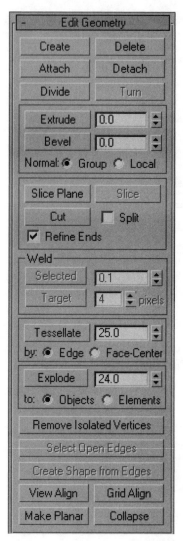

Figure 8.37 The Edit Geometry rollout for Edit Mesh and editable meshes. Only the commands for face-level editing are enabled.

Table 8.1

Mesh-Editing Commands and the Levels They Affect

COMMAND	VERTEX	EDGE	FACE	POLYGON	ELEMENT	OBJECT
Create	✓		✓	✓	✓	
Delete	✓	✓	✓	✓	✓	✓
Attach	✓	✓	✓	✓	✓	✓
Attach List						✓
Detach	✓		✓	✓	✓	
Break	✓					
Divide		✓	✓	✓	✓	
Turn		✓				
Extrude		✓	✓	✓	✓	
Chamfer	✓	✓				
Bevel			✓	✓	✓	
Slice	✓	✓	✓	✓	✓	
Cut		✓	✓	✓	✓	
Split	✓	✓	✓	✓	✓	
Weld	✓					
Tessellate		✓	✓	✓	✓	
Explode			✓	✓	✓	✓
Remove Isolated Vertices	✓	✓	✓	✓	✓	✓
Select Open Edges		✓				
Create Shape from Edges		✓				
View Align	✓	✓	✓	✓	✓	✓
Grid Align	✓	✓	✓	✓	✓	✓
Make Planar	✓	✓	✓	✓	✓	
Collapse	✓	✓	✓	✓	✓	
Flip			✓	✓	✓	
Unify			✓	✓	✓	
Smoothing Groups Tools			✓	✓	✓	
Material ID Tools			✓	✓	✓	
Edit Vertex Colors Tools	✓		✓	✓	✓	
Visibility		✓				

The Attach command joins objects together and turns them into a single object with one name and one set of object properties. Each of the attached objects becomes a sub-object element.

Attach works at any level of sub-object editing, as well as at the object level.

To attach an object:

1. Select an object (**Figure 8.38**).

2. Open the Modify panel.

3. Convert the object to an editable mesh, or apply an Edit Mesh modifier to it.

4. Enable a selection level, or work at the object level (the default).

5. In the Edit Geometry rollout, click Attach (**Figure 8.39**).

6. Click the object you want to attach.

    The second object attaches to the first. It is now an element within that object.

    If the objects are different colors, the attached element will inherit the color of the object (**Figure 8.40**).

    If the attached element has a different material, you will be given a choice as to how to incorporate it (**Figure 8.41**).

7. Click any other objects you want to attach.

8. Click the Attach button to turn off attach mode.

✔ Tips

- Clicking Attach List brings up a list of attachable objects so that you select the object that you want to attach by name.

- To smooth the seams between attached elements, use the Weld command (see the next task).

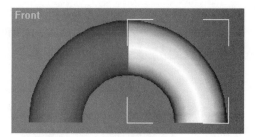

Figure 8.38 Select the mesh object that you want to attach other objects to.

Figure 8.39 Click Attach before attaching objects.

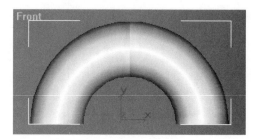

Figure 8.40 When you attach an object, it takes on the color of the object that it attaches to.

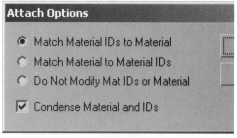

Figure 8.41 The Attach Options dialog box lets you choose how materials are combined.

EDITING MESH OBJECTS

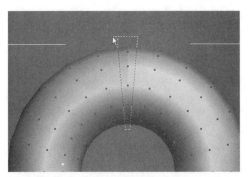

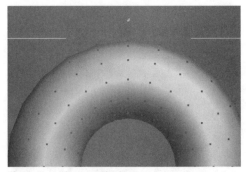

Figure 8.42 Selecting a group of vertices to weld.

Figure 8.43 Click Selected to weld the selection.

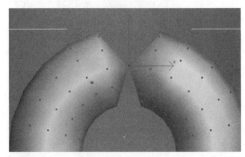

Figure 8.44 The smoothed seam.

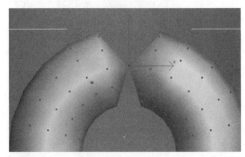

Figure 8.45 Collapse was used to weld all of the vertices on the seam into a single point.

Welding eliminates vertices within a certain distance of each other so that adjacent elements are united as one.

To weld a mesh:

1. Select an object.

2. Open the Modify panel.

3. Convert the object to an editable mesh, or apply an Edit Mesh modifier.

4. Enable Vertex-level selection.

5. Select a set of adjacent vertices by dragging a selection region around them (**Figure 8.42**).

6. In the Weld group of the Edit Geometry rollout, click Selected (**Figure 8.43**).

    Vertices that are within the threshold value (located to the right of the Selected button) are welded together.

    The elements are joined together into one, and the seam in between them is smoothed (**Figure 8.44**).

7. If the vertices that you selected are too far apart, a dialog box will appear to tell you that there are no vertices within the weld threshold distance. To resolve this, increase the weld threshold value and click Selected again.

    or

     Scale the vertices so they draw together. Then click Selected.

✔ Tip

- Collapse is like a super-powerful weld command that merges selected vertices into one vertex at the center of the selection (**Figure 8.45**).

The Break command is the opposite of Weld; it clones vertices and assigns them to adjoining faces. This allows you to pull faces apart from a corner where they had originally been joined.

To break a vertex:

1. 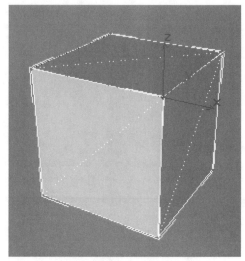 Select an object.

2. Open the Modify panel.

3. Convert the object to an editable mesh, or apply an Edit Mesh modifier to it.

4. Enable Vertex-level selection.

5. Select a vertex (**Figure 8.46**).

Figure 8.46 Selecting the corner of a box.

6. In the Edit Geometry rollout, click Break (**Figure 8.47**).

   The vertex is broken. You can now pull apart the adjoining faces (**Figure 8.48**).

✔ Tips

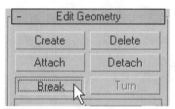

Figure 8.47 Click Break to clone the vertices.

- To break off a selection into a separate element, use the Detach command.

- Remove Isolated Vertices deletes vertices that are not connected to edges.

- View Align and Grid Align align selected vertices and faces to the plane of the view or the plane of the grid, respectively.

- Make Planar flattens the selection onto a plane whose normal is the average of all the normals of the faces attached to the vertices.

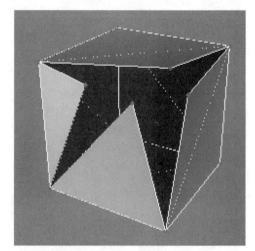

Figure 8.48 After moving the faces apart by dragging their vertices. The dark interior is a result of unchecking the Backface Cull display property.

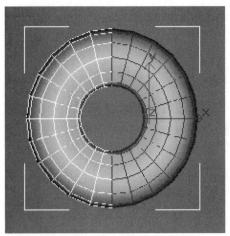

Figure 8.49 Selecting the right half of the torus.

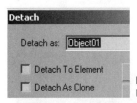

Figure 8.50
Click Detach to create a new object or element.

Figure 8.51
Detaching an object.

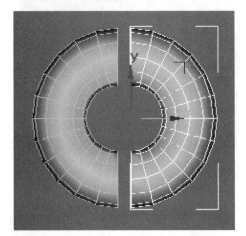

Figure 8.52 After exiting sub-object mode, you can select and move the new object.

Detach turns sub-object components into discrete elements, separate objects, or separate objects that are copies of the current selection.

To detach part of a mesh:

1. Select an object.

2. Open the Modify panel.

3. Convert the object to an editable mesh, or apply an Edit Mesh modifier to it.

4. Enable a selection level.

5. Select the sub-object components that you want to detach (**Figure 8.49**).

6. In the Edit Geometry rollout, click Detach (**Figure 8.50**).

   The Detach dialog box appears (**Figure 8.51**).

7. In the Detach dialog box, choose whether you want to detach the selection into a separate object (the default), an element, or a clone. (Clone copies the selection into a new object, ensuring that no geometry is removed from the original.)

8. Name the new object or clone in the Detach dialog box, or accept the default.

   The selection is detached. You can now select and move it independently (**Figure 8.52**).

Chamfering creates an edge or corner that appears to have been filed down.

Chamfering an edge splits an edge in two. Two new faces are created between the new edges. Adjoining faces subdivide accordingly.

To chamfer an edge:

1. Select an object.

2. Open the Modify panel.

3. Convert the object to an editable mesh, or apply an Edit Mesh modifier to it.

4. Enable Edge-level selection.

5. Select an edge (**Figure 8.53**).

6. In the Edit Geometry rollout, click Chamfer (**Figure 8.54**).

7. Drag the Chamfer spinner, enter a value in the Chamfer field, or click on the edge in the viewport and drag.

   The edge splits, chamfering the edge (**Figure 8.55**).

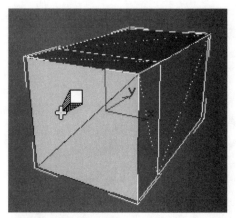

Figure 8.53 Select an edge.

Figure 8.54 Click Chamfer to start the chamfer operation.

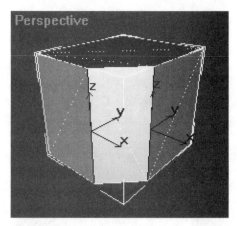

Figure 8.55 The chamfered edge.

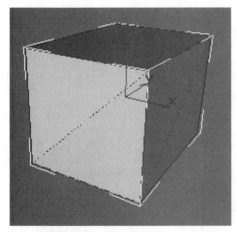

Figure 8.56 The chamfered vertex.

Chamfering a vertex splits a vertex into multiple vertices that move away from its original location down every edge that connects to it. New edges and faces are created automatically.

To chamfer a vertex:

1. Select a mesh object.

2. Open the Modify panel.

3. Convert the object to an editable mesh, or apply an Edit Mesh modifier to it.

4. Enable Vertex-level selection.

5. Select a vertex.

6. Click Chamfer.

7. Drag the Chamfer spinner, enter a value in the Chamfer field, or click on the vertex in the viewport and drag.

8. The vertex splits, chamfering the corner (**Figure 8.56**).

✔ Tip

- Chamfer vertex only creates new vertices on **visible** edges leading to the original vertex.

Extruding is a quick way to build geometry. You can extrude edges, faces, polygons, or elements. Use Extrude to add details to an existing model or to build a low-polygon model from scratch.

To extrude a polygon:

1. Select an object.

2. Open the Modify panel.

3. Convert the object to an editable mesh, or apply an Edit Mesh modifier to it.

4. Enable Polygon-level selection.

5. Click a polygon to select it.

6. In the Edit Geometry rollout, click Extrude (**Figure 8.57**).

7. Drag the polygon.

   or

   Drag the Extrude spinner.

   or

   Enter an Extrude value.

   The polygon extrudes from the surface of the mesh (**Figure 8.58**).

✔ Tips

- To extrude a multiple selection of faces or polygons in a single direction, choose Normal:Group. To extrude along individual face normals, choose Normal:Local.

- The Bevel command scales a selected face or polygon. By combining it with the Extrude command, you can create more complex profiles (**Figure 8.59**).

- Combining scale and move transforms with a polygon extrusion is a great way to create a low-poly model (**Figure 8.60**).

- New polygons created by extruding are not included in any smoothing groups.

Figure 8.57 Click Extrude to create new faces.

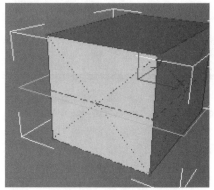

Figure 8.58 Extruding the front polygon of a box by dragging.

Figure 8.59 After combining Extrude with the Bevel command to vary the width of extrusion.

Figure 8.60 This low-poly jet fighter was created from a box using a series of Extrude commands.

EDITING MESH OBJECTS

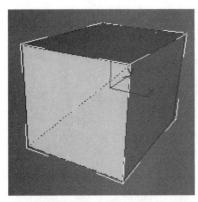

Figure 8.61 Selecting all the faces in a box to slice. Note that Edges Only is turned off.

Figure 8.62 Use Slice Plane to subdivide an object along a plane.

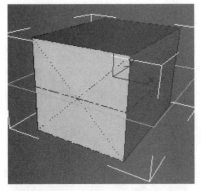

Figure 8.63 After clicking the Slice button, new edges appear along the Slice plane.

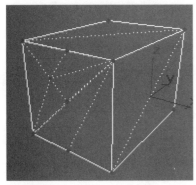

Figure 8.64 After dividing the edges on the front left polygon.

The Slice command divides a mesh in two.

To slice a mesh:

1. Select an object.

2. Open the Modify panel.

3. Convert the object to an editable mesh, or apply an Edit Mesh modifier to it.

4. Enable any sub-object selection level.

5. Select the sub-objects you would like to slice (**Figure 8.61**).

6. In the Edit Geometry rollout, click Slice Plane (**Figure 8.62**).

   The slice plane appears in the middle of the object. Like the Section object, it extends infinitely into space.

7. Place the slice plane where you want it to slice the object.

8. Click Slice.

   All edges and faces intersected by the slice plane are subdivided (**Figure 8.63**).

✔ Tips

■ The Split option divides an object into two separate elements by creating duplicate vertices at every point of intersection.

■ Create Shape from Open Edges selects all the open edges in a mesh object and clones them into a new shape. Used with the Slice command, it sections an object.

■ The Divide command divides edges as you click on them (**Figure 8.64**).

■ The Cut command divides all edges on the visible surface that you drag across.

■ The Turn command rotates an edge and connects it to the other vertices of the two faces it divides.

The Delete command deletes sub-object selections at any level.

To delete part of a mesh:

1. 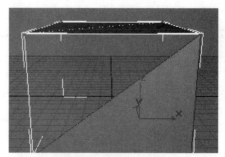 Select an object.

2. Open the Modify panel.

3. Convert the object to an editable mesh, or apply an Edit Mesh modifier to it.

4. Enable the selection level of the components you want to delete.

5. Select the part of the mesh that you want to delete (**Figure 8.65**).

6. Click Delete, or press the Delete key.

   If you are working at the Edge, Face, Polygon, or Element level, the Delete Face dialog box appears (**Figure 8.66**).

7. Click Yes.

   The selected part of the mesh is deleted (**Figure 8.67**).

✔ Tips

- Isolated vertices are usually considered junk. They do not render, but they do add unnecessary confusion to your model. The only time you want to keep them is when you want to build new faces off of them.

- If you have attached two objects that intersect one another, deleting the faces in the intersecting region will improve rendering performance.

- Use the Create command to rebuild faces and vertices that have accidentally been deleted.

Figure 8.65 Selecting the body of a teapot.

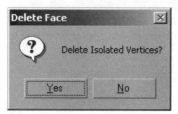

Figure 8.66 The Delete Face dialog box asks if you want to delete isolated vertices.

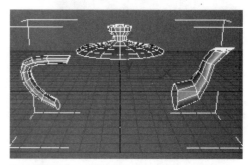

Figure 8.67 After deleting the body of the teapot.

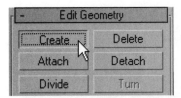

Figure 8.68 Click Create to start creating new geometry.

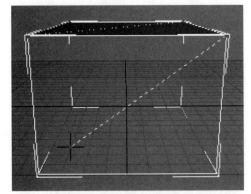

Figure 8.69 Click and drag from the first vertex counterclockwise to the second vertex.

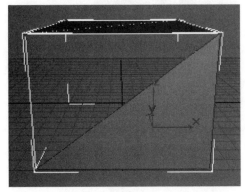

Figure 8.70 The new face appears on the front of the box.

The Create command gives you the ability to create new geometry from the ground up. With the Create command, you can create vertices, connect them with edges, and define faces and surfaces from scratch.

To create a face:

1. Select a mesh object that is missing some of its faces.

2. Open the Modify panel.

3. Convert the object to an editable mesh, or apply an Edit Mesh modifier to it.

4. Enable Face-level selection.

5. In the Edit Geometry rollout, click Create (**Figure 8.68**).

   The vertex points of the object appear.

6. Click one of the vertices that you want to use to build the face.

7. Move the cursor to the next vertex, proceeding counterclockwise.

   A "rubber-band line" stretches from the first point to the second (**Figure 8.69**).

8. Click the second vertex to set the second corner of the face.

9. Move the cursor to the final vertex, and click to anchor the last point of the face.

   The new face fills the hole in the mesh (**Figure 8.70**).

✔ Tips

- Click Auto Smooth in the Surface Properties rollout to smooth the face.

- Picking points in clockwise order builds a face whose normal points away from you.

- If a face does not appear when you build it, click Unify in the Surface Properties rollout to flip the face.

EDITING MESH OBJECTS

Editing Polymeshes

A **polymesh** is a close relative of the mesh object that has additional tools for selecting and editing sub-object components. Many familiar features—such as Extrude, Bevel, Tessellate, and Attach, to name a few—now have Settings dialogs that greatly improve workflow. Shrink, Grow, Ring, and Loop make sub-object selection quicker and more versatile. Tools such as Hinge From Edge, Extrude Along Spline, Remove [vertices], Connect, Inset, and others provide quick solutions to many common modeling tasks.

Polymesh Sub-Object Selection

Polymesh objects are made up of five types of sub-objects (**Figure 8.71**). Note that the face type is not included because faces are not individually selectable in polymeshes:

Vertex—A point location in space, defined by XYZ coordinates.

Edge—A straight line that connects two vertices.

Border—A closed sequence of edges that borders a hole.

Polygon—A closed sequence of three or more edges connected by a surface.

Element—A discrete set of contiguous polygons that share vertices with all of their neighbors.

As with mesh objects, you make polymesh sub-objects selectable by applying sub-object modifiers or by converting them to non-parametric objects called **editable polys**.

Converting a mesh to a polymesh creates borders from open edge sequences and joins faces into polygons. Invisible edges that triangulate the surface remain invisible by default.

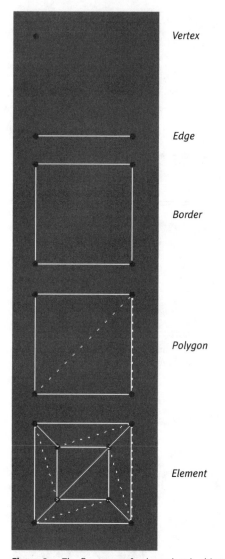

Figure 8.71 The five types of polymesh sub-objects.

EDITING POLYMESHES

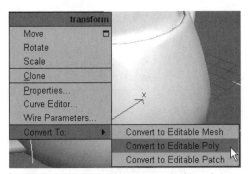

Figure 8.72 Convert an object to an editable poly in the Transform quad menu.

Figure 8.73 In the Modify panel, the editable poly replaces the original object type in the modifier stack.

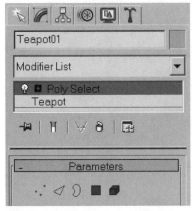

Figure 8.74 The Poly Select modifier is applied to the object.

To convert a mesh object to an editable poly:

1. Select a mesh object.

2. Right-click on the object.

3. In the Transform quad menu, roll the cursor over Convert To. Then choose Convert to Editable Poly from the pop-up menu (**Figure 8.72**).

   The object is converted to an editable poly (**Figure 8.73**). It is now selectable at a sub-object level.

✔ Tips

■ You can also convert a mesh object to an editable poly object by right-clicking on the name of the object in the modifier stack display and choosing Convert To: Editable Poly.

■ To control how faces are joined into polygons, and how many vertices they include, you use a Turn To Poly modifier. See the User Reference for more info.

The Poly Select modifier makes polymesh sub-objects selectable while preserving the object's creation parameters in case you want to adjust or animate them later.

To apply a Poly Select modifier:

1. Select an object.

2. Open the Modify panel.

3. Apply a Poly Select modifier from the Modifier list.

   The Poly Select modifier is applied to the object (**Figure 8.74**). The object is now selectable at the poly sub-object levels.

Vertex, edge, polygon, and element selection is the same for polymesh objects as it is for mesh objects. The only difference is that you have additional selection tools for manipulating selections and selecting borders.

To select a border sub-object:

1. Select an editable polygon or apply a Poly Select modifier to an object.

2. Optional: Enable Edged Faces or Wireframe viewport display.

3. Open the Modify panel.

4. In the stack display, click the plus (+) sign next to Editable Poly or Poly Select. Then choose Border from the drop-down list.

    or

    In the Selection rollout, click the Border sub-object button (**Figure 8.75**).

    or

    Right-click in a viewport and choose Border from the tools 1 quad menu.

    The border type becomes highlighted. Commands that can be applied at the border level become available below.

5. Ctrl + click or drag a selection region around the borders you want to select.

    The selected borders turn red (**Figure 8.76**).

✔ Tips

- Check Ignore Backfacing to prevent selection on the far side of a polymesh.

- Check By Vertex to select adjacent edges and faces when you click a vertex.

- You can import a selection from another sub-object level using the commands in the Get from Other Levels group of the Poly Select modifier.

Figure 8.75 Choosing Border level sub-object selection in the Modify panel.

Figure 8.76 The open edges of a teapot form borders that turn red when selected.

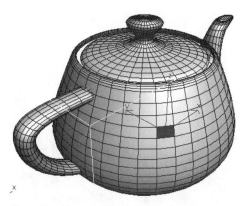

Figure 8.77 After selecting a single polygon.

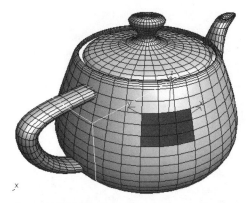

Figure 8.78 Clicking Grow expands the selection.

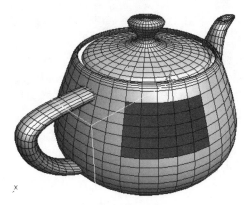

Figure 8.79 After clicking Grow a second time.

Shrink, Grow, Ring, and Loop are powerful tools for controlling sub-object selection.

Grow uniformly expands a sub-object selection to include its nearest neighbors.

Shrink has the opposite effect: It subtracts sub-objects at the boundaries of a selection.

To grow a selection:

1. Make a sub-object selection, such as a single polygon (**Figure 8.77**).

2. In the Selection rollout, click the Grow button.

   The selection expands to include adjacent sub-objects (**Figure 8.78**).

3. To further increase the selection, click the Grow button again (**Figure 8.79**).

   Sub-objects are added to the selection until an open edge is reached.

To shrink a selection:

1. Make a sub-object selection, like the one shown in **Figure 8.79**.

2. In the Selection rollout, click the Shrink button.

   The selected sub-objects along the outer edge of the selection become deselected, as in **Figure 8.78.**

3. To decrease the selection further, click the Shrink button again.

   Sub-objects are subtracted from the selection along its boundaries as in **Figure 8.77**. This continues as you click until they are all deselected.

✔ Tips

- The keyboard shortcut for Grow is Ctrl+Page Up. The keyboard shortcut for Shrink is Ctrl+Page Down.

- If there is more than one selection at any given sub-object level, all the selections will grow and shrink simultaneously.

POLYMESH SUB-OBJECT SELECTION

The Ring and Loop commands increase edge selection by selecting parallel edges.

Loop increases a selection of edges length-wise by propagating through four-way edge intersections or along open edges.

To loop a selection:

1. 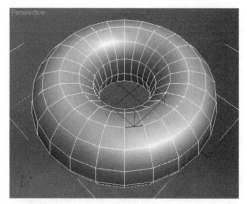 In a polymesh object, select an edge (**Figure 8.80**).

2. In the Selection rollout, click the Loop button (**Figure 8.81**).

   The selection expands lengthwise along the edge until the selection encircles the object or reaches an open edge (**Figure 8.82**).

✔ Tips

■ If there is more than one selection at any given sub-object level, the selections will all loop the object simultaneously.

■ The keyboard shortcut for selecting an edge loop is Alt + L.

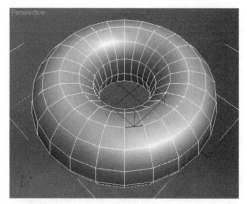

Figure 8.80 Selecting an edge in a torus that has been converted to a polymesh.

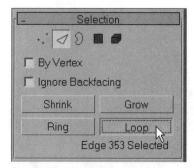

Figure 8.81 Click the Loop button.

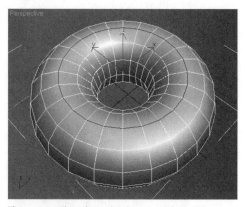

Figure 8.82 The edge selection expands until it makes a circle.

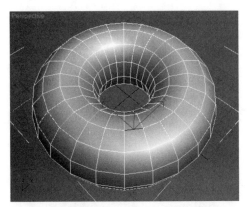

Figure 8.83 Selecting an edge in a torus that has been converted to a polymesh.

Figure 8.84 Click the Ring button.

Ring increases a selection of edges by adding parallel edges to the original selection.

To ring a selection:

1. In a polymesh object, select an edge or a border (**Figure 8.83**).

2. In the Selection rollout, click the Ring button (**Figure 8.84**).

   The selection expands to include all edges that are parallel to the current selection until the selection encircles the object or reaches an open edge (**Figure 8.85**).

✔ Tips

- If there is more than one selection at any given sub-object level, the selections will all ring the object simultaneously.

- The keyboard shortcut for selecting an edge ring is Alt + R.

- By applying both the Ring and the Loop commands, you can select all the parallel edges in an object (**Figure 8.86**).

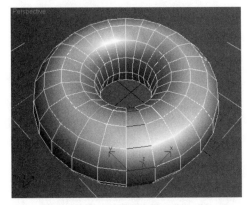

Figure 8.85 The edge selection expands until it surrounds the object.

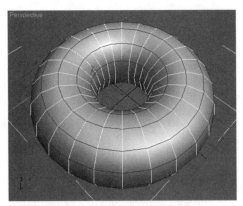

Figure 8.86 After selecting the ring of edges and then looping them. You get the same results by looping the edge selection and then ringing them.

POLYMESH SUB-OBJECT SELECTION

Editing Polymesh Objects

For polymesh editing, the commands in the Edit Geometry rollout apply to the object level and to all levels of sub-object selection. Most of the commands will be familiar from mesh editing: Create, Collapse, Attach, Detach, Slice Plane, Reset Plane, QuickSlice (an interactive variation on Slice Plane), Split, Cut, MeshSmooth, Tessellate, Make Planar, View Align, Grid Align, Hide Selected, Unhide All, Hide Unselected, and Named Selections Copy and Paste (same as Named Selection Sets for mesh sub-objects) (**Figure 8.87**). In addition, you are given three very handy global editing tools: Repeat Last repeats the last command, Constraints constrains sub-object transforms to other sub-objects, and a Full Interactivity option allows you adjust the feedback level of interactive tools. Show Cage is a display toggle that is specific to the Symmetry modifier.

Commands that are specific to each sub-object level appear in separate rollouts. Like the Edit Geometry commands, many will be familiar to you already. Other commands that are unique to polymesh editing or new to a corresponding sub-object level include:

Vertex: Remove, Extrude, Remove Unused Map Verts, Weight.

Edge: Remove, Insert Vertex, Connect, Weld, Target Weld, Create Shape From Selection, Weight, Crease, Edit Triangulation.

Border: Insert Vertex, Extrude, Chamfer, Cap, Connect, Create Shape From Selection, Weight, Crease.

Polygon: Insert Vertex, Outline, Inset, Retriangulate, Hinge From Edge, Extrude Along Spline, Edit Triangulation.

Element: Insert Vertex, Edit Triangulation, Retriangulate.

Table 8.2 shows the availability of editing commands at each sub-object level.

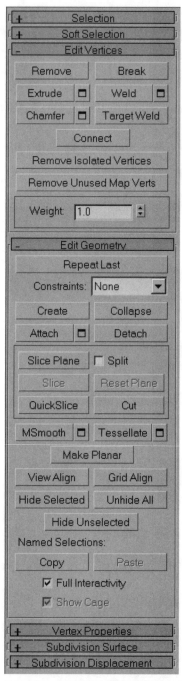

Figure 8.87 Polymesh editing tools include different rollouts for each level of sub-object selection. The tools in the Edit Geometry rollout, unlike mesh editing, apply to all levels of sub-object selection.

Table 8.2

Edit Poly Commands and the Levels They Affect

COMMAND	DIALOG	VERTEX	EDGE	BORDER	POLYGON	ELEMENT
Remove		✓	✓			
Insert Vertex			✓	✓	✓	✓
Extrude	✓	✓	✓	✓	✓	✓
Chamfer	✓	✓	✓	✓		
Bevel	✓				✓	✓
Outline	✓				✓	✓
Inset	✓				✓	✓
Flip					✓	✓
Split			✓			
Break		✓				
Weld		✓	✓			
Target Weld		✓	✓			
Cap				✓		
Connect	✓	✓	✓	✓		
Remove Isolated Vertices		✓				
Remove Unused Map Verts		✓				
Create Shape From Selection			✓	✓		
Weight		✓	✓	✓		
Crease			✓	✓		
Hinge From Edge	✓				✓	✓
Extrude Along Spline	✓				✓	✓
Retriangulate					✓	✓
Edit Triangulation			✓	✓	✓	✓

▫ indicates interactive command mode option with dialog box controls.

Note: Right-clicking cancels all interactive commands.

The Insert Vertex command places a vertex into an edge or polygon.

To insert a vertex into a polygon:

1. Enable polygon or element level selection.

2. Optional: Turn on the display of invisible edges in the Object Properties dialog box by clearing the Edges Only check box in the Display Properties area.

3. In the Edit Polygon or Edit Element rollout, click Insert Vertex (**Figure 8.88**).

4. Click on the surface of a polygon (**Figure 8.89**).

   The vertex is inserted under your cursor. The polygon subdivides into smaller polygons.

To insert a vertex into an edge:

1. Enable edge or border level selection.

2. In the Edit Edge or Edit Border rollout, click Insert Vertex.

3. Click on an edge.

   The vertex is inserted under your cursor. The edge subdivides into two edges and adjacent polygons are retriangulated (**Figure 8.90**).

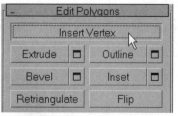

Figure 8.88 The Insert Vertex command is available at the Edge, Border, Polygon, and Element levels.

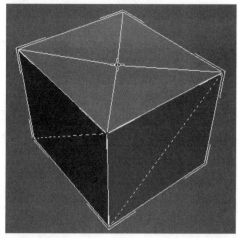

Figure 8.89 Inserting a vertex into a polygon on the top surface of a box. The top is now divided into four triangular-shaped polygons instead of a single quad.

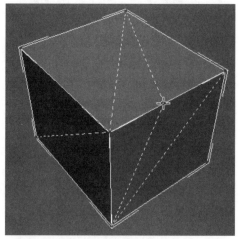

Figure 8.90 Inserting a vertex into an edge. The edge subdivides into two edges; the adjacent polygons are retriangulated but remain whole.

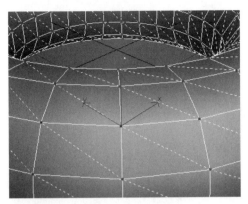

Figure 8.91 Selecting a vertex on a torus.

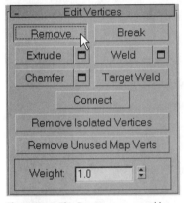

Figure 8.92 The Remove command is found at the vertex level (for removing vertices) and the edge level (for removing edges.)

The Remove command deletes a vertex and retriangulates the mesh to maintain surface continuity.

To remove a vertex:

1. Optional: Turn on the display of invisible edges in the Object Properties dialog box.

2. Select a vertex (**Figure 8.91**).

3. In the Edit Vertex rollout, click Remove (**Figure 8.92**).

   The vertex is removed from the surface of the polymesh. The polygons around it are redrawn to maintain the continuity of the polymesh surface (**Figure 8.93**).

   Compare this to pressing the Delete key to delete a vertex, which creates a hole (**Figure 8.94**).

✔ Tips

- The Remove command can also be used at the Edge level to remove an edge.

- The keyboard shortcut for removing a vertex is the Backspace key.

- Certain modeling operations can leave isolated map vertices that cannot be used for mapping. When these appear in the UVW Map editor, you use Remove Unused Map Verts to get rid of them.

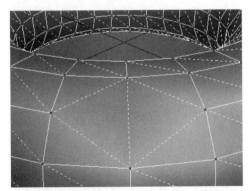

Figure 8.93 After removing the vertex, the program joins adjacent polygons and retriangulates them.

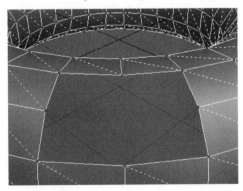

Figure 8.94 Pressing the Delete key also removes the vertex -- and the surrounding polygons with it.

When you manipulate a polymesh long enough, triangulation errors can appear in the surface. To correct them, you can use the Retriangulate command to make the program correct triangulation automatically. If this does not work to your satisfaction, Edit Retriangulation enables you to make your corrections manually.

To retriangulate a polymesh:

1. Select an object that has triangulation errors.

2. 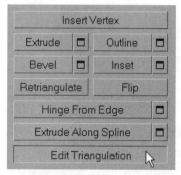 Enable polygon or element level selection.

3. In the Edit sub-object rollout, click Edit Retriangulation (**Figure 8.95**).

4. Click a vertex that needs to be retriangulated. Then move the cursor to the vertex you want to triangulate (connect) to (**Figure 8.96**).

5. Click the second vertex.

   The polymesh retriangulates (**Figure 8.97**).

Figure 8.95 The Edit Retriangulation command is available at the Edge, Border, Face, and Element levels.

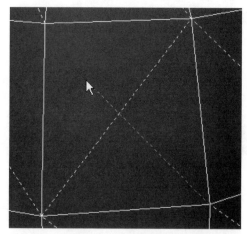

Figure 8.96 Click on a vertex you want to retriangulate. Then move and click on a second vertex.

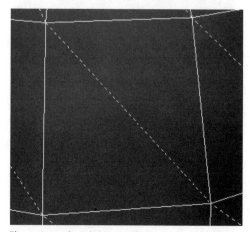

Figure 8.97 After clicking on the second vertex, the mesh retriangulates.

EDITING POLYMESH OBJECTS

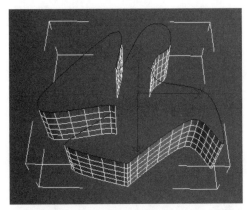

Figure 8.98 After selecting a border sub-object.

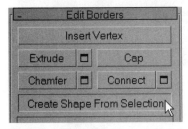

Figure 8.99 Click Create Shape From Selection.

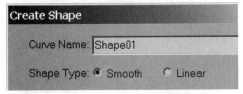

Figure 8.100 The Create Shape dialog box allows you to name the new shape, and determine its type.

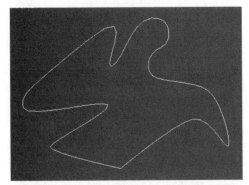

Figure 8.101 The new shape is an editable spline that you can use to begin a new modeling operation.

When you need to make an object that exactly fits another, Create Shape From Selection helps get you started.

To create a shape from a selection:

1. Make an edge or border selection (**Figure 8.98**).

2. In the Edit Edge or Edit Border rollout, click Create Shape From Selection (**Figure 8.99**).

   The Create Shape dialog box appears (**Figure 8.100**).

3. In the Create Shape dialog box, enter a name for the new shape object. Then choose a shape type. Smooth produces smoothly curved segments made from Bézier vertices. Linear produces angular segments made from corner vertices. Then click OK.

   An editable spline is created. To see it, press H on your keyboard. Then use the Select Object dialog box and the move tool to select the shape and move it away from the original object (**Figure 8.101**).

✔ Tip

- Use the border level Cap command to close holes and eliminate open edges. Like the Cap Holes modifier, the Cap command can be invaluable for fixing broken meshes and preparing a mesh for Boolean operations.

EDITING POLYMESH OBJECTS

Using the edit command mode settings, you can interactively perform critical modeling tasks with greater confidence and precision.

The Outline command proportionally scales a polygon up or down, just like the Bevel mesh editing command.

To outline a polygon:

1. Select a polygon (**Figure 8.102**).

2. In the Edit Polygon rollout, click the Outline Settings button, which is just to the right of the Outline button.
The Outline Polygons dialog box appears (**Figure 8.103**).

3. In the Outline Polygons dialog box, drag the Outline Amount spinner to set the amount of scaling.
The polygon is scaled (**Figure 8.104**).

4. To make another Outline without closing the settings dialog box, click Apply and repeat step 3. Otherwise, click OK to complete the Outline command.

✔ Tips

- The Inset command duplicates a polygon and proportionally scales it down, so that it nests inside the original polygon (**Figure 8.105**).

- You can switch between settings dialog boxes without closing them by clicking their respective settings buttons.

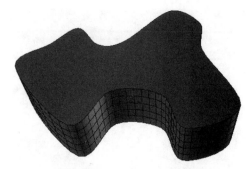

Figure 8.102 Selecting the polygon that forms the top plane of this object.

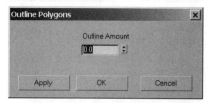

Figure 8.103 The Outline Polygons dialog box allows you to set the scale amount of a selected polygon.

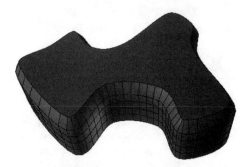

Figure 8.104 The polygon is scaled down.

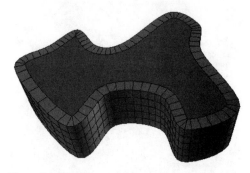

Figure 8.105 Insetting a polygon preserves the original outline and creates a scaled-down duplicate.

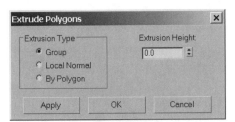

Figure 8.106 The Extrude Polygons dialog box has settings for height and extrusion type.

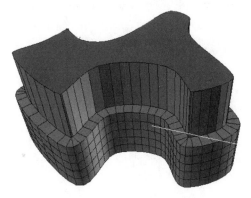

Figure 8.107 After extruding the inset polygon.

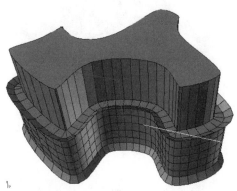

Figure 8.108 After extruding the outer edges of the original object.

Figure 8.109 From left to right: Extruding the same selection by Group, by Local Normal, and by Polygon.

The Extrude command is available at the vertex, edge, border, and polygon levels.

To extrude a polygon:

1. Select a polygon, such as the inset polygon in Figure 8.110.

2. In the Edit Polygon rollout, click the Extrude Settings button.

   The Extrude Polygons dialog box appears (**Figure 8.106**).

3. In the Extrude Polygons dialog box, drag the Extrusion Height spinner to set the height of the extrusion.

   The polygon is extruded (**Figure 8.107**).

4. To make another Extrusion without closing the settings dialog box, click Apply and repeat step 3. Otherwise, click OK to complete the extrusion.

✔ Tips

- Unlike mesh editing, the polymesh Extrusion command allows you extrude vertices and borders. Extruding a vertex creates pyramid-shaped extrusions. Extruding edges or borders rims them with a new layer of polygons (**Figure 8.108**).

  The keyboard shortcut for Extrude mode is Shift+E.

- If you are extruding a multiple selection of polygons, you can extrude them:

  By Group (the average direction of the selected polygon's normals)

  By Local Normal (each in the direction of its individual normal and scaled to create a continuous surface) or

  By Polygon (also by individual normal but without scaling up the polygons so that each one is extruded separately) (**Figure 8.109**).

EDITING POLYMESH OBJECTS

271

The Bevel command combines extrusion with Outline-type scaling to give you the convenience of two commands in one.

To bevel a polygon:

1. Select a polygon (**Figure 8.110**).

2. In the Edit Polygon rollout, click the Bevel Settings button.

   The Bevel Polygons dialog box appears (**Figure 8.111**).

3. In the Bevel Polygons dialog box, drag the Height spinner to set the height of the extrusion.

   The polygon is extruded (**Figure 8.112**).

4. Drag the Outline spinner to scale the polygon.

   The polygon is scaled, creating a beveled form (**Figure 8.113**).

5. To make another bevel without closing the settings dialog box, click Apply and repeat step 3. Otherwise, click OK to complete the bevel operation.

6. To bevel a multiple selection of polygons, choose a bevel type in the Bevel Type area of the Bevel Polygons dialog box. (See "To extrude a polygon" on the previous page for a description of these parameters.)

✔ Tip

■ The keyboard shortcut for Bevel mode is Shift+Ctl+B.

Figure 8.110 Selecting the central polygon of a plane.

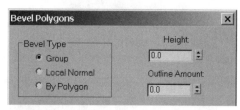

Figure 8.111 The Bevel Polygons dialog box has inputs for both height and outline amount.

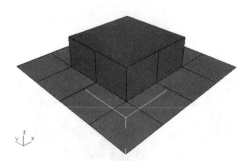

Figure 8.112 After extruding the polygon by setting the height of the bevel.

Figure 8.113 After scaling the polygon by setting the outline amount to complete the bevel operation.

Figure 8.114 Selecting the central polygon of a plane.

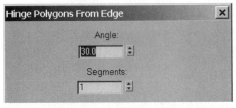

Figure 8.115 The Hinge Polygons From Edge dialog box has settings for the hinge angle and number of segments.

Figure 8.116 After extruding the polygon by setting the height of the bevel.

Figure 8.117 After scaling the polygon by setting the outline amount to complete the bevel operation.

The Hinge From Edge command combines a polygon extrusion with a rotation.

To hinge a polygon from an edge:

1. Select a polygon (**Figure 8.114**).

2. In the Edit Polygon rollout, click the Hinge From Edge Settings button.

   The Hinge From Edge dialog box appears (**Figure 8.115**).

3. In the Hinge From Edge dialog box, click the Pick Hinge button. Then click on one of the outside edges of the polygon. This will be the hinge.

4. Drag the Amount spinner up or down.

   The polygon rotates outward or inward using the hinge edge as the axis of rotation (**Figure 8.116**).

5. To make sides of the extrusion curve, increase the number of segments (**Figure 8.117**).

Extrude Along Spline gives you all the bells and whistles: polygon extrusion, rotation, tapering, twisting, and an extrusion path.

To extrude a polygon along a spline:

1. Select a polygon (**Figure 8.118**).

2. In the Edit Polygon rollout, click the Extrude Along Spline Settings button.

   The Extrude Polygons Along Spline dialog box appears (**Figure 8.119**).

3. In the Extrude Polygons Along Spline dialog box, click Pick Spline. Then click a spline.

   The polygon is extruded along the spline. Its initial appearance may be very rough, due to the low default segments value.

4. Increase the number of segments until the extrusion deforms as smoothly as needed. Then adjust the angle of extrusion. Check Align to Face Normal if you want the base of the extrusion to project from the object at a 90° angle. To rotate the extrusion in a different direction, drag the Rotation spinner.

5. Use the Taper Amount, Taper Curve, and Twist spinners to adjust the amount of tapering, convexity, concavity, or twist of the extrusion. Increase the number of segments as needed (**Figure 8.120**).

6. To extrude other polygons using the same settings, Ctrl+Click on them.

   The polygons extrude simultaneously (**Figure 8.121**).

✔ Tip

- Lofting is a powerful modeling tool that projects a shape of any form along the path of another shape. For more information, see Chapter 10, "Compound Objects."

Figure 8.118 The initial polygon and spline.

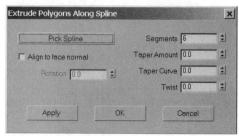

Figure 8.119 The Extrude Polygons Along Spline dialog box gives you multiple ways to customize an extrusion.

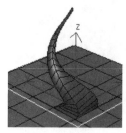

Figure 8.120 After extruding, rotating, tapering, curving, and twisting the polygon.

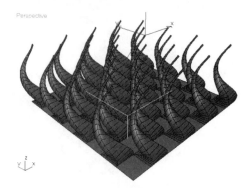

Figure 8.121 Extruding every other polygon on the plane creates a hairlike group of creepy tentacles.

EDITING SHAPES

Figure 9.1 Shapes were used to create the profiles of the apple, stem, seed, and core.

Shapes are primarily used as the source objects for 3D geometry, including flying logos for television, low-polygon models for 3D games, architectural and mechanical models, and morph targets for morph animation. They are also used as motion paths for animation and distribution paths for placing objects in a scene (**Figure 9.1**).

To fine-tune a shape, you apply transforms, modifiers, or edit commands to a sub-object selection. Transforms are mostly used for adjusting the curvature of a shape, although they can come in handy for arranging sub-objects within a shape. Modifiers are rarely applied at the sub-object level; more often they are applied at the object level after shapes have been edited.

Shape Sub-Objects

Shapes have three types of sub-objects that you can edit (**Figure 9.2**):

 Vertex–A point location in space, defined by XYZ coordinates.

 Segment–A straight or curved line that connects two vertices.

 Spline–A set of vertices and segments that connect them.

Sub-Object Selection

You edit shapes by applying transforms, modifiers, or edit commands to a sub-object selection. To make shape sub-objects selectable, you apply a spline sub-object modifier to the shape, or you convert it to an **editable spline.**

Converting a shape object to an **editable spline** preserves the object in its current state by changing it from a parametric object to an explicit description of sub-object components (**Figure 9.3**). Creation parameters and any modifiers that have been applied to the object are discarded.

(Note: Editable splines are really editable shapes, rather than a new object type. The same goes for the Edit Spline modifier; it is really a shape modifier and cannot be applied to any other type of object.)

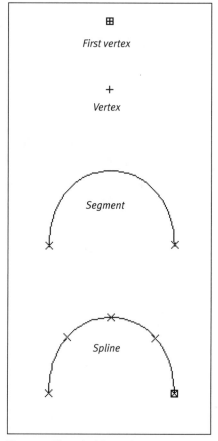

Figure 9.2 The sub-objects of a shape.

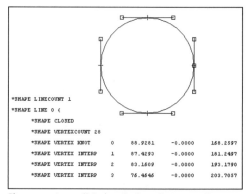

Figure 9.3 An explicit description of a teapot. Note the coordinate locations of the vertices and their face grouping sequences.

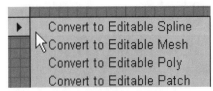

Figure 9.4 Converting an object to an editable spline in the transform quad menu.

Figure 9.5 In the Modify panel, the editable spline appears in the modifier stack display, replacing the original object type.

As with mesh objects, the method that you use to make a shape sub-object selectable depends on what you intend to do with it. If you need an object that has as little memory overhead as possible, you convert it to an editable spline. If you will need to adjust or animate its creation parameters, you apply a Spline Select or Edit Spline modifier.

Applying an Edit Spline modifier or converting an object to an editable spline allows you to apply modifiers, transforms, or built-in editing commands to sub-object selections.

Select modifiers only allow you to apply modifiers to the sub-object selection. Their purpose is to pass sub-object selection data up the modifier stack and preserve the selection for future rounds of editing.

To convert a shape object to an editable spline:

1. Select a shape object.

2. Right-click on the object.

3. In the Transform quad menu, roll the cursor over Convert To. Then choose Convert to Editable Spline from the pop-up menu (**Figure 9.4**).

   The object is converted to an editable spline (**Figure 9.5**).

✔ Tip

- You can also convert shape objects by right-clicking on the name of the object in the modifier stack display and choosing Convert To: Editable Spline.

The Spline Select and Edit Spline modifiers allow you to select shape sub-objects and preserve parameters at the same time.

Applying a Volume Select modifier converts a shape to a mesh object, so you cannot use it for editing shapes.

To apply a shape sub-object modifier:

1. Select an object.

2. Open the Modify panel.

3. Apply a Spline Select or Edit Spline modifier (**Figure 9.6**).

    The shape sub-object modifier is applied to the object (**Figure 9.7**).

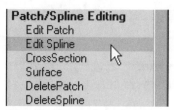

Figure 9.6 Choose a Select or Edit modifier from the Modifier drop-down list.

Figure 9.7 The modifier appears above the object in the stack display. Its parameters appear in the area below.

SHAPE SUB-OBJECTS

St. Basil's Cathedral
Karl Raade, 2001

Image courtesy of Karl Raade
karl@lucaslearning.com

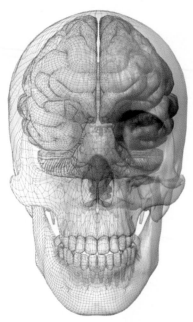

Brain and Skull
Darin Hakes, 1999
Image courtesy of Viewpoint Corporation
darin.hakes@viewpoint.com

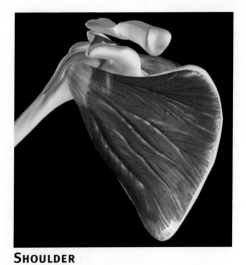

Shoulder
Michele Matossian, 1998
Image courtesy of UCSF School of Medicine, Department of Radiology
3d@lightweaver.com

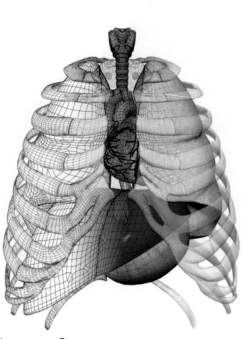

Internal Organs
Darin Hakes, 1999
Image courtesy of Viewpoint Corporation
darin.hakes@viewpoint.com

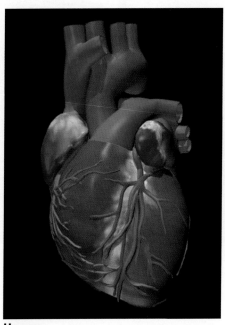

Heart
Sean Curtis, 1998
Image courtesy of Viewpoint Digital
sean.curtis@viewpoint.com

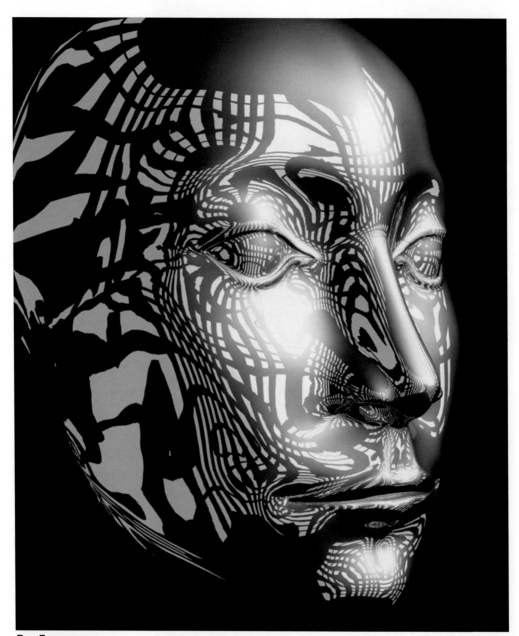

RAYFLECTION
Bradford Stuart, 1999

Image courtesy of Autodesk, Inc.
brad.stuart@autodesk.com

MAY THE BLESSINGS BE
Clark Heist, 1998

Image courtesy of Clark Heist
clark.heist@autodesk.com

GOD IS GREAT. GOD IS GOOD.
Clark Heist, 1998

TAJ MAHAL Michele Matossian, 1997

CHRISTMAS TREE Grant Heath, 1998

Image courtesy of Grant Heath *grant.heath@viewpoint.com*

CADACEUS Michele Matossian, 2002

PRAIRIE Bob Prokopp, 1997

APPLES AND CHEESE Michele Matossian, 2001

CLOUDBANK Michele Matossian, 2004

THE U.S.S. JOHN SHAFT Karl Raade, 1997

SCI-FI CHAIN REACTION Blur Studio, 1999

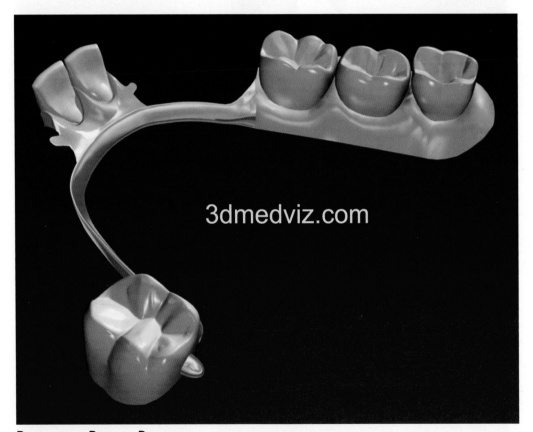

REMOVABLE PARTIAL DENTURE
Michele Matossian, 2002

ADOBE HOUSE   Michele Matossian, 2004

FOR THE CAUSE Blur Studio, 1999

HARLEY
Darin Hakes, 1999
Image courtesy of Viewpoint Corporation
darin.hakes@viewpoint.com

REPAIR SHOP
Darin Hakes, 2000
Image courtesy of Viewpoint Corporation
darin.hakes@viewpoint.com

GUNFIGHT FANTASY
Colby Acree, 2001
Image courtesy of Viewpoint Corporation.
colby.acree@viewpoint.com

CHAMELEON Jared Trulock, 1998

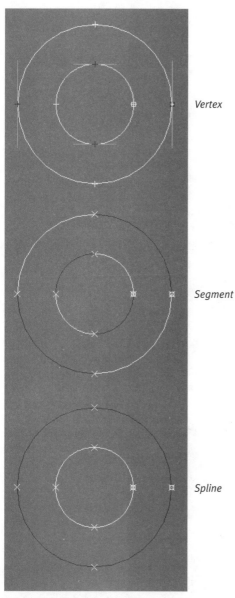

Vertex

Segment

Spline

Figure 9.8 Sub-object selections created at each of the three levels of selection.

Once you convert an object to an editable spline, or apply a spline sub-object modifier to it, you can make a sub-object selection (**Figure 9.8**). Different selections can exist simultaneously at each sub-object level.

Methods of sub-object selection include:

◆ Clicking

◆ Dragging a selection region

◆ Choosing a named selection set that you created from a previous selection of that sub-object type

As with object selection, you can:

◆ Add to a sub-object selection by holding down the Ctrl key

◆ Subtract from a selection by holding down the Alt key

◆   Lock and unlock sub-object selections

◆ Invert sub-object selections

However, most of the time you will only need to select one vertex at a time.

As with mesh object selection, you can:

◆ Cycle through sub-object selection levels by pressing the Insert key

◆ Import a selection from another level using the Spline Select modifier

Sub-object selection can be performed only when the Modify panel is open and a level of sub-object selection is chosen. When you are in a sub-object selection mode, object selection in the viewport is disabled.

SHAPE SUB-OBJECTS

To make a vertex selection:

1. 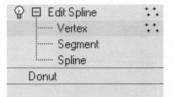 Select a shape.

2. Open the Modify panel.

3. Convert the shape to an editable spline or apply an Edit Spline modifier to it.

4. In the stack display, click the plus (+) sign next to the Edit Spline modifier or the editable spline. Then choose Vertex from the drop-down list (**Figure 9.9**).

   or

   Click the Vertex button in the Selection rollout.

   or

   Right-click in a viewport and choose Vertex from the tools1 quad menu.

   The vertex type becomes highlighted. Commands that can be applied at that level become available below.

   In the viewports, vertex ticks appear as "+" shapes along the spline. The first vertex is marked by a square.

5. Click or drag a selection region around the vertex you want to select (**Figure 9.10**).

   The vertices turn red, indicating that they are selected. If you selected a Bézier vertex, Bézier handles appear (**Figure 9.11**).

✔ Tips

- To cycle through sub-object selection levels, press the Insert key.

- Every vertex is numbered from first to last as an alignment aid for lofting. To display vertex numbers, check Show Vertex Numbers in the Display area of the Selection rollout.

Figure 9.9 Enabling vertex-level selection in the stack display.

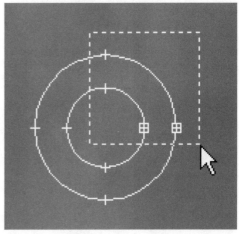

Figure 9.10 Dragging a selection region around some vertices in a donut.

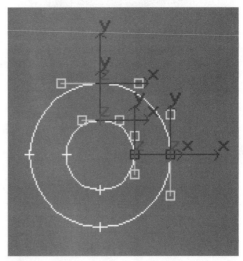

Figure 9.11 The vertices turn red and sprout Bézier handles.

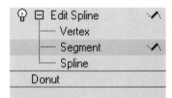

Figure 9.12 Enabling segment-level selection in the stack display.

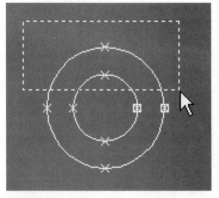

Figure 9.13 Dragging a selection region around segments in a donut.

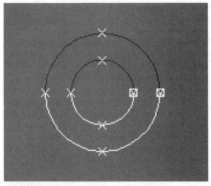

Figure 9.14 The selected segments turn red.

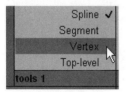

Figure 9.15 Choosing a selection level in the Tools 1 quad menu.

To make a segment selection:

1. Select a shape.

2. Open the Modify panel.

3. Convert the shape to an editable spline or apply an Edit Spline modifier to it.

4. In the stack display, click the plus (+) sign next to the Edit Spline modifier or the editable spline. Then choose Segment from the drop-down list (**Figure 9.12**).

   or

   Click the Segment button in the Selection rollout.

   or

   Right-click in a viewport and choose Segment from the tools1 quad menu.

   The segment type becomes highlighted. Commands that can be applied at that level become available below.

   In the viewports, vertices turn into "X"s. The first vertex is marked by a square.

5. Click or drag a selection region around the segments you want to select (**Figure 9.13**).

   The segments turns red, indicating that they are selected (**Figure 9.14**).

✔ Tip

- You can also choose shape sub-object selection levels from the Tools 1 quad menu (**Figure 9.15**).

SHAPE SUB-OBJECTS

To make a spline selection:

1. Select a shape.

2. Open the Modify panel.

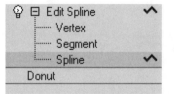

Figure 9.16 Enabling spline-level selection in the stack display.

3. Convert the shape to an editable spline, or apply an Edit Spline modifier to it.

4. In the stack display, click the plus (+) sign next to the Edit Spline modifier or the editable spline. Then choose Spline from the drop-down list (**Figure 9.16**).

   or

   Click the Spline button in the Selection rollout.

   or

   Right-click in a viewport and choose Spline from the tools1 quad menu.

   The spline type becomes highlighted. Commands that can be applied at that level become available below.

   In the viewports, vertices appear as "X"s. The first vertex is marked by a square.

5. Click or drag a selection region around the spline you want to select (**Figure 9.17**).

   The spline turns red, indicating that it is selected (**Figure 9.18**).

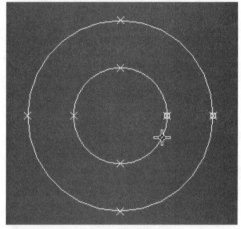

Figure 9.17 Clicking a spline in a donut.

✔ Tips

- In the Select Segment rollout of the Spline Select modifier, Get Vertex Selection, Get Segment Selection, and Get Spline Selection create a selection based on adjacent sub-objects that are selected on other levels.

- To access spline sub-object selection mode from the keyboard, press Ctrl + B.

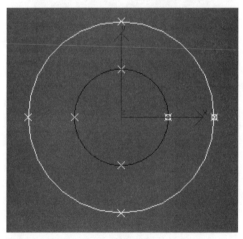

Figure 9.18 The selected spline turns red.

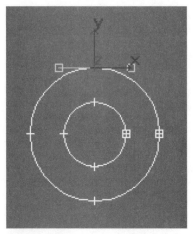

Figure 9.19 The vertex at the top of the donut is selected.

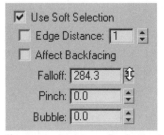

Figure 9.20 Applying soft selection to adjacent vertices.

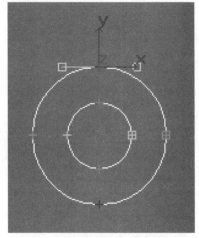

Figure 9.21 The soft selected change color to indicate the intensity of selection.

You can soft select spline sub-objects with an Edit Spline modifier, or within an editable spline, in order to control the affect of edit commands. Soft selection is not passed up the modifier stack and is not available with Spline Select.

To see an example of soft selection in action, see "To adjust the curvature of a shape" in the next section.

To make a soft selection:

1. Make a vertex-level sub-object selection with an Edit Spline modifier or within an editable spline (**Figure 9.19**).

2. Open the Soft Selection rollout.

3. Check Use Soft Selection. Then drag the Falloff spinner to adjust the degree of selection (**Figure 9.20**).

    The sub-objects in range of the soft selection change colors from red to orange to yellow to blue as you increase the falloff value. Red indicates the hottest selection where commands will be applied at full intensity; blue indicates the coolest selection where the effect of commands will diminish (**Figure 9.21**).

4. If you want to change the falloff pattern, apply Pinch and Bubble to the selection.

Adjusting Curvature

The manipulation of shapes, and splines in general, is all about controlling curvature. Curvature controls are a property of vertices that control the curvature of neighboring segments. Because segments cannot bend more than 2° between steps, the number of steps in each segment governs the smoothness of its curve.

You adjust the curvature of segments by moving vertices, moving vertex controls, or converting to different vertex types:

◆ **Corner types** produce straight line segments that protrude at any angle on either side of the vertex.

◆ **Smooth types** produce gradually sloping curves and have no controls that you can adjust.

◆ **Bézier types** have two control handles that can be dragged to affect each adjacent segment.

◆ **Bézier Corner types** have two control handles that can be dragged independently. Use this type to create sharp corners and curved segments.

For an illustration of each vertex type, see **Figure 9.22**.

Usually, the easiest way to adjust Bézier controls is by dragging them with the Move tool. You can also rotate and scale Bézier controls, but you can accomplish the same effect using the Move tool, and with better control. Rotating and scaling Smooth and Corner vertices has no effect.

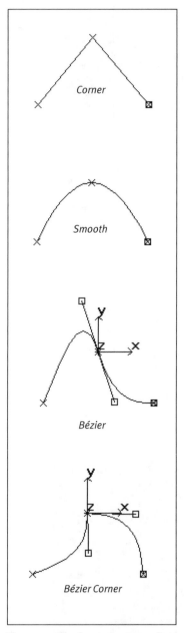

Figure 9.22 The four vertex types allow you to control the curvature of a spline.

ADJUSTING CURVATURE

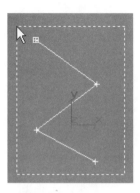

Figure 9.23 Selecting all the vertices in a jagged line.

Figure 9.24 Choose a vertex type in the Tools 1 quad menu.

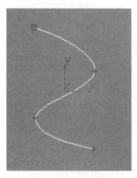

Figure 9.25 After converting the vertices to the Smooth type.

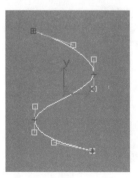

Figure 9.26 Bézier handles will now allow you to adjust the curve.

Converting a vertex changes its type. This produces different options for curving adjacent segments or making them straight.

To convert a vertex:

1. Select the line.

2. Open the Modify panel.

3. Enable Vertex level selection.

4. Click on the vertex you want to convert. To convert multiple vertices at once, drag a selection region around them (**Figure 9.23**).

5. Right-click on a selected vertex.

6. In the Tools 1 quad menu, choose a vertex type from Corner, Smooth, Bézier, or Bézier Corner.

   To produce the most evenly rounded curves, choose Smooth (**Figure 9.24**).

   The vertices convert to the new type, and the segments adjacent to the vertex adjust accordingly (**Figure 9.25**).

✔ Tip

■ To produce smooth, adjustable curves, convert vertices to the Smooth type before converting them a second time to Bézier (**Figure 9.26**).

   If the handles are too close to the vertex to select easily, convert the vertex to smooth type, and then convert it back to Bézier.

ADJUSTING CURVATURE

285

You adjust the curvature of a shape by adjusting vertices along its path.

To adjust the curvature of a shape:

1. Select a shape with the Move tool.

2. Open the Modify panel.

3. Enable Vertex-level selection.

4. Convert the shape to an editable spline or apply an Edit Spline modifier to it.

5. Select a vertex that is adjacent to the segments you want to adjust (**Figure 9.27**).

6. Optional: Soft select the vertex by increasing the selection falloff.

7. Move the vertex.

   The adjacent segments scale and bend as you move the vertex (**Figure 9.28**).

   If you applied soft selection to the adjacent vertices, they will deform as well (**Figure 9.29**).

8. To adjust curvature with more precision, convert the vertex to a Bézier or Bézier Corner vertex. Then move the Bézier control handles toward, away from, or around the vertex.

   The curvature of the segments adjacent to the vertex adjust (**Figure 9.30**).

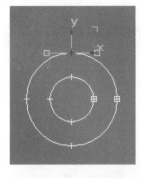

Figure 9.27 After selecting the vertex.

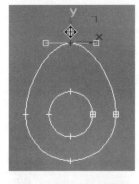

Figure 9.28 Moving the vertex affects the adjacent segments.

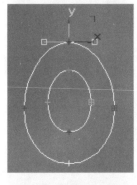

Figure 9.29 Soft selection spreads the effect of the deformation.

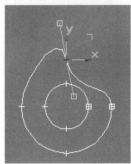

Figure 9.30 Dragging Bézier handles gives you precise control over curvature.

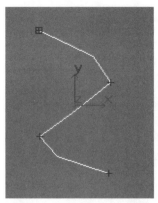

Figure 9.31 Selecting a line that has only one step between vertices.

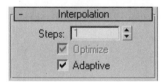

Figure 9.32 After checking Adaptive, the Steps and Optimize parameters become unavailable.

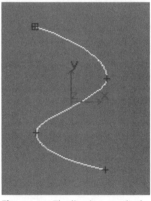

Figure 9.33 The line is smoothed as a result of adding more steps in between the vertices.

You smooth a curve at the shape level by increasing the number of steps between vertices. By checking Adaptive, you can increase the number of steps in such a way that they are distributed more liberally along tighter curves.

To smooth a shape:

1. Select a shape (**Figure 9.31**).

2. In the Modify panel, open the Interpolation rollout of the shape.

3. Increase the number of steps.

   or

   Check Adaptive (**Figure 9.32**).
   The shape becomes smoother (**Figure 9.33**).

✔ Tip

- Checking Adaptive disables the Optimize and Steps parameters, and introduces a lot of steps. If you are planning to extrude or lathe a shape, it is probably better not to use Adaptive because the resulting mesh will be more complex than needed. (Lofts have their own Optimize and Adaptive controls, so they are not affected by the complexity of the shapes that generate them.)

ADJUSTING CURVATURE

Editing Shapes

Shape objects can be edited at the vertex, segment, spline, and object levels. When you choose a selection level, the editing commands for that level become available in the Modify panel (**Figure 9.34**). You can also access spline editing commands from the Tools 2 quad menus.

Object-editing commands act upon the entire shape. They attach shapes, create lines, and insert vertices. The object level is the only level that allows you to attach multiple objects from a list.

The Attach, Attach Multiple, Create Line, Insert, Hide, Unhide All, and Delete commands can be used at every sub-object level. In addition, the following commands are specific to certain levels:

Vertex-specific commands are the most abundant. They include Break, Refine, Weld, Connect, Make First, Fuse, Cycle, Cross Insert, Fillet, Chamfer, Bind, and Unbind.

Segment-specific commands are the fewest in number. They include Break, Refine, Divide, and Detach.

Spline-specific commands are similar to element commands in that they affect discrete shapes within a spline. They include Reverse, Outline, Boolean, Mirror, Trim, Extend, Close, Detach, and Explode.

Table 9.1 shows the availability of editing commands at each sub-object level.

Figure 9.34 The Geometry rollout for Edit Spline and editable splines.

Table 9.1

Spline-Editing Commands and the Levels They Affect

COMMAND	VERTEX	SEGMENT	SPLINE	OBJECT
Create Line	✓	✓	✓	✓
Break	✓	✓		
Attach	✓	✓	✓	✓
Attach Multiple	✓	✓	✓	✓
Refine	✓	✓		
End Point Auto-Welding	✓	✓	✓	✓
Weld	✓			
Connect	✓	✓		
Insert	✓	✓	✓	
Make First	✓			
Fuse			✓	
Reverse	✓			
Cycle	✓			
CrossInsert	✓			
Fillet	✓			
Chamfer	✓			
Outline			✓	
Boolean			✓	
Mirror			✓	
Trim			✓	
Extend			✓	
Hide	✓	✓	✓	
Unhide All	✓	✓	✓	
Bind	✓			
Unbind	✓			
Delete	✓	✓	✓	
Close	✓		✓	
Divide	✓	✓		
Detach		✓	✓	
Explode			✓	

SPLINE-EDITING COMMANDS

End Point Auto-Welding is available at all levels.

To attach a shape:

1. 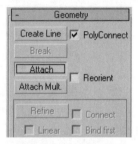 Select a shape (**Figure 9.35**).

2. Open the Modify panel.

3. Convert the shape to an editable spline or apply an Edit Spline modifier to it.

4. In the Geometry rollout, click Attach (**Figure 9.36**).

5. Click the shape you want to attach (**Figure 9.37**).

   The second shape is attached to the first.

6. Continue clicking shapes to attach them, or click Attach to end attach mode.

✔ Tips

- Clicking Attach Mult. brings up a list of attachable shape objects so that you can attach multiple shapes at one time.

- To attach shapes as you create them, uncheck the Start New Shape checkbox on the Shape creation menu (**Figure 9.38**).

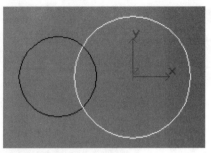

Figure 9.35 Select a shape object.

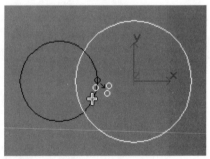

Figure 9.36 Click Attach in order to add another shape to the object.

Figure 9.37 Click a second shape to attach it to the first.

Figure 9.38 Unchecking Start New Shape allows you to attach shapes as you create them.

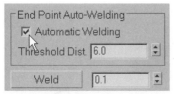

Figure 9.39 Enable automatic welding.

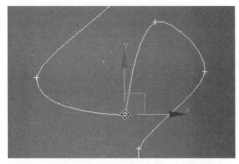

Figure 9.40 Move one end point on top of another.

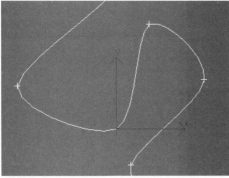

Figure 9.41 After welding the vertices into one, the spline smoothes across the weld.

Welding joins the end points of attached splines into a single vertex. You can use it for modeling, connecting motion paths, or cleaning up 2D drawings that are imported from CAD programs.

To weld vertices:

1. Select a shape.

2. Open the Modify panel.

3. Convert the shape to an editable spline, or apply an Edit Spline modifier to it.

4. Enable Vertex-level selection.

5. In the End Point Auto-Welding area of the Geometry rollout, enable Automatic Welding (**Figure 9.39**).

6. Move one of the end points onto the other so that they coincide (**Figure 9.40**).
   The vertices weld and become one vertex (**Figure 9.41**).

✔ Tips

■ You can also use the Weld command to set a weld threshold and weld selected vertices.

■ A quick way to tell if coincident vertices in a spline are welded is to click Show Vertex Numbers in the Selection rollout and see if there is only one number at the vertex.

■ The Fuse command brings vertices together without welding them.

The Break command cuts a spline apart at a vertex point.

To break a spline:

1. 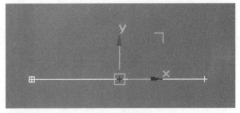 Select a shape.

2. Open the Modify panel.

3. Convert the shape to an editable spline, or apply an Edit Spline modifier to it.

4. Enable Vertex-level selection.

5. Select a vertex where you want to break a spline (**Figure 9.42**).

6. In the Geometry rollout, click Break.

   The vertex is cloned and converted to a first vertex. You can now move the vertex apart from its clone (**Figure 9.43**).

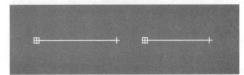

Figure 9.42 Select a vertex to break.

Figure 9.43 After you break a spline, you can separate the cloned vertices.

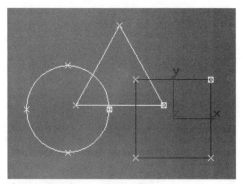

Figure 9.44 Select a spline.

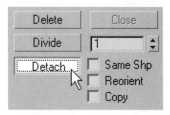

Figure 9.45 Click Detach to separate a sub-object selection.

The Detach command reverses the Attach command by detaching segments or splines into separate shapes.

To detach a spline:

1. Select a shape.

2. Open the Modify panel.

3. Convert the shape to an editable spline, or apply an Edit Spline modifier to it.

4. Enable Spline-level selection.

5. Select the spline you want to detach (**Figure 9.44**).

6. In the Geometry rollout, click Detach (**Figure 9.45**).

7. Click OK to accept the default name for the detached shape.

   The spline is detached to a new shape.

✔ Tips

- You use the same procedure at the segment level to detach a segment.

- Explode is a fast way to detach segments or splines all at once. You can explode to detached shapes or to attached splines. Explode only works at the spline level.

EDITING SHAPES

Connect builds a straight line segment between two end points of a spline, regardless of the tangent values of the vertices that connect.

To connect two vertices:

1. 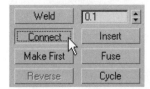 Select a shape.

2. Open the Modify panel.

3. Convert the shape to an editable spline, or apply an Edit Spline modifier to it.

4. Enable Vertex-level selection.

5. Select an end vertex (**Figure 9.46**).

6. In the Geometry rollout, click Connect (**Figure 9.47**).

7. Drag the mouse cursor from the selected vertex to another end vertex (**Figure 9.48**).

   The vertices are connected by a segment (**Figure 9.49**).

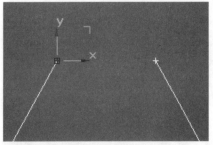

Figure 9.46 Select an end vertex to connect.

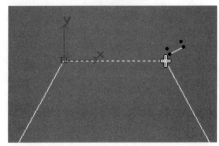

Figure 9.47 Click Connect.

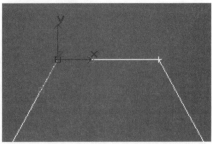

Figure 9.48 Drag a connection from the first end vertex to the next.

Figure 9.49 After connecting the two vertices, a straight segment is drawn between them.

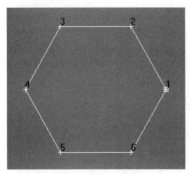

Figure 9.50 The first vertex of the NGon is on the right.

Figure 9.51 Use Make First to reorder the vertices.

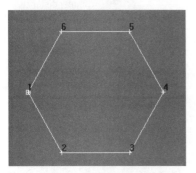

Figure 9.52 Now the first vertex of the NGon is on the left. The numbering still proceeds counterclockwise.

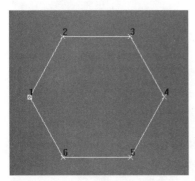

Figure 9.53 After using the Reverse command, the numbering proceeds clockwise.

Every shape has a first vertex at one end, or in the middle if it is a closed shape. The first vertex is important for determining the beginning of a motion path or a loft path.

The Make First feature allows you to choose which vertex of a shape is first.

To set a first vertex:

1. Select a shape.

2. Open the Modify panel.

3. Convert the object to an editable spline, or apply an Edit Spline modifier to it.

4. Enable Vertex-level selection.

5. In the Selection rollout, click Check Show Vertex Numbers.

   Vertex numbers appear by each vertex, numbering the vertices in order from beginning to end. The first vertex has a square around it (**Figure 9.50**).

6. Select a vertex at the end of an open spline, or anywhere on a closed spline.

7. Click Make First in the Geometry rollout (**Figure 9.51**).

   The selected vertex becomes the first vertex (**Figure 9.52**).

✔ Tips

- Clicking the Cycle button advances a vertex selection to the next vertex in a spline. If the shape contains more than one spline, the selection will cycle from one spline to the next and then back to the beginning.

- The Reverse command reverses the direction, or vertex order, of a single spline. The Reverse command is available only at the Spline selection level (**Figure 9.53**).

Chamfer splits a vertex into two vertices and spreads them apart evenly. If the vertex is on the corner of a shape, the corner is filed down.

To chamfer a vertex:

1. 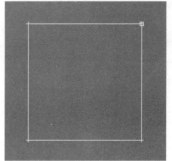 Select a shape that has a Corner vertex type (**Figure 9.54**).

2. Open the Modify panel.

3. Convert the shape to an editable spline, or apply an Edit Spline modifier to it.

4. Enable Vertex-level selection.

5. Select a vertex.

6. In the Geometry rollout, click Chamfer (**Figure 9.55**). Then drag the Chamfer spinner.

   or

   Enter a value to set the chamfer distance.

   or

   Drag the vertex upward in the viewport.

   The vertex splits into two vertices, which spread apart along the length of the spline. If they are on a corner, they chamfer the corner (**Figure 9.56**).

✔ Tip

- Fillet works the same way as the Chamfer command, except that it rounds a corner to an arc (**Figure 9.57**).

Figure 9.54 A rectangle is a good shape to use to learn about Chamfer and Fillet.

Figure 9.55 Use the Chamfer spinner to set the chamfer distance.

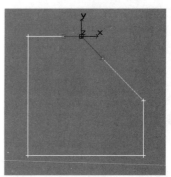

Figure 9.56 The rectangle corner after chamfering.

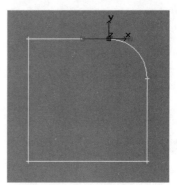

Figure 9.57 Fillet produces a rounded corner.

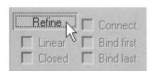

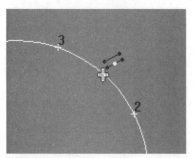

Figure 9.58 Use Refine to add new vertices to a spline.

Figure 9.59 The Refine cursor tells you that you can click to add a vertex.

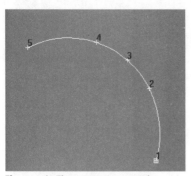

Figure 9.60 The new vertex stays in numeric sequence with the rest.

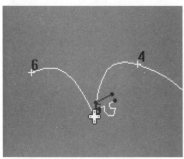

Figure 9.61 Use Insert to add a vertex and move it at the same time.

You refine a shape by adding vertices to it. This makes curved shapes bend more smoothly. If the refined shape is extruded, lathed, or lofted, the resulting shape object will have more faces.

To refine a shape:

1. Select a shape.

2. Open the Modify panel.

3. Convert the shape to an editable spline, or apply an Edit Spline modifier to it.

4. Enable Vertex-level selection.

5. In the Geometry rollout, click Refine (**Figure 9.58**).

6. Place the cursor over a segment.

   The cursor changes to the Refine cursor (**Figure 9.59**).

7. Click the spline at the point where you would like to add the vertex.

   A new vertex appears, subdividing the segment you clicked on. If the vertex numbers are visible, they update accordingly (**Figure 9.60**).

✔ Tips

- You can add as many vertices as you want as long as the Refine button is active.

- You cannot create a stand-alone vertex. Vertices must always be connected to at least one segment in a spline.

- The Insert command allows you to add vertices and move them (**Figure 9.61**).

- CrossInsert adds two vertices at the juncture of two intersecting splines. It does not connect, weld, or fuse them.

- Divide is a segment-level command that adds a vertex to the middle of a segment.

You delete shape sub-objects with the Delete command, or by pressing Delete on your keyboard.

To delete any part of a shape:

1. Select a shape object.

2. Open the Modify panel.

3. Convert the shape to an editable spline, or apply an Edit Spline modifier to it.

4. Enable a sub-object selection level.

5. Select the part of the spline that you want to delete (**Figure 9.62**).

6. Press the Delete key, or click the Delete button in the Geometry rollout.

   The selection is deleted (**Figure 9.63**).

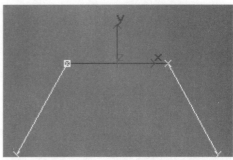

Figure 9.62 Select the portion of the object that you want to delete.

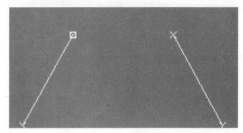

Figure 9.63 After deleting the segment.

Figure 9.64
Dragging the Outline spinner. A positive number offsets to the inside of the spline; a negative number offsets to the outside.

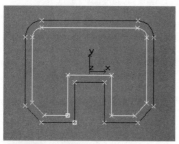

Figure 9.65 An outline has been added to the spline.

Figure 9.66 Because the profile was enhanced using Outline, the vase will have thickness when lathed.

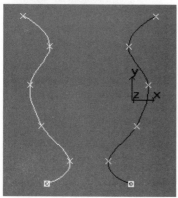

Figure 9.67 Use Mirror to flip or clone a spline.

The Outline command offsets a spline subobject a specified distance from the original.

Outline is used in architectural modeling to add thickness to walls. You can also use it to add thickness to a lathed object.

To outline a spline:

1. Select a shape object that contains one or more splines.

2. Open the Modify panel.

3. Convert the shape to an editable spline, or apply an Edit Spline modifier to it.

4. Enable Spline-level selection.

5. Select the spline you want to outline.

6. Drag the Outline spinner, drag the spline, or enter a value to specify the distance between the original spline and the outline (**Figure 9.64**).

   A new spline is created that outlines the spline you selected. This spline remains part of the shape (**Figure 9.65**).

✔ Tips

- If you want to offset the spline and its outline an equal distance on either side of the original, activate the Center checkbox.

- Outline the profile of a vase to add thickness to the vase when it is lathed (**Figure 9.66**).

- The Mirror command flips splines vertically, horizontally, or both. It also gives you the option of cloning your spline (**Figure 9.67**).

EDITING SHAPES

299

Spline Boolean operations combine overlapping spline sub-objects and delete portions based on how they overlap. Each of the spline sub-objects that you operate on is referred to as an **operand.**

 Union—Deletes the overlapping portion of splines that intersect.

 Subtraction—Deletes the part of the first spline that overlaps the second, and the part of the second spline that does not overlap the first.

 Intersection—Deletes the non-overlapping portion of intersecting splines.

To perform a Boolean operation:

1. Select a compound shape object that has two or more overlapping splines.

2. Open the Modify panel.

3. Convert the shape to an editable spline, or apply an Edit Spline modifier to it.

4. Enable Spline-level selection.

5. Select a spline sub-object to be the first operand (**Figure 9.68**).

6. In the Geometry rollout, click Boolean (**Figure 9.69**).

7. Click a Boolean button to choose a Boolean operation.

8. Click a spline sub-object to be the second operand (**Figure 9.70**).

   The Boolean operation is performed on the two operands (**Figure 9.71**).

9. Continue clicking the operands and changing the boolean operation until the shape is complete (**Figure 9.72**).

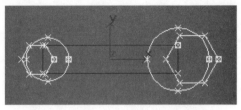

Figure 9.68 Select the rectangle to be the first operand. The other shape sub-objects are two circles and two NGons.

Figure 9.69 Click Boolean and choose an operation. Here, the Union operation is selected.

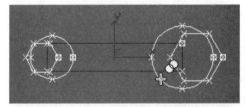

Figure 9.70 Clicking the second operand.

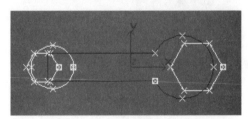

Figure 9.71 After performing a Boolean union on the first circle, the overlapping portions of the rectangle and circle disappear.

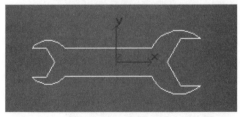

Figure 9.72 After the second circle is added and the NGons are subtracted, the final product is a wrench template, which can then be extruded.

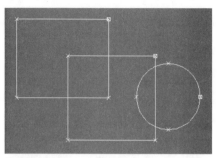

Figure 9.73 This is a single shape made up of two rectangles and a circle.

Figure 9.74 The Trim button turns yellow when it is active.

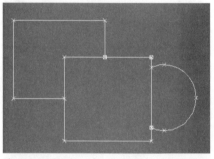

Figure 9.75 The lines inside the center spline are trimmed away.

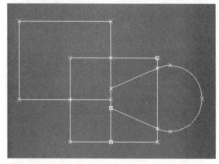

Figure 9.76 The lines are extended until they intersect with a spline.

Trim deletes the portion of a shape that extends beyond the area of intersecting spline sub-objects.

The Trim command has the same requirement as Boolean operations in that the splines you are working with must be part of the same shape.

To trim a shape:

1. Select a compound shape object that has at least two overlapping splines (**Figure 9.73**).

2. Open the Modify panel.

3. Convert the shape to an editable spline, or apply an Edit Spline modifier to it.

4. Enable Spline-level selection.

5. Click the Trim button (**Figure 9.74**).

6. Select the lines that you want to remove (**Figure 9.75**).

The lines are trimmed up to where they intersect the nearest spline.

✔ Tips

■ Click the Extend button, and see what happens when you click the lines that you just trimmed (**Figure 9.76**).

■ Note that you do not have to select one of the splines to use Trim or Extend. You simply activate the button and start picking lines you want trimmed or extended.

EDITING SHAPES

301

COMPOUND OBJECTS

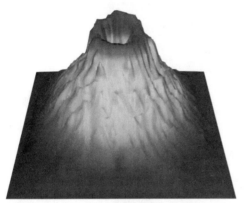

Figure 10.1 This terrain model of a volcano was created with actual contour line data.

Compound objects combine two or more objects into one. They greatly assist complex modeling operations and facilitate certain animation techniques, such as 3D morphing. 3ds max 6 ships with ten types of compound objects: Boolean, Connect, Scatter, Shape-Merge, Terrain, Conform, Loft, Morph, BlobMesh, and Mesher. BlobMesh and Mesher are primarily for use with particle systems and are not covered in this book.

Compound objects combine some of the best characteristics of modifiers and arrays. With compound objects, you can deform, cut, join, remove, and extrude surfaces. You can create ordered or random arrays of clones. You can also create surface terrain models from contour lines (**Figure 10.1**).

When you apply a Compound Object command to individual objects, the objects become operands of the compound object operation—meaning that they are operated upon. Compound Object commands cannot be used to select the first object, so you must select an object before choosing a Compound Object command. Commands for creating compound objects are found in the drop-down menu of the Create/Geometry branch.

Creating Boolean Objects

Boolean algebra was invented by British mathematician George Boole in order to manipulate sets of numbers. In 3D graphics, Boolean operations are applied to objects in order to manipulate their forms. This chapter covers Boolean operations for mesh objects. For spline Booleans, see Chapter 9, "Editing Shapes."

Boolean operations treat mesh objects as sets of faces that can be added or subtracted from each other. They always work on two objects. The first object that you select is called **operand A**. The second object is called **operand B**. The result is determined by how the operands intersect and the type of Boolean operation you select (**Figure 10.2**):

◆ **Union**—Combines both operands into one object and removes intersecting faces.

◆ **Subtraction (A-B)**—Subtracts the volume of operand B from the volume of operand A. Builds an interior surface on operand A by adding the enclosed faces of operand B to it. The rest of operand B's faces are deleted.

◆ **Subtraction (B-A)**—Subtracts the volume of operand A from the volume of operand B. This operation uses faces from operand B to cover the hole that would otherwise remain.

◆ **Intersection**—Deletes the nonintersecting volume of the two operands and uses the faces of the interpenetrating surfaces to build a new object.

◆ **Cut**—Cuts open the surface of operand A with the volume of operand B. No faces from operand B are added to operand A. Instead, faces are refined, split, or deleted in operand A along the intersection of its surface with operand B.

Figure 10.2 Boolean operations between a cube and a sphere.

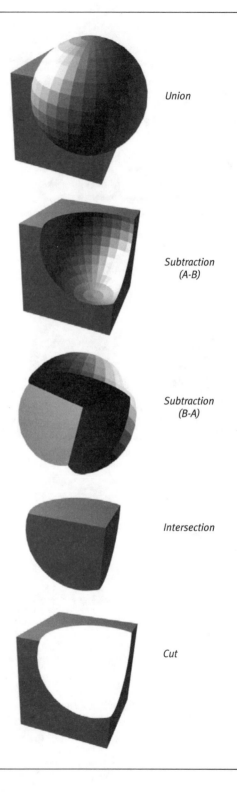

Union

Subtraction (A-B)

Subtraction (B-A)

Intersection

Cut

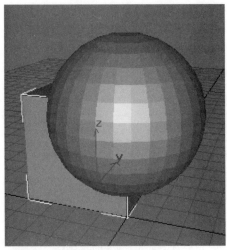

Figure 10.3 Select the first operand.

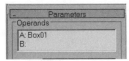

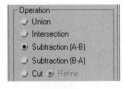

Figure 10.4
The Parameters rollout shows the selected object assigned to operand A.

Figure 10.5 Subtraction (A-B) is the default Boolean operation.

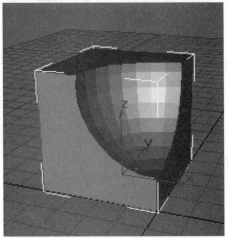

Figure 10.6 The sphere has taken a bite out of the box.

Subtraction is the most commonly used Boolean operation.

To perform a Boolean subtraction:

1. Position two mesh objects so that they intersect.

2. Select the object you want to operate on (**Figure 10.3**).

3. In the Create panel, open the Geometry sub-panel and choose Compound Objects from the drop-down list. Then click Boolean in the Object Type rollout.

   The Boolean rollout appears. The selected object is already assigned to operand A (**Figure 10.4**).

4. In the Parameters rollout, choose Subtraction (A-B) (**Figure 10.5**).

5. Click Pick Operand B, and click the intersecting object.

   The volume of the second object is subtracted from the first (**Figure 10.6**).

6. To subtract the first object from the second, click Subtraction (B-A).

✔ Tip

■ Boolean operations sometimes fail to work properly, although they have improved significantly since the program was first released. However, it is still a good idea to hold your scene (using Edit > Hold) before performing a Boolean operation. That way, if the operation fails, you can retrieve the scene from the hold file using Edit > Fetch. For more information on how to make Boolean operations a success, see the tips for performing successful Boolean operations later in this section.

CREATING BOOLEAN OBJECTS

The product of a Boolean intersection looks like the piece you drilled out in a subtraction. If the operands do not intersect, both disappear.

To perform a Boolean intersection:

1. 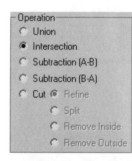 Position two mesh objects so that they intersect.

2. Select one of the objects (**Figure 10.7**).

3. Apply a Boolean command.

4. In the Parameters rollout, choose Intersection (**Figure 10.8**).

5. Click Pick Operand B, and then click the second object.

   The non-intersecting faces are removed, leaving the intersection of the two objects (**Figure 10.9**).

✔ Tip

■ To change Boolean operations interactively so that you can compare the effect of each, click on the different operations in the Parameters rollout.

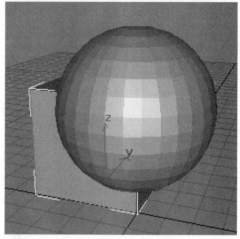

Figure 10.7 Select an operand. It doesn't matter which object you pick.

Figure 10.8 Choose the Intersection operation.

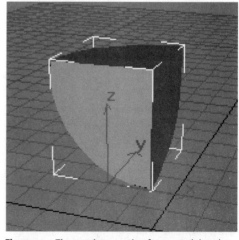

Figure 10.9 The non-intersecting faces are deleted.

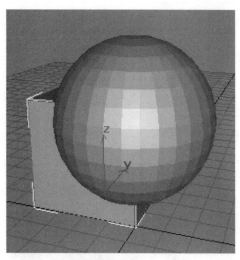

Figure 10.10 Position the two objects, and then select the one you want to cut.

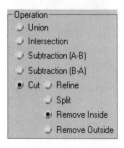

Figure 10.11 Choose the Cut > Remove Inside operation.

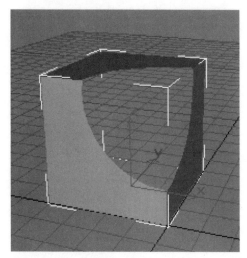

Figure 10.12 The sphere cuts a hole in the box without leaving any faces.

The Boolean cut operation has four variations:

- **Refine**—Adds new faces to operand A where it intersects the surface of operand B.

- **Split**—Adds two sets of new faces to operand A where it intersects the surface of operand B. Each of these sets of faces is used to define a separate element in the mesh so that the mesh can easily be split apart.

- **Remove Inside**—Deletes faces from operand A that are enclosed by the volume of operand B. This option works like Subtraction, except that it does not add faces to operand A.

- **Remove Outside**—Deletes faces from operand A that are not enclosed by the volume of operand B. This option works like Intersect, except that it does not add faces to operand A.

To perform a Boolean cut:

1. Position two mesh objects so that they intersect.

2. Select the object you want to cut (**Figure 10.10**).

3. Apply a Boolean command.

4. In the Parameters rollout, choose Cut and Remove Inside (**Figure 10.11**).

5. Click Pick Operand B, and then click the second object.

   The first object is cut by the second one (**Figure 10.12**).

Boolean operands can be animated after a Boolean operation has been performed. The results can be elegant and magical to watch and have a wide variety of applications.

To animate a Boolean:

1. Select a Boolean object. For this example, use an object that has been created by subtraction.

2. Open the Modify panel.

3. In the Display area, check Result + Hidden Ops (**Figure 10.13**).

   The hidden operand appears in wireframe (**Figure 10.14**).

4. In the modifier stack display, click the plus sign next to the word Boolean. Then click Operands (**Figure 10.15**).

5. ![Auto Key] Click Auto Key.

6. Drag the time slider to a new position.

7. Drag the wireframe operand all the way through the solid operand (**Figure 10.16**).

8. In the Display area, check Result.

9. ![play] Click Play Animation.

   The hole created by the hidden operand moves smoothly through the solid operand.

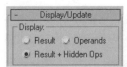

Figure 10.13 In the Modify panel, check Result + Hidden Ops.

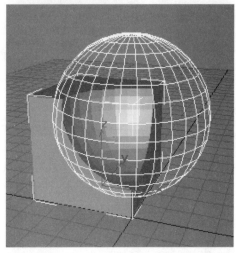

Figure 10.14 You can now see the wireframe sphere that was subtracted from the box.

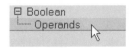

Figure 10.15 Turning on Sub-Object lets you manipulate and animate Boolean operands.

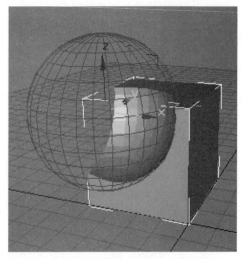

Figure 10.16 The space created by the subtracted operand seems to move through the solid operand.

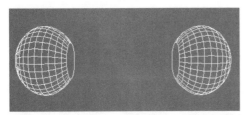

Figure 10.17 Positioning the objects so the holes face each other.

Figure 10.18
The selected object is assigned to be operand 0.

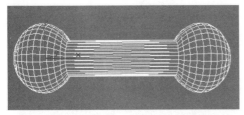

Figure 10.19 The result of connecting two spheres.

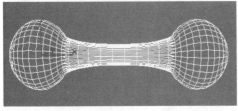

Figure 10.20 The result of adjusting the number of segments and tension setting.

The Connect command can connect two or more mesh objects by building bridges between holes in their surfaces. Use Connect to create architectural structures, furniture, handles, tools, and other manufactured objects. You can also use Connect to connect fingers to a hand or to connect appendages to a torso.

To create a Connect object:

1. Create two mesh objects.

2. Make a hole in the surface of each object by deleting some sub-objects or by performing a Boolean cut operation.

   For symmetrical output, create one object with a hole and then mirror/clone it.

3. Position the objects so that the holes face each other within a 90-degree angle (**Figure 10.17**).

4. Select one of the objects.

5. From the Create/Geometry drop-down list, choose Compound Objects > Connect.

   The Connect rollout appears. The selected object is assigned as operand 0 (**Figure 10.18**).

6. Choose a clone type for your next operand.

7. Click Pick Operand, and click the second mesh object.

   A mesh structure bridges the gap between holes in the operands (**Figure 10.19**).

8. Smooth the bridge in the middle and at either end by checking Bridge and Ends.

9. Increase the number of segments and adjust the tension to make the bridge bulge or shrink (**Figure 10.20**).

309

The Scatter objects operation distributes clones of a source object over the surface or within the volume of a distribution object.

To create a Scatter object:

1. Select or create a mesh object to scatter.

2. 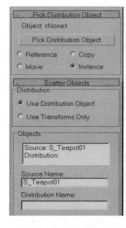 From the Create/Geometry drop-down list, choose Compound Objects > Scatter.

    The Scatter rollout appears. The selected object is assigned to be the source object (**Figure 10.21**).

3. Choose a clone type.

4. Click Pick Distribution Object. Then click a mesh object to be the distribution object.

    The source object positions itself on the surface of the distribution object.

5. In the Source Object Parameters group, enter a value for the number of duplicates.

    Clones of the source object arrange themselves evenly over the surface of the distribution object (**Figure 10.22**).

6. Try each of the distribution methods by clicking the radio buttons in the Distribution Object Parameters group (**Figure 10.23**).

    All Vertices, All Edge Midpoints, and All Face Centers ignore the Duplicates value and create regular arrays (**Figure 10.24**).

✔ Tip

- To create a random distribution of objects within a volume, use a mesh object that encloses volume as the distribution object and check Volume in the Distribution Object Parameters group.

Figure 10.21 The Scatter panel shows the selected object assigned as the source.

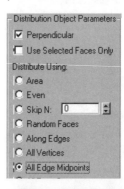

Figure 10.22 The result of scattering teapots on a planar surface.

Figure 10.23 Setting All Edge Midpoints in the Scatter panel.

Figure 10.24 The result of scattering teapots on a planar surface using the All Edge Midpoints option.

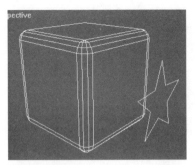

Figure 10.25 Getting a star shape ready to merge onto a ChamferBox.

Figure 10.26 The ShapeMerge panel shows the ChamferBox assigned as the Mesh operand.

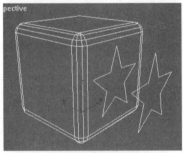

Figure 10.27 The star shape has been embedded into the ChamferBox surface.

Figure 10.28 Using Cookie Cutter to cut shapes out of a mesh.

You use the ShapeMerge command to embed shapes in a mesh surface or to cut shapes out of it. The faces, vertices, and edges created by embedded shapes are automatically selected at the sub-object level so that you can easily extrude, bevel, or assign materials to them.

To perform a ShapeMerge operation:

1. Position a shape over the surface of a mesh object (**Figure 10.25**).

2. Select the mesh object.

3. From the Create/Geometry drop-down list, choose Compound Objects > ShapeMerge.

   The ShapeMerge rollout appears. The mesh object is assigned as the Mesh operand (**Figure 10.26**).

4. Choose a clone type and click Pick Shape. Then click the shape.

   The shape is projected onto the surface of the mesh along the shape's local negative Z axis (**Figure 10.27**).

5. Choose Cookie Cutter to cut the area enclosed by the shape out of the mesh surface. Check Invert to cut the surface away from the embedded shape area (**Figure 10.28**).

✔ Tip

- To learn how to assign different colors to embedded shapes, see "To create a Multi/Sub-Object material" in Chapter 13, "Materials."

CREATING BOOLEAN OBJECTS

311

Terrains are 3D models that you make from contour line data. Terrains create landscapes for building sites, shadow studies, grading plans, and games. If you do not have any contour line models of landscapes, you can make one using an array of closed splines, with each level being slightly smaller and more elevated than the previous one.

To create a terrain:

1. Import a contour line data set, or create your own set of concentric shapes or splines (**Figure 10.29**).

   If you create your own set, uncheck Start New Shape so they will all be one shape. You can also use the Attach Multiple command of an editable spline to make all the shapes into a single editable spline.

2.  From the Create/Geometry drop-down list, choose Compound Objects > Terrain.

   The Terrain rollout appears (**Figure 10.30**). The contour lines are **skinned**— that is, a surface forms over them—and turned into a terrain (**Figure 10.31**). Note that complex contour lines may take awhile to skin.

3. If any contour lines were skipped, click Pick Operand and click the contour line.

4. You can assign colors to each level of the terrain in the Color by Elevation rollout (**Figure 10.32**).

✔ Tip

■ To reduce the complexity of the mesh, open the Simplification rollout and choose Use $^1/_2$ of Lines or Use $^1/_4$ of Lines for vertical simplification, or choose Use $^1/_2$ of Points or Use $^1/_4$ of Points for horizontal simplification.

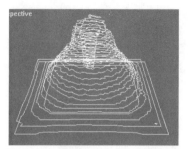

Figure 10.29 Using splines as the terrain contour lines.

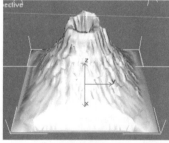

Figure 10.30 The shape is assigned as Op o in the Terrain panel.

Figure 10.31 The Terrain compound object forms a volcano from the splines.

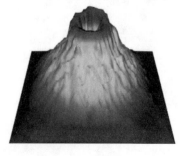

Figure 10.32 Using Color by Elevation to assign realistic shades to the volcano surface.

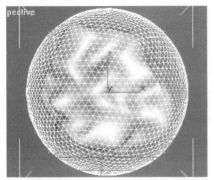

Figure 10.33 A GeoSphere encloses the Wrap-To object in preparation for creation of a Conform object.

Figure 10.34
The Conform panel shows the GeoSphere assigned as the Wrapper object.

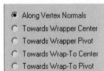

Figure 10.35 Choosing Along Vertex Normals causes the wrapper vertices to move inward perpendicular to the object surface.

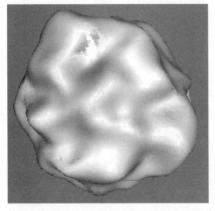

Figure 10.36 The GeoSphere is wrapped around the Wrap-To object and conforms to its surface.

Conform objects are compound objects created by "wrapping" the vertices of one object around the vertices of another. This causes the surface of the first object, called a **Wrapper object**, to conform to the surface of the second, the **Wrap-To object**. By placing the Wrapper object around the Wrap-To object, you can roughly duplicate the form of the Wrap-To object as if you were creating a very thin mold.

To create a Conform object:

1. Create an object. This will be your Wrap-To object.

2. Create a GeoSphere that is slightly larger than the Wrap-To object, and position it so it surrounds the first object. This will be your Wrapper object (**Figure 10.33**).

3. From the Create/Geometry drop-down list, choose Compound Objects > Conform.

   The Conform rollout appears. The selected outer object is assigned as the Wrapper object (**Figure 10.34**).

4. In the Vertex Projection Direction group, choose Along Vertex Normals (**Figure 10.35**).

5. In the Update group (near the bottom of the Parameters rollout), check Hide Wrap-To Object.

6. Click Pick Wrap-To Object, and choose a clone option.

7. Press H. Then select the inner object from the Select Object dialog box.

   The Wrapper object wraps around the Wrap-To object (**Figure 10.36**).

✔ Tip

■ Use Conform objects to make text lie on the surface of a mesh object.

Lofting Objects

Lofting is an incredibly versatile means of modeling and animating 3D forms. The term lofting comes from early methods of ship-building in which the hull of a ship was constructed from a series of cross-sections, or ribs, placed along its length. A structure called a loft supported the hull while the ribs were hoisted into place. The process of hoisting the ribs into the loft gave rise to the term lofting.

As in the shipbuilding days of yore, lofting in 3ds max creates a 3D object by placing cross-section shapes along a path. But instead of hoisting wooden ribs into a hull, lofting places shapes along a spline path. As each shape is added to the path, the loft builds a surface, or skin, to accommodate the different outlines of each (**Figure 10.37**).

A loft path can be angular or curved, open or closed, flat or three-dimensional, but it must be a single continuous spline. Shapes made up of more than one spline, such as a donut, cannot be used as a path. In contrast, shapes that you use as cross-sections of the loft can be made up of single or multiple splines. If splines are nested inside of each other, then each nested layer will be lofted together (**Figure 10.38**).

To loft an object, you start with either a path or a shape. If you start with a path and then get the cross-section shapes, the shapes will be arranged perpendicularly along the length of the path. If you start with a shape and then get a path, the path will be positioned along the local Z-axis of the shape. For this reason, starting with the path and then getting the shapes is usually preferred, because it is easier to predict where the loft will be built.

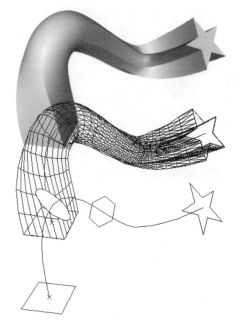

Figure 10.37 Using four shapes on a curved path to create an unusual lofted object.

Figure 10.38 Using nested splines to loft an object with a hole through it.

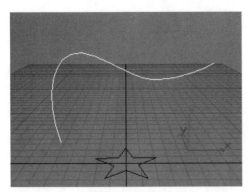

Figure 10.39 Selecting a spline line for the loft path.

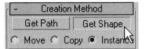

Figure 10.40 The Loft panel provides Get Path and Get Shape functions.

Figure 10.41 The mouse cursor is over a valid shape for lofting.

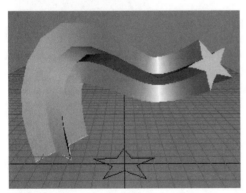

Figure 10.42 The shape is lofted along the entire path.

To loft an object with Get Shape:

1. Select a valid shape for a path (**Figure 10.39**).

2. From the Create/Geometry drop-down list, choose Compound Objects > Loft.

   The Loft rollout appears. If the selected spline shape is not a valid path, the Get Shape button will be dimmed.

3. Click Get Shape, and choose a clone option. Accept the default option, Instance, if you plan to edit or animate the loft later (**Figure 10.40**).

4. Move the cursor over a shape.

   If the shape is valid, the cursor changes to a loft cursor (**Figure 10.41**). If the shape is invalid, the reason the shape is invalid is displayed in the prompt line.

5. Click the shape.

   The loft object appears. The shape, or a clone of it, is placed at the first vertex of the path and extruded along its length (**Figure 10.42**).

✔ Tips

- If you want to try lofting a different shape, click a new shape immediately after step 5. The new shape replaces the last shape you picked.

- Lofting a short line along a curved line creates a ribbon. Applying a two-sided material shades the ribbon on both sides.

- If you use shape objects that are made up of more than one spline, all shapes in the loft must contain the same number of splines, and the shapes must have the same nesting order, which is the number of splines that nest within.

LOFTING OBJECTS

315

To loft an object with Get Path:

1. Select a valid cross-section shape (**Figure 10.43**).

2. From the Create/Geometry drop-down list, choose Compound Objects > Loft.

   The Loft rollout appears. If the selected spline shape is not a valid shape, the Get Path button will be dimmed.

3. Click Get Path and choose a clone option (**Figure 10.44**).

4. Place the cursor over a shape you want to use as a path. Accept the default option, Instance, if you plan to edit or animate the loft later.

   If the shape is valid as a path, the cursor changes to a loft icon.

5. Click the shape.

   The loft appears, aligned to the local Z axis of the shape. The first vertex of the path is positioned at the pivot point of the shape (**Figure 10.45**).

✔ Tips

- If you want to try lofting a different path, click Get Path and click a new path. The new path replaces the last path you picked.

- To flip the orientation of the path so that it follows the negative Z axis of the shape, hold down the Ctrl key when you click Get Path.

- Lines that are created by dragging Bézier end points generate uneven segment divisions, or steps, when used as paths (**Figure 10.46**). Converting the end points of the line to another vertex type and relofting the object corrects this problem.

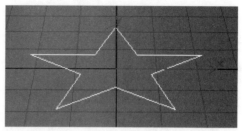

Figure 10.43 Selecting a valid shape for lofting.

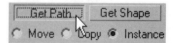

Figure 10.44 Activating the Get Path button using the Instance clone option.

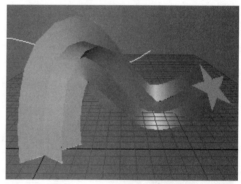

Figure 10.45 A loft generated using Get Path starts at the first shape.

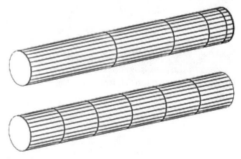

Figure 10.46 A loft path with uneven segment divisions uses Bézier end points (top); the problem is corrected by using Corner end points (bottom).

LOFTING OBJECTS

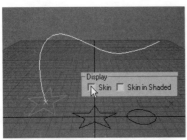

Figure 10.47 Turning off the skin display so you can see the loft path and shapes.

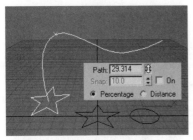

Figure 10.48 A small yellow X marks the point on the path where a new shape will be added.

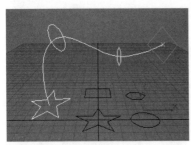

Figure 10.49 After adding a circle, an NGon, and a square to the path.

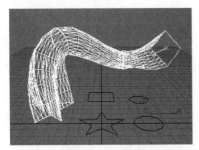

Figure 10.50 The skin of the loft object follows the contours of the shapes.

You adjust the shapes, path, skin, and surface rendering of a loft in the Modify panel.

To add shapes to a loft:

1. Select a loft object.

2. Open the Modify panel.

3. In the Display group of the Skin Parameters rollout, uncheck Skin.

    The surface of the loft is hidden, making the path and shapes easier to see (**Figure 10.47**).

4. In the Path Parameters rollout, drag the Path spinner upward. Click Percentage or Distance to view the Path setting as a percentage along the path or as a distance in current units. Enable Snap if you want to snap to even intervals along the path.

    As you change the Path value, a yellow X moves along the path from the first shape to a new position, or level, on the path. This marks where the next shape will be added (**Figure 10.48**).

5. Click Get Shape, and choose a clone option.

6. Click a shape.

    The shape, or a clone of it, is placed on the path at the current path level.

7. Repeat steps 4 through 6 until you have added all the shapes to the path that you want (**Figure 10.49**).

8. Turn Skin back on to see the results (**Figure 10.50**).

LOFTING OBJECTS

317

To replace shapes:

1. Select a loft object (**Figure 10.51**).

2. Open the Modify panel.

3. Open the Skin Parameters rollout, and turn off the skin display.

   The surface of the loft is hidden.

4. Open the Path Parameters rollout, and navigate the path level to the shape you want to replace. Click one of the following:

   Pick Shape: Enables you to pick a shape by clicking it in the loft.

   Next Shape: Moves up a level to the next shape in the path.

   Previous Shape: Moves back a level to the previous shape in the path.

5. Click Get Shape, and click the shape you want to insert at that level.

   The new shape replaces the old shape in the loft (**Figure 10.52**).

6. Repeat steps 4 and 5 until you have replaced all the shapes you want to replace (**Figure 10.53**).

7. Turn Skin back on to see the results (**Figure 10.54**). To see how the loft looks in shaded mode, turn on Smooth + Highlights.

✔ Tip

■ You can also replace a path if you use Get Path to select the new path.

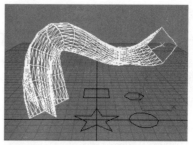

Figure 10.51 Selecting a loft object before replacing its shapes.

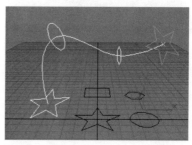

Figure 10.52 The star shape has replaced the original square at the end of the loft.

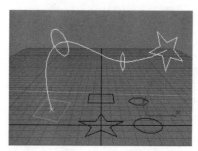

Figure 10.53 The square now replaces the star shape at the beginning of the path.

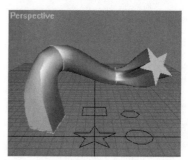

Figure 10.54 A shaded display of the finished loft.

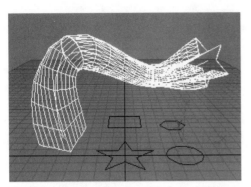

Figure 10.55 Set the viewport to Wireframe before adjusting skin complexity.

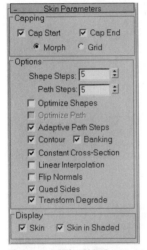

Figure 10.56 The Skin Parameters rollout lets you adjust skin complexity.

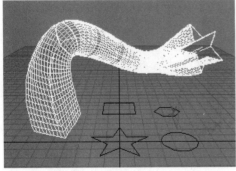

Figure 10.57 Increasing Shape Steps and Path Steps yields a better-looking, more complex loft object.

Adjusting skin complexity

Two factors govern the complexity of a loft:

◆ **Shape steps** are the number of segment divisions in the skin between each vertex of a cross-section shape. The number of shape steps determines the radial complexity of the loft.

◆ **Path steps** are the number of segment divisions in the skin between each cross-section shape on the path. The number of path steps determines the longitudinal complexity of the loft.

To adjust skin complexity:

1. Select a loft object, and set the viewport display to Wireframe (**Figure 10.55**).

2. Open the Modify panel.

3. Open the Skin Parameters rollout (**Figure 10.56**). By default, the Shape Steps and Path Steps are each set to 5.

4. Increase or decrease Shape Steps or Path Steps to increase or decrease the complexity of the loft (**Figure 10.57**).

✔ Tips

■ To optimize the number of path steps automatically, check Optimize Path. This checkbox is available only when Path Steps is selected in the Path Parameters rollout.

■ To generate the best-looking skin, check Adaptive Path Steps. This option is available only when Percentage or Distance is selected in the Path Parameters rollout.

■ Contour and Banking cause path steps to turn with the path in a flat plane and in 3D. Constant Cross-Section causes corners to be mitered correctly. These are all good options to leave checked.

LOFTING OBJECTS

319

Editing Lofts

The sub-object components of a loft are the path of the loft and its cross-section shapes. You edit loft objects by editing shapes and paths at the sub-object level or by manipulating instances of the sub-object shapes used to create the loft.

Manipulating the original shapes is usually the easiest solution. Just select a shape, open the Modify panel, and edit, modify, or adjust the shape's creation parameters. Transforms are not passed on from original shape objects to instanced loft sub-objects unless you place them in an XForm modifier.

Loft sub-object editing commands are limited to aligning and cloning loft components, but once you are in sub-object mode, you can move, rotate, and scale cross-section shapes. You can also rotate paths along their Z axes. Because loft sub-object selections are not passed up the modifier stack, any modifiers that are applied at the sub-object level will have the unexpected result of modifying the entire loft.

The following exercises explain how to edit loft shape sub-objects. You edit loft path sub-objects in much the same way, but you are limited to rotating and cloning them. Deleting a path deletes the entire loft object.

To select a loft shape:

1. Select a loft object.

2. Open the Modify panel and turn off the skin display.

3. In the stack display, click the plus sign next to the word Loft. Then choose Shape from the sub-object level drop-down list (**Figure 10.58**).

4. Click a loft shape in a viewport.
   The shape is selected (**Figure 10.59**).

Figure 10.58 At the Shape sub-object selection level, you can manipulate the loft object's shapes interactively.

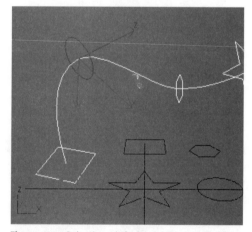

Figure 10.59 Selecting a loft shape in the viewport.

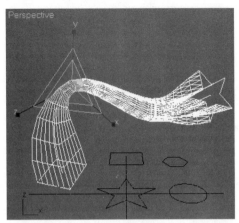

Figure 10.60 Scaling and moving the circle changes the dimensions of the loft object.

Figure 10.61 The Put To Scene dialog box lets you specify a name for the cloned shape.

To remove a loft shape:

1. Select a loft shape.

2. Click the Delete button, or press the Delete key.

The shape is removed from the loft object.

To transform a loft shape:

1. Select a loft shape.

2. Move, rotate, or scale the shape.

The shape is transformed in its local coordinate system. The skin updates to match the new position, orientation, or scale of the shape (**Figure 10.60**).

To clone a loft shape:

1. Select a loft shape.

2. Click Put in the Shapes Commands rollout.

The Put To Scene dialog box appears (**Figure 10.61**).

3. Name the new shape, and then click OK.

The copy or instance appears in the viewport at the origin of the home grid.

To align loft shapes to the path:

1. Select a loft.

2. Open the Modify panel.

3. Select the Shape sub-object level.

   The Shape Commands rollout appears (**Figure 10.62**).

4. Click the Compare button.

   The Compare window appears. A cross marks the position of the path as you look down its length.

   Click Pick Shape, and click a shape to bring it into the Compare window.

   Click Reset to clear the window.

   The first vertex of each shape in the window is marked by a small square (**Figure 10.63**).

5. In the viewport, select the shape or shapes you want to align.

6. In the Shape Commands rollout, use the buttons to align the shape to the path.

   The selected shapes change alignment to the path. The new alignment is shown in the Compare window (**Figure 10.64**). The loft object updates in the viewports (**Figure 10.65**).

✔ Tips

- Lofting typically aligns the first vertex of each shape, but if the shapes vary widely in shape or complexity, these vertices may get out of alignment. The result is a loft that twists or stretches unpredictably. Use the Compare window to check and realign the first vertex of each shape.

- Fine-tune your alignment by moving or rotating shapes at the sub-object level.

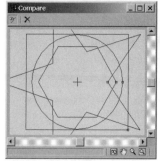

Figure 10.62 The Shape Commands rollout provides access to the Compare functions.

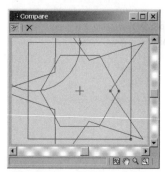

Figure 10.63 The Compare window shows you how shapes align to the path.

Figure 10.64 After changing the alignment of the circle.

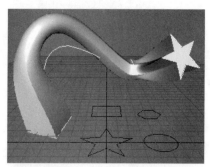

Figure 10.65 The loft moves above its path to follow the circle.

EDITING LOFTS

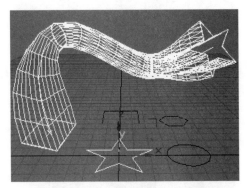

Figure 10.66 To animate a loft, you can animate the shapes used to create the loft.

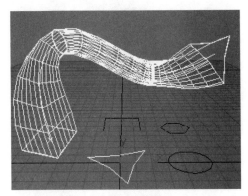

Figure 10.67 The loft animates as the star changes shape.

You can animate lofts at the object level or at the sub-object level. At the object level, you animate a loft object as you would any other mesh object. At the sub-object level, you animate a loft strictly by animating instances or originals of the loft path and shapes. Applying transforms or modifiers directly to loft sub-objects does not generate any animation keys and has no effect on the loft object over time.

To animate a loft:

1. Select an original or instance of a loft shape or path (**Figure 10.66**).

2. Open the Modify panel.

3. Click Auto Key.

4. Drag the time slider to a new position.

5. Modify or transform the shape or path by changing its creation parameters or applying a modifier and changing the parameters of the modifier. An XForm modifier should be used for transforms (**Figure 10.67**).

6. Click Play Animation.

   The loft changes over time.

Morphing Objects

3D morphing is a method of animation in which an object called a **seed** object changes shape to match a series of target objects. It is often used in character animation to change facial expressions and mouth position for lip-synching (**Figure 10.68**).

You can apply mesh morphing, patching, or NURBS to objects. The prerequisite for morphing mesh objects is that all target objects must have the same number of vertices as the seed object. This is because morphing moves the vertices of the seed object to corresponding vertices in the target objects. If the number of vertices is unequal, the morph animation will not work.

How do you model objects into different shapes with the same number of vertices? There are three main ways:

◆ Modify clones of a geometry primitive.

◆ Create mesh objects from splines that have identical numbers of vertices using the Extrude, Lathe, or Loft command.

◆ If you want to morph existing mesh models that have unequal vertices, clone a high-density GeoSphere and make Conform objects of each seed or target object.

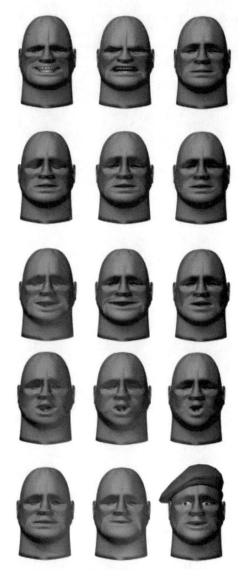

Figure 10.68 This figure from the 3ds max 6 tutorial (Commander_Lake_Tut_1.max) morphs from one expression to another.

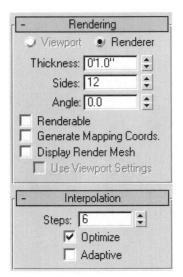

Figure 10.69 Use the Interpolation rollout to set a spline's vertex count.

Once you have learned the basics of morphing, I recommend that you learn how to use the Morpher modifier for more sophisticated tasks. The advantage of the Morpher modifier is that it can be added repeatedly to the modifier stack, and it has over 100 channels for assigning morph targets, as well as allowing for percentages of channels to be mixed to create complex targets.

To go along with the Morpher modifier, the Morph material assigns materials to different channels of the Morpher modifier, allowing you to morph between materials. For instructions on applying Morpher modifiers and Morph materials, see the 3ds max 6 online help files.

To set the number of vertices on a spline:

1. Create a spline object, such as a line.

2. Open the General Interpolation rollout of the spline (**Figure 10.69**).

3. Uncheck Optimize and Adaptive.

4. Set the number of steps.

    The number of vertices is set.

MORPHING OBJECTS

To extrude or lathe seed and target objects:

1. 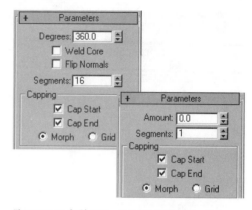 Select a spline shape.

2. Apply an Extrude or Lathe modifier. The Extrude or Lathe rollout appears (**Figure 10.70**).

3. Set the number of segments.

4. If you use the Lathe modifier, make sure Weld Core is unchecked.

5. Set Capping to Morph.

   This arranges cap faces in a predictable pattern for morphing.

6. Repeat steps 1 through 5 using a spline with an equal number of vertices. Make sure that the Segments value is the same each time.

Figure 10.70 (left) Using Lathe to generate morph objects; (right) Using Extrude to generate morph objects.

To loft seed and target objects:

1. Select a spline shape.

2. Loft the shape along a path.

3. In the Skin Parameters rollout, uncheck Optimize Shapes and Adaptive Path Steps, and set Capping to Morph (**Figure 10.71**).

4. Repeat steps 1 through 3 using loft shapes and paths with the same number of vertices.

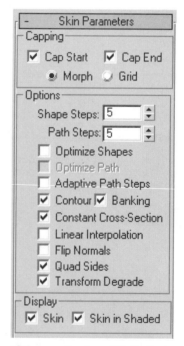

Figure 10.71 Use these Skin Parameters settings when creating morph objects.

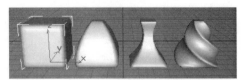

Figure 10.72 The ChamferBox is used as the seed object and thus appears first in the morph animation.

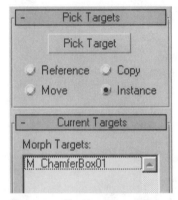

Figure 10.73 The Morph Targets list shows the ChamferBox as the first target.

Figure 10.74 After all the morph targets have been picked, they appear in the list in the order that they'll appear in the morph animation.

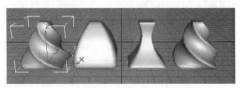

Figure 10.75 The ChamferBox morphs into each shape in turn, ending up as the twisted box.

To create a morph animation:

1. Create a seed object and some target objects for morphing.

2. Select the seed object (**Figure 10.72**).

3. From the Create/Geometry drop-down list, choose Compound Objects > Morph.

   The Morph rollout appears. In the Current Targets rollout, the seed object appears at the top of the Morph Targets list (**Figure 10.73**).

4. Click Pick Target, and choose a method for creating targets from your originals: Reference, Move, Copy, or Instance.

5. Click the morph target objects in the viewports.

   The target objects are added to the Morph Targets list (**Figure 10.74**).

6. Highlight the next target to which you want to morph the seed object.

7. Drag the time slider to the frame number or time where you want to set the first morph animation key. Note that it is not necessary to turn on the Auto Key button.

8. Click Create Morph Key.

   A key appears in the Track Bar at the current frame number or time.

9. To preview the animation, scrub the time slider back and forth. The seed object morphs to the target object automatically (**Figure 10.75**).

10. Repeat steps 6 through 9 until you are finished.

AEC Objects

AEC objects are complex objects designed for architectural, engineering, and construction visualization. Object types include Walls, Doors, Windows, Stairs, Railings, and Foliage.

"Smart" Walls are Walls that automatically create openings for Doors and Windows that intersect their surfaces and are linked to them. By default, Walls are set to 96 units high and 5 units deep, which is similar to the American construction standard of 8′ long sheets of half inch plywood and sheet rock built on a 2″ × 4″ wood or metal frame.

To create a Wall:

1. 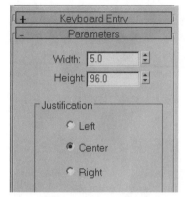 From the Create/Geometry drop-down list, choose AEC Extended > Wall.
   The Wall rollouts appear (**Figure 10.76**).

2. Optional: Turn on 3D Snaps and set snaps to Grid Points and Grid Lines.

3. In the Top viewport, click and drag the first wall of the house. By default, it is 5 units wide.

4. Click to complete the wall. Then move and click to define the second wall.
   The corners of the walls are "cleaned up" automatically, so that the joints are neat.

5. Continue moving the cursor and clicking to define more walls.

6. To enclose a room, snap the end of the last wall to the beginning of the first wall.
   The Weld Points dialog box appears (**Figure 10.77**). Choose Yes.

7. Right-click to end wall creation.
   The wall is created (**Figure 10.78**).

8. In the Parameters rollout, adjust the width and height of the Wall. Use the Justification buttons to align the Wall to the right, left, or center of its perimeter.

Figure 10.76 The default wall size is 5 units wide by 96 units high, similar to standard American construction.

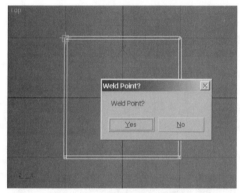

Figure 10.77 If you snap the last wall to the first at a 90° angle, you are given the option to weld their vertices.

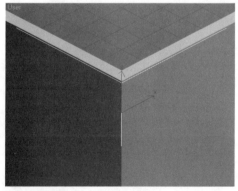

Figure 10.78 The walls as seen from a User viewport. Note how clean the corner joints appear.

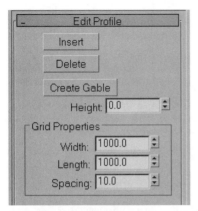

Figure 10.79 The Edit Profile rollout enables you to create gables by altering the profile of a Wall.

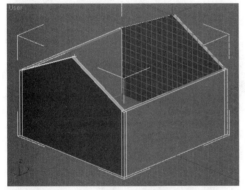

Figure 10.80 The Create Gable command alters the profile of a Wall by inserting a vertex and moving it.

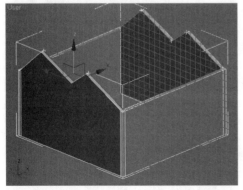

Figure 10.81 Creating custom gables by inserting and moving vertex points and snapping them to the grid.

Gables are walls that rise to a point in order to support a peaked roof. By editing a Wall at the Profile sub-object level, you can create simple A-frame or design custom gables.

To adjust the profile of a Wall:

1. Select a Wall.

2. Open the Modify panel.

3. In the stack display, open the Wall sub-object rollout and choose Profile (**Figure 10.79**).

4. Click on a straight section of the Wall that you want to build the gable on. The section, which is known as a Profile sub-object, is selected. A construction grid appears that is aligned to the Profile.

5. In the Edit Profile rollout, set the Height of the gable. Then click Create Gable. A vertex is inserted at the midpoint of the top of the profile and moved to the height you specified, creating a gable.

6. Click the opposite section of the wall. Then click Create Gable. A second vertex is inserted, and a matching gable appears (**Figure 10.80**).

7. To customize a Wall profile, use the Insert and Delete commands to insert and remove vertices from the Wall. Then use the Move tool to position them. For more precise placement, set the grid dimensions and grid spacing. Then snap the vertices to the grid (**Figure 10.81**).

✔ Tip

■ To allow for uneven ground, select a Segment sub-object. Then adjust the Bottom Offset and Height so that just the bottom of the Wall segment is raised.

AEC OBJECTS

3ds max 6 provides six types of Windows. If you snap a Window to the edges of a Wall, the program links the Window to the Wall and subtracts an opening for the Window.

To create a Window:

1. 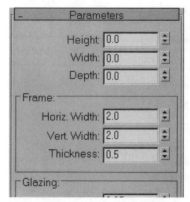 From the Create/Geometry drop-down list, choose Windows. Then choose a Windows type.

2. In the Creation Method rollout, make sure Width/Depth/Height is selected (**Figure 10.82**).

3. Turn on 3D Snaps. Then clear all snaps and enable Edge snaps only.

4. In the Perspective viewport, snap to the outer top edge of a Wall.

5. Click and drag along the edge of the Wall. Release to set the width of the Window (**Figure 10.83**).

6. Move the cursor across the top of the Wall and snap it to the other side. Then click to set the depth of the Window.

7. Move the cursor down until it snaps to the bottom of the wall. Then click to set the height of the Window.
   A hole that matches the dimensions of the Window is subtracted from the Wall. The front of the Window pops into view.

8. In the Parameters rollout, adjust the height, width, and depth of the Window.

9. Reposition the Window by dragging it in the XY plane or along the X axis (**Figure 10.84**).

   The opening in the Wall follows the Window as long as the Window intersects the Wall.

✔ Tip

■ 3ds max 6 ships with pre-built materials for each type of AEC object. For more information, see Chapter 13, "Materials."

Figure 10.82 These Window parameters are the same for every Window type.

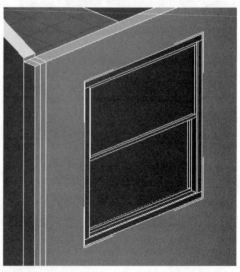

Figure 10.83 Snapping a Window to the top of a Wall.

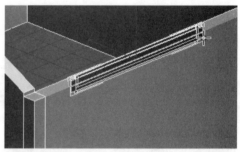

Figure 10.84 After sizing and positioning the Window.

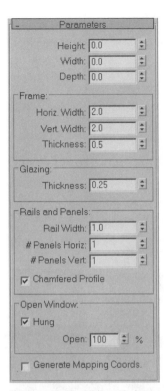

Figure 10.85 The Sliding Window
Parameters rollout. All Window
types include settings for Frame,
Glazing, Rails and Panels.

To adjust a Window:

1. Open the Modify panel and select the Window (**Figure 10.85**).

2. If the Window is not a Fixed Window, use the Open spinner to open the Window.

3. In the Frame group, set the dimensions of the window frame. Then set the thickness of the glass in the Glazing group.

4. Adjust the number of mullions and window panes by setting the number of Panels. Use the Width parameter to set the width of the mullions. Check Chamfered Profile to chamfer the edges of the mullions (**Figure 10.86**).

5. For Projected Windows, adjust the panel height. For Pivot Windows, adjust the and pivot direction (**Figure 10.87**).

Figure 10.87 The six Window types. From left to right:
Casement, Sliding, Projected, Fixed, Awning, Pivoted.

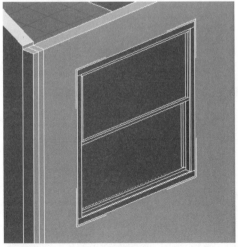

Figure 10.86 After adjusting a Sliding Window.

With 3ds max 6, you can create Pivot, Bifold, or Sliding Door objects that automatically open and shut. If you snap a Door to the edges of a Wall, the program links the Door to the Wall and automatically subtracts an opening for the Door.

To create a Door:

1.  From the Create/Geometry drop-down list, choose Doors. Then choose a Doors object type.

2. In the Creation Method rollout, make sure Width/Depth/Height is selected and Allow Non-vertical Door Jambs is unchecked (**Figure 10.88**).

3. Turn on 3D Snaps. Then clear all snaps and enable Edge snaps only.

4. In a User viewport, snap to the top outer edge of a Wall.

5. Click and drag along the snapped edge. Release to set the width.

6. Move the cursor across the top of the Wall and snap to the other side. Then click to set the depth of the Door (**Figure 10.89**).

7. Move the cursor down to the bottom of the Wall. When the cursor snaps to the bottom edge, click to set the height.

   A door-sized hole is subtracted from the Wall, causing the Door to pop into view.

8. In the Parameters rollout, adjust the height, width, and depth of the Door (**Figure 10.90**).

✔ Tips

- Flip Swing makes a door swing outward instead of inward. Flip Hinge moves the pivot point to the other side of the door if Double Door is unchecked.

- A door handle is usually placed about 3' above the ground for a 7' door.

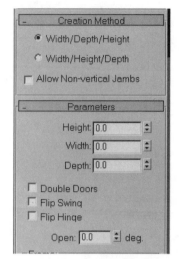

Figure 10.88 A Pivot Door has the same parameters as a Bifold Door. Sliding Doors flip front to back and side to side.

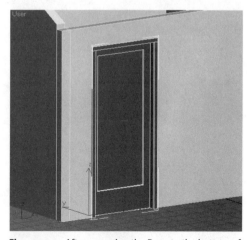

Figure 10.89 Snapping the Door to the Wall.

Figure 10.90 After snapping the Door to the bottom of the wall and setting the height of the Door to 84."

AEC OBJECTS

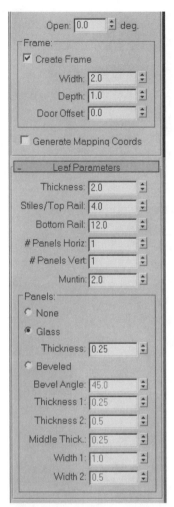

Open: 0.0 ⬧ deg.

Frame:
☑ Create Frame

Width: 2.0 ⬧
Depth: 1.0 ⬧
Door Offset: 0.0 ⬧

☐ Generate Mapping Coords

Leaf Parameters

Thickness: 2.0 ⬧
Stiles/Top Rail: 4.0 ⬧
Bottom Rail: 12.0 ⬧
Panels Horiz: 1 ⬧
Panels Vert: 1 ⬧
Muntin: 2.0 ⬧

Panels:
○ None
◉ Glass
Thickness: 0.25 ⬧
○ Beveled
Bevel Angle: 45.0 ⬧
Thickness 1: 0.25 ⬧
Thickness 2: 0.5 ⬧
Middle Thick.: 0.25 ⬧
Width 1: 1.0 ⬧
Width 2: 0.5 ⬧

Figure 10.91 The remaining parameters are the same for all three Door types.

To adjust a Door:

1. Reposition the door by dragging it in the XY plane or along the X axis. The Wall opens and reseals behind it.

2. Open the Modify panel to access the Door settings (**Figure 10.91**).

3. In the Leaf Parameters rollout, set the number of vertical and horizontal panels and experiment with the Panels settings.

4. Drag the Open spinner to open the door.

5. In the Parameters rollout, use the check boxes to create a double door or to adjust the direction of the door swing and the left or right placement of the hinge. Use the Frame group to adjust the size of the frame or offset the hinge (**Figure 10.92**).

✔ Tips

- If you animate the Open parameter, it will automatically be controlled by a Bézier curve so that the Door speeds up as it opens and slows down as it closes.

- To animate a door handle, create an arc that matches the doorswing and constrain the handle to follow the path. Then copy the controller from the Open (degrees) track of the Door and paste it on the Percent track of the handle and set the final key of this function curve to 100%.

Figure 10.92 Finished Pivot, Bifold, and Sliding Doors illuminated by a Sunlight system. (See Chapter 11, "Lights.") Multi/Sub-Object Materials from the AecTemplate.mat material library have been applied to each door.

AEC OBJECTS

3ds max 6 ships with a library of 13 pre-built plants that automatically generate leaves, trunks, flowers, and other parts that are a tremendous time-saver for landscaping sites.

To create Foliage:

1. From the Create/Geometry drop-down list, choose AEC Extended. Then click Foliage. The Foliage rollouts appear.

2. In the Favorite Plants rollout, find a plant that you like. Then drag the plant into a viewport, or click the plant and then click in a viewport (**Figure 10.93**).

3. In the Parameters rollout, adjust the height of the plant. Click the New Seed button to generate a new variation of the plant from a random number seed (**Figure 10.94**).

4. Adjust the Density and Pruning of the plant. For faster rendering, reduce Density and increase Pruning. For fuller-looking plants, increase Density and reduce Pruning.

5. In the Show group, choose whether to generate Leaves, Fruit, Flowers, Trunk, Branches, or Roots.

6. Adjust the Viewport Canopy settings to set the viewport display. The Canopy is the low-resolution transparent sheath that surrounds the top of the plant.

7. Set the level of rendering detail in the Level-of-Detail group (**Figure 10.95**). Then render the scene.

✔ Tip

■ Foliage objects come pre-mapped with Multi/Sub-Object materials. To adjust the colors, pick the material from the object using the eyedropper. For more information, see Chapter 13, "Materials."

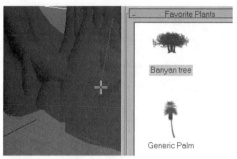

Figure 10.93 Dragging a Banyan Tree from the rollout of Favorite Plants.

Figure 10.94 The first thing you will need to do is adjust the height of the plant. To create a new variation on the plant, click the New button next to the Seed parameter, or type in a number.

Figure 10.95 A Banyan tree in full leaf, rendered at the High level of detail. Have fun playing with this!

AEC OBJECTS

LIGHTS

Figure 11.1 Light conveys mystery and magic.

In nature, light flows like a luminous tide, revealing and concealing form. Light radiates, reflects, refracts, reacts, and softly diffuses into air. Light is warm or cool, high or low, near or far, bright or dim, harsh or soft. These qualities make a scene happy, sad, harsh, soft, romantic, dull, mundane, or mysterious (**Figure 11.1**).

In the digital world, illumination is a calculated affair. Rendering algorithms, normal alignments, G-buffers, and Z-buffers determine the display of light and shadow. Where calculation fails, the eye of the artist must compensate.

The best lighting effects are achieved by artists who make themselves students of nature. Artists who study scene painting, drawing, photography, and cinematography develop sensitivity, awareness, and a practiced eye.

This chapter outlines the light sources available in 3ds max and how to control them.

Illuminating Scenes

In addition to making scenes more beautiful, working with light has practical applications. For instance, suppose you create a model of an office building for a prospective client. The client will want to see what it will look like under different lighting conditions. How will the building cast shadows? How will shadows be cast upon it? At what angle will light enter the windows at different times of the day and year?

The color and angle of a light place a scene in time and space. For morning or evening scenes, make the sun a warm color such as yellow, orange, or red. Then place the light source at a low angle (**Figure 11.2**). Cooler white lights placed at a high angle suggest the sun shining at midday. To make a mid-day scene more interesting, add clouds to the sky and project shadows from them (**Figure 11.3**). Fill lights above the ground should be blue or gray to match the sky. Fill lights below the ground should be green or brown to match the earth.

For night scenes, use a cool blue-white tint to suggest the light of the moon and stars (**Figure 11.4**). If there is fog, streetlights create warm, hazy cones of illumination. If there is a large or brightly colored object in the scene, match a nearby light to that color to create the effect of light radiating off of its surface.

Indoor lights also have color. Use warm, yellow colors for incandescent and halogen lights. Use a cold yellow-green color for fluorescent lighting. Be sure to create some fill lights to match the overall colors of the walls and carpets.

Figure 11.2 Morning in the mountains: Angled light, long shadows.

Figure 11.3 Midday in the hills: Cloud shadows add interest.

Figure 11.4 Moonlight in the desert: Stars in the sky and water create a feeling of space.

ILLUMINATING SCENES

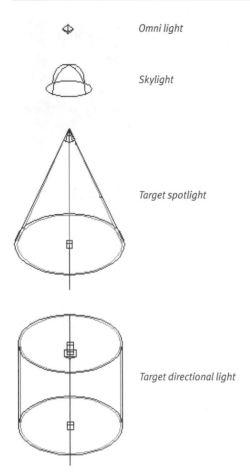

Omni light

Skylight

Target spotlight

Target directional light

Figure 11.5 The basic light types. Free spotlights and free directional lights look the same as their targeted counterparts, minus the target box.

Figure 11.6 The Lights branch of the Create panel.

Creating Lights

As in nature, illumination in 3ds max is the product of a complex interaction of lights and objects. To participate, lights and objects must be placed so that there is a direct line of sight between them, and objects must be renderable.

3ds max 6 offers four basic types of lights (**Figure 11.5**):

◆ **Omni light**—Radiates light in all directions from a single source point.

◆ **Skylight**—Simulates diffuse outdoor lighting from the dome of the sky.

◆ **Spotlight (target and free)**—Illuminates an area within a cone, similar to a stage light. Target spotlights point at a target that you aim. Free spotlights have no target, so they can be maneuvered more easily.

◆ **Directional light (target and free)**—Like spotlights, directional lights use a cone of illumination, except that the cone sides are parallel. This is because directional lights have parallel rays, while spotlights spread light from a single source point.

You create basic lights in the Lights branch of the Create panel (**Figure 11.6**).

New to 3ds max 6 are the **mr area omni** and the **mr area spot light** types. Designed to work with mental ray, max 6's advanced new ray tracing rendering engine, these lights are variations on the basic omni and spot light types. To learn more about mental ray, please refer to the 3ds max 6 New Features Guide and the 3ds max 6 User Reference.

CREATING LIGHTS

In addition to the basic light types, there are two types of lighting systems that you create in the Systems branch of the Create panel:

♦ **Sunlight system**—A hybrid light source that combines a free directional light with a Compass object to simulate the position of the sun as it moves across the sky over time.

♦ **Daylight system**—A hybrid light source that combines the direct light of the sun with the scattered light of the sky to produce realistic outdoor lighting that changes over time. Daylight systems use an advanced type of lighting called photometric lights by default (see sidebar).

By default, shadow casting is turned off for basic lights and turned on for lighting systems. Ambient light, the diffuse background light of a scene that fills in shadow areas, is turned off by default.

When you start building a scene in 3ds max, the default lighting has no direction. No matter which viewport you look in, the light appears brightest on the sides of the objects that face you. This lighting configuration was designed to make modeling easier, as the object facing you in the middle of the viewport is always fully lit.

There is a second default lighting configuration that places two omni lights along a diagonal through the world origin, from top-left-front to below-right-back. This lighting is more realistic and interesting.

Photometric Lights

Photometric lights simulate realistic lighting based on physical measurements of light intensity. 3ds max offers eight types of photometric lights: target point lights, free point lights, target linear lights, free linear lights, target area lights, free area lights, IES skylights, and IES sunlights. For more information on photometric lights and their settings, see the 3ds max 6 User Reference.

CREATING LIGHTS

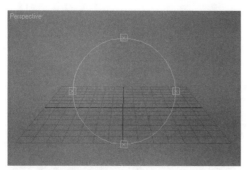

Figure 11.7 When you build a scene on a grid that is parallel to the viewport, it makes it easier to position lights around it.

Figure 11.8 The practice scene consists of light-colored objects.

Figure 11.9 This setting creates two default lights that you can later add to the scene from the Views menu.

Figure 11.10 The ActiveShade viewport renders the new default lighting.

Lighting requires a bit of finesse. To make the process easier, you will start by creating a practice scene, and then add lights to it until the scene is fully illuminated.

To create a practice scene:

1. Rotate the Perspective view so that the front of the grid is parallel to the bottom of the viewport (**Figure 11.7**).

2. In the Perspective viewport, create some light-colored objects and place them near the origin. Then place a white plane underneath (**Figure 11.8**).

   The light colors of the objects will make it easier to see the effects of light.

3. With the Perspective viewport still active, open the Viewport Configuration dialog box by right-clicking a viewport label and choosing Configure, or right-clicking any viewport control button.

4. In the Rendering Method tab panel, check Default Lighting and select 2 Lights (**Figure 11.9**). Then click OK.

5. Change the Perspective viewport to an ActiveShade viewport by choosing ActiveShade Viewport in the Rendering menu, or by right-clicking the viewport label and choosing ActiveShade under Views.

   The ActiveShade viewport renders the scene (**Figure 11.10**).

6. In the Front viewport, zoom out and pan so you will have plenty of room to place lights around the scene.

7. Choose File > Save, and name your scene Practice.max.

8. Choose File > Save As, and name your scene Practice00.max. This will serve as a back-up copy in case you accidentally save over your scene.

339

Like other objects, you create light objects by clicking and dragging. As soon as you create a light, the default lighting is turned off and the new light illuminates the scene.

A common way of lighting scenes is to use a bright **key light** for primary illumination of a scene, and one or more **fill lights** to make the dark edges of forms more discernable.

In the next three exercises, you'll create a spotlight for your key light and an omni light for your fill light, and then add a direct light to serve as an accent light.

To create a target spotlight:

1. Open Practice.max.

2.  In the Create panel, open the Lights sub-panel.

3. In the Object Type rollout, click Target Spot.

4. In the Front viewport, click in the upper-left corner to create the spotlight. Then drag to the center of the scene to create the target and aim the light (**Figure 11.11**).

   The spotlight illuminates the objects within its cone. The default lights are turned off (**Figure 11.12**).

5. In the General Parameters rollout, enable Shadows (**Figure 11.13**).

   The objects cast shadows. If the ActiveShade viewport does not show the shadows, right-click in the viewport and choose Initialize from the Tools quad menu.

   The viewport is redrawn. Shadows appear in the ActiveShade viewport and in rendered views (**Figure 11.14**).

6. Save the scene as Practice01.max.

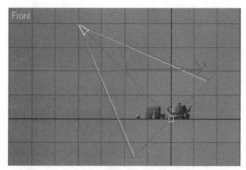

Figure 11.11 A target spotlight has a source, a cone of illumination, and a target.

Figure 11.12 The cone of illumination delimits the pool of light.

Figure 11.13 After enabling shadows for the spotlight.

Figure 11.14 The objects cast shadows based on the position of the source.

Figure 11.15 The Multiplier increased to 1.25.

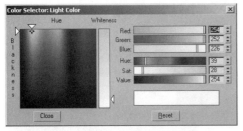

Figure 11.16 Selecting a color for the light.

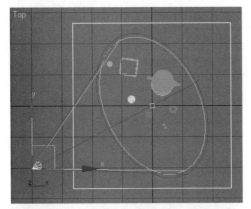

Figure 11.17 After positioning the light to the front of the scene.

Figure 11.18 After repositioning the light and its target.

There are many parameters you can adjust on a light, but the settings that you usually adjust right away are the intensity, color, position, and aim. Additional light settings are explained in the sections on shadow casting and controlling illumination.

To adjust a target spotlight:

1. Open Practice01.max.

2. Select the spotlight.

3. Open the Modify panel.

4. In the Intensity/Color/Attenuation rollout, increase the Multiplier to 1.25, or just enough to brighten the scene without washing it out (**Figure 11.15**).

5. In the Intensity/Color/Attenuation rollout, click the white color swatch.

6. In the Color Selector: Light Color dialog box, select a color using the Blackness, Hue, and Whiteness sliders, or type in the RGB or HSV amounts (**Figure 11.16**).

7. In the Top viewport, select and move the light so that it is about 30 in front of the scene (**Figure 11.17**).

8. Right-click on the light and choose Select Light Target from the Tools 1 quad menu.

9. Move the target to the origin. You can do this easily by right-clicking the X, Y, and Z spinners of the Transform Type-in boxes on the status bar, while in Absolute mode.

10. Render your scene to see the result (**Figure 11.18**).

11. Adjust the light further until you are satisfied. Then save your scene.

CREATING LIGHTS

341

Omni lights are made up of a single component that radiates in all directions. They are the simplest type of light to create and control.

To create an omni light:

1. Open Practice01.max.

2. In the Create panel, open the Lights sub-panel.

3. In the Object Type rollout, click Omni.

4. In the Front viewport, click in the lower-right corner to create the omni light (**Figure 11.19**).

   The objects in the scene are lit from below and to the right. The plane does not block the light because its surface normals face away from the light (**Figure 11.20**).

5. In either the Top or Left viewport, move the omni light slightly in back of the scene so it is opposite the spotlight (**Figure 11.21**).

6. In the Intensity/Color/Attenuation rollout, reduce the Multiplier of the light to around .5, or just enough to dimly illuminate the dark sides of the objects.

7. Render the scene to see the result (**Figure 11.22**).

8. Save the scene as Practice02.max.

✔ Tip

- To add the two default lights to the scene, open the Viewport Configuration dialog box by right-clicking on any viewport control button. In the Rendering Options area of the Rendering Method tab panel, enable Default Lighting and 2 Lights. Close the dialog box and choose Views > Add Default Lights to Scene. Two omni lights named DefaultFillLight and DefaultKeyLight are added to the scene, and can be adjusted like any other lights.

Figure 11.19 After creating the omni light in the Front viewport.

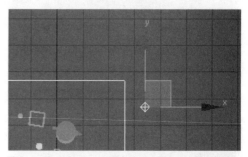

Figure 11.20 The scene is now lit from below right.

Figure 11.21 After moving the omni light into position.

Figure 11.22 The key light and fill light illuminate the objects from the front left and back right.

CREATING LIGHTS

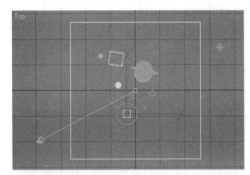

Figure 11.23 Place the free directional light directly over an object.

Figure 11.24 When you first set the directional light, it may be too bright.

Figure 11.25 After adjusting the lights and turning on cast shadows.

Free lights are aimed without using a target. This makes them easier to animate.

Free spotlights and directional lights are created with a single click. The light is automatically aimed at the grid of the viewport in which you clicked (the construction grid).

To create a free directional light:

1. Open Practice02.max.

2. In the Create panel, open the Lights sub-panel.

3. In the Object Type rollout, click Free Direct.

4. In the Top viewport, click on top of an object that you would like to highlight.

   The free directional light appears in the viewport on top of the object (**Figure 11.23**).

5. In the Front or Left viewport, move the directional light above the object.

   The light singles out the object with additional illumination (**Figure 11.24**).

6. Open the Modify panel. In the Intensity/Color/Attenuation rollout, reduce the Multiplier of the directional light so that it doesn't bleach out the object. Try a setting of around .5.

7. In the General Parameters rollout, check On in the Shadows area to enable shadow casting for the directional light.

8. Select the spotlight. Then reduce its intensity multiplier to around 1.1.

9. Render the scene to see the result (**Figure 11.25**).

10. Save the scene as Practice03.max.

✔ Tip

■ Decreasing a Multiplier setting to a negative value causes a light to remove illumination from a scene.

CREATING LIGHTS

A skylight acts as a dome of light to create the illusion of outdoor lighting. No matter where you place a skylight, it always illuminates the scene from above.

To create a skylight:

1. Open Practice.max.

2. 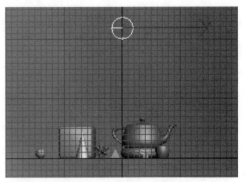 In the Create panel, open the Lights sub-panel.

3. In the Object Type rollout, click Skylight.

4. Click in any viewport.

    The skylight appears in the viewport (**Figure 11.26**).

5. Choose Rendering > Advanced Lighting > Light Tracer from the menu bar.

6. In the Advanced Lighting tab panel of the Render Scene dialog box, choose Light Tracer from the drop-down menu.

    The Light Tracer rollouts appear and become active (**Figure 11.27**).

7. To make the scene more realistic, choose Render > Environment and change the Environment Background color to light gray.

8. Click the ActiveShade viewport to activate it.

9. From the Main toolbar, choose Quick Render (Production).

    The scene renders line by line. When it is done, the skylight diffusely illuminates the scene from above. Faint shadows gather below each object (**Figure 11.28**).

10. Save as Practice04.max.

✔ Tip

- To increment a file name by +01, click the plus sign (+) in the Save File As dialog box.

Figure 11.26 Placing a skylight in the scene.

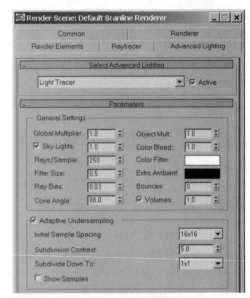

Figure 11.27 The Light Tracer controls skylights.

Figure 11.28 The skylight diffusely illuminates the scene from above.

CREATING LIGHTS

Figure 11.29
The Sunlight system positions the sun according to the time, date, and geographical location that you set.

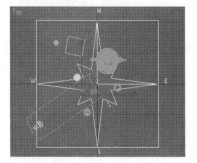

Figure 11.30 The compass sets the direction; the light illuminates the scene.

Figure 11.31 Picking a new location from the list.

Figure 11.32 Sunlight casts crisp shadows.

A sunlight system is a combination of a free directional light and a compass rose that sets the orientation of the system. Ray-traced shadows are on by default.

To create a sunlight system:

1. Open Practice.max.

2. In the Create panel, open the Lights sub-panel.

3. In the Object Type rollout, click Sunlight. In Control Parameters rollout, the time and date control the position of the sun along with a geographical location (**Figure 11.29**).

4. In the Top viewport, click and drag to create a compass rose of any size.

5. Move the cursor up or down to set the orbital distance of the sun. Then click to create the light (**Figure 11.30**).

6. In the Control Parameters rollout, set the time, date, and time zone for the light. You can also set latitude and longitude, or pick a location by clicking Get Location (**Figure 11.31**).

7. Open the Directional Parameters rollout in the Modify panel, and uncheck Overshoot. Then increase the Hotspot/Beam until the cone of illumination encompasses the entire scene, so that shadows will appear throughout.

8. Click the ActiveShade viewport. Then click Quick Render (Production). Sunlight floods the scene. The ray-traced shadows are crisp and precise (**Figure 11.32**).

9. Save as Practice05.max.

✔ Tip

■ After creating a sunlight system, you change its settings in the Motion panel.

CREATING LIGHTS

A daylight system combines sunlight and skylight into one integrated system.

To create a daylight system:

1. Open Practice.max.

2. In the Create panel, open the Lights sub-panel.

3. In the Object Type rollout, click Daylight.

   The Control Parameters rollout appears. It looks just like a Sunlight System rollout.

4. In the Top viewport, click and drag to create a compass rose. Then move the cursor up or down and click to set the orbital distance of the daylight assembly head (**Figure 11.33**).

5. In the Control Parameters rollout, set the time, date, and time zone for the light. You can also set the latitude and longitude, or pick a location by clicking Get Location.

   This positions the sun in the sky.

6. Choose Rendering > Advanced Lighting > Light Tracer or press 9 on your keyboard.

7. In the Advanced Lighting tab panel of the Render Scene dialog box, choose Light Tracer.

8. Choose Render > Environment. Then choose a Background color for the sky.

9. In the Exposure Control rollout, choose Automatic Exposure control from the drop-down menu. Then Activate the ActiveShade viewport, and click Render Preview (**Figure 11.34**).

10. Adjust the exposure as needed. Then click Quick Render (Production).

    Sunlight and daylight illuminate the scene (**Figure 11.35**).

11. Save as Practice06.max.

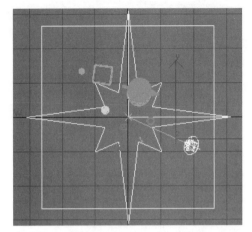

Figure 11.33 The compass orients the daylight assembly head to the location.

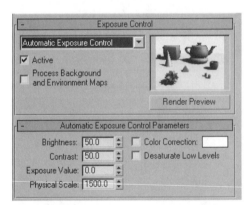

Figure 11.34 You adjust exposure in the Environment dialog box.

Figure 11.35 The final scene is illuminated with both sunlight and skylight.

Figure 11.36 Shadow map shadows have soft edges.

Figure 11.37 Area shadows produce soft, atmospheric shadows.

Figure 11.38 Ray-traced shadows have hard edges.

Figure 11.39 Advanced ray-traced shadows use anti-aliasing to produce soft edges.

Casting Shadows

There are four types of shadows that the scanline renderer can project from a light:

◆ **Shadow maps** are bitmaps that are projected from a light. They are created by the scanline renderer during a pre-rendering pass of the scene and applied during rendering. Shadow maps give shadows a soft edge, as if they are being diffused by the atmosphere.

Shadow maps are the default shadow type for most lights (**Figure 11.36**).

◆ **Area shadows** simulate shadows that are cast from an illuminated area or volume. They use anti-aliasing to produce soft, atmospheric shadows and they support opacity and transparency mapping (see Chapter 14, "Maps," for more information) (**Figure 11.37**).

◆ **Ray-traced shadows** are calculated by tracing a ray from source to object. Sharper and more precise than shadow-map shadows, ray-traced shadows are usually slower to render. Ray-traced shadows are perfect for architectural shadow studies, which is why they are the default shadow type for sunlight systems. Like area shadows, ray-traced shadows support opacity and transparency mapping, but they do not support soft shadows (**Figure 11.38**).

◆ **Advanced ray-traced shadows** are a variation of ray-traced shadows that use less RAM for rendering. They can use anti-aliasing to produce soft edges (**Figure 11.39**).

The fifth type of shadow, the **mental ray shadow map,** can only be used with the mental ray renderer. If mental ray shadow maps are used with the scanline renderer, no shadows will be rendered.

Once you select a shadow type, you can adjust its color, density, and position, plus other qualities specific to that type. The adjustments that you make to a shadow determine the speed at which it will render.

To change shadow type:

1. Open Practice02.max.

2.  Render the scene to see what the shadows look like (**Figure 11.40**).

3. Select the spotlight.

4. Open the Modify panel.

5. In the General Parameters rollout, choose a shadow type from the drop-down list (**Figure 11.41**).

6. Render the scene to see the result (**Figure 11.42**).

✔ Tip

- Ray-traced shadows render more slowly when you use them with omni lights. If possible, use ray-traced shadows with spotlights or directional lights instead. If you still need the effect of an omni or directional light, check Overshoot so the shadows will only be calculated within the cone.

Figure 11.40 The practice scene has soft shadow mapped shadows.

Figure 11.41 Changing the shadow type to Ray Traced Shadows.

Figure 11.42 The ray-traced shadows are more crisp and precise.

Figure 11.43 Before and after adjusting a shadow map.

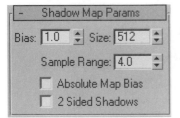

Figure 11.44 The Shadow Map Params rollout provides the means to correct shadow maps.

Figure 11.45 Increasing the map size and sample range focuses the shadow. Adjusting the map bias brings the shadow bank into alignment. To make the gap between the teapot and its lid disappear, check 2 Sided Shadows.

Shadow maps sometimes appear blurry, faint, or detached from the objects that cast them. Shadow-map parameters help you fix these problems (**Figure 11.43**):

◆ **Bias**—Offsets shadows from the object that casts them. Lowering the Bias value moves shadows closer to the object.

◆ **Size**—Controls the resolution of a shadow by setting the size of the bitmap that generates the shadow. Increasing this parameter sharpens shadow edges and increases rendering time.

◆ **Sample Range**—Controls the sharpness of shadows by averaging different sized areas of the shadow map. If a shadow smudges, streaks, or creates moiré patterns, the Sample Range setting is probably too high. A Sample Range setting that is too low creates jagged shadows.

◆ **Absolute Map Bias**—Determines how the map bias is computed in relation to the rest of the scene. Use this option to end flickering shadows in an animation.

◆ **2 Sided Shadows**—Causes surfaces to cast shadows as if they were double sided.

To get the most accurate feedback, render the scene after you change each parameter.

To adjust a shadow map:

1. Select a light that has a problematic shadow map, such as the spotlight in Practice02.max.

2. Open the Modify panel.

3. Open the Shadow Map Params rollout (**Figure 11.44**).

4. Increase the Size and the Sample Range to improve the resolution of the shadow. Then decrease the Bias until the shadows touch the objects that cast them (**Figure 11.45**).

5. Save the scene.

CASTING SHADOWS

Ray Traced shadows produce hard-edged shadows that rarely need correcting. Like shadow map shadows, they allow you to adjust the shadow bias and render 2-sided shadows. In addition, the Max Quadtree Depth setting controls the rendering speed of ray-traced shadows by setting the maximum size of the data structure that generates them.

Advanced Ray-Traced shadows allow you to add anti-aliased edges and control their smoothness. You can also add noise to the shadows to offset shadow artifacts.

For more information on shadow parameters for each of the shadow types, open the 3ds max 6 User Reference and go to Contents > Lights and Cameras > Lights > Rollouts for Specific Shadow Types.

To speed up rendering of ray-traced shadows:

1. Open Practice05.max. Then select Sun01 (**Figure 11.46**).

2. 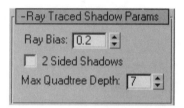 Open the Modify panel.

3. Open the Ray Traced Shadow Params menu (**Figure 11.47**).

4. Increase the Max Quadtree depth.

5. Render the scene.
   The scene renders faster.

Figure 11.46 This sunlit scene has ray-traced shadows that are slow to render.

Figure 11.47 Ray Traced shadows have few parameters. For faster rendering, increase Max Quadtree Depth.

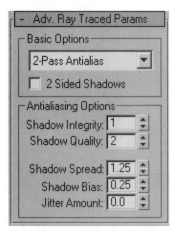

Figure 11.48 The Adv. Ray Traced Params rollout allows you to set options for anti-aliasing and adding noise to ray-traced shadows.

To anti-alias ray-traced shadows:

1. In the General Parameters rollout, convert the shadows of the Sun01 object to advanced ray-traced shadows.

2. Open the Adv. Ray Traced rollout (**Figure 11.48**).

3. Increase the Shadow Integrity to 5 and the Shadow Quality to 10. Then increase the Shadow Spread to 4.

4. Render the scene (**Figure 11.49**).

5. Continue to play with the parameters until you get the effect that you like. Be sure to try increasing the Jitter Amount to see what it looks like when you add noise to the shadow.

Figure 11.49 The anti-aliased shadows have softer edges.

CASTING SHADOWS

You can set shadow color for all types of shadows independently of the color of the light. Use this feature to simulate reflected color from nearby objects or from secondary light sources such as the sky.

To set shadow color:

1.  Select a light that casts shadows (**Figure 11.50**).

2. Open the Modify panel.

3. Open the Shadow Parameters rollout.

4. Click the Color swatch (**Figure 11.51**).

5. Choose a color in the Color Selector: Shadow Color dialog box (**Figure 11.52**).

6. Render the scene. The shadow changes color (**Figure 11.53**).

Figure 11.50 The object casts a black shadow.

Figure 11.51 Click the color swatch.

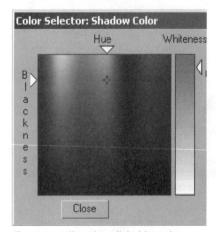

Figure 11.52 Choosing a light-blue color.

Figure 11.53 The shadow changes to light-blue.

CASTING SHADOWS

Figure 11.54 The object casts a shadow of Density = 1.0.

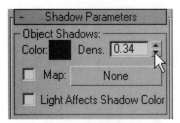

Figure 11.55 Decreasing the density of the shadow.

Figure 11.56 The shadow lightens.

The Density parameter sets the value, or darkness, of the shadows without affecting their hue and saturation. Use this feature to fill in shadows or to make them more transparent.

To set shadow density:

1. Select a light that casts shadows (**Figure 11.54**).

2. Open the Modify panel.

3. Open the Shadow Parameters rollout.

4. Set the Density value of the shadow (**Figure 11.55**).

5. Render the scene.
   The shadow becomes darker or lighter (**Figure 11.56**).

✔ Tips

■ To mix the color of the light with the shadow color, check Light Affects Shadow Color in the Shadow Parameters rollout.

■ To project a map into a shadow, check Map, click the None button, and choose a map.

CASTING SHADOWS

Shadow casting is an arrangement between three parties: a light and an object that cast shadows, and an object that receives them.

If you turn off the shadow-casting property of an object, it will not cast shadows for any light.

To turn off shadow casting for an object:

1. Open a scene that is illuminated by a light (**Figure 11.57**).

2. Select an object that is casting a shadow.

3. Right-click on the object, and choose Properties from the Transform quad menu.

4. In the Object Properties dialog box, uncheck Cast Shadows (**Figure 11.58**).

5. Click OK.

6. Render the scene to see the results (**Figure 11.59**).

✔ Tip

■ To prevent any shadows from falling across an object, uncheck Receive Shadows in its Object Properties dialog box (**Figure 11.60**).

Figure 11.57 In this scene, the teapot overshadows the tube.

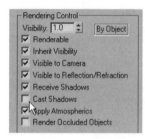

Figure 11.58 Turning off cast shadows for a teapot.

Figure 11.59 After turning off the teapot's shadow, the tube stands out.

Figure 11.60 The tube stands within the teapot's shadow but is not shaded by it.

CASTING SHADOWS

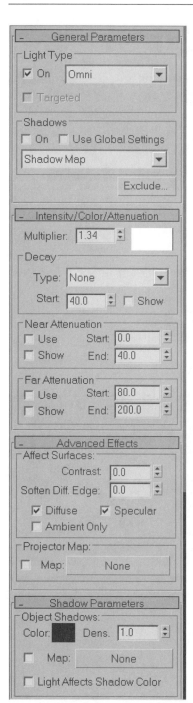

Figure 11.61 Different light types have many of the same parameter settings.

Controlling Illumination

Controlling illumination is essential to creating realistic scenes. The following parameters fine-tune the effects of light (**Figure 11.61**):

- **Light Type On**—Enables illumination.
- **Light Type**—Sets the light type.
- **Targeted**—Enables a target.
- **Cast Shadows On**—Enables shadow casting.
- **ShadowType**—Sets the shadow type.
- **Include/Exclude**—Determines which objects are illuminated by the light.
- **Multiplier**—Controls the intensity, or brightness, of a light.
- **Light Color**—Sets the hue, saturation, and value of a light.
- **Decay**—Diminishes the intensity of a light over its entire attenuation range.
- **Attenuation**—Fades the light at either end of its range.
- **Hot Spot/Beam and Falloff/Field**—Sets the inner and outer boundaries of the cone of illumination.
- **Contrast**—Sets the contrast between ambient and diffuse areas of illumination.
- **Soften Diff. Edge**—Softens the edge between ambient and diffuse areas.
- **Diffuse**—Adds the light to diffuse (middle value) areas of illumination.
- **Specular**—Adds light to specular (high value) areas of illumination.
- **Ambient Only**—Adds light to the minimum level of scene illumination.
- **Projector Map**—Projects an image or animation into a scene.
- **Shadow Color**—Sets the hue, saturation, and value of a shadow.
- **Shadow Density**—Increases or decreases the value of a shadow.

CONTROLLING ILLUMINATION

By default, lights illuminate all objects within range. Turning off a light ends their illumination. Note that hiding a light does not turn it off.

To turn off a light:

1. Open Practice03.max (**Figure 11.62**).

2. 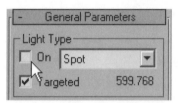 Select a light.

3. Open the Modify panel.

4. Uncheck the On box in the Light Type area of the General Parameters rollout (**Figure 11.63**).

   The light is turned off (**Figure 11.64**).

5. To turn the light back on, check the On box.

Figure 11.62 The practice scene before turning off the spotlight.

Figure 11.63 Uncheck the On box.

Figure 11.64 After turning off the spotlight, the scene is just illuminated by the direct light and the omni light.

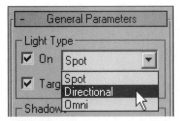

Figure 11.65 Changing the spotlight to a directional light.

Figure 11.66 The spotlight has been changed to a direct light, which is narrower at the far end of its cone.

You can convert a light from one type to another in the Modify panel. When a light changes type, the illumination from the new light type replaces the illumination from the old type.

To change a light type:

1. Open Practice03.max.

2. Select a light.

3. Open the Modify panel.

4. In the General Parameters rollout, choose a light type from the Light Type drop-down list (**Figure 11.65**).

   The new light type replaces the selected light, using the same basic settings.

   The name of the light remains unchanged. If the name of the light is Omni01 and you have just changed it to a target spotlight, this is probably a good time to rename it.

5. Activate the ActiveShade viewport, and render the scene.

   The new light type replaces the old and illuminates the scene (**Figure 11.66**).

✔ Tips

- When you convert an omni light to any other type of light, it points toward the grid of the viewport it was created in.

- The Targeted check box toggles a target on or off.

The Exclude command turns off the illumination of objects that are within range of a light. It can also turn off shadow casting.

To exclude objects from a light:

1. Open Practice02.max.

2. Select the spotlight.

3. Open the Modify panel.

4. Click Exclude in the General Parameters rollout (**Figure 11.67**).

   The Exclude/Include dialog box appears.

5. Make sure Exclude and Both are selected in the upper-right corner.

6. Select the names of the objects or group of objects you do not want to be illuminated or to cast shadows.

7. Click the >> button.

   The names of the objects are moved to the Exclude list on the right (**Figure 11.68**).

8. Click OK.

9. Render the scene.

   The excluded objects neither receive illumination nor cast shadows, giving them an air of mystery (**Figure 11.69**).

✔ Tips

- To remove objects from the exclude list, and end the exclusion of objects, click the Clear button.

- Using the Include button, you can selectively choose just those objects you want to include in a light. All other objects will be excluded automatically.

Figure 11.67 Click the Exclude button.

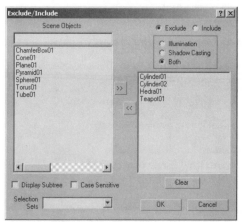

Figure 11.68 Turning off both illumination and shadow casting for the cylinders, hedra, and teapot.

Figure 11.69 Without shadows or major illumination, the excluded objects appear to float in the scene.

CONTROLLING ILLUMINATION

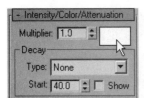

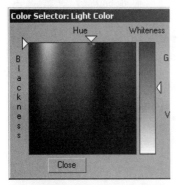

Figure 11.70 Click the color swatch.

Figure 11.71 Picking a color using the palette and whiteness slider.

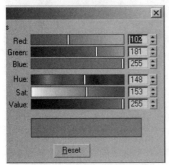

Figure 11.72 Picking the same color numerically.

Figure 11.73 Blue light gives the scene a more somber cast.

Color settings assign hue, value, and saturation to a light. The value of a color also affects its intensity. Brighter colors create brighter lights. Darker colors create dimmer lights.

To set color:

1. Open Practice02.max.

2. Select the spotlight.

3. In the Intensity/Color/Attenuation rollout, click the color swatch just to the right of the Multiplier (**Figure 11.70**).

4. Choose a color from the Color Selector dialog box. There are two basic methods:

   The most intuitive way to do this is to click in the Hue palette on the left and drag the Whiteness slider next to it (**Figure 11.71**).

   When precision is important, you can set numeric RGB or HSV values using the color sliders, input fields, or spinners on the right (**Figure 11.72**).

   As you change the color of the light, the lighting updates in the shaded viewports.

5. When you are satisfied with the result, close the Color Selector dialog box.

6. Render the scene to verify the results (**Figure 11.73**).

✔ Tip

- Light and color can be animated over time.

Global lighting commands shift the base intensity and color of all the lights in a scene, including the default lights.

Initially, the base intensity is set to 1.0 and the base color is set to white. Ambient light, which sets the minimum level of scene illumination, is set to black (no light). Changing these settings will affect the overall amount of color and illumination of the scene.

Because ambient light brightens darker values, increasing it reduces contrast across surfaces. Use this setting sparingly, so it does not wash out your scene.

To set global lighting:

1. Open Practice03.max (**Figure 11.74**).

2. Choose Rendering > Environment to open the Environment and Effects dialog box.

3. In the Global Lighting area, set the base intensity of the lights by adjusting the Level (**Figure 11.75**).

   The scene brightens or dims (**Figure 11.76**).

4. Reset the Level to 1.0, then click the Tint color swatch.

5. In the Color Selector: Global Light Tint dialog box, choose a hue and whiteness value.

   The color and intensity of the illumination updates.

6. Click the Ambient color swatch.

   The Color Selector changes to the Color Selector: Ambient Light dialog box.

7. Drag the Whiteness slider to set the minimum level of illumination. Then select a hue.

   Gradations of value become lighter throughout the scene and tinted by the hue that you selected (**Figure 11.77**).

Figure 11.74 Before changing the global lighting.

Figure 11.75 Reducing the global lighting level.

Figure 11.76 All the lights are dimmed.

Figure 11.77 Increasing the value of the ambient color reduces contrast in the scene.

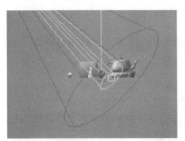

Figure 11.78 Adjust the hotspot and falloff in the spotlight parameters rollout.

Figure 11.79 The hotspot cone narrows more than the falloff cone.

Figure 11.80 The pool of light gains a softer edge.

Figure 11.81 The cone of the directional light narrows.

A light cone is actually made of two concentric cones: the inner core of illumination, or **hotspot**, and the outer edge of illumination, or **falloff**. Between these two cones the light forms a gradient from full intensity to zero.

To set the hotspot and falloff:

1. Open Practice03.max

2. Select the spotlight.

3. Open the Modify panel.

4. In the Spotlight Parameters rollout, decrease the Falloff/Field value (**Figure 11.78**). Then decrease the Hotspot/Beam value even more (**Figure 11.79**).

   In the ActiveShade viewport, the edge of the pool of light becomes softer (**Figure 11.80**).

5. Select the directional light.

6. In the Directional Parameters rollout, decrease the Falloff amount so that the hotspot and falloff cones shrink.

7. Render the ActiveShade viewport. The pool of light from the directional light becomes smaller, but its edges remain sharp (**Figure 11.81**).

✔ Tips

- Check Show Cone to display the cone even when the light is not selected.

- Checking Overshoot causes the light to ignore the boundaries of the hotspot and falloff cones and spread throughout the scene. Shadows, however, will be drawn within the cone of illumination only.

- Click Rectangle to make the pool of light rectangular or square. The Aspect parameter sets the aspect ratio of the length and width of the rectangle. The Bitmap Fit button will match the aspect ratio to an external bitmap, in case you want to project the map.

CONTROLLING ILLUMINATION

361

Projecting maps into a scene creates the illusion that there is more going on than meets the eye.

To project a map:

1. Open Practice02.max.

2. Select the spotlight.

3. Open the Modify panel.

4. In the Advanced Effects rollout, click the Projector Map button labeled None (**Figure 11.82**).

   The Material/Map Browser window appears.

5. Double-click Bitmap (**Figure 11.83**).

6. Choose a bitmap image using the Select Bitmap Image File dialog box. For this example, I chose the SCATR4.gif in the 3dsmax5/Maps/Lights folder.

   When you click Open, the bitmap image is projected by the spotlight onto the scene.

7. Increase the light multiplier to compensate for the reduced intensity of the bitmap.

8. Render the scene (**Figure 11.84**).

✔ Tips

- A black-and-white map that is designed to be used with a spotlight is called a **gobo map**.

- Try some of the other maps in the Material/Map Browser such as Brick, Cellular, Checker, Dent, Gradient Ramp, Perlin Marble, and Smoke (**Figure 11.85**).

Figure 11.82 Click the Projector Map button.

Figure 11.83 Double-click Bitmap in the Material/Map Browser.

Figure 11.84 The SCATR4 map projects spots of light and shadow.

Figure 11.85 Projecting a checker map that has been tiled in the Material Editor.

Figure 11.86 Check Use and Show for Far Attenuation.

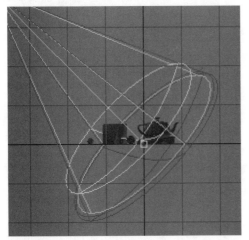

Figure 11.87 Setting the Far Attenuation range indicators.

Figure 11.88 The light falls off across the scene more dramatically.

Attenuation fades in a light near its source and fades out a light at the far end of its range.

To set attenuation:

1. Open Practice02.max.

2. Select the spotlight.

3. Open the Modify panel and the Intensity/Color/Attenuation rollout.

4. In the Far Attenuation group, check Use and Show (**Figure 11.86**).

   The far attenuation ranges appear. In the ActiveShade view, the light from the spotlight will disappear if the objects are out of the light's current attenuation range.

5. Drag the Far Attenuation spinners so that the Start and End ranges just enclose the scene objects (**Figure 11.87**).

6. Render the scene to see the final result (**Figure 11.88**).

✔ Tips

■ Because light can continue shining forever, it is a good idea to use far attenuation so that the program won't waste time making unnecessary calculations.

■ The Decay parameter increases the rate at which a beam of light diminishes as it moves away from its source.

Volume lighting is an atmospheric effect that is based on the real-world interaction between light and particulate matter such as fog, haze, dust, and smoke. It gives you the hazy glow of streetlights on a misty evening, the sweep of a lighthouse beacon on a foggy morning, or the rays of sunlight streaming through a window.

Volumetric lighting works with all types of light sources, although it is most commonly used with spotlights. Because volume lighting is a true 3D effect, you can render it only from viewports that use perspective projection.

To create a volume light:

1. Select a light that illuminates a scene.

2. Open the Modify panel.

3. Open the Atmospheres & Effects rollout. (Note: This rollout does not appear in the Create panel.)

4. Click the Add button (**Figure 11.89**).

5. Choose Volume Light from the Add Atmosphere or Effect dialog box (**Figure 11.90**). Then click OK.

6. Render the scene from a viewport that displays perspective, such as a Perspective, Camera, or Light viewport. The light is rendered volumetrically (**Figure 11.91**).

✔ Tips

- Decreasing the size of the hotspot can make a Volume Light easier to control.

- By animating attenuation, you can make a Volume Light "touch down" and "beam up."

- Combining a projector map with a Volume Light creates interesting results (**Figure 11.92**).

Figure 11.89 Click Add in the Atmospheres & Effects rollout.

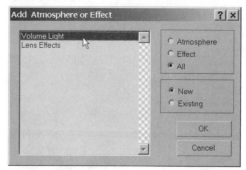

Figure 11.90 Add Volume Light to the spotlight.

Figure 11.91 The Volume Light renders in three dimensions.

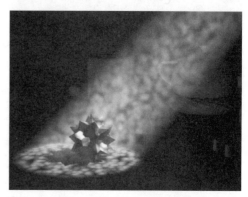

Figure 11.92 When added to a Volume Light, a Cellular map projects in three dimensions.

Figure 11.93
The Light viewport controls navigate Light viewports.

Navigating Lights

When you activate a light view, the viewport window controls change to a new set of navigation buttons called the light viewport controls (**Figure 11.93**). By navigating lights with the light viewport controls, you can fine-tune their placement and animate them over time.

The names of light viewport controls are based on traditional terms for making movies. For a complete description of the light viewport controls, see **Table 11.1**.

Table 11.1

Light Viewport Controls

ICON	NAME	DESCRIPTION
	Dolly Light	Moves light along its local Z axis or line of sight.
	Dolly Light + Target	Moves light and target along light's Z axis.
	Dolly Target	Moves target along light's Z axis.
	Light Hotspot	Changes the size of the hotspot.
	Light Falloff	Changes the size of the falloff.
	Roll Light	Rotates light around its Z axis.
	Zoom Extents All	Centers objects in all non-fixed viewports.
	Zoom Extents All Selected	Centers selected objects in all non-fixed viewports.
	Truck Light	Moves light and target parallel to the view plane.
	Orbit Light	Rotates light around its target.
	Pan Light	Rotates light. Target rotates around light.
	Min/Max Toggle	Toggles between viewport layout and full display.

Note: Free lights use virtual targets for the Dolly, Truck, Pan, and Orbit commands.

You can look at a scene from the point of view of a spotlight or a directional light.

To change a view to a light view:

1. Open a scene that has a spotlight or directional light in it.

2. Activate the viewport you want to change.

3. Type $ (Shift + 4).

    The Select Light dialog box appears (**Figure 11.94**).

4. Select a light, and click OK.
    The view in the viewport changes to the Light view (**Figure 11.95**).

Figure 11.94 The Select Light dialog box prompts you to choose a light.

Figure 11.95 The Light viewport shows how the scene looks from the standpoint of the light.

Figure 11.96 Open the Spotlight viewport.

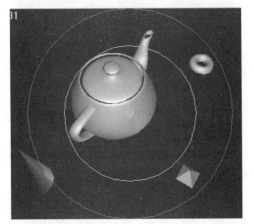

Figure 11.97 The scene enlarges in the viewport after you dolly the light closer to its target.

Figure 11.98 The pool of illumination shrinks.

To dolly a light:

1. Change a view to a Light view (**Figure 11.96**).

2. Click the Dolly Light button in the light viewport controls.

3. Drag the dolly cursor up or down in the Light viewport.

   The light moves in or out along its local Z axis, or "line of shine" (**Figure 11.97**).

   The pool of illumination shrinks or expands (**Figure 11.98**).

✔ Tips

- To dolly a target, choose Dolly Target from the Dolly Light flyout.

- To dolly a light and its target together, choose Dolly Light + Target from the same flyout.

The Truck command moves a light and its target across a scene parallel to the plane of the Light viewport.

To truck a light:

1. Open a scene with a light in it (**Figure 11.99**).

2. Change a view to a Light view.

3. ![hand icon] Click the Truck Light button.

4. Drag the panning hand across the Light viewport.

   The Light viewport moves across the scene (**Figure 11.100**).

   The cone of illumination moves as well (**Figure 11.101**).

Figure 11.99 The scene before you truck the light.

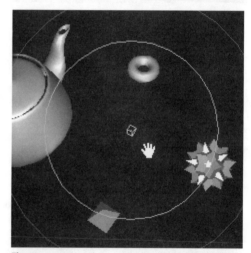

Figure 11.100 Use the panning hand to truck the light.

Figure 11.101 After moving the cone of illumination to the right.

Figure 11.102 Using a rectangular cone of illumination, the light projects a Brick map onto the scene.

Figure 11.103 After rolling the light about 50°.

Figure 11.104 The map rolls with the projector.

Roll rotates a light along its line of sight. This affects the scene only if the light casts a rectangular cone or uses a projector map.

To roll a light:

1. Open a scene that is lit by a rectangular cone of illumination (**Figure 11.102**).

2. Change a view to a Light view.

3. Click Roll Light.

4. Drag the roll cursor across the Light viewport.

   The light rotates around its depth axis (**Figure 11.103**).

   The pool of illumination, and any maps that are being projected, roll with the light (**Figure 11.104**).

Orbit Light moves a spot or directional light around its target. If the light is a free light, it uses a virtual target located at the end of the light cone.

To orbit a light:

1. Open a scene (**Figure 11.105**).

2. Change a viewport to a Light view.

3.  Click the Orbit Light button in the Light viewport controls.

4. Drag the cursor in the Light viewport.

   The light rotates around its target (**Figure 11.106**).

   The light orbits around the scene (**Figure 11.107**).

✔ Tip

- To align a light to a surface normal, select the light and choose Place Highlight from the Align flyout. Then click the object. The light aligns to the surface normal at the point where you clicked in order to set the highlight there. It remains at the same distance from the object. For more information on controlling highlights, see Chapter 13, "Materials."

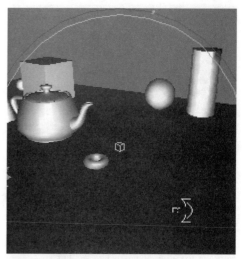

Figure 11.105 This scene is mainly lit from above and to the left.

Figure 11.106 Orbiting the light around its target.

Figure 11.107 The scene is now illuminated from above and to the right.

NAVIGATING LIGHTS

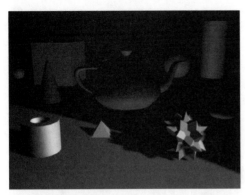

Figure 11.108 The light initially falls on the left front corner of the scene.

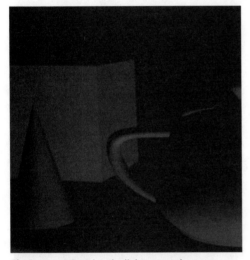

Figure 11.109 Panning the light across the scene.

Figure 11.110 The light sweeps across the scene.

Pan Light rotates a target around a light. If the light is a free light, it uses a virtual target located at the end of the light cone.

To pan a light:

1. Open a scene that is lit by a spotlight or a directional light (**Figure 11.108**).

2. Change a view to a Light view.

3. Click the Pan Light button in the Light viewport controls, located on the Orbit Light flyout.

4. Drag the cursor across the Light viewport.

   The Light view pans across the scene (**Figure 11.109**).

   The light sweeps across the scene (**Figure 11.110**).

NAVIGATING LIGHTS

Animating Lights

Lights are animated by keyframing or linking, or by assigning animation controllers to them (**Figure 11.111**).

Any numerical parameter of a light can be keyframed, including intensity, color, contrast, hotspot, falloff, attenuation, and shadow density. You can also keyframe the position and orientation of a light using the Move and Rotate transforms and the Light window controls. However, parameters that use checkboxes cannot be keyframed.

Linking a light to a moving object ensures that the light will illuminate the object or objects nearby—think running lights or headlights on a car. If the light is linked to a camera, the light will shine wherever the camera is pointed.

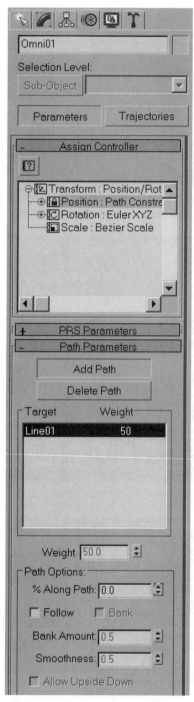

Figure 11.111 You animate a light to follow a path by assigning a path constraint to it.

ANIMATING LIGHTS

Figure 11.112 Linking the omni light to the hedra.

Figure 11.113 The hedra is lit from above and below.

Figure 11.114 When you move the hedra, the omni light and the target light follow it.

The Look At constraint turns a light into a searchlight that always points at a target object. Moving the target over time is an easy way to animate the light. (Use a non-rendering helper object such as a dummy or a point if you do not want the target to be seen.) 3ds max automatically assigns the Look At constraint to spotlights and directional lights, so all you need to do is tell the light where to look.

To make lights follow an object:

1. Open Practice03.max, and close the ActiveShade view. (Note: The scene may shift a little when you close the view.)

2. Link the omni light to the object above it (**Figure 11.112**).

3. Turn off the spotlight. Then increase the Multiplier of the directional light to 1.5 (**Figure 11.113**).

4. In the Modify panel, convert the directional light to a Target Direct type.

5. Open the Motion panel.

6. In the Look At Parameters rollout, click the Pick Target button. Then click the highlighted object.

7. Move the object. The lights follow the object (**Figure 11.114**).

By animating the intensity multiplier, you can make lights dim and brighten over time.

To animate light intensity:

1. Open Practice03.max.

2. Close the ActiveShade view.

3.  Pan the Perspective viewport so that an object is in the center of the composition.

4. Choose Tools > Light Lister.

5. In the Light Lister dialog box, turn off the spotlight. Then set the omni Multiplier to 0 (**Figure 11.115**). The scene dims (**Figure 11.116**).

6. Turn on the Auto Key button. Then drag the time slider to frame 50.

7. In the Light Lister, set the directional light multiplier to 1.5. Then set the omni light multiplier to .5 (**Figure 11.117**).

8. Drag the time slider to frame 100.

9. Set the intensity of both the directional light and the omni light to 0.

10. Play back the animation.

The lights brighten and dim.

✔ Tips

- To animate a light turning on and off, change the tangent type of the Multiplier keys to Step, or assign an On/Off controller to the Multiplier track.

- By cloning the directional light and adding volume and a projector map, you can create a transporter that beams up your objects (**Figure 11.118**).

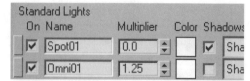

Figure 11.115 Light settings in the Light Lister utility.

Figure 11.116 Start with dim lighting.

Figure 11.117 As the overhead light brightens to full intensity, the fill light brightens with it.

Figure 11.118 Beam me up, Scotty!

Sidebar: ANIMATING LIGHTS

CAMERAS

Figure 12.1 Imaginative camera placement adds drama to your story.

In the previous chapters, you learned how to model and animate objects. With cameras, you determine how the audience views the scene.

Cameras make you the director of your own movie. To tell your story, you compose shots to show the part of the scene where the action takes place. As you become more experienced, you begin setting up shots from more informative, beautiful, mysterious, unusual, helpful, or surprising points of view (**Figure 12.1**).

This chapter explains how you create and adjust different types of cameras and how to use cameras to create effects. You will also learn how to animate cameras using keyframes and motion paths.

Viewing Scenes

Camera placement determines the composition of your final image. It tells the viewer what is important, and it places the viewer in the scene. By positioning a camera properly, you can transform a scene from mediocre to memorable.

If you want to make viewers feel as if they are participating in a scene, place the camera at eye level. For example, if you are designing an architectural walk-through, the eye-level camera creates the feeling that the viewer is actually taking a tour of the building (**Figure 12.2**).

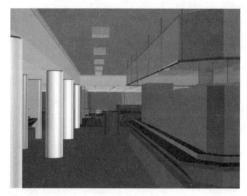

Figure 12.2 Proper camera placement makes viewers feel as if they are a part of the scene.

Maybe you are re-creating a car accident scene and you want to show what led up to the accident. You might position a camera so it gives viewers the idea that they are in a helicopter that is keeping pace with the vehicle. Placing a camera high above a scene creates an omnipotent point of view, like that of a narrator (or lawyer) telling a story (**Figure 12.3**). Adding a second camera at eye level places your witness on the scene (**Figure 12.4**).

Figure 12.3 Place the camera overhead, aiming downward, for a storytelling viewpoint.

Close-up shots give the impression of intimacy, like watching a character in a soap opera. Long shots create an impersonal feeling, like gazing across the vast sweep of the Western frontier. If you are working from an existing image, matching the shot may be the first step you take in creating a digital matte painting.

To create a feeling of insignificance, place the camera close to the ground, so that it is level with an ant's point of view. This gives the viewer the impression that everything is huge and overwhelming by making objects loom steeply overhead, as in **Figure 12.1**.

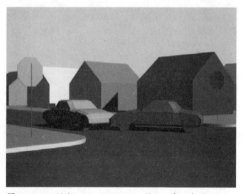

Figure 12.4 Using two vantage points often helps describe an incident better.

Effects such as fog and depth of field blurring are also controlled by camera placement (**Figure 12.5**).

Figure 12.5 Fog is an effect that is governed by camera placement.

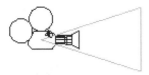

Figure 12.6 The camera cone is a pyramid whose tip is the camera. The target camera (top) displays a target at the focal length of the camera.

Figure 12.7 You can create two types of cameras in 3ds max: target cameras and free cameras.

Creating Cameras

A camera is a nonrendering object that displays a view of a scene. The location and direction of the view is determined by the position and orientation of the camera.

Just as illumination can be considered an effect of a light, displaying a view can be considered an effect of a camera. To delimit a view, cameras use a field of view cone similar to a light's cone of illumination. The main difference is a camera's cone is shaped like a pyramid. The angle of the cone ranges in arc from 0° to 175° across its width. The default field of view setting is 45°.

Like lights, cameras are either targeted or free (**Figure 12.6**):

❖ **Target Cameras**—Composed of a camera and a target component. Each component can move independently, but the camera always points at the target. This feature makes target cameras easy to aim.

❖ **Free Cameras**—Single-object cameras that use a virtual target. Free cameras move and rotate easily, which makes them better for animating complex camera movements.

As with other objects in 3ds max, you create cameras in the Create panel (**Figure 12.7**).

Target cameras are easy to create and aim. You just click and drag from camera to target.

To create a target camera:

1. Open a scene.

2. ![icons] Open the Cameras branch of the Create panel.

3. Click Target.

4. In the Top viewport, position the cursor where you want to place the camera. Use 3D Snap to align the camera precisely.

5. Click to create the camera, and drag to aim it. Release the mouse button to set the target (**Figure 12.8**).

6. Activate a viewport, and type C to change the viewport to a Camera viewport.

   The viewport displays the view from the camera (**Figure 12.9**).

7. Adjust the position and orientation of the camera by moving and rotating it.

8. Aim the camera by moving its target.

   To select a target quickly, right-click on the camera and choose Select Camera Target from the Tools1 quad menu.

✔ Tips

■ You can also change views to a Camera view using the viewport right-click menu.

■ To match a camera to a Perspective view, select the camera in the Perspective view-port and type Ctrl + C (**Figure 12.10**).

■ To create a target camera that is matched to a Perspective view, activate the Perspective viewport and type Ctrl + C.

■ To fine-tune the position of the camera, see "Navigating Cameras" later in this chapter.

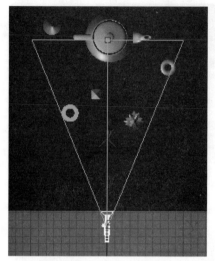

Figure 12.8 To aim a camera horizontally in your scene, create it in the Top viewport.

Figure 12.9 The initial view from the target camera.

Figure 12.10 After matching the camera to the Perspective view.

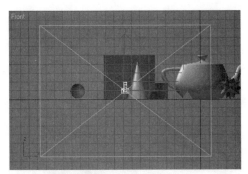

Figure 12.11 To point the free camera into your scene, create it in the Front viewport.

Figure 12.12 The initial view from the free camera. Note: The plane in these practice scenes is mapped with a Checker map. See Chapter 14, "Maps," for information on mapping objects.

Figure 12.13 The Select Camera dialog box lets you choose which camera to use.

Free cameras are easy to move. You create a free camera with a single click.

To create a free camera:

1. Open a scene.

2. Open the Cameras branch of the Create panel.

3. Click Free.

4. Click the location where you want to place the camera.

   The camera appears in the viewport, facing the active grid (**Figure 12.11**).

5. Activate a viewport and type C to see the view from the camera (**Figure 12.12**).

6. Move or rotate the camera to position and aim it.

   or

   Match the camera to the Perspective viewport as explained in the tip for creating a target camera.

✔ Tip

■ If the scene includes multiple cameras, and none are selected, typing C opens the Select Camera dialog box so you can choose which camera to use (**Figure 12.13**).

CREATING CAMERAS

The Align Camera command aligns a camera to the surface normal of an object.

To align a camera to an object:

1. Select a camera.

2. Choose Align Camera from the Align flyout in the Main toolbar.

3. Place the cursor on the surface of an object. Then click and hold down the mouse button.

   A blue normal appears to indicate the direction of alignment (**Figure 12.14**).

4. Drag the cursor until the normal points in the direction that you want to align the camera. Then release the mouse button.

   The camera aligns to the normal of the face that you clicked (**Figure 12.15**).

✔ Tips

- You can select a camera or its target from the camera viewport label right-click menu.

- To undo a camera movement, click Ctrl + Z.

You can also use an AutoGrid to align a free camera to the surface of an object while you are creating it (**Figure 12.16**). AutoGrid is not available for target cameras, but you can convert a free camera to a target camera after it has been created.

To convert a camera:

1. Select a camera.

2. Open the Modify panel.

3. Choose a new camera type in the Type drop-down list of the Parameters rollout (**Figure 12.17**).

Figure 12.14 Click and drag the Align Camera cursor to find a surface normal for aligning the camera.

Figure 12.15 The camera points at the teapot in line with the surface normal you selected.

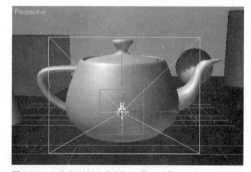

Figure 12.16 Use AutoGrid to align a free camera to an object upon creation.

Figure 12.17 Use the Type drop-down list to change the camera type.

CREATING CAMERAS

Figure 12.18 The Parameters rollout is the same for target and free cameras.

Adjusting Cameras

Target and free cameras have the same adjustments. The principle settings are lens size, clipping planes, environment ranges, depth of field, and motion blurring (**Figure 12.18**).

In 3ds max, the focal length of a camera can be adjusted by changing the size of its lens—just like with a real camera. When you change lenses, the focal length increases or decreases, and the field of view (FOV) widens or narrows.

The depth to which you can see in space is limited by two clipping planes: one near the camera and one farther away along its line of sight. Objects not enclosed by these planes are not visible from the camera (**Figure 12.19**).

When you add an effect called Standard Fog to your scene, the fog is limited to a near and far range from the camera. This range is called the Environment range, and it allows you to define the region in which fog can obscure the scene (**Figure 12.20**).

Depth of field and motion blurring imitate the effects of real cameras by blurring objects that are outside of a certain radius. The radius can be defined by the target distance or by a focal depth that you set especially for this effect.

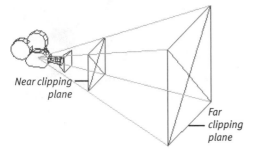

Figure 12.19 The clipping planes indicate which part of the scene the camera can see.

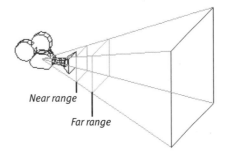

Figure 12.20 The environment range planes show where standard fog will render.

You set the focal length of a camera by adjusting the size of its lens. Lenses range in size from 0.1mm to 100,000mm. For convenience, you can pick from a set of nine stock lenses ranging from 15mm to 200mm. Changing the size of the lens inversely affects the FOV setting.

To set the focal length:

1.  Select a camera.

2. Type C to activate the view from that camera (**Figure 12.21**).

3. Open the Modify panel. The camera Parameters rollout appears.

4. Drag the Lens spinner up or down (**Figure 12.22**).

   or

   Click the Field-of-View tool in the Camera Viewport controls and drag up or down in a Camera viewport.

   As the focal length increases, the field of view decreases. Objects in the Camera view appear closer, and the perspective flattens (**Figure 12.23**).

   Decreasing the focal length increases the field of view and deepens perspective.

✔ Tip

- Select one of the stock lenses. The 15mm lens provides a wide-angle, fish-eye effect. At the other extreme, the 200mm lens zooms in tightly and flattens perspective.

Figure 12.21 Setting the scene for experimenting with focal length.

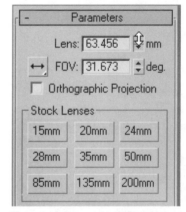

Figure 12.22 Increasing the lens size.

Figure 12.23 The camera zooms into the scene for a close-up shot.

ADJUSTING CAMERAS

Figure 12.24 Before changing the field of view.

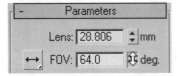

Figure 12.25 Increasing the field of view.

Figure 12.26 The camera zooms out, revealing more of the scene.

Figure 12.27 After checking Orthographic Projection, the Camera view looks like a User view.

The field of view sets the breadth of the Camera view in degrees of arc. Views can range from 0° to 175° across. The field of view is inversely proportional to the focal length.

To adjust the field of view:

1. Select a camera.

2. Type C to activate the view from that camera (**Figure 12.24**).

3. Open the Modify panel to access the camera parameters.

4. Drag the FOV spinner up or down (**Figure 12.25**).

   or

   Click the Field-of-View tool in the Camera Viewport controls and drag up or down in a Camera viewport.

   As the field of view increases, the focal length decreases. Objects in the Camera view appear further away, and the perspective flattens (**Figure 12.26**).

   Decreasing the field of view deepens perspective and makes objects appear closer.

✔ Tips

- The FOV Direction flyout changes how the program measures the field of view.

- Check Show Cone to display the FOV cone when the camera is not selected.

- To match a Camera view to a background image, check Show Horizon. Then align the horizon line of the camera to the horizon line of the background image.

- By animating the field of view, you can simulate the action of a zoom lens.

- Check Orthographic Projection to change the Camera view to an axonometric view (**Figure 12.27**).

ADJUSTING CAMERAS

Clipping planes define the region of visibility within a camera's view cone along its **depth axis**, or line of sight. Objects positioned outside of this region are invisible to the camera. If a clipping plane intersects an object, the object is cut away.

To adjust clipping planes:

1. Select a camera.

2. Open the Modify panel.

3. In the Clipping Planes group, check Clip Manually (**Figure 12.28**).

   The clipping parameters become available in the rollout. The far clipping plane appears in the cone of the camera as a red rectangle with red diagonal lines. The near clipping plane is not visible yet because it is set to 1.0.

4. Type C to activate the Camera view.

5. Adjust the near and far clipping planes by dragging their spinners.

   As you drag their spinners, the clipping planes move toward or away from the camera (**Figure 12.29**). In the Camera viewport, the front and/or back of the scene disappears (**Figure 12.30**).

✔ Tip

■ You can animate clipping planes to animate a cut-away view.

Figure 12.28 Turn on Clip Manually to set a specific clipping range.

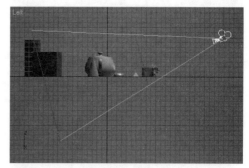

Figure 12.29 The clipping planes of this camera cut off the front and back of the scene.

Figure 12.30 The rendered scene is missing some geometry in the front and the back.

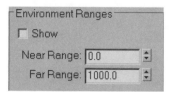

Figure 12.31 Turn on Show in the Environment Ranges group to display the environment range planes.

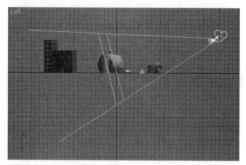

Figure 12.32 The environment range planes enclose the scene.

Figure 12.33 Fog renders just in between the environment range planes.

Standard Fog is an atmospheric effect that obscures objects as they move away from a camera. The Environment Range settings determine the near distance at which fog begins fading objects and the far distance at which it finally obscures them.

To set the environment range:

1. Open a scene with a camera in it.

2. Apply a Standard Fog effect to the scene. (This is explained in Chapter 15, "Rendering." Briefly: Choose Rendering > Environment. In the Atmosphere rollout, click Add. Then choose Fog, and click OK.)

3. Render the scene to view the effect.

4. Select a camera.

5. Open the Modify panel.

6. In the Environment Ranges group, check Show (**Figure 12.31**).

    The far range plane appears in the camera's view cone. The near range plane is set to zero, so it does not yet appear.

7. Drag the Near Range spinner to set the beginning of the fog.

    The light brown rectangle of the near range plane moves along the camera's line of sight.

8. Drag the Far Range spinner to set the point of full obscuration (**Figure 12.32**).

    The brown rectangle of the far range plane moves along the camera's line of sight.

9. Change to the Camera view by typing C.

10. Render the scene.

    The fog is rendered between the Near Range and the Far Range distances (**Figure 12.33**).

ADJUSTING CAMERAS

Depth of field is a multi-pass rendering effect that blurs foreground and background using a focal point that you specify.

To apply depth-of-field blurring:

1. Select a camera that views a scene.

2. Activate the Camera view.

3. Open the Modify panel.

4. In the Multi-Pass Effect group of the camera Parameters rollout, check Enable (**Figure 12.34**).

5. Click Preview.

   The Camera view wiggles for a few moments, and then stops. The view is shown in the camera viewport with a small amount of depth-of-field blur both in front and beyond the target distance.

6. Increase the Sample Radius slightly (**Figure 12.35**). Then click Preview.

   The Camera view shakes again. The depth-of-field blurring increases (**Figure 12.36**).

7. Adjust the Sample Radius and preview the image until the blurring is sufficient.

8. Click Quick Render to see the result.

   The Rendered Frame Window updates 12 times. Each time, the image gets brighter. When the rendering is complete, the image is blurred both in front and beyond the focal point (**Figure 12.37**).

✔ Tips

- To increase the offset amount of the blurred images, increase the Sample Bias.

- To adjust the focal point, adjust the target distance or uncheck Use Target Distance and enter a Focal Depth.

- To make the rendered image appear grainier, uncheck Normalize Weights or increase the Dither Strength.

Figure 12.34 Enable multi-pass rendering for the depth-of-field effect.

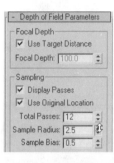

Figure 12.35 Increase the sample radius to increase the amount of blur.

Figure 12.36 Preview the image in the Camera viewport.

Figure 12.37 The image renders using multiple passes that are averaged together to create the blur effect.

ADJUSTING CAMERAS

Figure 12.38 Enable the motion blur effect for multi-pass rendering.

Figure 12.39 Increase the Duration and the Bias amounts.

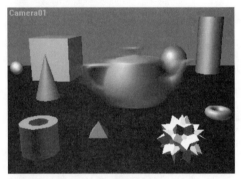

Figure 12.40 Preview the image in the Camera viewport.

Figure 12.41 After multiple passes, the scene is rendered with motion blur.

Motion blur is a multi-pass rendering effect that creates a trail behind a moving object.

To apply motion blur:

1. Select a camera that views an animated object.

2. Activate the Camera view.

3. Move the time slider so that the moving object is visible in the Camera viewport.

4. Open the Modify panel.

5. In the Multi-Pass Effect group, check Enable. Then choose Motion Blur from the Multi-Pass Effect drop-down menu (**Figure 12.38**).

6. Click Preview.

   The object moves for the period of one frame. The view is rendered with a small amount of motion blur both in front and beyond the target distance.

7. Increase the Duration (frames) parameter to increase the amount of blur.

8. Adjust the Bias amount to weight the blur toward the two preceding frames or the two succeeding frames (**Figure 12.39**).

9. Click Preview to preview the image in the Camera viewport (**Figure 12.40**).

10. Adjust your settings. Then do a Quick Render to see the result (**Figure 12.41**).

✔ Tips

- Clicking Preview has no effect if the Camera view is not activated.

- For a complete description of depth of field blurring and motion blur, look up multi-pass parameters in the User Reference.

ADJUSTING CAMERAS

387

Navigating Cameras

When you activate a Camera view, the viewport window controls change to a new set of navigation buttons called the Camera Viewport controls (**Figure 12.42**). By navigating cameras with the Camera Viewport controls, you can fine-tune their placement and animate them over time.

The names of Camera Viewport controls are based on traditional terms for making movies. For a complete description of the Camera Viewport controls, see **Table 12.1**.

Figure 12.42 The Camera Viewport controls navigate cameras.

Table 12.1

Camera Viewport Controls

Icon	Name	Description
	Dolly Camera	Moves camera along its local Z-axis, or line of sight.
	Dolly Camera + Target	Moves camera and target along camera's Z-axis.
	Dolly Target	Moves target along camera's Z-axis.
	Perspective	Dollies camera and changes its field of view.
	Roll Camera	Rotates camera around its Z-axis.
	Zoom Extents All	Centers objects in all non-fixed viewports.
	Zoom Extents All Selected	Centers selected objects in all non-fixed viewports.
	Field-of-View	Changes the angle of the camera lens.
	Truck Camera	Moves camera and target parallel to the view plane.
	Orbit Camera	Rotates camera around its target.
	Pan Camera	Rotates camera. Target rotates around camera.
	Min/Max Toggle	Toggles between viewport layout and full display.

Note: Free cameras use virtual targets for the dolly, truck, pan, and orbit commands.

Figure 12.43 The scene before dollying the camera.

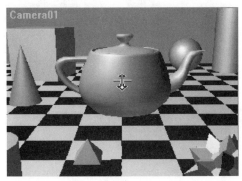

Figure 12.44 Dollying the camera into the scene.

Figure 12.45 After dollying in, the camera is closer, but the target remains in the same place.

The Dolly Camera command moves a camera toward or away from a scene by moving the camera along its line of sight.

To dolly a camera:

1. Select a camera.

2. Type C to change the active viewport to a Camera view (**Figure 12.43**).

3. Click the Dolly Camera button.

4. Drag the dolly cursor up or down in the Camera viewport (**Figure 12.44**).

   The camera moves along its Z (depth) axis, so that it moves closer to, or farther away from, the objects it views. The objects grow or shrink in the view (**Figure 12.45**).

✔ Tips

- Dolly Camera has two additional flyout commands:

  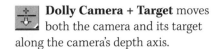 **Dolly Target** moves the target of the camera along its depth axis.

  Dolly Camera + Target moves both the camera and its target along the camera's depth axis.

- You can animate the dolly command to gradually approach a point of interest or to back away, revealing the whole scene.

The Truck Camera command moves a camera and its target across a scene parallel to the plane of the Camera viewport.

To truck a camera:

1. 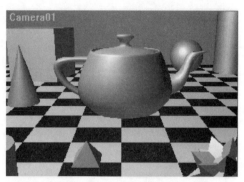 Select a camera.

2. Type C to change the active viewport to a Camera viewport (**Figure 12.46**).

3. Click the Truck Camera button.

4. Drag the panning hand across the Camera viewport (**Figure 12.47**).

   The camera moves across the scene (**Figure 12.48**).

✔ Tip

■ Animate the Truck Camera command to simulate the view from a train or the side window of a car.

Figure 12.46 The scene before trucking the camera.

Figure 12.47 Trucking the camera across the scene moves both the camera and its target.

Figure 12.48 Afterward, the camera looks at a different part of the scene.

Figure 12.49 The scene before rolling the camera.

Figure 12.50 Use Roll Camera to bank, or tilt, the camera around its depth axis.

Figure 12.51 After rolling the camera, the scene looks tilted.

Roll Camera rotates a camera along its line of sight, causing the scene to spin in the view.

To roll a camera:

1. Select a camera.

2. Type C to change the active viewport to a Camera viewport (**Figure 12.49**).

3. Click Roll Camera.

4. Drag the roll cursor left or right in the Camera viewport (**Figure 12.50**).

   The camera rotates around its depth axis. The scene rolls in the view (**Figure 12.51**).

✔ Tip

■ Animate a camera roll to simulate a car rolling over. By combing a roll with a Dolly Camera command, you can simulate a plane diving into a spin.

Orbit Camera rotates a camera around its target. If the camera is a free camera, it uses a virtual target located at the focal length of the camera.

To orbit a camera:

1.  Select a camera.

2. Type C to change the active viewport to a Camera view (**Figure 12.52**).

3. Click the Orbit Camera button.

4. Drag the cursor across the Camera viewport (**Figure 12.53**).

   The camera rotates around its target. Objects in the scene appear to spin around the target (**Figure 12.54**).

✔ Tip

■ To create a simple fly-by animation, try orbiting a target camera around a point of interest over time.

Figure 12.52 Before orbiting the camera.

Figure 12.53 Orbiting the camera under the scene.

Figure 12.54 After orbiting the camera under the scene, the plane doesn't render because its normals face upward.

NAVIGATING CAMERAS

Figure 12.55 Before panning the camera.

Figure 12.56 Panning pivots a camera and moves its target around it.

Figure 12.57 The camera faces a new direction.

Pan Camera rotates a target around a camera. If the camera is a free camera, it uses a virtual target located at the focal length of the camera.

To pan a camera:

1. Select a camera.

2. Type C to change the active viewport to a Camera view (**Figure 12.55**).

3. Click the Pan Camera button in the Orbit Camera flyout.

4. Drag the cursor across the Camera viewport (**Figure 12.56**).

   The camera pivots, and the Camera view sweeps across the scene (**Figure 12.57**).

✔ Tips

- Dragging the Pan Camera cursor up or down in the Camera view tilts the camera, as if you were looking up and down a tall building.

- With the Pan Camera command, you can animate a camera as it slowly surveys a scene. Establishing the scene in this way gives the viewer a sense of reference.

- By panning rapidly around the scene over time, you can make it seem as if the viewer is in a car spinning out of control.

The Field-of-View command changes the size of the camera lens. As the field of view gets wider, the scene begins to distort like a fish-eye lens. As the field of view gets narrower, the perspective flattens and the scene appears to have less depth.

To change the field of view:

1. Select a camera.

2. Type C to change the active viewport to a Camera view.

3. Render the view (**Figure 12.58**).

4. Click the Field-of-View button.

5. Drag the cursor up or down in the Camera viewport (**Figure 12.59**).

   The field of view increases or decreases (**Figure 12.60**).

Figure 12.58 Before changing the field of view.

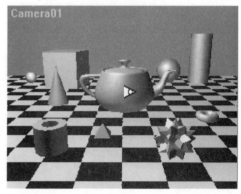

Figure 12.59 Dragging downward increases the field of view.

Figure 12.60 Afterward, you can see more of the scene, but the camera remains in the same place.

Figure 12.61 The scene with normal perspective.

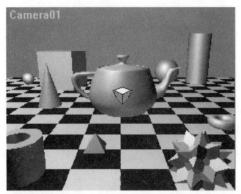

Figure 12.62 Increasing the perspective of the camera.

Figure 12.63 Exaggerated perspective adds a dramatic look to the scene.

The Perspective command dollies a camera and changes its field of view at the same time. This action preserves the essential composition of the scene while changing its perspective.

To change perspective:

1. Select a camera.

2. Type C to change the active viewport to a Camera viewport.

3. Render the view (**Figure 12.61**).

4. Click the Perspective button.

5. Drag the cursor up or down in the Camera viewport.

   The view changes perspective and zooms a bit (**Figure 12.62**).

6. Render the scene (**Figure 12.63**).

✔ Tip

■ Holding down the Ctrl key while changing perspective accelerates the change.

Animating Cameras

Cameras have a wide range of controls that can be animated. You can animate Camera Viewport controls, lens size, clipping planes, and depth-of-field controls. You can also animate a camera by keyframing it or assigning it to a motion path.

To keyframe a camera:

1. Select a camera.

2. Type C to change the active viewport to a Camera view.

3. Aim the camera and adjust its settings for the opening shot (**Figure 12.64**).

4. Click the Auto Key button.

5. Move the time slider to the right.

6. Adjust the camera by navigating it with the Camera Viewport controls, by moving and rotating the camera and its target, or by adjusting its parameters (**Figure 12.65**).

7. Set additional keys by moving the time slider and adjusting the camera (**Figure 12.66**).

8. Play the animation to review the timing and smoothness of any camera motion. Most of the time, the camera will be moving too fast, and its motion will be jerky.

9. Adjust the speed of the camera by moving its keys further apart. To slow down the entire animation, re-scale time in the Time Configuration dialog box.

✔ Tip

- Linking a camera and its target to a dummy object and then moving the dummy can make a target camera easier to position.

Figure 12.64 This opening shot of the front of a house gives the viewer a context to place the action in.

Figure 12.65 After trucking the camera to the left, and dollying it half way up the walkway.

Figure 12.66 The camera comes to a halt at the door, which begins to open, inviting the viewer inside.

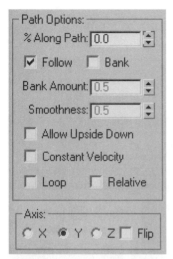

Figure 12.67 Check Follow, and choose an axis.

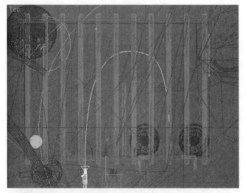

Figure 12.68 The camera looks down the path.

Figure 12.69 The camera walks the viewer through this firelit scene.

Walk-through animations are commonly used in architecture to show clients how the inside of a building will appear, but you can also use them to explore a landscape or any other type of scene.

To create a walk-through animation:

1. Create a line for the path of the camera that winds through your building or scene. For your first attempt, make the line parallel to the ground, and keep the curves as shallow as possible. Then position the line at eye-level.

2. Create a Free camera.

3. In the Animation menu > Constraints, assign a Path constraint to the camera. Then click the line.

   The camera moves to the first vertex of the line.

4. In the Motion panel, check Follow, and choose an axis of orientation. You may need to check Flip to make the camera look in the right direction (**Figure 12.67**).

   The camera looks down the animation path (**Figure 12.68**).

5. Type C to activate the Camera viewport. Then roll the camera until it is level.

6. Scrub the time slider to see what the camera sees as it moves down the path.

7. Rotate the camera to adjust its line of sight using the Rotate Transform Type-In dialog box. Do not use the viewport navigation buttons; these reset the % Along Path parameter.

8. Adjust the height of the camera by moving the path up or down.

9. Click Play Animation. The camera walks the viewer through the scene (**Figure 12.69**).

They say timing is everything. If your animation is too fast, the scene will whiz by before viewers get a chance to see it. If the animation is too slow, viewers will become bored.

Another key factor is composition. Frame your shots to show the most important details -- and the most flattering views.

By adjusting the timing and composition of your walk-through animation, you can tell a story that holds your viewer's attention while emphasizing the points you want to make.

To adjust a walk-through animation:

1. Create a walk-through animation.

2. Adjust the speed of your animation by changing the number of frames or by adjusting the % Along Path parameter.

3. Play the animation to see the results.

4. Adjust the timing of your animation by adding or subtracting frames, adding or subtracting keys, manipulating the camera path, or by moving keys in time. By adding keys and flattening the Percent function curve, you can make a camera slow down or pause (**Figure 12.70**).

5. Play the animation to see the results.

6. Make your camera tell the story more beautifully by adjusting its lens size, rotating it, or by navigating it with the camera viewport navigation tools.

   The camera reveals the high points of your scene (**Figure 12.71**).

7. Adjust lights and materials to complement your scene. Reposition objects as necessary to augment your composition (**Figure 12.72**).

8. When you are done, render your animation (**Figure 12.73**).

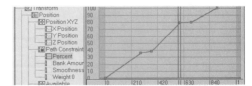

Figure 12.70 Creating pauses along the camera path.

Figure 12.71 Pausing to look at a painting.

Figure 12.72 Diagonals make dynamic compositions.

Figure 12.73 The final frame looks out the front window.

ANIMATING CAMERAS

Figure 12.74 Check Bank and set a Bank Amount.

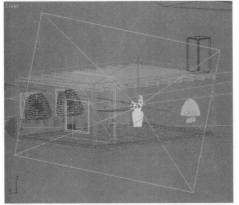

Figure 12.75 Banking makes the camera roll along the path at an angle.

Figure 12.76 The scene appears to tilt as the camera banks through the turns.

To animate the view from a race car, a swooping bird, or a fighter jet, you animate a free camera along a three-dimensional path and make the camera bank through the turns. Adding a LookAt constraint to the camera allows you to assign a separate target to the camera, such as a plane that is traveling by your side.

To create a fly-through animation:

1. Create a walk-through animation.

2. Adjust vertices along the path so that the path travels up and down as well as winding from left to right.

3. In the Path Parameters rollout, check Bank (**Figure 12.74**).

   The camera rolls around the path (**Figure 12.75**).

4. Activate the Camera view, and play back the animation.

   The camera rolls as it passes through the turns (**Figure 12.76**).

   To increase the amount that the camera rolls through turns, increase the Bank Amount.

5. To make the camera move more smoothly, ignoring minor irregularities in the motion path, increase the Smoothness parameter. Decrease this value to less than 3 if you want more of a jerky camera motion.

6. Continue to adjust and play back the animation until you are completely satisfied. Fly-by animations show the viewer how an object or area in a scene looks from different angles.

The default transform controller for a target camera is the LookAt constraint. LookAt constraints limit rotation to the depth axis so that a camera always looks at its target. When you combine a LookAt constraint with a Path constraint, creating a fly-by animation becomes smooth and painless.

To create a fly-by animation:

1. 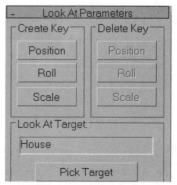 Create a spline shape for the path of the camera.

2. Position the shape above the objects.

3. Create a target camera.

4. In the Motion panel, open the LookAt Parameters rollout and click Pick Target. Then pick an object for the camera to look at (**Figure 12.77**). The camera rotates to look at the target.

5. From the menu bar, choose Animation > Constraints > Path Constraint.

   The cursor changes to a pick target cursor and is tethered to the camera by a dotted line.

6. Click a path. The camera moves to the first vertex of the path (**Figure 12.78**).

7. Type C to activate the Camera viewport.

8. Scrub the time slider.

   The camera flies by the target object (**Figure 12.79**).

9. In the Modify panel, adjust the field of view or other camera settings as needed.

10. Play back the animation to review the timing and composition. To change the beginning and end points of the animation, click the Auto Key button and adjust the Path constraint % Along Path parameter.

Figure 12.77 Pick an object to replace the camera target.

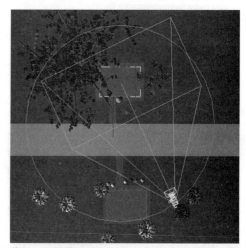

Figure 12.78 The camera keeps facing the target when it moves to the path.

Figure 12.79 The camera looks down as it flies by the house.

13

MATERIALS

Figure 13.1 All the objects in this scene use different materials.

Materials control how objects reflect and transmit light. They paint your scene with color, luminosity, transparency, and translucency, and they give objects their final finish: shiny or dull, glossy or matte, solid or wireframe, faceted or smooth (**Figure 13.1**).

Using the Material Editor, you can create and combine materials and add maps. As your material evolves, the Material Editor builds a hierarchy of sub-materials and maps called a **material tree**.

When you save your scene, material trees are stored in the .max file. You can also export them to custom libraries where they can be browsed and imported into other scenes.

Using the Material Editor

The Material Editor is divided into two main sections: the sample slot palette and button menus at the top (**Figure 13.2**) and the parameter rollouts underneath (**Figure 13.3**).

The sample slot palette is a high-resolution canvas for designing materials. Material controls along the edges of the palette allow you to browse, load, navigate, name, copy, save, and assign materials (**Table 13.1**). The parameter rollouts contain settings for building and adjusting material trees.

Table 13.1

Material Controls	
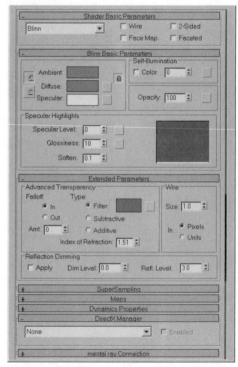	Sample Type
	Backlight
	Background
	Sample UV Tiling
	Video Color Check
	Make Preview
	Play Preview
	Save Preview
	Options
	Select by Material
	Material/Map Navigator
	Get Material
	Put Material to Scene
	Assign Material to Selection
	Reset Map/Mtl to Default Settings
	Make Material Copy
	Make Unique
	Put to Library
	Material Effects Channel
	Show Map in Viewport
	Show End Result
	Go to Parent
	Go Forward to Sibling

Active sample slot *Sample slot* *Material sample*

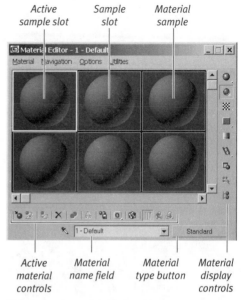

Active material controls *Material name field* *Material type button* *Material display controls*

Figure 13.2 The sample slots and button menus.

Figure 13.3 The material parameter rollouts contain settings for building and adjusting material trees. Rollouts vary according to material type.

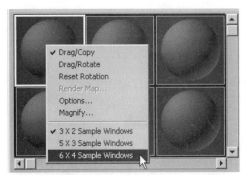

Figure 13.4 Choose 6 X 4 Sample Windows from the sample palette right-click menu.

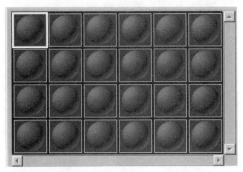

Figure 13.5 The palette refreshes, displaying 24 sample slots.

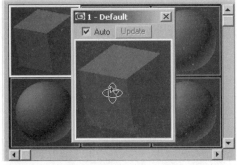

Figure 13.6 Rotate a sample cube by dragging in the sample slot.

Six sample slots appear in the palette by default, but there are actually 24 slots in all. View the rest by scrolling the bars to the right and bottom, or by changing the display.

To navigate the sample palette:

1. Click Material Editor in the Main toolbar.

   or

   Type M on your keyboard.

2. Drag the scroll bars below and next to the sample palette to view the other slots.

3. Click on a sample slot to activate it. Then right-click on the active sample slot.

4. In the sample slot right-click menu, choose 6 × 4 Sample Windows (**Figure 13.4**).

   The display refreshes to show 24 sample slots (**Figure 13.5**). Because all the sample slots are displayed, the scroll bars are disabled.

5. Right-click on the active sample slot, and choose 5 × 3 Sample Windows.

   The display updates to 15 sample slots. The scroll bars are re-enabled.

✔ Tips

- To magnify a sample slot, choose Magnify from the sample slot right-click menu, or double-click the slot. You increase the magnification of a sample slot by dragging a corner of its window.

- Using the Sample Type flyout, you can change the sample object to see how a material will look on an object that more closely matches the shape of your model. You can also import a custom object.
  For instructions, see "Creating a Custom Sample Object" in the User Reference.

- The Drag/Rotate option in the sample slot right-click menu allows you to rotate a sample object by dragging it (**Figure 13.6**).

The Material/Map Browser lets you browse for materials from material libraries, the Material Editor, and the current scene. You can also use the Browser to load materials and to select new material types.

To browse materials:

1. Open a scene that has some materials and maps in it, such as Earth.max, from the 3dsmax6\maps\Space folder.

2.  Open the Material Editor.

3. Click Get Material.

   The Material/Map Browser appears.

   Materials appear next to blue spheres. Maps appear next to green parallelograms (**Figure 13.7**).

4. In the Show group, uncheck Maps to hide the maps.

5. Choose a graphical display option by clicking an icon at the top of the Browser:

   View List + Icons

   View Small Icons

   View Large Icons

6. Choose a source to browse from.

   As you choose each option, the materials that are available at that location appear in the Material/Map Browser.

7. Scroll through the list and click on a material that interests you.

   A larger image of the material appears in the upper-left corner of the Material/Map Browser (**Figure 13.8**).

8. When you are done, choose File > Reset to reset the program and the material library.

Figure 13.7 The Material/Map Browser displays all the available materials and maps.

Figure 13.8 Click on a material to see a large thumbnail image.

USING THE MATERIAL EDITOR

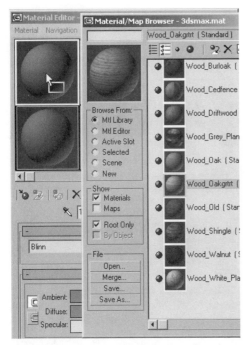

Figure 13.9 Drag a material from the list or from the large thumbnail.

Figure 13.10 The material is copied into the sample slot.

To adjust materials, you must first load them into the Material Editor.

To load a material:

1. Open the Material Editor.

2. Click Get Material.

   The Material/Map Browser appears.

3. Select a material and click Open.

4. Double-click your selection to load it into the active sample slot of the Material Editor.

   or

   Drag your selection from the Browser onto the sample slot of your choice (**Figure 13.9**).

   The material is loaded into the Material Editor (**Figure 13.10**).

5. Close the Material/Map Browser.

✔ Tip

- The File > New command does not reset the material library, so you can use the same materials in a new file.

The Material/Map Navigator shows how a material is constructed and provides access to settings at every level of the material tree.

To navigate a material tree:

1. Load a material into a sample slot.

2. Click the Material/Map Navigator button.

   The Material/Map Navigator appears. It displays the material tree of the currently active sample slot in list format (**Figure 13.11**).

3. To browse through the material tree visually, click a graphical display icon at the top of the browser.

4. Click the root or branch of a material tree (**Figure 13.12**).

   The Material Editor moves to the branch of the tree that you selected (**Figure 13.13**).

5. You can also navigate a material using the controls underneath the sample slots.

   Move to a deeper level by selecting from the drop-down list.

   Click Go to Parent to move up a level of the material tree.

   Click Go Forward to Sibling to move across the material tree to a different branch at the same level.

✔ Tip

- A red icon indicates that Show Map in Viewport has been enabled for a given branch of a material tree.

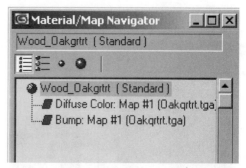

Figure 13.11 The Material/Map Navigator displays material and map trees.

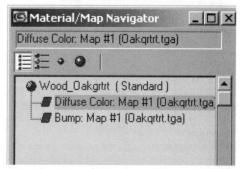

Figure 13.12 Click a branch of the tree to navigate the Material Editor.

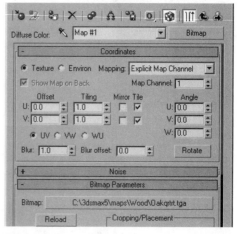

Figure 13.13 The Material Editor displays the branch of the tree that you selected.

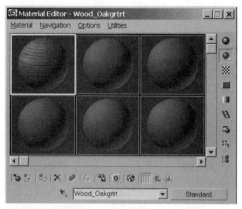

Figure 13.14 When you activate a sample slot, the name of its contents appears at the top of the Material Editor and in the material name field.

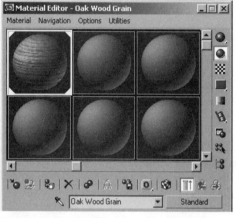

Figure 13.15 Changing the name of the material.

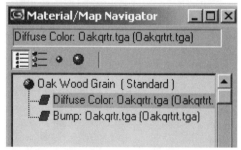

Figure 13.16 The new name appears in the Material/Map Navigator.

Names identify a material as being a unique entity that can be selected and manipulated.

To rename a material:

1. Activate a sample slot.

   The name of the material appears at the top of the Material Editor and in the material name field (**Figure 13.14**).

2. Highlight the name of the material in the material name field. Then enter a new name (**Figure 13.15**).

   The material is renamed.

3. Using the Material/Map Navigator, navigate to any branches of the tree that you would like to name.

4. Enter a new name in the name field.

   The branch of the material or map tree is renamed. The name appears in the Material/Map Navigator (**Figure 13.16**).

✔ Tip

■ As you build material trees, it helps to give each branch a descriptive name for easier reference.

USING THE MATERIAL EDITOR

You assign materials to objects by clicking or by dragging. When you assign a material to an object, the material becomes **hot**, meaning that the material is currently being used in the scene. Any changes that you make to a hot material instantly affect the object that it has been applied to.

To assign a material to an object by clicking:

1. Select one or more objects.

2. Select a material in the Material Editor.

3. Click Assign Material to Selection. The material is applied to the object. White triangles appear in the corners of the sample slot, indicating that the material is hot (**Figure 13.17**).

To undo a material assignment:

❖ Press Ctrl + Z.

To assign a material to an object by dragging:

❖ Drag a material from the Material Editor, Material/Map Browser, or the Material/Map Navigator onto an object (**Figure 13.18**).

The material is applied to the object and becomes hot. If the object is not selected, the corners of the sample slot turn gray instead of white (**Figure 13.19**).

✔ Tip

■ When you assign a mapped material to certain objects, you may be asked to supply mapping coordinates in order for the map to render correctly. See Chapter 14, "Maps," for more information.

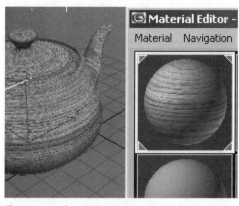

Figure 13.17 After clicking Assign Material to Selection, the material appears on the selected object and the corners of the sample slot turn white.

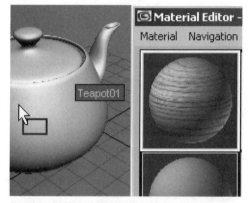

Figure 13.18 Drag the material onto the object.

Figure 13.19 Gray corners appear on the sample slot to indicate that the material is hot, but the object is not selected.

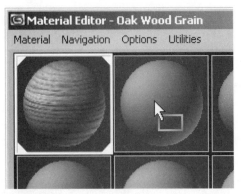

Figure 13.20 Drag the sample slot to copy it onto one of its neighbors.

Figure 13.21 The copy is warm, and the original is hot.

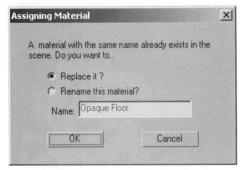

Figure 13.22 Assigning materials with duplicate names brings up this error message.

Often the best way to create a new material is by copying a sample slot and adjusting its contents. The root and branches of the copied material have the same names and settings as the original.

If the original sample slot is hot, the copy is considered **warm** until you rename it, assign it to an object, or click the Put Material to Scene button.

To copy a sample slot:

1. Drag a sample slot that contains the material or map you want to copy onto another sample slot (**Figure 13.20**).

   The material is copied to the slot, replacing its previous contents (**Figure 13.21**).

2. Rename the material.

✔ Tip

- Assigning a material to a scene that has a duplicate name brings up the Assigning Material dialog box (**Figure 13.22**). Renaming the material with a unique name prevents this message from reappearing.

Resetting clears the contents of a sample slot. Use the Reset Map/Mtl to Default Settings button when you want to make more room in the sample palette, or to remove materials and maps from the scene.

To reset a sample slot:

1. Select a sample slot.

2.  Click Reset Map/Mtl to Default Settings.

   If the map or material is warm or cool (i.e., not used in the scene), the Material Editor dialog box appears (**Figure 13.23**).

   If the map or material is hot, the Reset Mtl/Map Params dialog box appears (**Figure 13.24**).

3. Click Yes in the Material Editor dialog box.

   or

   Choose an option in the Reset Mtl/Map Params dialog box, and click OK.

   The sample slot is cleared. If you choose "Affect mtl/map in both the scene and the editor slot?" then the map or material is removed from the scene as well.

✔ Tip

■ You can remove a material from selected objects using the UVW Remove utility located in the More menu of the Utilities command panel.

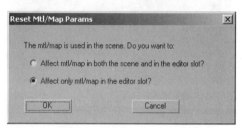

Figure 13.23 Click Yes to reset the warm or cool sample slot.

Figure 13.24 When you reset a hot material, you can choose whether to remove it from the objects it is assigned to, only in the material slot, or both.

USING THE MATERIAL EDITOR

Figure 13.25 The warm copy on the right is activated.

Figure 13.26 After you choose Put Material to Scene, the warm copy becomes hot and the hot original becomes warm.

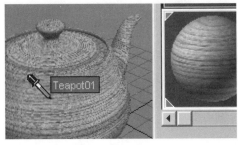

Figure 13.27 Picking a material from an object.

The Put Material to Scene button replaces a hot material with a warm copy of any material that has the same name.

The beauty of this arrangement is that you can make multiple copies of a material, make changes to the copies, and then substitute them for the original material by putting them to the scene. Using this method, you can freely experiment to find out which settings work best.

To put a material to a scene:

1. Activate a sample slot that contains a warm copy (**Figure 13.25**).

2. Click Put Material to Scene.

3. The warm copy becomes hot. The hot material becomes warm (**Figure 13.26**). All the objects that displayed the original material now display the hot copy.

4. If you want to edit a scene material that does not appear in the Material Editor, use the eyedropper to get it from the scene.

To pick a material from an object:

1. Activate an available sample slot.

2. Click the eyedropper icon.

3. Click on an object (**Figure 13.27**). The material that is assigned to the object appears in the sample slot.

✔ Tip

■ To make a hot material cool, so that it is disconnected from the objects it is assigned to, click Make Material Copy.

Using Material Libraries

3ds max 6 ships with 16 libraries of materials and maps. They are categorized by content, such as Wood, Brick, Stones, Sky, Ground, Metal, Space, and Backgrounds. The default material library that appears when you first open the browser is called 3dsmax.mat. All material libraries have this .mat extension.

To open a material library:

1. 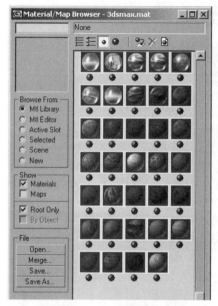 Open the Material/Map Browser.

2. Click the Mtl Library radio button.

   The maps and materials in the current material library are displayed in the window on the right. On the left, the File group appears in the list of browsing commands (**Figure 13.28**).

3. In the File group, click Open.

   The Open Material Library dialog box appears. It displays the material libraries in the 3dsmax 6\matlibs folder (**Figure 13.29**).

4. Select a library and click Open.

   The material library opens (**Figure 13.30**).

✔ Tips

- The Merge button merges materials from a library that you select into the library that is currently loaded.

- Save lets you save the currently loaded material library, including any materials or maps you have added to it.

- Save As lets you save the materials and maps in the list into a new library.

Figure 13.28 Viewing a material library. File commands appear at left.

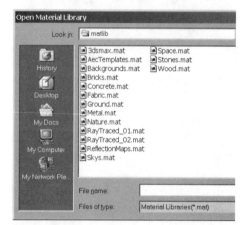

Figure 13.29 Material libraries are stored in the 3dsmax6\matlibs folder by default.

Figure 13.30 After opening the Space.mat library.

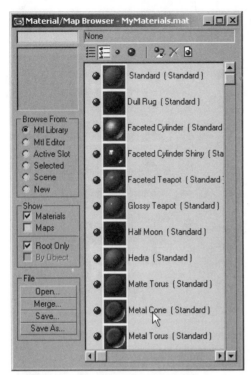

Figure 13.31 Viewing materials used in the scene in Figure 13.1.

Figure 13.32 Saving the scene materials to a library named Grayscale.mat.

A custom material library preserves your favorite materials and maps all in one place and keeps the master library from getting too large. I suggest that you create libraries by material category, such as Metallic or Architectural, or create separate libraries for different projects.

To create a library of scene materials:

1. Open a scene file in which materials have been assigned to objects.

   For practice, use one of the sample scene files that ship with the program.

2. Open the Material Editor.

3. Open the Material/Map Browser.

4. Click the Scene radio button.

   A list of just the materials that are used in the scene appears (**Figure 13.31**).

5. Click the Save As button.

   The Save Material Library dialog appears (**Figure 13.32**).

6. Enter the name of the new library, and click Save.

   Your new library contains all materials and maps used in the scene.

✔ Tips

- You can also create a custom library by loading an existing library using the Delete From Library button to get rid of the materials you don't want, and then saving it with a different name.

- Clicking Clear Material Library removes all materials from the currently loaded library. This does not affect the saved library file unless you click Save. Creating materials can take a lot of work. When you have a material that you like, put it in a custom material library.

USING MATERIAL LIBRARIES

413

To save a material to a library:

1. Activate the sample slot of the material or map you want to save (**Figure 13.33**).

2. 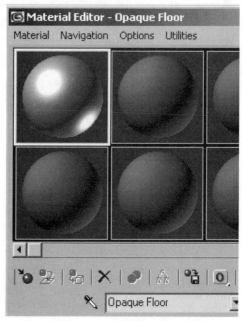 Open the Material/Map Browser.

3. Load the library you want to save the material or map into.

4. Click Put to Library.

   Confirm the name of the material (**Figure 13.34**).

   The material or map is saved.

✔ Tip

■ To delete a material from a library, select the material from the list in the library. Then click Delete From Library.

Figure 13.33 Activate the sample slot of the material you want to put to the library.

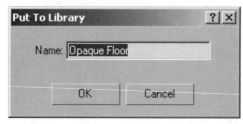

Figure 13.34 Adding a material to the current library.

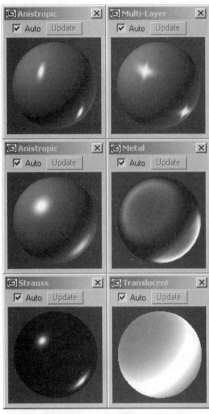

Figure 13.35 Variations on a Standard material.

Standard Materials

The default material in 3ds max 6 is the **Standard** material. But do not be misled by the name! Standard materials represent years of development that go back to the earliest DOS versions of 3ds max, when the program was named 3D Studio. Consequently, they have numerous controls and options for creating exquisitely beautiful and complex materials.

Standard materials start out with a solid, dull, and gray appearance. By setting basic parameters, you give them color, transparency, and brilliance (**Figure 13.35**).

A material color is actually made up of three colors that blend together (**Figure 13.36**):

◆ **Diffuse** color is the primary color of the material. It predominates when a surface is directly lit.

◆ **Ambient** color is the color of a material in the absence of direct light. It is strongly influenced by the ambient color of the environment.

◆ **Specular** color is the color of specular highlights. It appears only in areas of strong illumination.

For the next few exercises, create a simple scene, such as a teapot, a plane, and a spotlight.

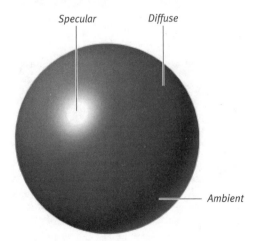

Figure 13.36 Materials have three basic colors that blend together.

The usual place to begin is to set diffuse color, as this will be the predominant color of the material.

To assign a color to a material:

1. Open a practice scene (**Figure 13.37**).

2. Select a material in the sample palette by activating its sample slot.

3. Click the Diffuse color swatch in the Blinn Basic Parameters rollout (**Figure 13.38**).

   The Color Selector dialog box appears.

4. Select a color by setting the Red, Green, and Blue amounts; by setting the Hue, Saturation, and Value amounts; or by setting the Hue and Whiteness amounts.

   The Diffuse color swatch updates to display the color that you chose. Ambient color is locked to Diffuse color by default, so the color is automatically copied from the Diffuse swatch to the Ambient swatch.

   The material sample object also changes hue (**Figure 13.39**).

5. Without closing the Color Selector, click the Specular color swatch and assign it a color. Then close the Color Selector dialog box.

6. Assign the material to an object.

   The object takes on the color of the material (**Figure 13.40**).

✔ Tips

- To unlock the Ambient and Diffuse colors, click the button to the left of the colors.

- To copy a color, drag the color swatch onto another.

- A quick way to create a Specular color is to copy the Diffuse color and then lighten it with the Whiteness slider.

Figure 13.37 A teapot is a good object for practicing on.

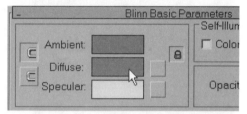

Figure 13.38 Click on the Diffuse color swatch.

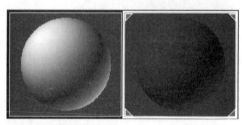

Figure 13.39 After changing a copy of the white material to dark gray.

Figure 13.40 The teapot turns dark gray when you assign the material to it.

Figure 13.41 Reduce the Opacity value to make the material more transparent.

Figure 13.42 Turning on the background makes it easier to interpret the sample.

The Opacity parameter sets the opacity of a material from opaque to transparent.

To make a material transparent:

1. Select a material.

2. ▦ Click the Background button.

   A multicolored test pattern appears in the background of the slot.

3. Drag the Opacity spinner downward (**Figure 13.41**).

   As you drag the spinner, the material becomes more transparent and the background becomes more visible through it (**Figure 13.42**).

4. 🔲 Apply the material to an object.

5. 🫖 Render the scene (**Figure 13.43**).

   The object is rendered partially to fully transparent. If shadow casting is enabled, the shadows appear dark and heavy.

6. To cast a shadow that adapts to the transparency of the object, change the shadow type of the key lights to Ray Traced Shadows (**Figure 13.44**).

✔ Tips

- You further control the darkness of shadows by adjusting the shadow density and shadow color of the light. You can also increase the self-illumination of the surface that the shadow is falling upon.

- Transparent materials are easier to see if you make them shiny by increasing the Specular Level and Glossiness values.

- 🔲 To assign a bitmap to the background of a sample slot, click the Options button. Then click the blank button next to the Custom Background option and navigate to the bitmap.

Figure 13.43 After assigning the transparent material to the teapot.

Figure 13.44 Ray Traced Shadows automatically adjust for transparency.

Self-Illumination sets the minimum ambient value of a material, regardless of the amount of light falling across its surface. Objects that are self-illuminated do not emit light or cast shadows.

To self-illuminate a material:

1. Select a material.

2. Increase the Self-Illumination amount (**Figure 13.45**).

   The material sample brightens (**Figure 13.46**).

3.  Assign the material to an object.

4. Render the scene (**Figure 13.47**).

✔ Tips

- To self-illuminate an object with a color, check the Color box.

- Self-illumination brightens objects and reduces contrast. If your self-illuminated objects start appearing too washed out, reduce the amount of self-illumination.

- Self-illumination materials can be a great timesaver because they do not have the rendering overhead of lights. Try substituting self-illuminated objects for decorative lights, such as running lights on a ship or plane.

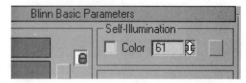

Figure 13.45 Increase the self-illumination of the material.

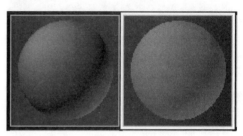

Figure 13.46 The dark values of the material brighten, reducing overall contrast.

Figure 13.47 After assigning the self-illuminated material to the teapot.

STANDARD MATERIALS

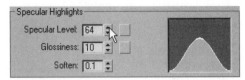

Figure 13.48 Increasing the Specular Level raises the specularity curve.

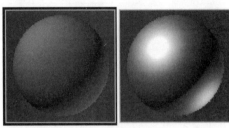

Figure 13.49 The shiny material has broad specular highlights.

Figure 13.50 After assigning the shiny material to the teapot.

Shininess is controlled by two settings: Specular Level and Glossiness.

Specular Level sets the intensity of the specular highlight. Higher values produce brighter highlights to make a surface appear shinier.

Glossiness controls the size of the specular highlight. Higher values produce a smaller highlight to simulate a high gloss surface.

To make a material shiny:

1. Select a material.

2. Increase the specularity of the material by increasing the Specular Level value (**Figure 13.48**).

   The highlights on the material sample brighten (**Figure 13.49**).

3. Assign the material to an object.

4. Render the scene.

   The object renders with a bright shine (**Figure 13.50**).

To make a material glossy:

1. Select a material.

2. Increase the Specular Level. Then increase the Glossiness value (**Figure 13.51**).

   The highlights on the sample material become smaller, polishing the sample sphere to a high gloss (**Figure 13.52**).

3. Assign the material to an object.

4. Render the scene.

   The object renders with a glossy luster (**Figure 13.53**).

✔ Tips

- You must set the Specular Level to a value greater than zero for the material to appear glossy.

- To turn off the secondary lighting of a material sample, click Backlight.

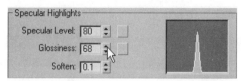

Figure 13.51 Increasing the Glossiness value narrows the specularity curve.

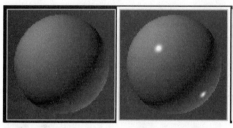

Figure 13.52 The glossy material has small, bright specular highlights.

Figure 13.53 After assigning the glossy material to the teapot.

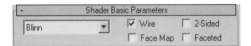

Figure 13.54 Check Wire in the Shader Basic Parameters rollout.

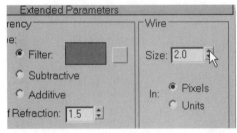

Figure 13.55 The material sample renders in wireframe.

Figure 13.56 Adjust the size of the wire and its units of measurement in the Extended Parameters rollout.

Figure 13.57 After assigning the wireframe material to the teapot.

The Shader Basic Parameter rollout offers four options for rendering surfaces: Wire, 2-Sided, Face Map, and Faceted.

The Wire option makes an object render in wireframe.

To make a wireframe material:

1. Select a material.

2. Open the Shader Basic Parameters rollout.

3. Check Wire (**Figure 13.54**).

    The material changes its display mode to wireframe (**Figure 13.55**).

4. Open the Extended Parameters rollout (**Figure 13.56**).

5. Select Pixels or Units to determine the measurement of the wireframe size. **Pixels** are pixels on your screen. **Units** are scene units that are rendered in perspective.

6. Set the size of the wireframe.

    The wireframe becomes thicker or thinner as you change the size.

7. Assign the material to an object.

8. Render the scene.

    The object renders in wireframe. If shadow casting is turned on, the object casts wireframe shadows. All other parameters, such as color and shininess, remain the same (**Figure 13.57**).

✔ Tips

- You can animate the Size parameter to make an object fill in or wither away over time.

- Wireframe materials sometimes look better if you also make them 2-Sided.

Faceted shading renders coplanar faces with a single intensity value that is even across all faces.

Because intensity gradations are not calculated, faceted materials render faster than smooth ones.

To make a material faceted:

1. Select a material.

2. Open the Shader Basic Parameters rollout.

3. Check Faceted (**Figure 13.58**).

   The material changes its display mode to faceted (**Figure 13.59**).

4.  Assign the material to an object.

5. Render the scene.

   The surface of the object renders with facets (**Figure 13.60**).

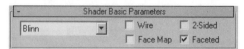

Figure 13.58 Check Faceted.

Figure 13.59 The material sample renders with facets.

Figure 13.60 After assigning the faceted material to the teapot.

Figure 13.61 Removing a lid from a teapot reveals that the inside is not rendered.

Figure 13.62 Check 2-Sided.

Figure 13.63 The inside of the teapot renders.

Figure 13.64 After applying a Swirl mapped material to each coplanar pair of faces.

The 2-Sided option makes a surface render on both the inside and outside. Because it shades both sides of each face, it takes longer to render.

To make a material two-sided:

1. Render an object that you can see the inside of, such as a teapot without a lid (**Figure 13.61**).

2. Select a material.

3. Open the Shader Basic Parameters rollout.

4. Check 2-Sided (**Figure 13.62**).

5. Assign the material to an object.

6. Render the scene.

   The surface of the object renders on both sides (**Figure 13.63**).

✔ Tip

- Check Face Map to apply the entire material to each polygon on a surface. When used with mapped materials, this can create fascinating patterns depending on the structure of the mesh object you apply it to (**Figure 13.64**).

  Mapping coordinates do not need to be applied to the object because the face map uses the XYZ coordinates of each face.

Shaders determine how surfaces are rendered. The default Blinn shader type is a good all-purpose shader that will create most of the effects that you need. For more specialized purposes, such as glass and metal shading, try using one of the other shader types that give you more control, such as Anistropic, Multi-Layer, or Metal.

Shader types for Standard materials include (**Figure 13.65**):

◆ **Anisotropic**—Calculates highlights from two different angles and renders them as ellipses. Good for creating hair, glass, or brushed metal.

◆ **Multi-Layer**—Similar to Anistropic, but with two highlights and two sets of highlight controls. Good for surfaces with more complex highlights.

◆ **Phong**—Calculates realistic highlights by averaging surface normals for every pixel. Good for creating strong, circular highlights.

◆ **Metal**—Creates sharply contrasting highlights with two peaks of specularity as found on metallic surfaces.

◆ **Blinn**—A variation on Phong that uses softer highlights by default. Good for rendering bump, opacity, shininess, specular, and reflection maps.

◆ **Oren-Nayar-Blinn**—A variation on the Blinn shader that has additional controls for creating matte surfaces with dull, rough highlights.

◆ **Strauss**—Creates sharply contrasting highlights like Metal, but with a single specular peak.

◆ **Translucent**—A variation on Blinn shading that scatters light within an object, like frosted glass.

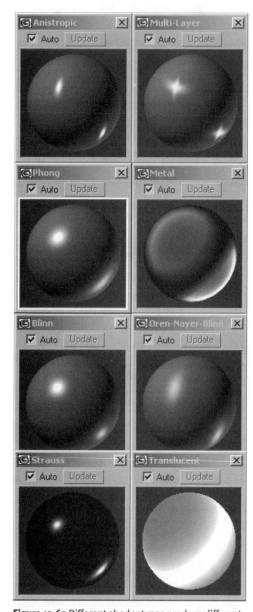

Figure 13.65 Different shader types produce different kinds of specular highlights.

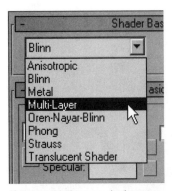

Figure 13.66 Choose a shader type from the drop-down list.

Figure 13.67 The Multi-Layer shader produces anisotropic highlights that you can orient to different angles.

To change the highlights of a material:

1. Activate a sample slot.

2. Choose a shader type from the Shader Basic Parameters drop-down menu (**Figure 13.66**).

   The new shader is applied to the material.

3. Adjust the Diffuse Color, Opacity, and Self-Illumination of the shader.

4. Adjust the specular highlight parameters of the shader.

   Set the Specular Level and Glossiness of the shader. (Strauss shaders have a single Glossiness parameter that also controls its specular level.)

   For Blinn, Oren-Nayar-Blinn, and Phong shaders, set the Soften value of the highlight.

   For Anisotropic and Multi-Layer shaders, set the width and orientation of the highlights by adjusting the Anisotropy and Orientation parameters.

   For the Strauss shader, use the Metalness parameter to adjust the contrast of the highlight.

5. Adjust the Diffuse Level of the Anisotropic shader, and then adjust the Diffuse Level and Roughness of the Multi-Layer shader.

6. Render the scene (**Figure 13.67**).

Compound Materials

Compound materials combine two or more materials to make a more complex material. They are primarily for combining mapped materials, but you can also use them for combining basic materials (**Figure 13.68**):

◆ **Architectural**—A Multi Sub-Object material (see below) that has built-in materials to match the material IDs of Doors and Windows objects.

◆ **Blend**—Combines two materials by mixing them together. Similar to a Mix map. See "To create a Mix map" in Chapter 14.

◆ **Composite**—Adds, subtracts, or mixes up to ten materials based on their opacity and composite amount.

◆ **Double-Sided**—Combines two materials by assigning them to either the front or back faces of an object. Similar to 2-Sided materials, except that you use different materials on either side.

◆ **Morpher**—Shifts materials from one to another. For use with a Morpher modifier.

◆ **Multi/Sub-Object**—A container for up to 1,000 materials that that can be applied to different parts of an object by matching material ID numbers of each material to the corresponding material ID numbers of faces on an object.

◆ **Shell Material**—A container for a material and a "baked" material that helps speed rendering for Direct 3D devices.

◆ **Shellac**—Combines two materials by assigning one to be a Base Material and the second to be a Shellac Material. By adjusting the Shellac Color Blend, you tint the Base Material with the Shellac Material.

◆ **Top/Bottom**—Combines two materials by assigning one to faces whose normals point upward and the other to faces whose normals point downward.

Blend

Composite

Shellac

Double-Sided

Top / Bottom

Multi / Sub-Object

Figure 13.68 The compound material types in this example combine a Checker-mapped material with a Cellular-mapped material.

Figure 13.69 Selecting a Blend material type in the Material/Map Browser.

Figure 13.70 Choosing to discard the old material removes the current material from the material slot. Keeping the old material incorporates it into your compound material as a sub-material branch.

Figure 13.71 The Material/Map Navigator displays the two sub-material branches of the Blend material tree.

For blending and layering patterns, the Mix and Composite map types are very effective tools. As a result, the Blend, Composite, and Shellac materials types are not used as often.

In addition to these compound materials, the Advanced Lighting Override, Ink 'n Paint, Lightscape, and mental ray materials all use advanced lighting features to help you achieve realistic surfaces. While these materials are beyond the scope of this book, I encourage you to experiment with them after you become familiar with the Ray Trace map and Ray Trace materials. These are introduced in Chapter 14, "Maps." (Note: The mental ray material does not appear unless the mental ray renderer is enabled in the Render Scene dialog box.)

To load a compound material:

1. Select an available material sample.

2. Click the Material Type button.
   The Material/Map Browser appears.

3. Select a compound material from the list of material types (**Figure 13.69**).
   The Replace Material dialog box appears (**Figure 13.70**).

4. Choose to discard the current material. Then click OK.
   The compound material is loaded into the Material Editor. In the Material/Map Navigator, the compound material appears at the top level of the hierarchy, which is the root of the material tree (**Figure 13.71**).

✔ Tip

■ If the Material/Map Browser is already open (after choosing Get Material), you access new material types by choosing Browse From: New and Show: Materials.

Double Sided materials assign a different material to each side of an object. These materials are Standard materials by default, but you can replace them with any other type.

To create a Double Sided material:

1. Click the Type button and load a Double Sided material into the Material Editor.

   The Material Editor adds two sub-material branches to the material tree (**Figure 13.72**).

2. Name the Double Sided material. The name "Double Sided" is sufficient.

3. In the Double Sided Basic Parameters rollout, click the Facing Material button (**Figure 13.73**).

   The Material Editor moves down one level to the Facing material branch.

4. Name the facing material. Then create a material for the front faces. You can set parameters, choose a shader type, and add maps to the Material as you would to any other Standard material.

5. Click Go Forward to Sibling. The Material Editor moves to the Back material branch.

6. Name and create a material for the back faces. Then click Go to Parent.

7. Assign the material to an object and render the scene. The outer faces of the object render with the Facing material. The inner faces of the object render with the Back material (**Figure 13.74**).

✔ Tip

■ To blend the materials together as if you are seeing through a thin wall, set the Translucency of the material as a percentage from 0 to 100.

Figure 13.72 Using the Material/Map Navigator to view the two sub-material branches of the Double Sided material tree.

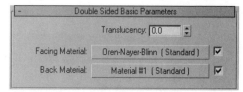

Figure 13.73 Click a button to access the material settings.

Figure 13.74 The Facing material is a shiny, black, semi-transparent Standard material. The Back material is light gray and slightly self-illuminated.

Figure 13.75 The Top/Bottom material contains two sub-material branches.

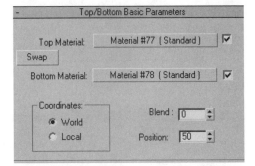

Figure 13.76 After designing your materials, choose a reference coordinate system and a Blend amount, and adjust their position.

Figure 13.77 The Top/Bottom material is positioned slightly over the middle of the teapot, and it is blended together slightly.

Top/Bottom materials assign two different materials to the top and bottom of an object.

To create a Top/Bottom material:

1. Load a Top/Bottom material into the Material Editor.

   The Material Editor adds two sub-material branches to the material tree (**Figure 13.75**).

2. Name the Top/Bottom material. The name "Top/Bottom" is sufficient.

3. In the Top/BottomBasic Parameters rollout, click the Top Material button (**Figure 13.76**).

   The Material Editor moves down one level to the Top material branch.

4. Name the Top material. Then create a material for the top faces. You can set parameters, choose a shader type, and add maps to the Material as you would to any other Standard material.

5. Click Go Forward to Sibling.

   The Material Editor moves to the Bottom material branch.

6. Name and create a material for the bottom faces. Then click Go to Parent.

7. Choose a coordinate system. World coordinates align the position of the material to world space, even as you rotate the object.

8. Assign the material to an object and render the scene (**Figure 13.77**).

✔ Tip

- To blend the materials together as if you are seeing through a thin wall, set the Translucency of the material as a percentage from 0 to 100.

Multi/Sub-Object materials allow you to assign multiple materials to an object. There are two ways to create Multi/Sub-Object materials: by assigning different materials to different faces and picking the material from the object, or by creating the material from scratch. Of these two methods, the first is simpler because it automatically assigns material ID numbers to faces as you assign materials to them.

To create a Multi/Sub-Object material:

1. Create three or four different materials (**Figure 13.78**).

2. Make a sub-object selection of faces, polygons, or elements.

3. Drag a material from a sample slot and drop it onto the selected faces.

4. Continue to select faces and apply materials to them. Then render the scene (**Figure 13.79**).

5. Adjust the position of the materials by making new selections and dragging materials onto them.

6. Exit sub-object selection mode.

7. Activate an unused sample slot.

8. Click the eyedropper next to the material name field. Then click the object.

   The Multi/Sub-Object material is loaded into the sample slot. Its rollout appears below. Each sub-material that creates a branch in the material tree is assigned a different material ID number (**Figure 13.80**).

9. To display the Multi/Sub-Object material on another object, assign the material to the object and assign corresponding material ID numbers to its faces.

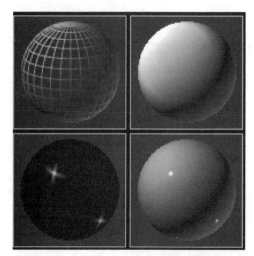

Figure 13.78 These four materials will be combined into one.

Figure 13.79 After assigning a different material to each element of the teapot.

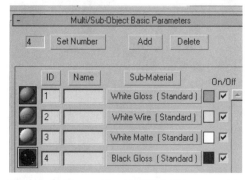

Figure 13.80 The resulting Multi/Sub-Object material has four sub-materials.

COMPOUND MATERIALS

Maps

Figure 14.1 The Taj Mahal is mapped with scanned photographs.

Maps make your scene look real. By introducing texture and pattern, maps put grain in wood, rust on metal, streaks in paint, and frost on glass. They paint a blush on rosy cheeks and draw cracks on a concrete sidewalk. To set the stage, maps put stars in the sky, reflect the moon in the water, and place a scene in India or Spain (**Figure 14.1**).

3D artists routinely "dirty up" their models with maps to make them look real. To give a boat the appearance of age, you add texture maps of peeled paint, and make the edges look cracked and broken. A spaceship that has been through the stresses of hyperspace needs burns, dents, shockwave patterns, and faded insignia.

Scanners, digital cameras, and photo CDs are indispensable to the serious 3D artist for capturing realistic details. To create custom maps, you should know at least one image-editing program, such as Adobe Photoshop.

About Maps and Mapping

A **map** is a pattern of color arranged in a rectangular array of bits (as in a bitmap) or described by a mathematical procedure (as in a procedural map).

You can add maps to lights, fog, backgrounds, materials, and other maps; however, you cannot assign a map directly to an object.

Mapping is a mathematical function or procedure that projects maps onto objects, effects, and backgrounds. Different mapping functions serve different purposes (**Figure 14.2**):

Texture mapping transfers the pattern of a bitmap or procedural map onto the surface of a 3D object.

Procedural mapping uses the coordinates of a surface to generate patterns and variations in two or three dimensions.

Bump mapping creates the illusion of surface roughness by perturbing normals using the intensity values of a map.

Displacement mapping uses the intensity values of a map to create "real" surface roughness by displacing faces.

Environment mapping surrounds objects with a map to quickly generate surface reflections. Environment background maps use billboard mapping to create a background that stays locked to the view.

Raytrace mapping simulates the action of photons by tracing a ray of light as it bounces from one object to another to create highly accurate surface reflections.

Texture

Procedural

Bump

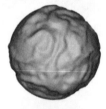

Displacement

Environment

Raytrace

Figure 14.2 Mapping functions create different types of surface effects.

Figure 14.3 As you choose each Browse From option, the maps that are available at that location appear in the Material/Map Browser.

Figure 14.4 A large thumbnail of the map appears in the upper-left corner of the Material/Map Browser.

Browsing Maps

When you add a map to another map, it builds a hierarchy called a map tree. Map trees can either stand alone, or be part of a material tree. When you save your scene, map trees are stored in the .max file, but the maps that they reference remain external. Maps also remain external when you store map trees in material libraries.

The Material/Map Browser lets you browse map trees and load maps from material libraries, the Material Editor, and the current scene. You can also use the Browser to load new map types.

To browse maps:

1. Open a scene that has some materials and maps in it, such as Earth.max.

2. ■ Open the Material Editor.

3. ■ Click Get Material.

   The Material/Map Browser appears.

4. Uncheck Materials in the Show area so that just maps are displayed.

5. Choose a display option by clicking an icon at the top of the Browser.

6. Choose a source to browse from (**Figure 14.3**).

7. Scroll through the list and click on any map that interests you (**Figure 14.4**).

In order to create and adjust maps, you must first load them into the Material Editor.

To load a map:

1. ![icon] Open the Material Editor.

2. ![icon] Click Get Material.

   The Material/Map Browser appears.

3. Select a map from any source.

4. Drag your selection from the Material/Map Browser onto a sample slot in the Material Editor (**Figure 14.5**).

   or

   Double-click the map to load it into the active sample slot.

   The map is loaded into the Material Editor (**Figure 14.6**).

5. Close the Material/Map Browser.

✔ Tips

- You can also load maps directly into materials. See "Adding Maps to Materials" later in this chapter.

- You can browse and load bitmaps from your system or the Web using the Asset Browser utility. To access, open the Utilities panel and click Asset Browser. Navigate to a folder that contains maps. Then choose Filter > All images from the Asset Browser menu to automatically generate and display thumbnail images of all the bitmaps in the current folder (**Figure 14.7**). To load a bitmap, drag a thumbnail onto a sample slot.

  Thumbnails of every image that you browse are stored in the 3dsmax6\abcache folder. To empty the cache or decrease its size, choose File > Preferences in the Asset Browser.

Figure 14.5 Drag the map onto a sample slot.

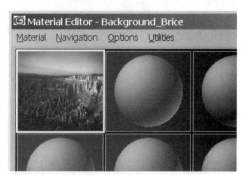

Figure 14.6 The map appears as a thumbnail image that fills the sample slot from edge to edge.

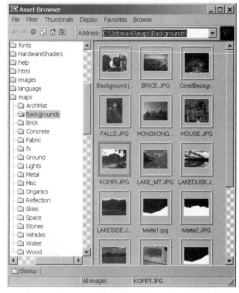

Figure 14.7 The Asset Browser allows you to browse and load bitmaps.

Figure 14.8 The Material/Map Navigator displays the components of a map tree.

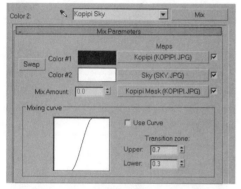

Figure 14.9 Select a branch in the map tree to view the parameter settings in its rollouts.

Figure 14.10 Giving each branch a descriptive name helps you navigate map trees more easily.

The Material/Map Navigator shows how a map is constructed, and provides access to map settings at every level of its tree.

To navigate a map tree:

1. Load a map into a sample slot, or load a material that contains a map tree.

2. Click the Material/Map Navigator button.

   The Material/Map Navigator appears. It displays the map tree of the currently active sample slot in list format (**Figure 14.8**).

3. To browse through the map tree visually, choose a graphical display option by clicking an icon at the top of the Navigator.

4. Click a branch in the map tree. The Material Editor moves to the branch of the tree that you selected (**Figure 14.9**).

5. You can also navigate a map using the controls underneath the sample slots.

   Move to a deeper level by selecting from the Material type field drop-down list.

   Click Go to Parent to move up the map tree one level.

   Click Go Forward to Sibling to move across the map tree to a different branch at the same level of the tree.

✔ Tips

- Red icons indicate that the Show Map in Viewport option is enabled.

- As you build a map tree, it helps to give each branch a descriptive name as you go along (**Figure 14.10**).

- To save a map to an open material library, click Put to Library.

Creating Maps

3ds max 6 ships with 33 different types of maps. Using the Material/Map Browser, you can browse map types by category (**Figure 14.11**):

- **2D Maps**—Two-dimensional bitmaps, procedural maps, or filters used for texture mapping and special effects.

- **3D Maps**—Solid texture procedural maps that can be used for special effects.

- **Compositors**—Maps that combine multiple maps into a single map.

- **Color Modifiers**—Maps that change the color output of a material or a map.

- **Other**—Maps that create reflections and refractions include all mental ray maps.

Most maps contain map buttons that allow you to add other maps to them. You can also click the map type button to turn the current map into a sub-map of a new map.

2D maps and 3D maps are applied in different ways. For a 3D map, the process is fairly simple: Take the XYZ coordinates from the surface of an object, and plug them into a procedure. The procedure returns a series of RGB values and assigns them to the XYZ location, creating a pattern. When you cut away part of the object using a Boolean operation, you see that the pattern continues in three dimensions (**Figure 14.12**).

Applying a 2D map to an object is not as straightforward because, like wrapping paper, the map may not fit very neatly onto the 3D surface. To make this process a little easier, the coordinates of the surface and the coordinates of the map are converted to UV mapping coordinates, in which U and V correspond to the width and height of both the surface and the map. To enable rotation, a third axis called W is added (**Figure 14.13**).

Figure 14.11 Maps come in a wide variety of patterns.

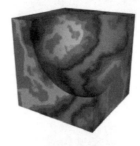

Figure 14.12
Subtracting part of a box reveals why 3D maps are called solid textures.

Figure 14.13
For UVW coordinates, the U axis corresponds to width, the V axis to height, and the W axis runs perpendicular to the UV plane.

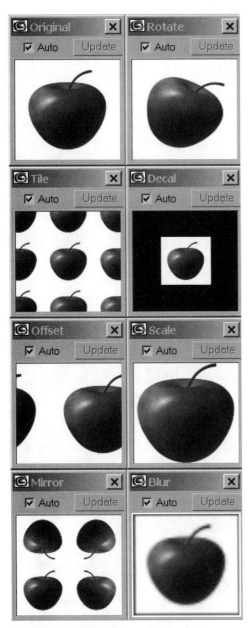

Figure 14.14 Adjusting the coordinates of a map changes its placement.

Common adjustments for 2D maps (2D), 3D maps (3D), or both include (**Figure 14.14**):

◆ **Texture** or **Environment** (2D)—Sets the mapping function that will be applied.

◆ **Source** (3D) or **Mapping** (2D)—Determines the mapping coordinate system. Explicit Map Channel uses the coordinates of the current map channel.

◆ **Show Map on Back** (2D)—Enables a map to appear on the back of an object when planar mapping projection is in use.

◆ **Map Channel**—Determines which set of mapping coordinates will be used by the object.

◆ **Axes**—Sets the direction in which a map is offset, tiled, mirrored, or rotated.

◆ **Offset**—Sets the distance that a map is moved, or offset, from its original location.

◆ **Tiling**—Scales a map. Values greater than 1 or less than -1 shrink a map and cause it to repeat. Values between 1 and -1 enlarge a map.

◆ **Tile**—Enables tiling.

◆ **Mirror** (2D)—Flips maps along their edges. If tiling is enabled, the map will repeat in a symmetrical pattern.

◆ **Angle**—Rotates a map around an axis.

◆ **Blur**—Blurs a map in world space depending on its distance from the view-plane. Helps prevent anti-aliasing.

◆ **Blur Offset**—Blurs a map in object space regardless of distance from the viewplane.

◆ **Rotate** (2D)—Rotates a map around its W axis.

CREATING MAPS

437

Bitmaps are 2D maps that import color and alpha channel information from an external bitmap or movie file. They also reference Adobe Photoshop filters and Premiere filters.

To create a Bitmap:

1.  Open the Material/Map Browser. Set Browse From to New and set 2D Show to Maps and 2D maps.

2. Drag a Bitmap onto an available sample slot.

3. In the Select Bitmap Image File dialog box, change Files of Type to All Formats. Then navigate to a map and open it (**Figure 14.15**).

4. In the Bitmap Parameters rollout, click View Image (**Figure 14.16**). Drag the handles in the corners and along the sides of the image to crop it. Then close the window and check Apply.

5. In the Coordinates rollout, adjust the placement of the Bitmap (**Figure 14.17**). See **Figure 14.14** to view the results:

   ▲ To offset the map horizontally or vertically, adjust the U or V Offset amount.

   ▲ To rotate the map, adjust the W angle.

   ▲ To tile the map so that it repeats across the surface horizontally or vertically, increase the U or V Tiling amounts.

   ▲ To mirror the map in either direction, check the U or V Mirror option.

   ▲ To create a decal, uncheck Tile and Mirror. To enlarge the width or height of the map, reduce the Tiling amount.

   ▲ Increase the Blur or Blur offset amount to make the map appear softer.

   ▲ To reload a map after it has been updated externally, click Reload.

   ▲ To eliminate moiré patterns on tiled maps, enable Summed Area in the Bitmap Parameters rollout.

Figure 14.15 Select a map from the 3dsmax6\Maps directory, or from an image file anywhere on your system.

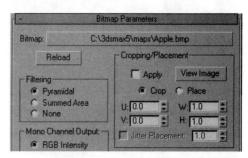

Figure 14.16 The Bitmap Parameters rollout controls how bitmap information is used.

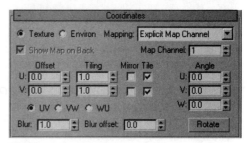

Figure 14.17 You adjust the placement of a Bitmap with the Coordinates rollout.

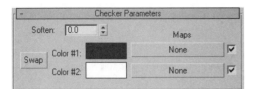

Figure 14.18 The Checker Parameters rollout allows you to choose checker colors or patterns.

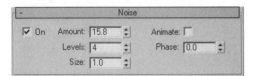

Figure 14.19 Use the Noise rollout to disturb the checker pattern.

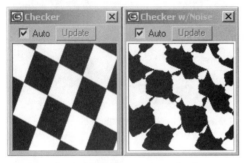

Figure 14.20 Left, tiling and rotating a Checker map. Right, after adding noise to the map.

Checker maps are 2D procedural maps that form a two-color checker pattern.

To create a Checker map:

1. Open the Material/Map Browser and check Show Maps and 2D maps.

2. Drag a Checker map onto an available sample slot.

3. In the Checker Parameters rollout, select a color for each checker (**Figure 14.18**).

   or

   Click the Maps button next to each color swatch to replace the color with a map.

4. If you want to blur the edges between the checkers, increase the Soften amount.

5. In the Coordinates rollout, adjust the placement of the map:

   ▲ Increase the U and V Tiling values to increase the number of checkers.

   ▲ Use the Offset and Angle coordinates to move and rotate the checkers.

6. To disturb the checker pattern, open the Noise rollout and check On. Then adjust the Amount, Levels (iterations), and Size of the noise (**Figure 14.19**).

   The edges of the checker pattern wiggle and wave (**Figure 14.20**).

✔ Tips

■ **2D maps** all have Noise rollouts. Many other maps types have noise built in.

■ **Tile maps** create brick and mortar patterns based on traditional brick-laying.

■ **Swirl maps** create two-color swirls that can be twisted, blurred, or mapped.

■ **Gradient maps** create a gradient of up to three colors that can be mapped.

■ **Gradient Ramp maps** create a wide spectrum of colors and patterns.

CREATING MAPS

439

A Noise map is a 3D map that creates random marks. Use Noise to roughen the colors of other materials and disturb the patterns of other maps.

To create a Noise map:

1. In the Material/Map Browser, check Maps and 3D maps in the Show area.

2. Drag a Noise map onto an available slot.

3. In the Noise Parameters rollout, set the Size of the noise, and select a Noise Type (**Figure 14.21**).

   Fractal noise produces a more abundant grain. Turbulent is a type of fractal noise that creates a craggier look (**Figure 14.22**).

4. Select colors for the noise pattern, or click the Maps buttons next to the color swatches to replace the color with a map.

5. To filter high- and low-intensity values, set the High and Low Noise Threshold amounts. By setting these values close together, you can simulate a starry sky (**Figure 14.23**).

6. To increase the resolution of fractal or turbulent noise, increase the Levels setting. This increases the number of iterations of the fractal function (**Figure 14.23**).

7. To change the pattern of the noise, change the Phase setting. Animating this parameter changes the pattern of the noise over time.

8. Use Blur or Blur offset when you want to soften noise.

✔ Tips

- **Falloff maps** have advanced controls for creating three-dimensional gradients.

- Depending on the functions that are used to generate them, 3D procedural maps create ordered patterns or random marks. Cellular, Marble, Perlin Marble, Planet, Water, and Wood maps create distinct patterns. Dent, Smoke, Speckle, Splat, and Stucco maps create random marks.

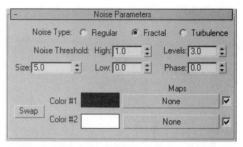

Figure 14.21 The Noise Parameters rollout allows you to set the size, type, color, and threshold parameters of the noise.

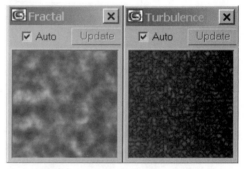

Figure 14.22 The Fractal and Turbulence options affect how the noise is shaded.

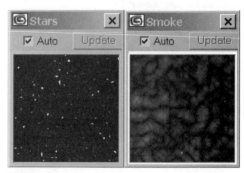

Figure 14.23 Use Noise maps to create starry skies and billowing smoke.

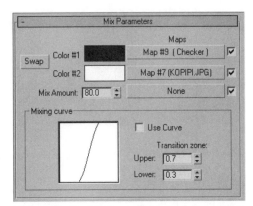

Figure 14.24 The Mix Parameters rollout allows you to blend colors and maps.

Figure 14.25 Mixing a Bitmap with a Checker map (left) and another Bitmap (right).

Figure 14.26 Placing a mask in the Mix Amount map button allows you to composite the island and the clouds without blending them.

A Mix map is a Compositor map that blends two maps together in varying proportions.

To create a Mix map:

1. In the Material/Map Browser, check Maps and Compositors in the Show area.

2. Drag a Mix map onto an available slot.

3. In the Mix Parameters rollout, select a color for each color swatch or build a compound map by adding a map to one or both map buttons.

4. Adjust the Mix Amount from 0 to 100% (**Figure 14.24**).

    The maps blend together in the proportion that you designate (**Figure 14.25**).

5. To limit the upper and lower threshold of mixing, click Use Curve. Then adjust the transition zones of the mixing curve.

✔ Tips

■ By adding a black-and-white mask to the mix amount, you can filter out areas of each map (**Figure 14.26**).

■ The **RGB Multiply map** combines two maps and multiplies their color and alpha channels together. Use this to combine two Bump maps together while retaining the strength of each.

■ The **Composite map** allows you to composite up to 1000 maps in layers using alpha channels for masking.

■ The **RGB Tint** adds a color tint to a material or map using separate channels for red, green, and blue.

■ The **Vertex Color map** enables the display of colors that have been applied to vertices. To learn more, look up the VertexPaint modifier and the Assign Vertex Colors utility.

■ For more information on these and other maps types, look up "maps" in the User Reference. Remember that you must enable a map type or choose Show All to see it in the Material/Map Browser.

Output maps allow you to adjust the hue, saturation, value, and alpha information of a map.

To adjust the output of a map:

1. In the Material Editor, select a map that you want to adjust.

   Bitmap, Cellular, Falloff, Gradient, Gradient Ramp, Mix, and Noise maps have Output rollouts built into them. To adjust the output of these map types, skip to step 5.

2. Click the Type button.

3. In the Material/Map Browser, click Show > Color Mods. Then click Output.

4. In the Replace Map dialog box, choose Keep old map as sub-map (**Figure 14.27**).

5. In the Output Parameters rollout, check the options you want to apply (**Figure 14.28**):

   ▲ Invert reverses the colors of the map like a color negative of a photo (**Figure 14.29**).

   ▲ Clamp limits the intensity of a map when you increase its RGB Level.

   ▲ Alpha from RGB Intensity generates an alpha channel from the intensity of the map's color channels.

   ▲ Enable Color Map allows you to use the graph at the bottom of the rollout to adjust the intensity range of a map.

6. Adjust the Output spinners.

   ▲ Output Amount controls the amount of the map that will be added to or removed from the composite map.

   ▲ RGB Offset lightens or darkens the map.

   ▲ RGB Level adjusts the saturation of the map.

   ▲ Bump Amount adjusts the bumpiness of a bump map independent of the Bump Amount parameter in the Maps rollout. This comes in handy for Bump maps when two maps are mixed together.

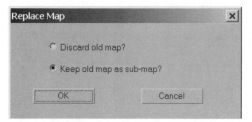

Figure 14.27 Choosing to keep a map as a sub-map adds another level to the material tree.

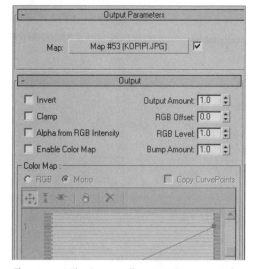

Figure 14.28 The Output rollout contains commands for altering the color properties of a map.

Figure 14.29 Checking the Invert option reverses map color information.

CREATING MAPS

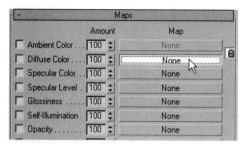

Figure 14.30 Click a Map button to load a map into it.

Figure 14.31 You build map and material trees by adding maps to map buttons.

Figure 14.32 Use the material name field drop-down list to navigate back up the material tree.

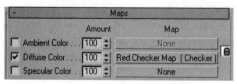

Figure 14.33 The name of the map appears on the Map button.

Adding Maps to Materials

You cannot assign a map directly to an object. Instead, you add maps to materials and assign mapped materials to objects.

Materials can use the complete color information of a map, or just its intensity (light and dark) values. When you add a map to a material, the name of the map appears on a button in the Maps rollout. The amount of influence that the Map has on the material is set by the Amount spinner.

Because grayscale maps use about one third less RAM than color maps, use grayscale copies whenever you don't need color information. Viewing maps in grayscale also makes it easier to predict their effects.

There are two ways you can add a map to a material: by clicking or by dragging.

To add a map to a material by clicking:

1. Select a material sample by activating an available sample slot.

2. Open the Maps rollout.

3. Click a map button (**Figure 14.30**). The Material/Map Browser appears.

4. In the Material/Map Browser, double-click a map type.
   The map is added to the material tree (**Figure 14.31**). The Material Editor moves to the new map branch.

5. Name the material branch and adjust it as needed.

6. To move back up the material tree, click Go to Parent, or choose the name of the material from the material name field drop-down list (**Figure 14.32**).
   The Maps rollout reappears. The name of the map appears on the map button that you clicked earlier (**Figure 14.33**).

7. To turn off a map, uncheck the box next to the map type in the Maps rollout.

The small gray buttons in the Basic Parameters rollout are duplicate map buttons that make it easier to add maps to the parameters.

To add a map to a material by dragging:

1. Select a material sample by activating an available sample slot.

2. Open the Maps rollout.

3. Drag a map from the sample palette or the Material/Map Browser, and drop it onto a map button in the Maps rollout or the Basic Parameters rollout (**Figure 14.34**).

   An "M" appears on the map button to indicate that a map has been added to it (**Figure 14.35**).

4. To adjust the parameters of the map, click the map button to navigate the Material Editor down to the map level.

✔ Tips

■ You can drag a map from one map button to another to instance, copy, or swap the map with another map (**Figure 14.36**). Instanced maps update whenever you change the parameters of any of the other instances.

■ When the map is turned off in the Maps rollout, the "M" on a small map button changes to a small "m" (**Figure 14.37**).

■ To clear a large or small map button, drag an empty map button over the map button you want to clear, or click the map button and choose NONE in the Material/Map Browser.

■ If you drag a map from the Asset Browser onto a material sample rather than onto a map sample or a material map button, it is automatically loaded into the Diffuse Color map button of the material.

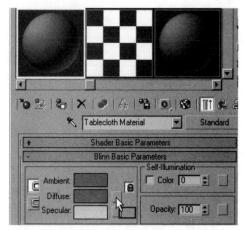

Figure 14.34 Dragging a Checker map onto the Diffuse map button.

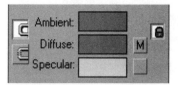

Figure 14.35 The "M" indicates that a map is loaded in the map slot.

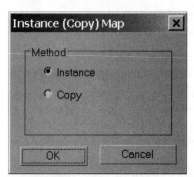

Figure 14.36 This dialog box allows you to instance, copy, or swap a map.

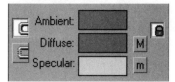

Figure 14.37 The small "m" indicates a map is inactive.

Figure 14.38 Adding a map to the Diffuse map button replaces the diffuse color of the material.

Figure 14.39 Click Show Map in Viewport to turn on viewport display of the map.

Figure 14.40 The diffuse map appears on the surface of the object.

Diffuse maps replace the overall diffuse color of a material with a map. Diffuse maps are often referred to as **texture maps**.

To add a Diffuse (texture) map:

1. Select a material sample.

2. In the Basic Parameters rollout, click the small gray button next to the Diffuse color swatch. Then select a map in the Material/Map Browser.

   or

   Drag a map onto the button.

   The map replaces the diffuse color of the material (**Figure 14.38**).

3. Adjust the parameters of the map.

   The map updates on the material sample.

4. Click Go to Parent. In the Maps rollout, drag the Amount spinner to adjust the amount of influence that the map has on the diffuse color.

5. Drag the panning hand downward on an empty part of the Maps rollout to access the Basic Parameters rollout.

   You can also use the thin scroll bar.

6. Adjust the material's basic parameters.

   To increase the brightness of a map, increase the self-illumination of the material.

   To assign face-mapping coordinates to the map, click Face Map in the Shader Basic Parameters rollout.

7. Assign the material to a mesh primitive, or to any other object that has mapping coordinates applied to it. (To learn how to apply mapping coordinates to objects, see the next section.)

8. Click Show Map in Viewport.

   The map appears on the surface of the object (**Figure 14.39**). If the map looks askew, right-click on the viewport label and choose Texture Correction.

9. Render the scene (**Figure 14.40**).

ADDING MAPS TO MATERIALS

Opacity mapping uses the intensity values of a map to calculate transparency. Lighter areas create more opaque surfaces. Darker areas create more transparent surfaces.

To add an Opacity map:

1. Select a material sample.

2. In the Basic Parameters rollout, click the small gray button next to the Opacity spinner. Then select a map in the Material/Map Browser.

   or

   Drag a map onto the button.

   Usually you choose a grayscale map that you have created specifically for this purpose. For practice, try using a Checker map (**Figure 14.41**).

3. Adjust the basic parameters of the material. For instance, you might want to make the material two-sided by checking 2-Sided.

4. Assign the material to an object.

5. Click Show Map in Viewport.

   The Opacity map appears as an opaque pattern on the surface of the object.

6. Click Go to Parent. At the root level, click Show Map in Viewport.

   If you are using OpenGL display, the object becomes transparent wherever the Opacity map is dark (**Figure 14.42**).

7. Render the scene.

   If you checked 2-Sided, the inside surface of the object is visible through the transparent parts of the outside surface (**Figure 14.43**).

✔ Tips

■ Opacity maps are great for filing down edges without adding extra polygons. And Ray Traced Shadows are cast from the edges of an object's Opacity map instead of from the edges of the object.

■ You can use the alpha channel of a 32-bit bitmap file to generate an Opacity map by setting Mono Channel Output to Alpha in the Bitmap Parameters rollout.

Figure 14.41 An Opacity map adds a transparent pattern to a white material.

Figure 14.42 You can get a good idea of how the object will render by viewing the Opacity map in the viewport.

Figure 14.43 Checking 2-Sided makes the inside of the object visible through the transparent areas on the outside. To make the inside easier to read, Receive Shadows has been turned off in the Object Properties dialog box.

ADDING MAPS TO MATERIALS

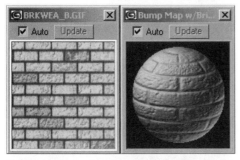

Figure 14.44 The bump map BRKWEA_B.GIF may be found in the 3dsmax6\Maps\Bricks folder.

Figure 14.45 Increasing the Bump amount increases the effect of the Bump map.

Figure 14.46 The surface of the teapot appears bumpy. The silhouette of the object is unaffected.

A Bump map creates the illusion of displacement by altering how a surface is shaded. Artists often add Bump maps to diffuse-mapped materials to make a texture-mapped surface look more convincing. For example, you could add a Noise map to make a surface look rougher, or a grayscale version of the texture map to make the bump pattern match the texture map.

You can also create your own Bump maps by scanning textured surfaces into Photoshop or Painter or by rendering images from 3ds max.

To add a Bump map:

1. Select a material sample and open the Maps rollout.

2. Add a map to the Bump map button (**Figure 14.44**).

3. ![icon] Click Go to Parent.

4. Increase the Bump amount until the effect of the Bump map is visible on the material sample (**Figure 14.45**).

5. ![icon] Assign the material to an object. Note: Bump maps are not displayed in the viewports.

6. ![icon] Render the scene (**Figure 14.46**).

   The surface of the object appears bumpy.

✔ Tips

- Reducing the Bump Amount to a negative number creates an inverted Bump map in which light values indent and dark values are raised.

- A quick way to create a Bump map is to drag an instance of the Diffuse map onto the Bump Map button.

- Noise and Dent Bump maps make a surface look coarse or dirty.

- To make a map displace geometry, add it to the Displacement Map button. Note that you will need to use a very dense mesh in order to obtain good results.

Applying Mapping Coordinates to Objects

Mapping coordinates wrap a two-dimensional map around a three-dimensional object by matching the coordinates of the map to the mapping coordinates of the object.

Mesh primitives and all compound objects, except Boolean objects, are automatically assigned mapping coordinates when they are created. Other types of objects must have mapping coordinates assigned to them by applying a UVW Map modifier.

While generating mapping coordinates is very convenient, the UVW Map modifier offers several advantages. First, it allows you to assign mapping coordinates to objects that cannot generate them, such as editable meshes. Second, it allows you to adjust object mapping coordinates, which in turn adjusts the placement of maps. Third, it allows you to change mapping channels in order to "tune in" different sets of material mapping coordinates. Finally, it allows you to choose a system of mapping projection using the gizmo of the UVW Map modifier, commonly known as a mapping gizmo.

The shape of a mapping gizmo determines the method of projection: planar, cylindrical, spherical, box, and so on (**Figure 14.47**). Map placement is further affected by the position, orientation, and scale of the gizmo.

For example, a planar gizmo projects a map in a single direction, like a projector. If the surface is not parallel to the plane of the gizmo, the map stretches as the surface turns away from it. To avoid stretching a map, choose a gizmo whose shape more closely resembles that of your object.

Figure 14.47 Map gizmos determine how a map is applied to an object. Planar is the default gizmo type.

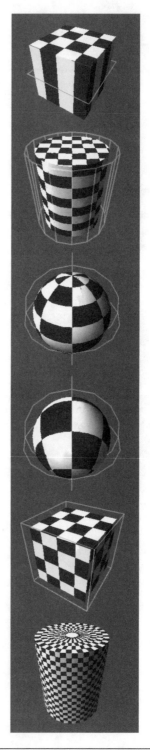

Planar

Cylindrical

Spherical

Shrink Wrap

Box

Face

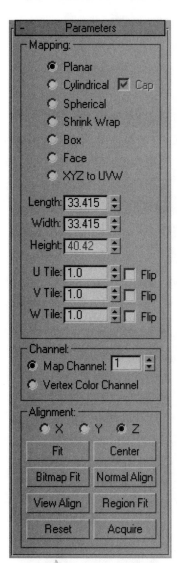

Figure 14.48 The UVW Map modifier adjusts the placement of a map on an object that it modifies. It does not adjust map placement for a material.

UVW Map modifiers have three groups of controls for assigning mapping coordinates (**Figure 14.48**):

◆ **Mapping**—Determines the shape and proportions of the mapping gizmo. Sets parameters for tiling and flipping maps.

◆ **Channel**—Allows you to create up to 99 sets of object mapping coordinates. To display a channel, the UVW mapping coordinates of an object must be set to the same channel as the UVW coordinates of the map that is applied to it.

◆ **Alignment**—Matches the position, orientation, or scale of a gizmo to maps, objects, or the world. Alignment controls include:

    ◆ **X, Y, and Z**—Aligns a mapping gizmo to the axes of the local coordinate system.

    ◆ **Fit**—Resizes a mapping gizmo to match the extents of an object. Try this first to prevent distortions of the map.

    ◆ **Center**—Realigns a mapping gizmo to the center of the selection.

    ◆ **Bitmap Fit**—Resizes a mapping gizmo in proportion to the size of a bitmap. Use this to prevent distortion of bitmaps after you have tried the Fit command.

    ◆ **Normal Align**—Aligns a mapping gizmo to a face normal by dragging the cursor over the surface of an object.

    ◆ **View Align**—Aligns a mapping gizmo to the current view.

    ◆ **Region Fit**—Allows you to drag out the dimensions of a mapping gizmo.

    ◆ **Reset**—Returns a mapping gizmo to its default alignment.

    ◆ **Acquire**—Matches the mapping coordinates of the current object to the mapping coordinates of an object that you pick.

Generate Mapping Coordinates is a base parameter found in the creation rollouts of mesh primitives, shape primitives, editable splines, lathed objects, and extruded objects.

To generate object mapping coordinates:

1. ![cursor] Select an object.

2. ![icon] Open the Modify panel and locate the Generate Mapping Coords parameter.

    For mesh primitives, go to the bottom of the Parameters rollout (**Figure 14.49**). The parameter is turned on by default.

    For lathed or extruded objects, go to the bottom of the Parameters rollout.

    For spline objects, open the Rendering rollout and check Renderable.

3. Check the box if it is not already checked. If the object is a spline object, check the Renderable box as well.

    Mapping coordinates are applied to the object. If a mapped material is applied to the object, the map will now render correctly.

✔ Tip

■ Some maps do not need additional mapping coordinates because they generate their own based on other input:

    3D maps (use the local coordinates of the object that they are applied to)

    Environment and Reflection/Refraction maps (use a combination of World and View coordinates)

    Face-mapped materials (use face coordinates from the object they are applied to)

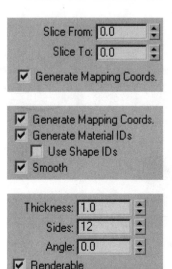

Figure 14.49 The Generate Mapping Coords. parameter for a primitive object (top), lathed object (middle), and a spline object (bottom).

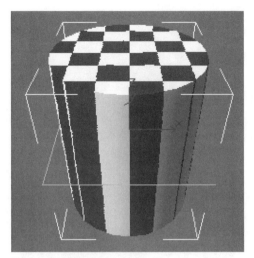

Figure 14.50 Planar mapping applies a map along an object's Z axis. The map stretches along the sides of the object.

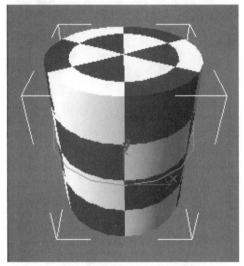

Figure 14.51 Spherical mapping wraps the map around the object and gathers it together at the poles of the sphere gizmo.

You assign mapping coordinates to an object by applying a UVW Map modifier and choosing a mapping gizmo. To fine-tune the placement of your coordinates, you can move, rotate, or scale the mapping gizmo.

To assign mapping coordinates to an object:

1. Select an object.

2. Apply a mapped material to the object so you can see the effect of different types of mapping coordinates. Make sure Show Map in Viewport is enabled for the map you want to display.

3. Apply a UVW Map modifier to the object.

   The modifier gizmo applies mapping coordinates to the object.

   Planar mapping coordinates are applied by default (**Figure 14.50**).

4. Select a gizmo type. Choose from Planar, Cylindrical, Spherical, Shrink Wrap, Box, Face, or XYZ to UVW (**Figure 14.51**).

5. To adjust the gizmo, use the Mapping and Alignment controls.

   or

   Select the gizmo in the stack display and transform it.

✔ Tips

- Scaling up a Spherical or Shrink Wrap gizmo makes the placement of the gizmo easier to see without changing its effect.

- Mapping coordinates are set to channel 1 by default. By changing channels in the UVW Map modifier, you can assign a different set of mapping coordinates to each channel.

APPLYING MAPPING COORDINATES TO OBJECTS

Using Environment Maps

Environment maps add context to a scene and make it more interesting. Use them to add background images at rendering time and to create surface reflections on objects.

As scene backgrounds, Environment maps provide additional visual information without your having to build everything that you see.

As surface reflections, Environment maps give objects a finishing touch. Reflections are explained in the section following this one.

To create an Environment map:

1. Load a map type into a sample slot.

   You can choose a simple 2D or 3D map, or build a compound map by mixing, masking, and mapping colors (**Figure 14.52**).

2. Adjust the parameters of the map type so that the image looks right toward you.

   To brighten the map, click the map type button and choose Output. Choose to keep the old map as a sub-map. Then increase the RGB Level or Output Amount (**Figure 14.53**).

3. Adjust the coordinates of the map. Pay particular attention to size and placement.

   For 2D maps, be sure to change the coordinates of all maps and sub-maps from Texture to Environment. Screen mapping, which matches a map to the viewplane of a camera, is the default (**Figure 14.54**).

    Hint: Use Go to Forward to Sibling to navigate the map tree.

✔ Tip

■ Use Screen mapping if you plan on using the Environment map as a background image for your scene. Use Spherical Environment, Cylindrical Environment, and Shrink-Wrap Environment to change the appearance of reflection maps.

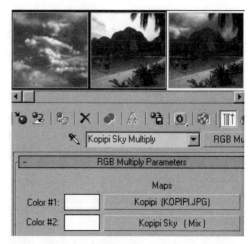

Figure 14.52 Any type of map can be turned into an Environment map.

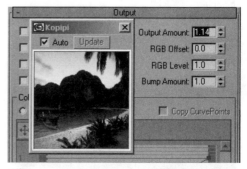

Figure 14.53 You often need to brighten a map before using it as an Environment map.

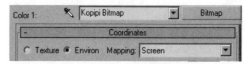

Figure 14.54 Choose the Environment option to turn a 2D map into an Environment map.

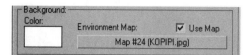

Figure 14.55 After loading the Environment map.

Figure 14.56 Use the viewport Background map and camera horizon to aid object placement.

Figure 14.57 The Environment map renders in the background of the scene.

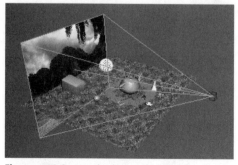

Figure 14.58 Create a background with a plane by matching it to the cone of a camera.

To add an Environment map to the background:

1. Choose Rendering > Environment.

   or

   Press 8.

2. In the Environment dialog box, drag a map onto the Environment Map button.

   or

   Click the button and choose a map with the Material/Map Browser.

   If you load a map from the Material Editor, choose to instance the map, so that you can edit it later as needed (**Figure 14.55**).

3. Press Alt + B. In the Viewport Background dialog box, check Use Environment Background and Display Background. Click OK.

4. Arrange your objects using the viewport background and camera horizon for reference (**Figure 14.56**).

5. Render the scene.
   The Environment map appears behind the objects (**Figure 14.57**).

6. To adjust the background, drag an instance of the map onto a sample slot in the Material Editor and adjust it there.

✔ Tips

■ To save rendering time, render objects in the back of your scene to a high-resolution bitmap image; then load the image into the Environment map as a background.

■ Because Environment Background maps are locked to the viewplane, they do not change perspective when you move the camera. If you need to use a background that is located in space, position a plane behind your objects so it is perpendicular to the line of sight of your camera. Then match the dimensions of the plane to the viewplane of the camera and assign it a mapped material that is not shiny and fully self-illuminated (**Figure 14.58**).

USING ENVIRONMENT MAPS

A Matte/Shadow material causes the environment background to show through an object. This enables you to cast shadows, add reflections, or place objects in the background.

To place an object in a background:

1. Load a map into the environment and viewport backgrounds of a scene.

2. Load a Matte/Shadow material into a material sample slot.

   The Matte/Shadow Basic Parameters rollout appears (**Figure 14.59**).

3. ![icon] Assign the material to an object. The object becomes a matte object.

4. ![icon] Position the matte object so that one of its edges matches an object in the background. Then place an object behind the matte object so that it emerges along the matched edge (**Figure 14.60**).

5. ![icon] Render the scene (**Figure 14.61**).

6. To make a matte object receive shadows, check Receive Shadows (**Figure 14.62**). Use the Shadow Brightness and Color parameters to make the shadow match the background image more closely.

Figure 14.60 Hiding part of an object behind the matte object.

Figure 14.61 When you render the scene, the partially hidden object appears to be inside the pictorial space of the background.

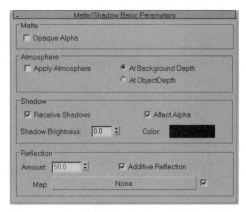

Figure 14.59 The Matte/Shadow material allows you to create a new environment for an object.

Figure 14.62 After checking Receive Shadows, the object appears to cast a shadow in the background.

Figure 14.63 The Taj Mahal is reflected in a Flat Mirror map.

Figure 14.64 This chemistry visualization uses refraction mapping for the water and the glass.

Reflection and Refraction

Everything that you see is an illusion of light. Earth, sun, sky, clouds, moon, stars, and every person, place, or thing is visible because of emitted or reflected light.

Reflections appear when a pattern of color is carried by rays of light from a shiny surface into your eyes (**Figure 14.63**). 3D programs create reflections by simulating the interaction of light and objects in nature.

To create reflections in 3ds max, you need to do three things:

◆ Assign a reflective material to an object.

◆ Surround the object with other objects, or an Environment map.

◆ Illuminate the scene so that light reflects off the object and into the viewplane.

You create reflective materials by adding a Reflect/Refract or a Raytrace map to a Standard material, adding a Flat Mirror map to a Standard material, or setting a Raytrace material to be reflective.

Reflection maps are locked to world coordinates so they will appear constant as objects move through them. They only appear to move when the camera you are viewing them with moves. Because reflections are not tied to objects, objects do not need to be assigned mapping coordinates in order to display reflections.

Refraction is a phenomenon that makes light bend when it passes through transparent objects. You can create refractions with a Reflect/Refract map or a Raytrace map, but I find the refractions that are produced by Raytrace material to be more satisfactory and easier to control (**Figure 14.64**).

The best way to create reflections on a flat surface is with a Flat Mirror map.

To create a reflection on a flat surface:

1. Select a plane that has a few objects sitting on it.

2. Open the Material Editor.

3. Select one of the sample slots.

4. Click the Reset Map/Mtl to Default Settings button to change the colors of the material to shades of gray.

5. Open the Maps rollout.

6. Click the Reflection Map button. The Material/Map Browser appears.

7. Select the Flat Mirror map type. The Flat Mirror Parameters rollout appears (**Figure 14.65**).

8. Click Assign Material to Selection.

9. Render the scene. The planar surface reflects the scene (**Figure 14.66**).

10. To change which side of the object reflects, check Apply to Faces with ID and change the ID number at right. This number corresponds to the Material ID number of the object's faces.

✔ Tips

- Flat Mirror maps work only when applied to coplanar faces of an object, usually the top side. To create reflections on more than one side, use a Multi/Sub-Object material and set each Flat Mirror map to a different material ID.

- An extruded shape also makes a good reflecting surface.

- Adding a little noise to a Flat Mirror map creates the appearance of ripples on water (**Figure 14.67**).

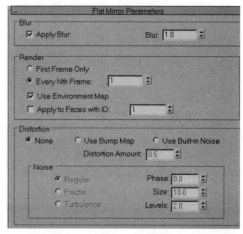

Figure 14.65 The rollout for a Flat Mirror map allows you to add an Environment map to the reflection, and to disturb the reflection with noise or a Bump map.

Figure 14.66 A Flat Mirror map makes a plane reflect the scene.

Figure 14.67 Adding noise creates a ripple effect.

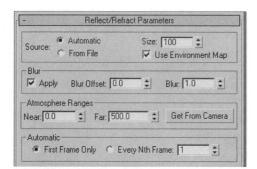

Figure 14.68 Use the Reflect/Refract map to create an automatic reflection.

Figure 14.69 Increasing the contrast of the material colors strengthens the reflection.

Figure 14.70 Reflections are usually secondary to the diffuse color of an object.

The fastest way to create reflections on a curved or irregular surface is with a Reflect/Refract map.

Reflect/Refract maps take snapshots of the scene from six directions and map them onto a surface using a cubic Environment map.

To create a reflection on a curved surface:

1. Select a material that you want to add reflections to.

2. Open the Maps rollout.

3. Add a Reflect/Refract map to the Reflection Map button.

4. In the Reflect/Refract Parameters rollout, make sure that the Source is set to Automatic and that Use Environment Map is checked (**Figure 14.68**).

5. Set the Blur or Blur Offset amount if you want the reflection to blur.

6. Apply the material to a curved or irregular surface.

7. Assign a Background map to the environment of a scene.

8. Activate a Perspective or Camera viewport. Then render the scene.

    A reflection of the scene appears on the surface of the object. The reflection mixes with the base color of the material, but it does not mix with its specular highlights.

9. To give the reflection more contrast, so that it looks like a mirror, set the Ambient and Diffuse colors to black and the Specular color to white (**Figure 14.69**).

10. To mix the reflection with the diffuse color of the object, reduce the Reflection Amount in the Maps rollout (**Figure 14.70**).

✔ Tip

■ If an object intersects the object you are working with, it may not appear in the reflection. Correct this by moving the object.

REFLECTION AND REFRACTION

Raytrace maps eliminate seams by tracing a series of paths, or rays, from every pixel that you see on the viewplane into the scene. As the rays bounce from one object to another, they accumulate color and lighting information that they use to paint surface colors and reflections.

Because they require more calculation than cubic environment mapping, ray-traced reflections take longer to render.

To create ray-traced reflections:

1. Select a material and open the Maps rollout.

2. Add a Raytrace map to the Reflection Map button.

3. In the Background area of the Raytracer Parameters rollout, choose a source of reflection mapping. To reflect the current environment map, choose Use Environment Settings. To reflect a solid color, choose the color swatch and pick a color, To reflect a map, including an external bitmap, click the map button. Spherical environment coordinates will automatically be assigned to the map (**Figure 14.71**).

4. 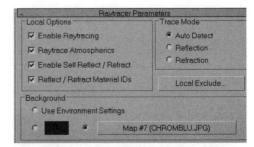 Apply the material to an object.

5. Activate a Perspective or Camera viewport. Then render the scene.
   A reflection of the scene appears on the surface of the object. This time the reflection does not have any seams.

6. Adjust the brightness, contrast, and tint of the reflection by changing the colors of the material and the Reflection Amount, or by changing the output of the Environment map (**Figure 14.72**).

7. To create a refraction instead of a reflection, load a Reflect/Refract map or a Raytrace map to the Refract Map button (**Figure 14.73**).

Figure 14.71 The Raytrace map rollout allows you to add an Environment Background map that encloses the surface of the reflecting object.

Figure 14.72 This highly polished reflection was created by adjusting the contrast of both the material and the map.

Figure 14.73 A Refraction map inverts the scene that surrounds the refracting object.

REFLECTION AND REFRACTION

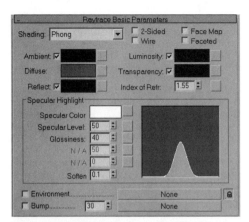

Figure 14.74 Setting Transparency to white is the same as making an object 100% transparent.

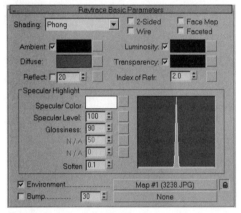

Figure 14.75 After adjusting the Raytrace Basic Parameters for a refracting crystal ball.

Figure 14.76 The ball reflects and refracts the scene.

Raytrace materials map reflections using the same ray-trace rendering engine as Raytrace maps. They have additional controls for creating refraction, transparency, translucency, and fog.

To create a refraction:

1. Click a sample slot.

2. Click the Type button, and choose Raytrace from the Material/Map Browser.

3. In the Raytrace Basic Parameters rollout, set the Transparency color to white, or 100% transparent (**Figure 14.74**).

4. Set the Index of Refraction to a value between 1.5 and 2, depending on if your crystal is made of glass, quartz, or diamond. Higher values increase the curvature of the refracted image.

5. Set the Specular Level to 100 and the Glossiness to 90.

6. To make the crystal ball reflect as well as refract, uncheck Reflect and increase the reflection amount by 5 to 20%. Higher amounts obscure the refracted image.

   If you are using an Environment map, you may need to offset the U coordinates of the map to eliminate the map seam.

7. Click the Environment map button and select the map that you want to refract.

   You can also drag a copy of the scene's Environment Background map onto this button (**Figure 14.75**).

8. Assign the material to a curved object, such as a sphere.

9. Render the scene (**Figure 14.76**).

✔ Tip

- For more information on Raytrace materials and how to adjust them, see the help files.

REFLECTION AND REFRACTION

15

RENDERING

Figure 15.1 The lens flare on the crystal ball was created with a rendering effect.

For thousands of years, artists have been drawing pictures. Starting with only a line, artists learned how to apply shading to form and color to light. After many centuries, they learned how to draw perspective: parallel perspective in the East, converging perspective in the West. Finally, in the twenty-first century, we are creating pictures out of our imaginations, using tools and media that could never have been foreseen. With 3ds max 6, artists can draw, paint, sculpt, and animate, and let the computer do the shading and perspective. For the first time, artists are working in a medium of light, moving bits of color and transparency and depth information through data channels and onto their screens. From the desktop to books, television, movies, and the Internet (not to mention new forms of multimedia production not even yet imagined), 3D graphics are here to stay.

This chapter shows you how to take the scenes you have created in your computer and send them out into the world. The basics of rendering still images are covered in Chapter 11, "Lights." This chapter picks up where that explanation leaves off, and demonstrates how to set image output size, how to render images to different types of file formats, how to render animations, and how to create atmospheric and post-process effects (**Figure 15.1**).

Rendering Scenes

The Render Types drop-down menu in the Main toolbar allows you to select parts of your scene for test rendering (**Figure 15.2**).

Figure 15.2 The Render Type drop-down list gives you eight ways to render a scene.

+ **View**—Renders the entire view.

+ **Selected**—Renders just the objects that you select. If there is an image in the Rendered Frame Window, the Selected type will render the selected objects on top of that image. Clicking Clear resets the Rendered Frame Window.

+ **Region**—Renders a rectangular region that you adjust. When you click the Render button, a dotted window with control handles appears in the viewport. Click the OK button in the lower-right corner of the viewport to render the contents of the window.

+ **Crop**—Renders a rectangular region and purges all other image data in the Rendered Frame Window.

+ **Blowup**—Renders a rectangular region and enlarges it to match the image size.

+ **Box Selected**—Renders the volume of the bounding box of the selection. Allows you to specify an image resolution.

+ **Region Selected**—Renders the region defined by the bounding box of a selection.

+ **Crop Selected**—Renders the region defined by the bounding box of the selection and crops out everything else.

As your scene renders, the Rendering dialog box appears (**Figure 15.3**). It indicates the progress of your rendering, frame by frame, and lets you know how long it took to render the last frame and how long it should take to render the rest of the animation. The Rendering dialog box also displays some of the settings used by the scanline renderer (**Figure 15.4**).

Figure 15.3 A fully expanded Rendering dialog box displays rendering progress, Render Settings, and gives you information about the contents of your scene.

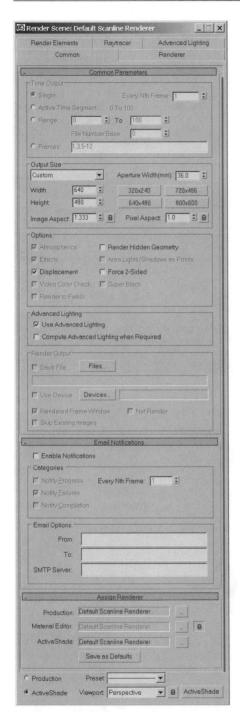

Figure 15.4 The Common panel of the Render Scene dialog box contains the most useful render settings.

You configure rendering options in the Render Scene dialog box (**Figure 15.4**). Five tab panels are contained within it. Of these, the most useful settings are found in the Common panel and the Renderer panel:

Common panel
Common Parameters rollout

Time Output group:

- ◆ **Single**—Renders a single image of the current frame.

- ◆ **Active Time Segment**—Renders the frames in the Active Time Segment.

- ◆ **Range**—Renders a specified sequence of frames.

- ◆ **Frames**—Renders non-sequential frames separated by commas, or sequences of frames separated by dashes.

- ◆ **Every Nth Frame**—Renders a sample of frames at regular intervals of N frames.

Output Size group:

- ◆ **Output size drop-down list**—Menu of 19 frame size options, including Custom.

- ◆ **Width**—Resolution in pixels of the width of the image output.

- ◆ **Height**—Resolution in pixels of the height of the image output.

- ◆ **Image Aspect**—Image aspect ratio of the image output.

- ◆ **Aperture Width(mm)**—Sets the aperture width of the camera that is assigned to render the scene. Changes the Lens size of the camera, but not its FOV.

- ◆ **Preset resolution settings**—Sets the image output to a preset resolution. To change a preset amount, right-click on the preset button or choose a new frame size from the Output Size drop-down list.

- ◆ **Pixel Aspect**—Displays or sets the pixel aspect size. This input is only available when the output size is set to Custom.

Common panel continued (**Figure 15.5**)

Options group:

◆ **Atmospherics**—Enables rendering of atmospheric effects.

◆ **Effects**—Enables rendering of rendering effects.

◆ **Displacement**—Enables rendering of displacement maps.

◆ **Video Color Check**—Verifies pixels are within range of PAL or NTSC thresholds.

◆ **Render to Fields**—Renders to two fields of alternating lines instead of to frames.

◆ **Render Hidden Geometry**—Renders hidden objects.

◆ **Area/Lights Shadows As Points**—Renders area lights and shadows faster by rendering them as point lights.

◆ **Force 2-Sided**—Renders both sides of objects regardless of material assignment.

◆ **Super Black**—Limits the darkness of pixels for video compositing.

Advanced Lighting group:

◆ **Use Advanced Lighting**—Renders light tracing and radiosity solutions.

◆ **Compute Advanced Lighting when Required**—Recalculates advanced lighting as needed on a per-frame basis.

Render Output group:

◆ **Save File**—Renders to an image file.

◆ **Use Device**—Sends rendered images to an output device such as video recorder.

◆ **Rendered Frame Window**—Renders to the Rendered Frame Window.

◆ **Net Render**—Renders animations over a network, including the Internet.

◆ **Skip Existing Images**—Prevents saving over existing sequences of image files.

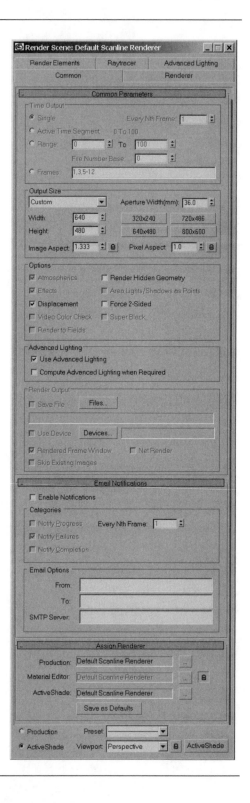

Figure 15.5 For your convenience, another look at the Common panel of the Render Scene dialog box.

RENDERING SCENES

Email Notifications rollout

◆ **Enable Notifications**—Sends an email to a specified address when triggered by a rendering event, as listed below.

Categories group:

◆ **Notify Progress**—Sends an email every time the number of frames specified in Every Nth Frame is rendered.

◆ **Notify Failures**—Sends an email if a rendering is not completed.

◆ **Notify Completion**—Sends an email if a rendering job is completed.

Email Options group:

◆ **From**—An email address that you enter, usually the person who initiates a job.

◆ **To**—An email address that you enter, usually the person you want to notify.

◆ **SMTP Server**—The IP address of the mail server.

Assign Renderer

◆ **Production**—Displays the name of the current production renderer.

◆ ▢—Assigns a renderer for production rendering.

◆ **Material Editor**—Displays the name of the Material Editor sample slot renderer.

◆ ▢—Assigns a renderer to the Material Editor sample slots.

◆ **ActiveShade**—Displays the name of the ActiveShade renderer.

◆ ▢—Assigns a renderer to the ActiveShade renderer.

◆ **Save as Defaults**—Saves the current renderer assignments to the default setting for the program.

Renderer panel

Default Scanline Renderer rollout

◆ **Mapping**—Enables rendering of maps.

◆ **Shadows**—Enables shadow rendering.

◆ **Enable SSE**—Enables rendering with Streaming SIMD Extensions. This speeds rendering for some CPU types.

◆ **Auto-Reflect/Refract and Mirrors**—Enables automatic Reflect/Refract and Flat Mirror maps.

◆ **Force Wireframe**—Renders objects in wireframe regardless of material settings.

◆ **Wire Thickness**—Sets wire thickness when Force Wireframe is enabled.

Antialiasing group:

◆ **AntiAliasing**—Enables anti-aliasing.

◆ **Filter maps**—Enables pyramidal and summed area filtering of bitmaps.

◆ **Filter drop-down list**—Menu of 12 anti-aliasing filters.

◆ **Filter size**—Sets the amount of blur for the Soften filter.

Global SuperSampling group:

◆ **Disable all Samplers**—Disables all SuperSample anti-alias rendering.

◆ **Enable Global Supersampler**—Applies the same supersampler to all materials.

◆ **Supersample Maps**—Supersamples Maps. Turn off to speed test rendering.

◆ **Sampler drop-down list**—Menu of four supersampling methods.

Object Motion Blur group:

◆ **Apply**—Enables object motion blur.

◆ **Samples**—Determines how many transparent copies are sampled. Maximum=32.

◆ **Duration (frames)**—Sets the number of frames used to compute blurring.

◆ **Duration Subdivisions**—Sets the number of transparent copies per frame.

Image Motion Blur group:

◆ **Apply**—Enables image motion blur.

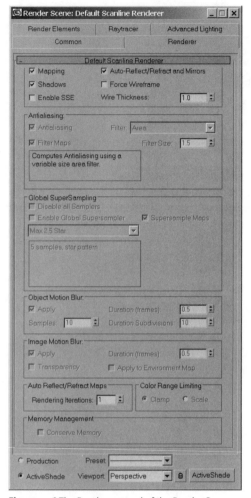

Figure 15.6 The Renderer panel of the Render Scene contains settings for the default scanline renderer.

Figure 15.7 The Output Size group gives you presets, customization settings, and more.

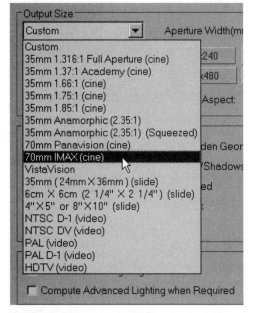

Figure 15.8 If you are rendering for a standard video or cinematic resolution, such as IMAX, choose from the Output Size drop-down list.

♦ **Transparency**—Applies image motion blur to transparent objects.

♦ **Duration (frames)**—Sets the number of frames used to compute blurring.

♦ **Apply to Environment Map**—Applies blurring of the environment map when it appears in reflections and refractions.

Color Range Limiting group:

♦ **Clamp**—Limits the range of RGB values.

♦ **Scale**—Limits the range of RGB hues.

Memory Management group:

♦ **Conserve Memory**—Saves 15 to 25% of memory at a cost of 4% of rendering time.

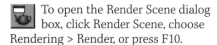 To open the Render Scene dialog box, click Render Scene, choose Rendering > Render, or press F10.

The Output Size settings in the Common tab panel determine the resolution of rendered images in pixel width and height. The default output size is 640 × 480 pixels.

To set the image output size:

1. 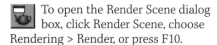 Open the Render Scene dialog box.

2. In the Output Size group, choose an output size by:

   Clicking a preset resolution button (**Figure 15.7**)

   or

   Entering values for Width and Height

   or

   Choosing a resolution from the Output Size drop-down menu (**Figure 15.8**).

✔ Tips

■ For faster test rendering, use a small image output size like 320 × 240 pixels.

■ Clicking the lock icon next to Image Aspect locks the Height and Width values to the image aspect ratio.

RENDERING SCENES

You can save rendered images to a wide variety of 2D file formats, including:

◆ **BMP (Windows Bitmap)**—The device-independent Windows image file format that can be displayed on any Windows-based system. It can be set to 8-bit (256 colors) or 24-bit (16.7 Million Colors) output.

◆ **TGA (Targa)**—A 32-bit compressed or uncompressed file format developed by Truevision that includes alpha channel transparency information as well as 24-bit RGB information. Used for video and print, this is the most accurate image file format you can render from 3ds max.

◆ **TIF (Tagged Image File Format)**—A 32-bit file format with a wide range of palette and color depth options that may be compressed. Originally a Macintosh format, it is commonly used in desktop publishing and by print service bureaus.

◆ **EPS (Encapsulated Post Script)**—A highly portable file format that allows you to specify print output parameters. Widely used in desktop publishing and by print service bureaus.

◆ **JPEG (Joint Photography Experts Group)**—A highly compressed 24-bit file format that creates a continuous-tone image with minimum data loss. Popular for use on the Internet.

◆ **PNG (Portable Network Graphics Specification)**—An Internet file format that can be set to 8-bit, 24-bit, 32-bit, or 48-bit (281 trillion colors). Includes options for alpha channel transparency and 8-bit or 16-bit grayscale output.

You assign a file name, file format, and destination for saved images in the Render Output File dialog box (**Figure 15.9**). This dialog box appears when you click the Files button in the Render Output group of the Render Scene dialog box Common panel.

Figure 15.9 The Render Output File dialog box allows you to save rendered output to one of nine different file formats.

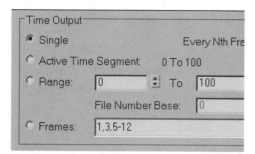

Figure 15.10 Save still image files by choosing Single in the Time Output group.

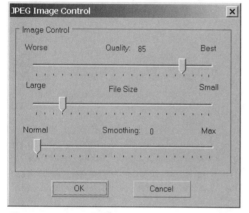

Figure 15.11 Image Control dialog boxes such as this give you additional options specific to the output file format you chose.

Figure 15.12 You can turn file saving on and off with the checkbox next to Save File.

To render an image to a file:

1. Open the Render Scene dialog box.

2. In the Time Output group, choose Single (**Figure 15.10**).

3. In the Output Size group, set the image output size.

4. In the Render Output group, click Files. The Render Output File dialog box appears.

5. In the Save as type drop-down list, choose a still file format.

6. Enter a name for the image.

7. Click Save.

   A configuration dialog box for that image file format appears (**Figure 15.11**). Note that clicking the Setup button brings up the same dialog box.

8. Set the image output parameters for the file format that you have selected. Then click OK.

   A check appears in the Save File check-box to let you know that the next render-ing will be saved to a file (**Figure 15.12**).

9. Click Render.

   The current frame renders to the Rendered Frame Window and the file you specified.

✔ Tips

- Remember to uncheck Save File in the Render Scene dialog box if you do not want the program to save over your image file the next time that you render.

- The keyboard shortcut for Quick Render is Shift + Q.

- The keyboard shortcut for Render Last (the last view rendered) is F9.

RENDERING SCENES

3ds max allows you to render multiple images of a single frame, or a series of still images from multiple frames. Such images are numbered sequentially, starting from 0000 up to the number of images rendered.

To render a series of images to file:

1. Open the Render Scene dialog box.

2. In the Time Output group, choose Active Time Segment, Range, or Frames (**Figure 15.13**).

3. If you chose Range, specify a range of files to render. If you chose Frames, enter the frames you want to render separated by a comma, or a sub-range using a hyphen between frame numbers.

4. To render every second, third, fourth, or fifth frame, and so on, increase Every Nth Frame to 2, 3, 4, or 5.

5. In the Render Output group, click Files. Then choose a still file format and name.

6. Click Save.

7. If prompted to do so, set the image output specifications. Then click OK (**Figure 15.14**).

8. Click Render.

   The frames that you selected render to the Rendered Frame Window and to the files that you specified (**Figure 15.15**).

✔ Tips

■ Alpha channel image files are commonly used for compositing images.

■ To create an animation composed of sequential bitmaps look up "IFL files" in the User Reference.

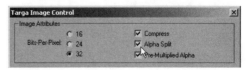

Figure 15.13 Choose the frames that you want to render from the animation.

Figure 15.14 Choosing Alpha Split in the Targa Image Control dialog box will cause the program to render a second set of files containing alpha channel information for each frame.

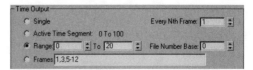

Figure 15.15 The rendered frames are automatically numbered in sequence.

3ds max 6 allows you to render to many different animation file formats, including:

- **AVI (Audio-Video Interleaved)**— Developed by Microsoft, AVI is the most common movie file format on the Windows desktop. This is the only movie file format that offers the option of rendering uncompressed frames.

- **CIN**—The Cineon bitmap movie file format developed by Kodak used to store a single frame of a motion picture or video data stream. In 3ds max, 32-bit files store RGB information in 10-bit color channels with no alpha channel.

- **MOV**—The Apple QuickTime standard. Because of their superior compression algorithms, QuickTime movies are often used on the Web.

- **FLC**—An 8-bit movie file format originally developed by Autodesk for Autodesk Animator. Because they do not store the parts of a frame that do not change, FLC files are small and fast.

- **SGI**—A bitmap file format created by Silicon Graphics. In 3ds max, you can load and save SGI files in 8-bit color or in 16-bit color with an alpha channel.

- **RLA (Run Length Encoded type A)**— Developed by Wavefront and promoted by SGI, this popular format supports arbitrary image channels used in post-production and effects work.

- **RPF (Rich Pixel Format)**—A newer format for creating arbitrary image channels that contain more channel options than the older RLA format.

Different compression methods are available for each format, depending on your need for quality versus file size. For basic experimentation, choose the AVI file format with Cinepak compression.

To render an animation to a movie file:

1. ![] Open the Render Scene dialog box.

2. Choose an image output size.

3. In the Time Output group, specify the frames you wish to render (**Figure 15.16**).

4. Choose a name and animation file format by clicking the Files button. When you click Save, the program prompts you to select a compression method or color palette (**Figure 15.17**).

5. Click Render.

   The frames render to a movie file. To play back the movie, choose File > View Image File and navigate to the file you just saved.

✔ Tips

- Render uncompressed AVI files or a series of Targa images if you are going to process the file later in another application.

- One of the best ***codecs***, or compression/decompression methods, for MOV files is Sorensen Video 3 (**Figure 15.18**).

- For faster test rendering, increase the value of Every Nth Frame. Setting this parameter to 2 renders every other frame.

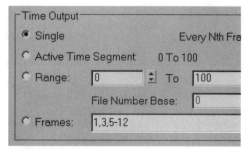

Figure 15.16 To render an animation, choose Active Time Segment, Range, or Frames.

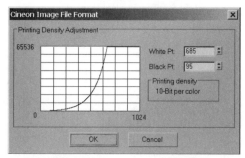

Figure 15.17 The Cinepak compression codec yields good results with AVI files.

Figure 15.18 Sorensen Video 3 offers fast, high-quality compression suitable for delivering video over the Internet.

RENDERING SCENES

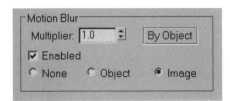

Figure 15.19 You must enable image motion blur in the Object Properties dialog box before it will be applied.

Figure 15.20 After setting image motion blur parameters in the Render Scene dialog box.

Figure 15.21 The moving train is blurred. The amount of blurring is proportional to the duration.

When the shutter of a real camera remains open for an extended period of time, any movement by the camera or the objects it views creates a blur.

Image motion blur simulates this effect by averaging images over multiple frames. For image motion blur to appear, either the object or the camera must be moving.

Image motion blur can also be applied as a rendering effect or multi-pass camera effect.

To render image motion blur:

1. Select the animated objects you want to blur. Then right-click on the selection and choose Properties from the Transform quad menu.

2. In the Motion Blur group of the Object Properties dialog box, check Enabled. Then click Image (**Figure 15.19**).

3. Click OK to save the changes and close the Object Properties dialog box.

4. Open the Render Scene dialog box.

5. Open the Renderer tab panel.

6. Adjust the Image Motion Blur Duration to set the number of frames that will be used to compute image motion blurring. Higher values increase blurring.

7. Check Apply to Environment Map to apply motion blur to reflections and refractions that use environment maps (**Figure 15.20**).

8. Click Render to render the scene.

   Moving objects that have image motion blur enabled are blurred along the path of their trajectories (**Figure 15.21**). If the camera is moving, everything in the scene that is not moving with the camera is blurred.

Object motion blur smoothes the appearance of moving objects by rendering multiple transparent copies for every frame that is averaged. It does not take into account the movement of cameras. The purpose is to make animations play back smoother on the computer, rather than to make moving objects look blurry.

To render object motion blur:

1. 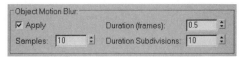 Select the animated objects you want to blur. Then right-click on the selection and choose Properties from the Transform quad menu.

2. In the Motion Blur group of the Object Properties dialog box, check Enabled. Then click Object (**Figure 15.22**).

3. Click OK to save the changes and close the Object Properties dialog box.

4.  Open the Render Scene dialog box.

5. Open the Renderer tab panel. Then adjust the Object Motion Blur Duration to set the number of frames that will be used to compute object motion blurring. Higher values increase blurring (**Figure 15.23**).

6. Adjust the number of Duration Subdivisions to set the number of transparent copies that are rendered within the Duration. Then, increase the number of Samples to set the amount of transparent dithering that occurs between copies. (This value must always be greater than or equal to the Samples level.)

7. Render the scene.

    Moving objects that have object motion blur enabled are blurred along the path of their trajectories (**Figure 15.24**).

✔ Tip

- For smoother video output, render to fields. (See "Fields" in the help files.) Note that you cannot render AVI files to fields.

Figure 15.22 You must enable object motion blur in the Object Properties dialog box before motion blur will be applied.

Figure 15.23 After setting object motion blur parameters in the Render Scene dialog box.

Figure 15.24 The moving train is blurred. The number of blurred copies is equal to the number of duration subdivisions.

Figure 15.25 Volume light and volume fog add a little magic to an ordinary scene.

Rendering Effects

Rendering effects can be applied during the initial rendering pass or added post-process in successive passes and updates. Atmospheric rendering effects are always added during the first pass. Effects listed in the Effects tab of the Render Scene dialog box are always added post-process—i.e., after the initial rendering pass.

Atmospheric Effects

Atmospheric effects are visual effects that create the illusion of fog, fire, smoke, and clouds. These effects appear when you render your scene.

Using the Environment tab of the Render Scene dialog box, you can create the following effects (**Figure 15.25**):

- **Fog**—Adds smoke and fog effects to a scene. There are two kinds of fog:

  Standard fog fades objects toward the front or back of a view.

  Layered fog fades objects toward the top or bottom of a perspective or camera view. You can also make fog constant throughout a view.

- **Volume fog**—Creates swirling smoke, fog, and cloud effects.

- **Volume light**—Adds swirling smoke and fog to a light beam, creating the illusion of headlights on a foggy night or spotlights in a smoky theater.

- **Fire effect**—Creates smoke, fire, and explosion effects, including candles, campfires, fireballs, nebulae, and clouds. Fire is animated by default.

You define the extent of an atmospheric effect in different ways.

◆ Standard fog is defined by the environment ranges of the camera.

◆ Layered fog is defined by the horizon of the camera and a layered fog parameter settings.

◆ Volume light is defined by the cone of illumination of a light.

To limit the range of volume fog and fire effects, you create an object called an **atmospheric gizmo** and assign it to the effect. Atmospheric gizmos can be box-shaped, spherical, or cylindrical.

To create a gizmo:

1. Activate a Perspective viewport or a Camera viewport.

2. 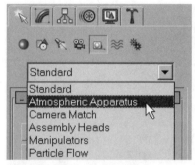 Open the Create panel, and click the Helpers sub-panel.

3. From the drop-down menu, choose Atmospheric Apparatus (**Figure 15.26**).

4. Click a gizmo button.
   The parameters of the gizmo appear below (**Figure 15.27**).

5. Drag out the gizmo in a viewport.
   For SphereGizmos, check the Hemisphere parameter to make the gizmo a hemisphere (**Figure 15.28**).

6. Set the dimensions of the gizmo by adjusting its Radius value. Other values are available for non-sphere gizmos.

7. Use the Move and Rotate tools to position the gizmo.

8. Use the Non-Uniform Scale tool to alter the proportions of the gizmo.

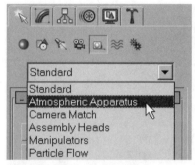

Figure 15.26 Choose Atmospheric Apparatus from the Helpers sub-panel.

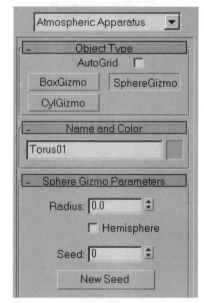

Figure 15.27 Choose a SphereGizmo.

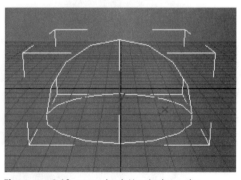

Figure 15.28 After you check Hemisphere, the SphereGizmo is cut in half.

RENDERING EFFECTS

Figure 15.29 Open the Effects tab panel of the Environment and Effects dialog box.

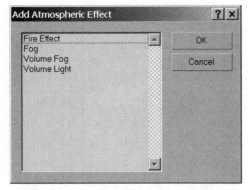

Figure 15.30 Choose an atmospheric effect from the Add Atmospheric Effect list.

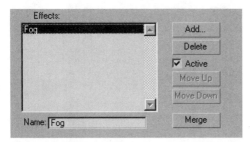

Figure 15.31 The Effects list lets you activate and deactivate individual effects.

To add an atmospheric effect:

1. Choose Rendering > Environment.

   The Environment and Effects dialog box appears.

2. Open the Effects panel (**Figure 15.29**).

3. Click the Add button.

   The Add Atmospheric Effect dialog box appears (**Figure 15.30**).

4. Double-click an effect.

   The atmospheric effect is added to the scene.

   The name of the effect appears in the Effects list (**Figure 15.31**). Active is checked by default. The Parameters rollout for the effect appears below.

5. If you have added a Fire Effect or Volume Fog effect, click Pick Gizmo. Then click a gizmo to define the boundaries of the effect.

✔ Tips

- To delete an effect, select the name of the effect from the Effects list and click the Delete button.

- To disable an effect temporarily, select the name of the effect from the Effects list and uncheck Active.

RENDERING EFFECTS

You can create two kinds of fog: standard fog, which fades the scene along your line of sight, and layered fog, which creates a vertical gradation between the earth and sky.

To create standard fog:

1. 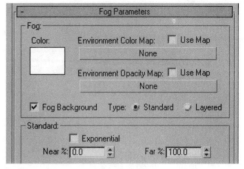 Select or create a camera.

2. Set the Environment Ranges of the camera to define the region that will be affected by the fog.

3. Activate the Camera viewport.

4. Open the Effects of the Render Scene dialog box, and add a Fog effect.

   The Fog Parameters rollout appears (**Figure 15.32**).

5. Choose Standard fog.

6. Render the scene to see the effect of the default settings.

7. Adjust the parameters of the fog.

   Adjust the Near % and Far % values to fade a scene from the near range to far range or vice versa. Check Exponential to increase the rate at which the fog effect obscures the scene (**Figure 15.33**).

8. Render the scene to see the effects of each adjustment.

✔ Tips

- You can change the color of the fog by clicking the Color swatch in the Fog Parameters rollout.

- Uncheck Fog Background if you don't want the fog to fade out the background (**Figure 15.34**).

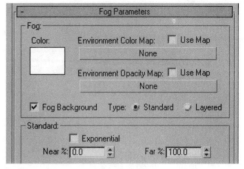

Figure 15.32 Use the Fog Parameters rollout to change the fog color, extents, and other parameters.

Figure 15.33 This scene uses the default settings for Standard fog.

Figure 15.34 Turn off Fog Background for an unrealistic effect in which the scene objects are affected by fog, but the background is not.

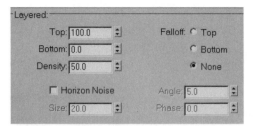

Figure 15.35 Layered fog parameters include Top, Bottom, and Horizon Noise to control the placement and edges of a layer of fog.

Figure 15.36 The layered fog obscures the ground, but not the sky.

Figure 15.37 After adding the same map that is used in the environment background to the environment color of the Layered fog, the furniture appears to sink in the grass.

Layered fog always lies parallel to the world XY plane—that is, parallel to the top view. It only renders from Perspective viewports.

To create layered fog:

1. Activate a Perspective or Camera viewport.

2. Open the Environment and Effects dialog box, and add a Fog effect.

3. In the Fog Parameters rollout, choose Layered fog.

   The layered fog parameters become enabled (**Figure 15.35**).

4. Render the scene to see the effect of the default settings.

5. Set the upper extent of the fog in World units by adjusting the Top parameter. Then set the lower extent of the fog by adjusting the Bottom parameter.

6. Set the density of the fog. A higher number results in more opaque fog.

7. Check Horizon Noise, and set a value for the Size of the Fog. Then set the Angle of the fog in degrees as measured from the camera horizon.

8. Render the scene (**Figure 15.36**).

✔ Tips

■ To make fog fall off at a faster rate, choose Top or Bottom Falloff.

■ Adding a map to the Environment Opacity Map button varies the opacity of the fog.

■ Adding a map to the Environment Color Map button applies a texture map to fog. If you use the same map in the background, it can make objects appear to sink into the environment (**Figure 15.37**).

RENDERING EFFECTS

479

Volume fog uses noise to create an uneven distribution of fog.

To create volume fog:

1. 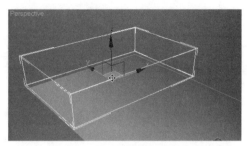 Create an atmospheric gizmo.

2. Position the gizmo in the scene where you want the fog to be (**Figure 15.38**).

Figure 15.38 Positioning a BoxGizmo in a scene.

3. Open the Environment and Effects dialog box and add a Volume Fog effect (**Figure 15.39**).

4. In the Volume Fog Parameters rollout, click Pick Gizmo. Then click the gizmo.

5. Render the scene to see the effect of the default settings.

6. Adjust the opacity of the fog by increasing or decreasing the Density value.

    Check Exponential to decrease the opacity of the fog more rapidly with distance.

7. Adjust the size and granularity of the fog using the Step Size and Max Steps spinners.

8. To decrease brightness and contrast, increase the Uniformity value.

    To increase brightness and contrast, choose Fractal or Turbulence noise.

    To reverse the areas of opacity and transparency, check Invert.

    To make fog render in discrete patches, increase the Low Noise Threshold amount and decrease the High Noise Threshold amount.

9. Render the scene (**Figure 15.40**).

✔ Tip

■ The Phase and Wind parameters churn and blow fog over time. Wind from the sets the wind direction. Wind Strength sets the Wind speed. If there is no wind, the fog will churn in place.

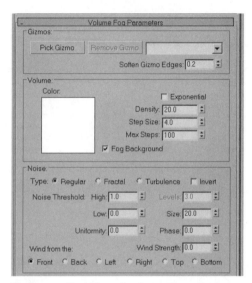

Figure 15.39 The Volume Fog Parameters rollout allows you to pick a gizmo, control opacity, and add noise to the fog effect.

Figure 15.40 By adding Noise and using the BoxGizmo, the volume fog creates a cloud bank.

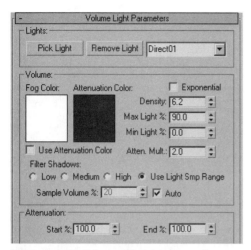

Figure 15.41 The Volume Light Parameters rollout contains settings that are similar to volume fog. It also allows you to control attenuation.

Figure 15.42 When combined with shadow map shadows, volume light creates 3D shadows.

Figure 15.43 Volume light created the rays of sunshine entering from a hole in the ceiling.

In Chapter 11, you learned how to add volume to a light. Now you'll learn how to adjust the light as well.

To adjust a volume light:

1. Select a volume light and open the Modify panel. Then click Setup in the Atmospheres & Effects rollout.

   or

   Open the Environment and Effects dialog box and add a volume light effect. Then pick a light.

   The Volume Light Parameters rollout appears (**Figure 15.41**).

2. Render the scene to see the effect of the default settings.

3. Adjust the Fog Color and Density of the effect. Set the minimum and maximum intensity of the light by setting the Minimum Light % and Maximum Light %.

4. Control the attenuation of the light with Attenuation Multiplier, Use Attenuation Color, and Attenuation Start and End.

5. To add noise to the light so that it looks like fog, check Noise On, and adjust the noise parameters. See "To create volume fog" in the User Reference for a full explanation of the volume fog parameters.

6. Render the scene (**Figure 15.42**).

✔ Tips

- To create volumetric shadows, use shadow maps rather than Ray Traced Shadows.

- Use volume light to make a dramatic statement about space (**Figure 15.43**).

- Use volume light to put a glow around an omni light. The Glow Lens Effect (covered in the next section) provides a more convincing glow effect.

RENDERING EFFECTS

The fire effect creates flames, fireballs, smoke, and explosions that animate automatically. Fire renders only from perspective-type views.

To create a fire effect:

1. Create an atmospheric gizmo and position it in the scene.

2. Open the Environment and Effects dialog box, and add a Fire Effect.
   The Fire Effect Parameters rollout appears (**Figure 15.44**).

3. Click Pick Gizmo, and click the gizmo.

4. Render the scene to see the effect of the default settings.

5. Adjust the color and shape of the fire. Choose Tendril to make campfire flames, or Fireball to make rounder balls of fire. Increase the Stretch amount to make the flames straighter and taller. You can also scale the gizmo to stretch the flames.

6. Increase the Regularity amount to make the flames more uniform.

7. Adjust the characteristics of the fire. Increase the Flame Size and Density amounts to make the flames larger and brighter. Increase the Flame Detail and Samples amounts to give the flames more distinct edges.

8. Render the scene (**Figure 15.45**).

✔ Tip

- Using the Motion and Explosion parameters, you control how the fire burns, including the rate that it burns, whether or not it explodes, the timing of the explosion, whether or not the explosion produces smoke, and so forth. To see a complete description of Fire parameters, look up "Fire" in the help files.

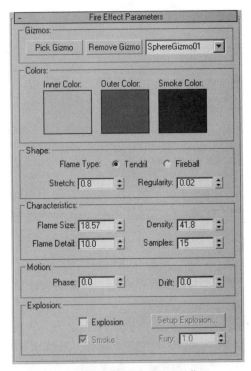

Figure 15.44 The Fire Effect Parameters rollout controls the appearance of flames, fireballs, explosions, and smoke.

Figure 15.45 Two fire effects and two gizmos were used to produce this burning bowl of oil.

Figure 15.46 Rendering effects are applied to scene renderings directly in the Rendered Frame Window.

Post-Process Effects

Render Effects are a collection of post-process effects that are added to images in the Rendered Frame Window immediately after they are rendered (**Figure 15.46**). Render Effects include:

◆ **Lens Effects**—Simulates effects that are created by a camera lens and a bright light. Use this effect to create glows, starbursts, streaking, and rainbows.

◆ **Blur**—Blurs an image uniformly, along one or two axes or from a center point. Includes advanced parameters for blurring different parts of an image.

◆ **Brightness and Contrast**—Changes the brightness and contrast of an image.

◆ **Color Balance**—Shifts the color balance of a rendered image using CMY/RGB sliders.

◆ **Depth of Field**—Blurs foreground and background along the line of sight while preserving focus with in a central region.

◆ **File Output**—Takes a snapshot of a scene and saves the image to a file or returns the image to the Effects stack for further processing.

◆ **Film Grain**—Applies noise to a rendered image, like the grain on old film.

◆ **Motion Blur**—Applies directional blurring in order to create the illusion that objects are moving past the camera.

Most effects give you the option of including or excluding background images from the effect. Because the effects are evaluated in sequence, the Effects list is also called the Effects stack.

To add a rendering effect:

1. Choose Rendering > Effects.

   The Effects panel of the Environment and Effects dialog box appears (**Figure 15.47**).

2. Click Add.

   The Add Effect dialog box appears (**Figure 15.48**).

3. Choose the effect you want, and click OK.

   The rendering effect is added to the scene.

   The name of the effect appears in the Effects stack (**Figure 15.49**). Active is checked by default. The Parameters rollout for the effect appears below.

4. Click Update Scene.

   The scene renders in the Rendered Frame Window. After a pause, the effect is applied.

5. Adjust the effect. Then click Update Effect.

   The effect updates in the Rendered Frame Window.

✔ Tips

- Check Interactive to automatically update effects as you change settings.

- Effects are evaluated in order from the top to the bottom of the stack. To change the order of evaluation, highlight an effect and click Move Up or Move Down.

- To delete an effect, select it from the Effects list and click the Delete button.

- To disable an effect temporarily, select the effect and uncheck Active.

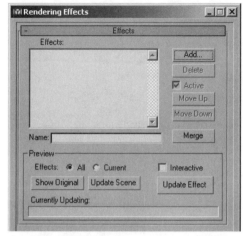

Figure 15.47 Use the Rendering Effects dialog box's Add button to create new effects.

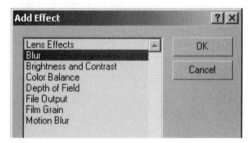

Figure 15.48 Choosing an Effect.

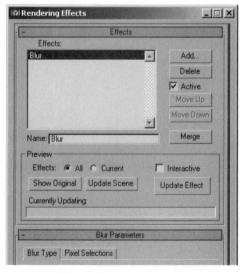

Figure 15.49 The effect is added to the Effects list.

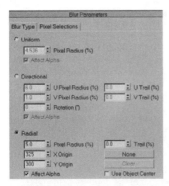

Figure 15.50 The Blur Parameters rollout allows you to choose from three different types of blurring.

Figure 15.51 After applying directional blur to the U direction in the amount of a 6% U Pixel Radius.

Figure 15.52 After applying a radial blur of 7% Pixel Radius using the house as a focal node.

The Blur effect blurs an image after it has been rendered.

To add blur:

1. Choose Rendering > Effects and add a Blur effect.

   The Blur effect is added to the Effects stack. The Blur Parameters rollout appears (**Figure 15.50**).

2. Click Update Scene.

   The scene renders from the active viewport. After a short pause, a strong Blur effect is applied to the image. The Blur effect is quite strong.

3. Reduce the Pixel Radius % to decrease the amount of the blur. Then click Update Effect.

4. Choose the Directional option. Adjust the U and V directional blurring to make the image blur along one or two axes. Then click Update Effect to see the result (**Figure 15.51**).

5. Choose the Radial option, and update the scene. Then adjust the Pixel Radius % to control the amount of radial blur. Use the X Origin and Y Origin to locate the center of blurring, or click the button labeled "None" and then click an object to use as a focal point. Check Use Object Center to assign the pivot point of the object as the focal point of the effect. Then click Update Effect (**Figure 15.52**).

✔ Tips

- Trails add "direction" to your blur by weighting it more heavily toward one side or another.

- When checked, Affect Alpha blurs the edges of the alpha channel. To view this effect, click Display Alpha Channel in the Rendered Frame Window.

- To blur an image more selectively, use the settings in the Pixel Selections tab panel. For information, see "Blur rendering effect" in the help files.

A Depth of Field effect blurs the foreground and background of a scene. The area that remains in focus is called the depth of field.

To add depth of field blurring:

1. Choose Rendering > Effects and add a Depth of Field effect.

   The Depth of Field Parameters rollout appears (**Figure 15.53**).

2. In the Depth of Field Parameters rollout, click Pick Node. Then click an object in the scene to be the focal point.

3. Click Update Effect.

   The scene blurs outside the depth of field (**Figure 15.54**).

4. In the Focal Parameters group, choose Custom. Adjust the strength of the blurring by modifying the Horizontal and Vertical Focal Loss settings.

   To set the range of the depth of field in front of and behind the focal point, adjust the Focal Range. Objects outside of this range will be blurred.

   To set the distance from the focal point at which blurring reaches its full amount, adjust the Focal Limit.

5. To use a camera target as the focal node of the depth of field, click Pick Camera and select a camera in the scene. Then choose Use Camera in the Focal Parameters group and set the Horizontal and Vertical Focal Loss settings.

6. Click Update Effect.

   The scene blurs outside of the depth of field that is established by the camera target (**Figure 15.55**).

   To move the depth of field closer or farther away, use the Dolly Target command in the Camera viewport.

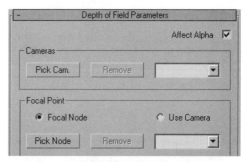

Figure 15.53 The Depth of Field Parameters rollout controls the placement of the depth of field and the amount of blurring outside the field.

Figure 15.54 Using the house in the middle ground as a focal node blurs the foreground and background.

Figure 15.55 After shifting the focus to the camera that targets the sports car, everything behind it blurs.

Figure 15.56 Enable image motion blur in the Object Properties dialog box.

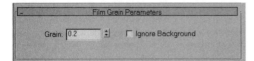

Figure 15.57 Adjust the amount of blurring by changing the Duration amount.

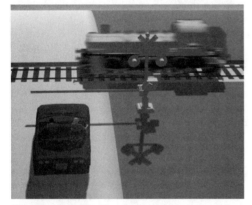

Figure 15.58 Motion blur simulates how real-world cameras sometimes blur fast-moving objects.

The Motion Blur effect adds image motion blur to your scene. Image motion blur can also be applied from the Render Scene dialog box, and from the camera as a multi-pass camera effect.

To add image motion blur:

1. Select some moving objects to blur. Then right-click on the selection and choose Properties from the Transform quad menu.

2. In the Motion Blur group of the Object Properties dialog box, check Enabled. Then click Image (**Figure 15.56**).

3. Click OK to save the changes and close the Object Properties dialog box, and choose Rendering > Effects. Then add a Motion Blur effect to the scene.

   The Motion Blur Parameters rollout appears (**Figure 15.57**).

4. Set the amount of motion blur that you want by changing the Duration amount.

5. Click Update Effect.

   Objects that have image motion blur enabled and that are moving in relation to the camera during the current frame are blurred along the path of their trajectories (**Figure 15.58**).

✔ Tips

- For faster rendering, leave Work with transparency unchecked unless you are having trouble blurring either transparent objects or the objects behind them.

- When you apply image motion blur from more than one place, the effects are added together, rather than replaced.

- A small amount of image motion blur is applied from the Render Scene dialog box by default. To turn off this effect, uncheck Apply in the Image Motion Blur group in the Renderer tab's Default Scanline Renderer rollout.

RENDERING EFFECTS

Film Grain makes a rendered image look old and weathered, like the graininess you see on old movie films.

To add film grain:

1. Choose Rendering > Effects and add a Film Grain effect.

   The Film Grain Parameters rollout appears (**Figure 15.59**).

2. Check Interactive.

   The scene renders in the Preview window. A small amount of grain is added.

3. Increase the Grain setting.

   The image becomes grainier (**Figure 15.60**).

✔ Tip

■ If you do not want the background image to be affected by the grain, check Ignore Background (**Figure 15.61**).

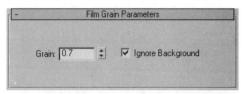

Figure 15.59 The Film Grain Parameters rollout sets the contrast of the grain and determines whether the grain will applied to the background.

Figure 15.60 A grain appears throughout the image.

Figure 15.61 After checking Ignore Background, the grain appears only on the motorcycle and its shadow. Note that the shadow, which was projected onto a matte object, is considered foreground, but the rest of the matte object is ignored as background.

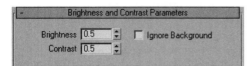

Figure 15.62 The Brightness and Contrast Parameters rollout sets the brightness and contrast of a rendered image.

Figure 15.63 After increasing Brightness to .75, the motorcycle brightens but retains good contrast.

Figure 15.64 After applying .25 Brightness and .75 Contrast and checking Ignore Background.

The Brightness and Contrast effect changes the brightness and/or contrast of a rendered image.

To change brightness and contrast:

1. Choose Rendering > Effects and add a Brightness and Contrast effect.

   The Brightness and Contrast Parameters rollout appears (**Figure 15.62**).

2. Check Interactive.

3. Set the Brightness and Contrast amounts. Check Ignore Background to leave the background values intact (**Figure 15.63**).

4. Try reversing the Brightness and Contrast amounts to see what happens (**Figure 15.64**).

The Color Balance effect shifts the color balance of a rendered image using CMY/RGB sliders.

To shift the color balance:

1. Choose Rendering > Effects and add a Color Balance effect.

The Color Balance Parameters rollout appears (**Figure 15.65**).

2. Check Interactive.

3. Set the color balance by dragging the sliders (**Figure 15.66**).

✔ Tips

■ Checking Preserve Luminosity preserves the range of values, but does not preserve their distribution across the range (**Figure 15.67**).

■ The color channel buttons at the top of the Rendered Frame Window allow you to view how much of each color is added.

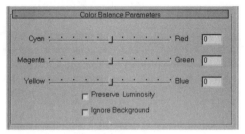

Figure 15.65 The Color Balance Parameters rollout allows you to adjust the amount of each color.

Figure 15.66 After shifting the color balance, the luminance values of the image are affected.

Figure 15.67 Checking Preserve Luminosity and Ignore Background helps restore luminance values.

RENDERING EFFECTS

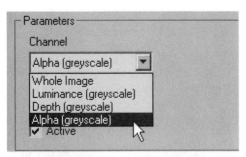

Figure 15.68 Setting the File Output channel.

Figure 15.69 A shadow cast on a Matte/Shadow material appears in the alpha channel.

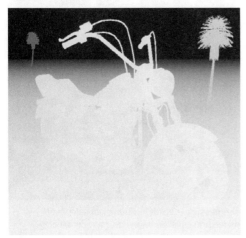

Figure 15.70 The depth channel information displays objects that are closer as being lighter.

The File Output effect saves the current state of an image to a separate file as it is processed in the Effects stack. You can save out the whole image, alpha, luminance, or depth channel information. Effects that are listed below the File Output effect will not be applied to the image.

◆ **Alpha**—Sends transparency information to the Render Effects stack in the form of a grayscale image. Environment background maps return as black.

◆ **Luminance**—Sends the light to dark color information as a grayscale image to the Render Effects stack.

◆ **Depth**—Sends a grayscale image of scene geometry that is within the clipping range of the camera, or in between two depth ranges that you specify. Objects that are closer to the camera appear lighter, while objects that are further away appear darker.

To render a channel:

1. Choose Rendering > Effects and add a File Output effect.

   The File Output Parameters rollout appears.

2. Click Files. Then choose a location, name, and file format to render to.

3. Open the Channel drop-down menu, and choose a channel (**Figure 15.68**).

4. Click Update Scene.

   The channel is rendered to the output file that you specified (**Figure 15.69**).

5. Change the channel selection and the output file name. Then click Update Scene (**Figure 15.70**).

✔ Tip

■ The Affect Source Bitmap option feeds the output file back into the Effects stack.

Lens Effects simulate the effects that are created by a camera lens and a bright light. They include Glow, Ring, Ray, Auto Secondary, Manual Secondary, Star, and Streak.

To add lens effects:

1. Choose Rendering > Effects and add a Lens Effect.

   The Lens Effects Parameters rollout appears.

2. Add the effects you want to apply by selecting them in the left window and clicking the right arrow button.

   The selected effects move to the right window (**Figure 15.71**).

3. In the Lens Effects Globals rollout, click Pick Light and then select a light.

4. Click Update Effect to see the effect of the default settings.

5. Adjust the global size and intensity of the lens effects.

6. Adjust the size, color, and intensity of individual effects. To access the parameters of an effect, click the name of the effect in the right window of the Lens Effects Parameters rollout then open the effects Element rollout.

7. Click Update Effect (**Figure 15.72**).

✔ Tip

■ Lens Effects can create magical effects (**Figure 15.73**). To learn more, look up "Lens Effects" in the User Reference.

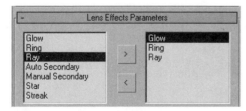

Figure 15.71 Adding lens effects to a scene.

Figure 15.72 After combining the Glow, Ring, and Ray lens effects with a starry sky.

Figure 15.73 The star is a universal symbol of divine presence. For more information, please see www.youareyourpath.com. This image appears on the monthly message of November.

RENDERING EFFECTS

A

Icons

Figure A.1 Lens Effects create mystical effects when combined with universal symbols, such as the cross.

3ds max is full of buttons and cursors. To help you keep track, here is a list of all the icons I used in creating this book.

Table A.1

Main Toolbar			
	Undo		2D SnapToggle
	Redo		2.5D SnapToggle
	Select and Link		3D SnapToggle
	Unlink Selection		Angle Snap Toggle
	Bind to Space Warp		Percent Snap
All	Selection Filter		Spinner Snap Toggle
	Select Object		Named Selection Sets
	Select by Name		Named Selection Sets dropdown
	Rectangular Selection Region		Mirror Selected Objects
	Circular Selection Region		Align
	Fence Selection Region		Normal Align
	Lasso Selection Region		Place Highlight
	Crossing Selection		Align Camera
	Window Selection		Align to View
	Select and Move		Layer Manager
	Select and Rotate		Curve Editor (Open)
	Select and Uniform Scale		Open Schematic View
	Select and Non-Uniform Scale		Material Editor
	Select and Squash		Render Scene
View	Reference Coordinate System	View	Render Type dropdown
	Use Pivot Point Center		Quick Render (Production)
	Use Selection Center		Quick Render (Active Shade)
	Use Transform Coordinate Center		
	Select and Manipulate		

Table A.2

Axis Constraints

X	Restrict to X
Y	Restrict to Y
Z	Restrict to Z
XY	Restrict to XY Plane
YZ	Restrict to YZ Plane
ZX	Restrict to ZX Plane

Table A.3

Extras

	Keyboard Shortcut Override Toggle
	AutoGrid
	Array
	Snapshot
	Spacing Tool

Table A.4

Named Selection Sets

	Create New Set
	Remove
	Add Selected Objects
	Subtract Selected Objects
	Select Objects in Set
	Select Objects By Name
	Highlight Selected Objects

Table A.5

Command Panels

	Create Panel
	Modify Panel
	Hierarchy Panel
	Motion Panel
	Display Panel
	Utilities Panel

Table A.6

Create Panel

	Geometry
	Shapes
	Lights
	Cameras
	Helpers
	Space Warps
	Systems

Table A.7

Modify Panel	
	Pin Stack (Off)
	Pin Stack (On)
	Show End Result (Off)
	Show End Result (On)
	Make Unique
	Make Unique (Active)
	Remove Modifier From the Stack
	Configure Modifier Sets
	Open/Close Sub-Object Drop-Down List
	Active Mode or "On"
	Inactive Mode or "Off"
	Off in Viewport
	Off in Renderer

Table A.8

Sub-Object Levels	
	Vertex
	Edge
	Face
	Polygon
	Element
	Vertex
	Edge
	Border
	Polygon
	Element
	Settings
	Vertex
	Segment
	Spline
	Union
	Subtraction
	Intersection

Table A.9

Text Functions	
I	Italic
U	Underline
	Align Left
	Center
	Align Right
	Justify

Table A.10

Status Bar Controls	
	Mini Curve Editor Toggle
	Selection Lock Toggle
	Absolute Mode Transform Type-In
	Offset Mode Transform Type-In
	Set Keys
Auto Key	Toggle Auto Key Mode
Set Key	Toggle Set Key Mode
Key Filters...	Open Filters Dialog
	Go to Start
	Previous Frame
	Previous Key
	Play Animation
	Play Selected
	Stop Animation
	Next Frame
	Next Key
	Go to End
	Key Mode Toggle
	Time Configuration

ICONS

Table A.11

Viewport Window Controls
Zoom
Zoom All
Zoom Extents
Zoom Extents Selected
Zoom Extents All
Zoom Extents All Selected
Region Zoom
Field-of-View
Pan
Arc Rotate
Arc Rotate Selected
Arc Rotate SubObject
Min/Max Toggle

Table A.13

Camera Viewport Controls
Dolly Camera
Dolly Camera + Target
Dolly Target
Perspective
Roll Camera
Zoom Extents All
Zoom Extents All Selected
Field-of-View
Truck Camera
Orbit
Pan Camera
Min/Max Toggle

Table A.12

Light Viewport Controls
Dolly Light
Dolly Light + Target
Dolly Target
Light Hotspot
Light Falloff
Roll Light
Zoom Extents All
Zoom Extents All Selected
Truck Light
Orbit Light
Pan Light
Min/Max Toggle

Table A.14

Camera Controls
Field of View Direction (Horizontal)
Field of View Direction (Vertical)
Field of View Direction (Diagonal)

Table A.15

Material Editor	
	Get Material
	Put Material to Scene
	Assign Material to Selection
	Reset Map/Mtl to Default Settings
	Make Material Copy
	Make Unique
	Put to Library
	Material Effects Channel
	Show Map in Viewport
	Show End Result (Inactive)
	Show End Result (Active)
	Go to Parent
	Go Forward to Sibling
	Material Map Navigator
	Select by Material
	Options
	Make Preview
	Play Preview
	Save Preview
	Video Color Check
	Sample UV Tiling
	Sample UV Tiling
	Sample UV Tiling
	Sample UV Tiling
	Background
	Backlight
	Sample Type
	Sample Type
	Sample Type
	View List
	View List + Icons
	View Small Icons
	View Large Icons
	Update Scene Materials from Library
	Delete From Library
	Clear Material Library
	Pick Material from Object

Table A.16

Schematic View	
	Display Floaters
	Select
	Connect
	Unlink Selected
	Delete Objects
	Hierarchy Mode
	References Mode
	Always Arrange
	Arrange Selected
	Free All
	Free Selected
	Move Children
	Expand Selected
	Collapse Selected
	Preferences
	Go to Bookmark
	Delete Bookmark

Table A.17

Rendered Frame Window and Render Scene	
	Save Bitmap
	Clone Rendered Frame Window
	Enable Red Channel
	Enable Green Channel
	Enable Blue Channel
	Display Alpha Channel
	Monochrome
	Clear
RGB Alpha	RGB Alpha
	Color Selector
	Choose Renderer
	Lock to Current Renderer

Table A.18

Curve Editor

	Filters			Lock Selection
	Move Keys			Snap Frames
	Move Keys Horizontal			Parameter Curve Out-of-Range Types
	Move Keys Vertical			Show Keyable Icons
	Slide Keys			Show All Tangents
	Scale Keys			Show Tangents
	Scale Values			Lock Tangents
	Add Keys			Pan
	Draw Curves			Zoom Horizontal Extents
	Reduce Keys			Zoom Horizontal Extents Keys
	Set Tangents to Auto			Zoom Value Extents
	Set In Tangents to Auto			Zoom
	Set Out Tangents to Auto			Zoom Time
	Set Tangents to Custom			Zoom Values
	Set In Tangents to Custom			Zoom Region
	Set Out Tangents to Custom			Zoom Selected Object
	Set Tangents to Fast			Show Selected Key Stats
	Set In Tangents to Fast			Constant
	Set Out Tangents to Fast			Cycle
	Set Tangents to Slow			Loop
	Set In Tangents to Slow			Ping Pong
	Set Out Tangents to Slow			Linear
	Set Tangents to Step			Relative Repeat
	Set In Tangents to Step			
	Set Out Tangents to Step			
	Set Tangents to Linear			
	Set In Tangents to Linear			
	Set Out Tangents to Linear			
	Set Tangents to Smooth			
	Set In Tangents to Smooth			
	Set Out Tangents to Smooth			
	Previous Key			
	Next Key			
	Copy to Previous Key			
	Copy to Next Key			

Table A.19

Lofting	
	Pick Shape
	Previous Shape
	Next Shape
	Pick Shape
	Make Symmetrical
	Display X Axis
	Display Y Axis
	Display XY Axes
	Swap Deform Curves
	Move Control Point
	Move Control Point
	Move Control Point
	Scale Control Point
	Insert Corner Point
	Insert Corner Point
	Mirror Horizontally
	Mirror Vertically
	Rotate 90 CCW
	Rotate 90 CW
	Delete Control Point
	Reset or Reset Curve
	Delete Curve
	Get Shape
	Generate Path
	Normal Bevel

Table A.20

File Save	
	Save and Increment +01

Table A.21

Cursors	
	Select and Link
	Bind to Space Warp
	Select Object
	Select Object (Over Object)
	Move
	Rotate
	Uniform Scale
	Non-Uniform Scale
	Squash
	Align
	Normal Align
	Place Highlight
	Align Camera
	Zoom
	Zoom All
	Zoom Region
	Pan
	Arc Rotate Free Rotation
	Arc Rotate Spinning Rotation
	Arc Rotate (when on handles)
	Field-of-View
	Dolly
	Perspective
	Roll
	Truck
	Orbit
	Pan
	Light Hotspot
	Light Falloff

KEYBOARD SHORTCUTS

Keyboard shortcuts are a major time-saver and worth taking some time to master. To help you get started, I have listed them by function, and I include nearly every default shortcut found in the main user interface. I also note some useful shortcuts that you can assign yourself.

To see a complete alphabetical list of shortcuts, assign your own hotkeys, and save them to a file, choose Customize > Customize User Interface > Keyboard.

Table B.1

Scene File Operations	
SHORTCUT	NAME
Ctrl + Z	Undo Scene Operation
Ctrl + Y	Redo Scene Operation
Ctrl + S	Save File
Ctrl + N	New Scene
Ctrl + O	Open File
Alt + Ctrl + H	Hold
Alt + Ctrl + F	Fetch
F1	Display Help Files

Table B.2

UI Display	
SHORTCUT	NAME
Alt + 6	Show Main Toolbar Toggle
Ctrl + X	Expert Mode Toggle
2	Modify Panel

Table B.3

Changing Views	
SHORTCUT	NAME
F	Front View
V + K	Back View
V + R	Right View
L	Left View
T	Top View
B	Bottom View
P	Perspective User View
U	Axonometric User View
C	Camera View
Shift + 4	Spotlight/Directional Light View
G	Hide Grids Toggle
Alt + W	Maximize Viewport Toggle
D	Disable/ Viewport
Shift + Z	Undo Viewport Operation
Shift + Y	Redo Viewport Operation
Alt + B	Viewport Dialog
Alt+Shift+Ctrl+B	Update Background Image
`(Accent Grave)	Redraw All Views

Table B.4

Viewport Navigation		
SHORTCUT	BUTTON	NAME
Alt + Z		Zoom Mode
assignable		Zoom All Mode
Alt + Ctrl + Z		Zoom Extents
assignable		Zoom Extents Selected
Shift + Ctrl + Z		Zoom Extents All
Z		Zoom Extents All Selected
Ctrl + W		Zoom Region Mode
assignable		Field-of-View Mode
Ctrl + P		Pan View
Alt+Middle Mouse Button		Arc Rotate
Alt + W		Min/Max Toggle
Alt + Q		Isolate Selection
[		Zoom Viewport In
]		Zoom Viewport Out

Table B.5

Object Selection and Display

SHORTCUT	NAME
Ctrl + A	Select All
Ctrl + D	Select None
Ctrl + I	Select Invert
H	Select-by-Name Dialog
Spacebar	Selection Lock Toggle
Page Up	Select Ancestor
Page Down	Select Child
Ctrl + F	Cycle Selection Method
Insert	Sub-Object Selection Level Cycle
1	Vertex Level Selection
2	Edge Level Selection
3	Face Level Selection
4	Polygon Level Selection
5	Element Level Selection
F2	Shade Selected Faces Toggle
F3	Wireframe/Smooth+Highlights Toggle
F4	View Edged Faces Toggle
assignable	Box Mode Selected Toggle
Shift + F	Show Safeframes Toggle
Shift + C	Hide Cameras Toggle
Shift + L	Hide Lights Toggle
Shift + H	Hide Helpers Toggle
Shift + P	Hide Particle Systems Toggle
Shift + G	Hide Geometry Toggle
Shift + W	Hide Space Warps Toggle
G	Hide Grids Toggle
Shift + S	Hide Shapes Toggle
assignable	Hide Selection
assignable	Hide Unselected
assignable	Hide by Name
assignable	Hide by Hit
assignable	Hide Frozen Objects Toggle
assignable	Unhide by Name
assignable	Freeze Selection
assignable	Unfreeze All
Alt + X	Display as See-Through Toggle
7	Polygon Counter

Table B.6

Transforms

SHORTCUT	BUTTON	NAME
X		Transform Gizmo Toggle
=		Transform Gizmo Size Up
-		Transform Gizmo Size Down
F5	⬛	Restrict to X
F6	⬛	Restrict to Y
F7	⬛	Restrict to Z
F8		Restrict Plane Cycle
W	✥	Move Mode
E	↻	Rotate Mode
Ctrl+E	⬛ ⬛ ⬛	Scale Cycle
F12		Transform Type-In Dialog Box
S	⬛	Snap Toggle
Alt+S		Snaps Cycle
A	⬛	Angle Snap Toggle
Shift + Ctrl + P	⬛	Snap Percent Toggle
assignable	⬛	Spinner Snap Toggle
assignable	⬛	Mirror Tool
Alt + A	⬛	Align
Alt + N	⬛	Normal Align
Ctrl + H	⬛	Place Highlight
assignable	⬛	Align Camera
assignable	⬛	Align to View
Ctrl + C		Create Camera from View
assignable	⬛	Array
assignable	⬛	Snapshot
Shift + I	⬛	Spacing Tool

Table B.7

Animation

SHORTCUT	BUTTON	NAME
Home	◄◄	Go To Start Frame
End	►►	Go To End Frame
. (period)	►►	Next Frame
, (comma)	◄◄	Previous Frame
assignable	◄	Next Key
assignable	►	Next/Previous Key
N	Auto Key	Auto Key Mode Toggle
'	Set Key	Set Key Mode
K	o—	Set Keys
/	►	Play Animation
/	►	Play Selected
/	❚❚	Stop Animation
\		Sound Toggle
assignable		Time Configuration

Table B.8

Rendering

SHORTCUT	BUTTON	NAME
M		Material Editor
8		Environment and Effects
9		Render Scene: Default Scanline Renderer
assignable		Texture Correction (Redraw Maps)
Shift + Q		Quick Render
F9		Render Last
F10		Render

INDEX

INDEX

INDEX